POETRY AND POLITICS

THE LIFE AND WORKS OF JUAN CHI
A.D. 210–263

Poetry and politics

THE LIFE AND WORKS OF JUAN CHI
A.D. 210–263

DONALD HOLZMAN

Sous-Directeur d'Etudes
Ecole des Hautes Etudes en Sciences Sociales, Paris

CAMBRIDGE UNIVERSITY PRESS

CAMBRIDGE

LONDON – NEW YORK – MELBOURNE

CAMBRIDGE UNIVERSITY PRESS
Cambridge, New York, Melbourne, Madrid, Cape Town, Singapore, São Paulo, Delhi

Cambridge University Press
The Edinburgh Building, Cambridge CB2 8RU, UK

Published in the United States of America by Cambridge University Press, New York

www.cambridge.org
Information on this title: www.cambridge.org/9780521102568

First published 1976
This digitally printed version 2009

A catalogue record for this publication is available from the British Library

Library of Congress Cataloguing in Publication data
Holzman, Donald.
Poetry and politics.
(Cambridge studies in Chinese history, literature and institutions)
Bibliography: p.
Includes index.
1. Juan, Chi, 210–263. I. Juan, Chi, 210–263
II. Title.
PL2664.J8Z69   895.1'1'2[B]   75-27798

ISBN 978-0-521-20855-0 hardback
ISBN 978-0-521-10256-8 paperback

CONTENTS

For Paul Demiéville

M'insegnavate come l'uom s'etterna:
e quant'io l'abbia in grado, mentr'io vivo
convien che nella mia lingua si scerna.
Inferno XV, 85–7.

PREFACE

I began work on Juan Chi many years ago and submitted a thesis containing the translation of his pentameter poetry to Yale University as part of the requirement for a Ph.D. degree in 1953. I realize now how bold such an attempt was and how inaccurate my translation was bound to be. For Juan Chi is one of the most difficult of the great Chinese poets to understand in any depth. His vocabulary is relatively small, his grammar deceptively simple, but his meaning is frustratingly difficult to grasp. 'We hear his words with our ears and see them with our eyes, but his emotions reach out beyond the confines of the universe', as Chung Jung said in his famous appreciation of Juan Chi. This 'reaching out' is as exhilarating as the obscurity of much of the verse is frustrating, and, once intrigued, the reader is naturally stimulated to try to deepen his understanding of the poet and to dissipate his frustrations. This book is my attempt to do just that, to study Juan Chi in all his complexity, ignoring none of the contradictions or difficulties he presents.

But if he is so obscure, if even the Chinese reader finds much of his poetry needs extended commentary, why attempt to present him to a Western audience? There are many reasons. In the first place, his poetry is, by any estimation, among the best ever written in China. He is, in the second place, at the head of the great tradition of classical poetry, immediately after Ts'ao Chih, who died when Juan Chi was twenty-two years old; he is thus an essential figure for the understanding of the poetry that follows him, poetry that is, as is well known, a mosaic of traditional allusions inspired by new individual talents. But, most important, he is a poet of a very special quality: he expresses with unsurpassed passion and intensity an aspect of the Chinese ethos that is inherent, to a greater or lesser degree, in all Chinese poets and which they instinctively associate with him. Juan Chi yearned to participate in the political life of his country, and it is his inability to do so honorably, without betraying his legitimate ruler, that forced him to lament in verse, to proclaim his attachment to higher moral values and his disgust with the vile opportunism he saw about him. The purity of his yearning, the gigantic, cosmic sweep of his dreams of heroic grandeur, awaken a sympathetic reaction in the poets who follow him. Anyone truly interested in Chinese poetry must spend some time with Juan Chi, must be initiated into this kind of passionate political commitment which was of prime importance for the great majority of Chinese men of letters and which remains so to the present day.

In spite of the beauty and interest of his verse, Juan Chi, probably because of his obscurity, has remained somewhat of a poet's poet, or at least an acquired taste. I sometimes wonder if the extremely warm response I have always received from Chinese (and Japanese) scholars when I told them I was studying Juan Chi was not due, in part at least, to the special quality of his verse, destined only for the happy few. Whatever the reason, I have benefited greatly from conversations about Juan Chi and from readings of his poetry and prose with a great number of specialists. All of them have given unstintingly of their time and knowledge and I should like to mention them here, in rough chronological order, by way of thanking them: Li T'ien-yi, Yoshikawa Kōjirō, Honda Wataru, Ogawa Tamaki, Yeh Chia-ying, Shen Hung-i, Fukunaga Mitsuji, Jao Tsung-i, Paul Demiéville, J. R. Hightower, and A. R. Davis. At an early stage in my work, and again towards the end of it, I was enabled by the Ford Foundation and the American Council of Learned Societies — Social Science Research Council to spend two years in the Far East.

The Chinese foreword by Professor Jao Tsung-i 饒 宗 頤 was written after I received the first proofs and it has been impossible for me to include a translation of it here. Professor Jao, whose knowledge and appreciation of Juan Chi's life and works are, I believe, unrivalled today, presents a wealth of new material in the two short pages covered with his elegant calligraphy. He draws attention to remarks on Juan Chi by Li Chih 李 贄 (1527—1602) in his *Ts'ang shu* 藏 書 and by Tu-ku Chi 獨 孤 及 (725—777) in a eulogy contained in *Ch'üan T'ang-wen* 384, pp. 7a—8a; emphasizes the importance of Juan Chi's *I ching* studies, insisting that in his understanding of the *I ching* as an aid to actual living Juan Chi should be placed above Wang Pi and Chung Hui; sees a familial affiliation in the thought of Juan Wu, Juan Yü and Juan Chi, but stresses the fact that Juan Chi's thought and the thought of his period in general is much more abstract and metaphysical than that of the older generation; suggests that perhaps 'Liu-tzu' mentioned in the 'Essay on music' (below, p. 88) refers to Liu Shao 劉 劭, an older contemporary philosopher; and notes that Tu-ku Chi, in his eulogy, refers to an essay by Juan Chi that is no longer extant and is mentioned nowhere else, which suggests that many more of Juan Chi's works were available in T'ang times than are today. Professor Jao's final praise, counting me as a latter-day intimate of Juan Chi, is the kindest that he, of all people, could make.

13 March 1976   D.H.

侯苦思孟著阮嗣宗生活与作品既殺青是歲三月初余抵巴黎得先覩其校樣喜而

為之序曰侯君謂史家月旦嗣宗殊不多觀余見李贄藏書列阮於隱者薄別具

卓識獨孤及為阮公嘯臺頌稱公以全德生於襄世而逃禮逃用晦德忘己徜讀通

易論知阮公固湛于易其説大人之義以為宗實者德之主明夫天道者不欲

害乎人德者不憂夫是之謂全德故曰作智造巧者害于物明是考非者危

其身論莊曰逃禮逃用實正顯諸仁而藏諸用此大人之至德非於易旨深有

體會蓋胱踐履之昌克綠此宣輔嗣之辭十逸辯士季之偏識互體其出處語默

不識物情樞機之發泥夫大道者可同日而語哉魏志載李東家誡引易括囊元咎

籍用白茅慎之至四稱天下之至慎其惟嗣宗乎每与之言之及玄遠而未嘗臧否人物

真可謂至慎者矣嗣宗之慎終身凜凜冰之戒又非得于易而何耶也説贊譽王戎目

阮文業清倫有鑒識文業著書謂之阮子興杜恕言相觀才性鍾會之撰四本論才性離

合之異必受其影響其人即嗣宗之従父世而嗣宗又瑀著文賢論亦以品衡人才文翔

眾人一時橫為名篇今覽嗣宗之言若云繁稱是非諍貿追文者述固之論此故至

人情其盾而潤其文支其師揚文質家學可溯焉文兼元瑜西藻人物仍是東

漢以來清談鑒識之舊學至劉勰而尋其總結若嗣宗則與首集皆尚玄遠

又絕口不臧否人物意于立功立事抗志九悵之間寄情八莫之表於名教有所不

屑去人而入天獨趨于神理玉始以來玄學之韓撥其在益乎阮公著樂論乃推劉

于之間向不知劉子為誰氏考助傳云著樂論十四篇給即劬乎又獨孤氏頌云袞莫

大于矯時死名於是有而此于文此篇嚴輯且無其月唐時為人傳誦知阮文之不

存首尚多也凡此瑣瑣書未及快蕘用署昭其剩義君書疏理邃密援警引

穎古之務盡行見不脛而走阮公心事千載之下難以情測得君此書術如

陰薶二華掃阮公方靈一自當驚知己於千古也已

一九七六年三月十月饒宗頤時客巴黎

The Wei emperors and the
Ssu-ma usurpers

Ts'ao Ts'ao 曹操, 155–220
Ts'ao P'i 曹丕, Emperor Wen 文, 186–226
Ts'ao Jui 曹叡, Emperor Ming 明, 204–239
Ts'ao Fang 曹芳, Emperor Fei 廢,
  Prince of Ch'i 齊王, 231–274
Ts'ao Mao 曹髦, Emperor Shao 少,
  Duke of Kao-kuei hsiang 高貴鄉公, 241–260
Ts'ao Huan 曹奐, Emperor Yüan 元, 245–302

Ssu-ma I 司馬懿, 179–251
Ssu-ma Shih 司馬師, 208–255
Ssu-ma Chao 司馬昭, 211–265
Ssu-ma Yen 司馬炎, Emperor Wu 武, first emperor of the Chin 晉,
  236–290

INTRODUCTION

The third century A.D. was one of the great turning points in Chinese history, a period of changes in all aspects of human life. The poet we are going to study in the following pages was very much a product of his times, very much aware of the changes taking place about him, and he responded to them so strongly in his life and in his works that in a way he has become their embodiment: the ambiguities and contradictions he shows in regard to politics, to society and to the main currents of contemporary philosophy are in great part products of his historical milieu. They are what make it so difficult to study him, and so rewarding.

That poet is named Juan Chi 阮 籍 (polite name, or *tzu*, Ssu-tsung 嗣 宗) and he lived from 210 to 263, through the crucial decades of the changes that were to transfigure China. The very name of his poetic masterpiece, a long series of eighty-two poems, gives us a clue to his originality and his complexity. He called his poems 'Yung-huai shih' 詠 懷 詩, 'Poems which sing of my innermost thoughts'. The title had never been used before (although it almost immediately became the name of a poetic genre), nor had any poet ever given as much of himself in his verse: Juan Chi's 'innermost thoughts' cover a wider range of experience and probe more deeply into the mind than any poet had previously attempted. His poems are ambiguously committed to the political conflict he lived through and comment closely, by innuendo, on current events; at the same time they are deeply concerned with ultimate values, both moral and religious. But this concern for current events has produced some of the most obscure poetry ever written in China. The style is 'simple' and direct, as one would use when speaking straight from the heart, but it is often extremely hard, often impossible, to understand the allusions to contemporary figures. One commentator (probably one of the 'Five Officials', *wu-ch'en*) in a prefatory note to the selection of these poems that appears in the medieval *Anthology* (*Liu-ch'en chu Wen hsüan* 23, p. 1a) says that 'only the author himself could plumb their depths'. Juan Chi's innermost thoughts include his feelings towards the men in power, the usurpers of the Wei imperial throne or their underlings, and his outrage can only find ex-

[1]

pression in what, for want of a better term, I have called 'satire', a usually humorless satire, more like Dante's castigation of his Florentine enemies than the mordant and witty verse that usually goes under that name.

The obscurity and complexity of Juan Chi's verse and his outlandish actions in society have given rise to conflicting interpretations of his character, his ideals and his thought. For many, he is a Taoist iconoclast; for others a pure Confucian; a hero for some, a villain for others. There is a real consensus of opinion among the best critics, but even their view is a complex one. This complexity and lack of unanimity make it impossible or at least premature to treat Juan Chi in an impressionistic way, in a Lytton Strachey-like biography aimed at underlining his place in history and literature through the artistic impression of some salient events in his life or characteristic literary works. For the first full length study of such a controversial figure it has seemed to me to be imperative to present all that can be known of his life and works so that the reader can judge for himself.

Ideally this presentation should be chronological, taking into account any changes in attitude brought about through age and experience. These changes surely occurred, but the almost total lack of dated works makes any hypothesis very hazardous. I have therefore been forced to arrange the biographical material and the works more or less arbitrarily into three categories: politics (chapters 1–3), society (chapters 4–6), and the inner life (chapters 7–11). This is arbitrary because Juan Chi, like most poets, does not think in categories and, since social life and politics were constantly at the forefront of his mind, they color almost all his works. Politics especially obsessed him. A brief look at his family background and at contemporary events will help explain why.

The Juan family, into which Juan Chi was born in 210, had its ancestral home in Wei-shih in the commandery of Ch'en-liu, a town some thirty-five kilometers to the south of what is now K'ai-feng in the province of Honan. It was a rich family and traditionally Confucianist,[1] but, unless we believe what we read in obviously legendary genealogies,[2] it does not seem to have been of very great antiquity. Juan Chi's grandfather, Juan Tun 阮 敦,[3] is the first member of the family to be mentioned in history, but all we know of him is that he was the local magistrate in Chi-wu (near Ning-ling, Honan) where, early in 190, the great warlord and founder of the Wei dynasty, Ts'ao Ts'ao, first raised troops.[4]

We know much more, however, about Juan Chi's father, Juan Yü 阮 瑀, whose accomplishments in several fields have earned him a secure, if modest, place in China's history.[5] A musician, pupil of the great scholar Ts'ai Yung 蔡 邕 (131–192), he was a member of a very famous group of Chinese literary men, the 'Seven Masters of the Chien-an (196–220) Era'. As a poet he is generally considered one of the dimmer if not the dimmest lights of the group, but the dozen or so of his poems that remain are not, in their rugged simplicity, without merit. He was, in any case, more renowned for his prose, and in particular for his letters,[6] during his own lifetime: 'A great many of the letters and official edicts of the Military Government were written by Ch'en Lin and Juan Yü.'[7] The first emperor of the Wei dynasty, in a famous letter describing each of the Seven Masters, speaks of the 'delight produced by the grace and elegance of Juan Yü's missives', and elsewhere he speaks of them as being 'outstanding in our times'.[8] We see Juan Yü in action, writing a letter for the head of the Military Government, Ts'ao Ts'ao (who was himself a very great writer), in an anecdote that makes his letter-writing ability almost legendary.

> Ts'ao Ts'ao once had Juan Yü write a letter to Han Sui. At the time Ts'ao Ts'ao had gone out a short distance [from his camp] and Juan Yü, who was accompanying him, wrote out the entire draft on horseback. When he had finished he presented it and Ts'ao Ts'ao, holding his brush in his hand ready to correct it, finally found that he was unable to add or to delete anything.[9]

Juan Yü seems to have been devoted to Ts'ao Ts'ao. After refusing a secretarial post under Ts'ao Hung, Ts'ao Ts'ao's younger brother, he occupied several posts under Ts'ao Ts'ao, all directly under his supervision and all, technically at least, very minor, fifth or seventh grade posts. He was *chün-shih chi-chiu* 軍師祭酒 (post created in 198) and Secretary, *chi-shih* 記室, in Ts'ao Ts'ao's headquarters when the latter was *ssu-k'ung* 司空.[10] His last post seems to have been in the Department of Granaries, *ts'ang-ts'ao* 倉曹,[11] attached to the *ssu-k'ung*'s bureau. These posts were extremely modest, but it is probable that, during the disorders that accompanied the fall of the Han dynasty, a subordinate post under Ts'ao Ts'ao was more important than its official rank might lead one to believe. The post in the Department of Granaries must have been particularly crucial in connection with the 'agricultural colony' (*t'un-t'ien* 屯田) system Ts'ao Ts'ao inaugurated in 196, when he first became *ssu-k'ung*. The only other person known to have occupied the post, Liu Yeh 劉曄, who died around 234, became one of the most important officials in the government at the time of Ts'ao Jui, Emperor Ming.[12]

When Juan Yü died in 212, Ts'ao P'i, son of Ts'ao Ts'ao and first emperor of the Wei dynasty, was so moved by the plight of his widow that he wrote a poem to express his commiseration:

> Juan Yü and I were friends of old, but the span of life destiny allotted to him was short, and he died an early death.[13] I cannot think of the

orphans he has left behind without being sorely afflicted. That is why I have written this *fu* expressing the sadness and pain of his wife and children. I have commanded Wang Ts'an and the others to write too.[14]

Both Ts'ao P'i's and Wang Ts'an's poems remain, and they are touching tributes to a bereaved woman.

In spite of what seems to be Juan Yü's obvious attachment to the Ts'ao family, there is an amusing story, surely apocryphal, about his refusal to join Ts'ao Ts'ao's Military Government:

> Ts'ao Ts'ao, constantly hearing of Juan Yü's fame, called him to office, but he failed to respond. When, after repeated urgings, he fled into the mountains, Ts'ao Ts'ao had the mountain set on fire. They caught Juan Yü and sent him to Ts'ao Ts'ao who summoned him to an audience. Ts'ao Ts'ao was giving a great reception during his campaign against Ch'ang-an. Angered when Juan Yü refused to talk to him, he had him sent to the ranks of the musicians. But Juan Yü was well versed in music and knew how to play the zither, so he strummed on its strings and sang, improvising the following refrain as he went along:

> With grandeur ope's the Gate of Heav'n:
>   Great Wei responds to fortune's move!
> The Blue Umbrell' o'er Nine States circles:
>   The West regrets its Eastward move.
> A knight doth die for his dear friend
>   And women play for those they love:
> If Bounty and Right be far widespread,
>   Will not revolt unheard of prove?

> The refrain was made with such rapidity, the music was so uncommonly beautiful, that he was considered to surpass all assembled. Ts'ao Ts'ao was greatly pleased.[15]

The 'Blue Umbrella' and 'Nine States' of the third line are somewhat contradictory. According to Han ritual,[16] 'a carriage with a blue umbrella [or blue canopy]' was given as a present to sons of the emperor when they received principalities. But only the emperor himself was supposed to make the rounds of the Nine Provinces forming the Chinese empire. If the poem were genuine, this could have been construed as unsubtle flattery of Ts'ao Ts'ao, prematurely treated as accomplishing the emperor's duties while only in a 'princely' position (although he actually became Prince of Wei only in 216).

The anecdote, however, not only contradicts other sources[17] which state that Juan Yü, after refusing Ts'ao Hung's advances, accepted Ts'ao Ts'ao's freely, it also contains impossible anachronisms: Ts'ao Ts'ao took the title 'Duke of Wei' only in 213,[18] the year after Juan Yü's death; the latter could not, therefore, speak of 'Great Wei' with reference to Ts'ao Ts'ao. The letter written to Han Sui, moreover, must have been written before Ts'ao Ts'ao's campaign against Ch'ang-an, for it was Han Sui's defeat that permitted his attack on the capital. The historian who invented this anecdote was probably repeating a story typical of the period into which he introduced the name of Juan Yü as Latter Han local color.[19]

The very fact that this anecdote is apocryphal gives it a certain universality; the state of affairs it describes, the flight from official service of a prominent man, was almost standard behavior.[20] It is easy to see why. Juan Yü lived during one of the most chaotic periods China has ever known. The fall of the great Han dynasty meant the collapse of order, of the classical system of government, of thinking, and of morality. It brought with it rebellions that caused enormous loss of life. But it was not to flee from the perils of war and revolution that the best of the officials shied away from public life; it was because public life had become, as it always becomes in such a period, corrupted, and serving in it meant turning one's back on traditional law and order and following some upstart warlord whose whims and whose suspicion of his subaltern officers were often more murderous than the local rebellions themselves.

Juan Yü chose to serve Ts'ao Ts'ao, the warlord who, ostensibly, won, and we might imagine that his son would simply inherit his father's influence and serve the new Wei dynasty. Ts'ao Ts'ao did not, however, win a definitive victory. The dynasty he established, like the Republic established in 1911, was only an interregnum and before many years had passed, precisely at the moment Juan Chi was ready to enter public office, the new dynasty found itself face to face with another warlord whose family was destined, during the second half of Juan Chi's lifetime, to overthrow the Wei and establish a new empire.

This new warlord was named Ssu-ma I. He and his sons turned the political world during the last twenty years of Juan Chi's lifetime into something close to a living nightmare. The disloyalty, the hypocrisy and the cruelty of their methods have made them infamous in Chinese history. Some sixty years after Juan Chi's death, around 323, the following scene was enacted, a dramatic retrospective illustration of the events that took place under his very eyes.

> Wang Tao 王 尊 (267–330) and Wen Ch'iao 温 嶠 (288–329) were in attendance upon Emperor Ming (299–325) who asked Wen Ch'iao to tell him how his ancestors [the Ssu-ma usurpers] won the throne. Wen Ch'iao remained silent. After a bit, Wang Tao said: 'Wen Ch'iao is young and knows little of those things. Allow me to tell them to Your Majesty.' Wang Tao then related the whole story in detail: the foundation of the dynasty by Ssu-ma I, how he exterminated the famous

intellectuals and their families and surrounded himself with his own faction, up to the end of the regency of Ssu-ma Chao and the affair of the Duke of Kao-kuei-hsiang, [the young Wei emperor Ssu-ma Chao had assassinated in 260]. When Emperor Ming had heard him out he covered his face and buried it on the throne, saying: 'If it is as you have said, how will We be able to keep the imperial title for long?'[21]

1
THE EARLY WEI EMPERORS

Politics was at the center of Juan Chi's preoccupations, as it was of almost all Chinese poets of the Middle Ages. In the fourth and fifth centuries, indeed, ten of the greatest poets of the age were executed for political reasons,[1] and a concern for politics, a yearning for participation in the life of the court at the center of the civilized world, can be felt in most of the poetry of the time, even in the bucolic poetry of the greatest poets of them all, T'ao Yüan-ming and Hsieh Ling-yün. There can be no doubt that Juan Chi was tormented by the state of contemporary political life and that his poetry reflects that torment to a very high degree. Many of the Chinese critics who have studied him see only this aspect of his work and they are surely wrong to neglect the philosophical and religious aspirations he expresses; but the political concern is there and, however obscure his satirical verses must forever remain and however ultimately unsatisfactory our analyses of them must be, we must begin by trying to understand as much of Juan Chi's attitude towards contemporary politics as we can.

The earliest commentator of his poetry, Yen Yen-chih 顏 延 之 (384–456), a poet who also lived during a period of dynastic change, has already underlined this aspect of his poetry:

> It is said that Juan Chi wrote his songs because he lived during the reign of Ssu-ma Chao, in constant fear that some catastrophe might befall him.

And then he adds:

> Juan Chi personally served a dynasty in disorder and was in constant fear of being slandered and meeting disaster. That is why he expressed himself in song, and that is why each time he sighs, lamenting his life, although his aim is to criticize and reprimand [men in public life], his style is full of obscurities. Many centuries later, it will be difficult to fathom his true intentions. Therefore I have explained the main ideas in these verses in a general way and touched on their hidden meanings.[2]

This is a sobering view of the problem: less than two centuries after Juan Chi's death one of the most competent contemporary men of letters admits that it was no longer possible to give any but the most general outline of the satirical meaning of these poems. However humble this declaration may make us, it is clear that politics animates much of Juan Chi's verse and that it is there that we must begin our investigation.

In reading the anecdotes referring to Juan Chi's participation in the politics of his time, we have the impression that he is constantly attempting to withstand a figurative if not a literal 'smoking out' by the central authorities, as his father is said to have done some years before. The first time he enters history, sometime after 225,[3] when he was perhaps no more than sixteen years old, he is shying away from any involvement in political affairs. We see him visiting the governor of his home province, Wang Ch'ang 王 昶 (d. 259), a protégé of the powerful Ssu-ma I[4] and the founder of the most famous family of the Middle Ages, the Wang family of T'ai-yüan.

> Juan Chi once went with his uncle to Tung-chün[5] where the governor of Yen-chou, Wang Ch'ang, asked to have an interview with him. When he had been with Juan Chi a whole day long and was unable to get a word out of him, Wang Ch'ang was abashed and filled with admiration for him. He felt that, as far as he was concerned, Juan Chi was unfathomable.[6]

We are tempted to find Juan Chi slightly unfathomable too (and not with the laudatory overtones of the Chinese term), until we remember that an interview with one's provincial governor (even at the age of sixteen) meant that one was being 'rated' for the beginning of an official career.[7] Juan Chi's silence was his first refusal to enter politics and his first demonstration that he was not in any way an ordinary man, that he had no intention of docilely following the normal course of promotion to make his way in an official career.

We next see Juan Chi in politics some ten years later, in 239. But it is important, first, to study the general political developments up until that time. In 225 the son of Ts'ao Ts'ao, Ts'ao P'i, had been emperor of the Wei dynasty for about five years and had proved himself incapable of conquering the south and west of China, where two other kingdoms had been formed out of the debris of the Han empire: the kingdoms of Wu in the south and of Shu in the west. Ts'ao P'i was also inept in consolidating his own position in his northern kingdom of Wei, the most important, by far, of the Three Kingdoms. Instead of utilizing his own family in strategic posts throughout the empire[8] and in the capital (his brilliant brothers Ts'ao Chih and Ts'ao Chang, for example), he showed himself distrustful of their loyalty and insisted on keeping all authority in his own hands, giving important posts to lower officials. His aim in acting in this way was to build up a strong central government and thus thwart the feudalistic or at least centrifugal tendencies (endemic throughout Chinese history) which the Han dynasty, in spite of the bloodiest repressions of the local princes, had never been able to supress completely, and which the fall of the dynasty had strongly accentuated. This anti-feudalistic attitude weakened the power and prestige of the imperial family greatly. Ts'ao P'i died on 26 June 226 and was succeeded by his son, Ts'ao Jui, who continued in this same manner, relying on lesser officials instead of on his own family. To make matters worse, he engaged in the construction of costly and luxurious palaces and assembled harems, oppressing the people and weakening his personal prestige.

Ts'ao Jui died in 239 without any male offspring of his own. Like his father, Ts'ao Jui seemed to fear seizure of imperial power by his own family more than usurpation by outsiders and he chose a child of unknown origin to succeed him on the throne.[9] Before he died he also appointed two co-regents to assist his young successor: a distant relative (son of a nephew of Ts'ao Ts'ao), Ts'ao Shuang 曹 爽 , and an old and successful general, Ssu-ma I. The latter, who was descended from an ancient and powerful family of landowners, was soon brushed aside, but only for a short while. Ten years later, in 249, he came back from retirement, took all power into his own hands and began the process that was to end, sixteen years later, in the usurpation of the dynasty by his grandson, Ssu-ma Yen, first emperor of the Chin.

As Ts'ao Jui was the last adult to reign as emperor of the Ts'ao-Wei dynasty, his responsibility for its rapid decline was surely very great. Juan Chi was personally familiar with the events of his reign because they occurred during his own adolescence and youth (from his sixteenth to his twenty-ninth year of age), and he might very well have been inspired to comment on them in his poetry. There are two poems that I believe may be hidden commentaries on Ts'ao Jui's reign, Poems 31 and 29. We have no way of knowing when any of Juan Chi's poems in regular meters (*shih*) were written. It is probable, however, that unless he was endowed with remarkable foresight, these two poems date from sometime after the purge of 249, when Ssu-ma I's ambitions became clear and the fall of the Wei dynasty inevitable. Here is the first of the two poems:

31

I yoke up my carriage and leave the city of Wei,
 Turn towards the south and gaze at the Woodwind Terrace.
The sound of flutes and pipes remains there still,
 But where, oh where is the king of Liang?
5 He fed his knights on husks and bran

And housed his sages amidst the weeds;
But before his songs and dances ended
The soldiers of Ch'in had come, and come again.
'The Narrow Forest is no longer mine;
10   My scarlet palaces are covered with dust and grime,
My armies defeated below Hua-yang,
My body become ashes and earth.'

The first two words of the poem subtly suggest two lines of the *Shih ching*, two lines common to *Shih ching* 39 and 59:

I yoke up my carriage and go out roaming
In order to dissipate my sadness

The 'city of Wei' (literally, 'capital of Wei'), as we see in line 2, refers to Ta-liang, the capital of the ancient state of Wei, but contemporary readers would naturally think first of Lo-yang, capital of the Ts'ao-Wei dynasty. The words 'Woodwind' (literally, 'blowing') Terrace in the second line, however, show the reference is to ancient Ta-liang (which was called Chün-i during Juan Chi's time and is the present K'ai-feng), because this terrace (according to *Shui-ching chu* 22, p. 47) was located to the southeast of the town, on the other side of an ancient canal. It is this terrace, or what was left of it in the third century A.D., 'a mound some hundred paces square standing alone to the east of the "Shepherds' Swamp" ', that inspires the poem. Juan Chi seems to iden-tify it with the Fan 泛 Terrace, scene of a famous treaty in 336 B.C.[10] and of a probably fictional meeting between the King of Wei-Liang and his lords de-scribed in the *Chan-kuo ts'e* (Crump translation, No. 303). Juan Chi seems clearly to be thinking of the *Chan-kuo ts'e* anecdote in his poem. In it, the king is seen entertaining at a drinking party in the Fan Terrace when one of his guests, the Duke of Lu, makes a speech warning him against dissipation. According to the duke, too much wine, too much attention to fine cooking, too many women, or too much time spent 'in a high pavilion looking upon beautiful scenery' were fatal to a kingdom; in fact, any one of these things would suffice to ruin a kingdom altogether. He ends his harangue on a more personal note, accusing the king of dissipation and naming his poisons, in-cluding the 'Narrow Forest' which provides part of the 'beautiful scenery' that is so harmful to busy rulers.

Juan Chi has disregarded chronology in his poem to heighten the dramatic effect. The king of the Fan Terrace in the *Chan-kuo ts'e* anecdote is thought to be King Hui of Liang, the famous ruler who received Mencius in 336 B.C. and who reigned from 370 to 333. The battle at Hua-yang (some seventy kilo-meters southeast of K'ai-feng) took place in 273, and the final fall of the Wei-Liang took place only in 225, over a century after the death of King Hui. In

Juan Chi's poem we see the kingdom crumble before our eyes and seem almost to hear the sound of the flutes and pipes still lingering about the terrace.[11] (Apart from the personal pronoun in line 9 — commonly used in historical narrative to mean 'our side' or 'our hero' — there is no assurance that the last lines are to be put in the king's mouth as I have done, following *yüeh-fu* tradition.) The telescoping of chronology not only heightens the dramatic effect of this poem, it also makes the poem more susceptible to satirical interpretation. Ch'en Hang has said Juan Chi is 'using the old as a metaphor for the new', and that he is satirizing Ts'ao Jui's addiction to dissipation and disregard for the civil and military aspects of his reign. He, however, 'did not lose his country to an enemy state, as the King of Liang did, but rather to a powerful villain', Ssu-ma I.

Poem 31 probably gains in interest when read, on one level, as a description of the decline of the Ts'ao-Wei dynasty, but it can very well stand on its own. It belongs to a well defined category of poems in Chinese that takes its inspiration from the sight of some old monument and preaches the fragility of all worldly things, and its satire may be considered as only secondary. This cannot be said of the following poem, no. 29, because it is so obscure as to be incomprehensible without some sort of satirical key. The critics suggest Ts'ao Jui furnishes that key and I believe they are right. But the poem remains extremely obscure, and the most obscure of the entire series. Here is a literal translation:

29

Long ago I roamed in Ta-liang
    And climbed to the top of Mt Huang-hua.
Kung-kung lives there in black darkness,
    His high towers reaching to blue heaven.
5   The secluded wastelands stretch on and on
    And make me think, in sadness, of the one I pity.
But who is the one I pity?
    One who saw things clearly, but who tried to shine with only his
        own cleverness.
The Winged Dragon sank in Chi-chou;
10   The Goddess of Drought was unable to sleep.
He gave himself over to prodigality, scorning the morals of the times,
    And he cannot be said to have prolonged his years!

The most important thing about this poem is that it is so obscure that (unless the text is hopelessly corrupt) it must surely be a satire. It proves, if such proof were needed, that Juan Chi felt it necessary to express himself cryptically about something, and that something, in view of contemporary history, was almost surely politics and the change in dynasty that was taking place under his eyes. But even knowing and admitting all this, Poem 29 resists complete interpretation. My own explanation is based on Huang Chieh's, but it, too, seems to me to be so arbitrary as not even to merit the adjective 'probable': 'possible' is about the best that can be said for it.

Ta-liang, in line 1, as we have seen in the preceding poem, was the capital of the ancient Wei kingdom, located near the present K'ai-feng, far south of the old bed of the Yellow River. We can say, with Ch'en Hang, 'Ta-liang is symbolic of the Ts'ao-Wei dynasty'. But what are we to make of the next place name, Huang-hua? According to the commentary of *Shih chi* 43, p. 49, by Chang Shou-chieh 張 守 節 , it is the name of a mountain on the north side of the Yellow River. The *Shui-ching chu* 9, p. 81, is more precise, speaking of a Huang-hua Valley, whose northern wall was seventeen *li* high, located just north of the present Mt Lin-lü 林 慮 in the northernmost corner of Honan on the Shansi border. This would make it almost exactly one hundred and fifty kilometers from Ta-liang. In other opening, *yüeh-fu* inspired, couplets of this kind (Poems 9, 16, 31 and 64) Juan Chi makes the object of his roaming much closer to his point of departure. Perhaps it is not too far-fetched to see Ta-liang as symbolic of Ts'ao Ts'ao's capital, Yeh, some fifty kilometers to the east of Mt Huang-hua. This is Huang Chieh's and Ku Chih's interpretation (although the latter needlessly and unconvincingly complicates matters) and it helps us to understand the following lines. Kung-kung is a famous mythological hero who 'built a tower for the Emperors north of the K'un-lun Mountains' (*Shan-hai ching* 8, p. 2a; 17, p. 4b); he himself never reigned, but, like Ts'ao Ts'ao, was the ancestor of a dynasty (*Shan-hai ching* 18, p. 8b). And Ts'ao Ts'ao, too, is famous for the three towers he built in the northern part of the western wall of Yeh.[12] It is perhaps from one of these towers that Juan Chi looks out at the desolate countryside (dynastic decay?) and thinks of the man he pities. The remainder of the poem is concerned with this unnamed figure. Lines 8 to 10 are the most difficult to interpret, line 8 being particularly obscure, whichever of the two variant texts one follows. The text I have followed implies that the 'man pitied' was intelligent, but relied too much on his own intelligence without consulting or using others. The other text, *ying tzu-jan* 應 自 然 , would imply his intelligence was natural, hereditary. The Winged Dragon in line 9 is another mythological hero. The text of line 10 does not read 'the Goddess of Drought' at all, but 'the fabulous woman'. I have followed Huang Chieh and read 妭 (a variant for 魃) for the 妖 of the text because the Winged Dragon, the Goddess of Drought and Kung-kung all figure in a myth described in the *Shan-hai ching* 17, pp. 4b–5b, and the two former are linked together by Chang Heng as examples of officials who work harmoniously together for their sovereign.[13]

The *Shan-hai ching* describes a battle Ch'ih-yu 蚩 尤 waged against the Yellow Emperor. The latter first sent the Winged Dragon against Ch'ih-yu in 'the wilds of Chi-chou' and then, when the dragon was in danger of being beaten by the gods of the wind and the rain, he sent down his daughter, Pa, the Goddess of Drought, who stopped the rain and allowed Ch'ih-yu to be killed. Juan Chi not only alludes to this battle, but to the fates of the Winged Dragon and the Goddess of Drought. By saying the former 'sank in Chi-chou' and the latter 'was unable to sleep' he is probably referring to the fact that both these figures were unable to go back up to heaven after their battles. The Winged Dragon is said (by Kuo P'u, *Shan-hai ching* 14, p. 6a) to live underground since he could no longer return to heaven, and the Goddess to be established 'north of the Red River' (*Shan-hai ching* 17, p. 5b).[14] The invocation of these two mythological figures thus alludes to the refusal of the subject of the poem, the 'man pitied', to rely on others: even after having conquered the Yellow Emperor's enemies, the Winged Dragon and the Goddess of Drought were not allowed to go back to his heavenly court. And the last two lines of the poem describe the subject's profligacy and (personal or dynastic) short life.

With the exception of Ch'en Hang, all the critics think this poem satirizes Ts'ao Jui. Chu Chia-cheng, Chiang Shih-yüeh, Tseng Kuo-fan and Wu Ju-lun, however, all follow the Ming critic Yang Shen who, in his *Shih-hua pu-i*,[15] attempts to show that the poem satirizes the disorder brought to Ts'ao Jui's harem and court by his Empresses Mao and Kuo. Yang Shen quotes a story from the *Chan-kuo ts'e*, that I have not been able to find there, but which seems to be based upon *Shih chi* 43, pp. 48 and 49, to defend his thesis. His explanation has the merit of accounting for line 2, but almost nothing else! According to Ch'en Hang, the Goddess of Drought symbolizes Ssu-ma I, and the Winged Dragon the Ts'ao clique he put to death in the series of purges begun in 249. Huang Chieh's explanation accounts for many more of the baffling lines of this baffling poem and corresponds well with what we know of Ts'ao Jui's character. He was indeed extremely intelligent, authoritarian, unwilling to share his power with men worthy of it, and the sumptuous palaces he had built rivalled those of 'Shih-huang', the 'First Emperor' of the Ch'in and of Emperor Wu of the Han. His early death at the age of thirty-five also corresponds well to the last line of the poem.

The co-regency Ts'ao Jui set up before he died very soon proved unworkable. Ssu-ma I and Ts'ao Shuang were too completely unlike and represented such different political philosophies that they were unable to cooperate in any manner. The former, after being 'kicked upstairs' to a meaningless but very highly graded post, retired from the court and devoted his activities, significantly, to the army. All we know of the politics of this period and of the tendencies of the Ts'ao Shuang and Ssu-ma I factions has been irreparably falsified by the historians who first described them under the strict censorship of the Ssu-ma. The partisans of Ts'ao Shuang are shown as frivolous reformers, effeminate and profligate, with no understanding of political affairs and with a ruinous penchant for idle metaphysical speculation. The Ssu-ma clique, on the contrary, is shown as being made up of traditionalistic political realists who quoted the holy Confucian Canon in their speeches and followed more or less Machiavellian methods in their acts. We know almost nothing of the reforms the Ts'ao Shuang group attempted to put into practice. The censorship exercised by the Ssu-ma when they assumed complete power as the Chin dynasty was so thorough that nothing remains, except violent criticism of Ts'ao Shuang and his clique from the high officials — the Old Guard — whose positions were perhaps menaced by the new reforms.[16] But, whatever real qualities these reforms may have had, they were probably doomed to failure. Thanks to the rigorous anti-feudalism of all the Ts'ao sovereigns, the reformists had no power in the provinces; instead of using the imperial princes as regional satraps or at least provincial governors, they were assigned to their principalities as if to prisons. One can imagine that Ssu-ma I had powerful friends among the regional aristocracy. In the capital itself it seems he had built up strong support in the army which he had led repeatedly in major battles since the early days of the dynasty. The balance of forces and the political ineptitude of the reformists were perhaps only symptoms of a deeper tendency working in favor of Ssu-ma I and the regional aristocracy, a tendency towards local autonomy, a tendency away from the strong and centralized government that the Ts'ao dynasty had attempted to establish since it came to power.

From the beginning of his administrative career until its very end, Juan Chi was in the service of the leaders of the Ssu-ma clan. His first post, obtained in 239, was that of a low (sixth grade) advisory official, *ts'ung-shih chung-lang* 從 事 中 郎 , in the bureau of Ssu-ma I. In that year, the first of the co-regency with Ts'ao Shuang, Ssu-ma I had been made *t'ai-fu* 太 傅 , a very high, but mainly honorific post that, Ts'ao Shuang hoped, would take from him the direct control of current affairs. The acceptance of this post of *ts'ung-shih chung-lang* in 239 does not mean that Juan Chi in any way supported Ssu-ma I's dynastic ambitions or that he was disloyal to the reigning house of Wei. Ssu-ma I's pretensions became clear only many years later when, perhaps, it was already too late for Juan Chi to disassociate himself from him and his family. In any case, this first post, and all his succeeding posts, in spite of their relatively low status, kept Juan Chi in the center of political life, in the bureaus of those who were to become the de facto rulers of the state.

Juan Chi was called to a new office when, on 1 September 242, Chiang Chi
蔣 濟(d. 249) became *t'ai-wei* 太 尉, one of the highest consultative posts
in the administration.[17] 'The *t'ai-wei* Chiang Chi, hearing that Juan Chi had
outstanding talents, called him to office. Juan Chi went to the municipal
offices and presented a memorandum.'[18] This memorandum refusing Chiang
Chi's appointment became a classic, the model for such letters of renunciation
of official life. It is included in the medieval 'Anthology of literature', *Wen
hsüan*, and one sentence, 'I am soon to set about ploughing on the sunny side
of the eastern flooded fields . . . ', is alluded to at least six times in the
'Anthology' alone by later writers who have paid it the homage of using it in
their own compositions. The letter opens with a typical, if rather violent,
polite salutation.

Letter to Lord Chiang

My guilt [in daring to write to you] is worthy of death, worthy of
death! I humbly beg to remark that because my illustrious Lord unites
all the virtues in his person he now occupies a most exalted position;
brilliant men all look up to him, and superior intelligences make their
way towards him. The day he set up his headquarters everyone counted
upon becoming a subaltern in it, but when the letters of appointment
were sent out, your servant was the first to receive one. When [the
commoner] Tzu-hsia dwelt on the banks of the Hsi, Wen, Marquis of
Wei, treated him with the utmost deference;[19] when Tsou-tzu lived in
the shade of Millet Valley, Prince Chao shared his carriage with him.[20]
Now, the reason that princes, lords and great men demean their persons
and lower themselves to men who wear common cloth, who dwell
humbly and who gird themselves with belts of simple, tanned leather,[21]
is that these men are endowed with the true Way [the *tao*]. I have the
virtues of neither Tsou nor Tzu-hsia, and I have their rusticity: it is in
no way fitting that I should be selected.

In order to keep from occupying an important official post, I am
soon going to set about ploughing on the sunny side of the eastern
flooded fields and send out my taxes of millet.[22] I am sick and exhausted with carrying firewood and the strength of my legs is not great: I
could not bear to accept your command to fill an official position. I beg
you, take back your misplaced bounty and you will add even greater
luster to your impeccable nominations![23]

But it was not so easy to refuse one of the highest officials in the land. We are
told further that

Chiang Chi had been afraid that Juan Chi would not come at all, so that,
when he received his memorandum, he quite happily sent a flunkey to
fetch him. But Juan Chi had already left. Chiang Chi was furious. Then

> Juan Chi's fellow townsmen all reasoned with him and he finally took
> up his post. Later he returned home with the excuse that he was ill.[24]

Five years later, in 247, Ts'ao Shuang, who had attempted from the beginning of the co-regency to by-pass Ssu-ma I in all government affairs, took over
all governing power. Ssu-ma I, who had been extremely active as general of
the army during this period, proclaimed himself sick and retired to await a
propitious moment to counter-attack. There can be little doubt that Juan Chi
was in the center of the political scene of his day, for at this very time, Ts'ao
Shuang and his clique attempted to enrol him on their side. They were no
more successful than Chiang Chi. The Minister for State Affairs, *shang-shu*,
was the famous philosopher Ho Yen 何 晏 , Ts'ao Shuang's closest aide.
Around 247[25] Juan Chi 'became Secretary of the Minister for State Affairs,
shang-shu lang, but after a short time he again vacated his post because of illness.'[26] Perhaps when Ho Yen was unable to keep Juan Chi in his bureau
Ts'ao Shuang himself tried, for 'when Ts'ao Shuang took over the government,
he summoned Juan Chi to act as a Military Aide, *ts'an-chün*, but he refused
because of illness and hid himself away in the country.[27] In a little more than
a year Ts'ao Shuang was killed. The people of the times admired Juan Chi's
foresight.'[28]

In 249 Ssu-ma I came back from his 'retirement' to take his revenge on
Ts'ao Shuang and his clique. On 5 February, when Ts'ao Shuang and his
brothers had gone with their imperial relatives to visit the family tombs to the
north of Lo-yang, Ssu-ma I had the city gates closed, mobilized the army, and
took up a strategic position on the pontoon bridge across the River Lo. His
ostensible reason for these acts was that he wanted to depose the Ts'ao
Shuang clique because they had proven themselves irresponsible and thus 'disloyal' to the emperor. Many of the men in power seem to have believed Ssu-
ma I. The *t'ai-wei* Chiang Chi (to whom Juan Chi wrote the famous letter just
quoted) went so far as to send a letter to Ts'ao Shuang vouching for Ssu-ma
I's lack of ulterior motives. That Chiang Chi was convinced of Ssu-ma I's loyalty to the reigning dynasty seems clear, because his death some months later
is attributed to his chagrin for having been an unwilling tool in the capture
and execution of Ts'ao Shuang. However humbly he played his role before
249, Ssu-ma I annihilated his political opponents with such violence that it
became obvious he was the new man in power.

> Ssu-ma I carried out his massacres on a large scale. When he killed Ts'ao
> Shuang, he exterminated all his associates and the three branches of
> their families [their paternal and maternal relations and their in-laws].
> He made no distinction between male and female, young and old: their
> mother-in-law's sisters and their daughters-in-law all were killed.[29]

A source of doubtful value adds: 'In a single day's carnage the number of famous men in the empire was cut in half.'[30]

The excellent fifth-century commentator of the *San-kuo chih*, P'ei Sung-chih 裴 松 之, criticizes the author of this last passage for being too 'original', for not sticking closely enough to traditional accounts. But it is quite possible that his testimony is true here. The Ts'ao family in general and Ts'ao Shuang in particular surrounded themselves with brilliant and independent intellectuals (the 'famous men' if the citation), and had done so since the time of their great ancestor, Ts'ao Ts'ao. This imperial support of what we would probably call 'independent intellectual activity' helped bring about a veritable literary and philosophical renaissance that was to have far-reaching effects in the history of Chinese thought. The regency of Ts'ao Shuang in particular, the period from 240 to 249 that goes under the name 'Cheng-shih' 正 始 , was famous for its philosophical conversations called 'pure talk', *ch'ing-t'an* 清 談 , and for its intellectual activity in general: it was to be remembered throughout the Middle Ages as an ideal age when Chinese thinkers had the freedom and felt the need to reconstruct their whole traditional philosophy.[31] The triumph of Ssu-ma I put an end to this freedom and brought a return to Confucian traditionalism.

Were there economic tensions or 'contradictions' between the Ssu-ma and the Ts'ao cliques, as recent Chinese scholars have attempted to prove?[32] Were the Ts'ao really the representatives of the 'smaller landed gentry', 'progressive forces' acting against the economically superior, 'reactionary' old landed magnates led by the Ssu-ma? It is very difficult, if not impossible, to know; we have so little information about the actual distribution of wealth in the third century. We do know, however, that beginning in the late Han and throughout the Middle Ages, indeed until the end of the T'ang, China was ruled by an 'aristocracy' of 'noble families', proud of their origins and extremely careful to preserve their 'nobility' by intermarrying with families of their own rank. The members of the Ts'ao family were, without any doubt, close to being pariahs, since they were descended from the adopted son of a eunuch, and the marriage alliances they contracted were with women of the lowest reaches of society.[33] It is very probable that, whatever their economic strength, they did belong to a social class very inferior to the Ssu-ma. What rank did Juan Chi's family occupy in this society? Were they, too, members of the 'middle and small landed gentry', and thus socially, economically and intellectually allied to the Ts'ao camp as has been suggested?[34] We shall see that Juan Chi's family was a powerful one, but how powerful, and with what allegiances we do not know. The whole problem is very complex and probably impossible to solve with any assurance. What we do know of the tendencies of the two opposing groups, the anti-feudalism of the Ts'ao, and their 'liberal', 'heretical' intellectual views, compared with the traditionalistic Confucianism and the insistence upon the feudalistic 'Doctrine of Names' of the Ssu-ma, shows that there were in all probability economic, social and intellectual conflicts inspiring their animosities. In any case, Ssu-ma I's victory in 249 hastened the tendency towards a new kind of feudalism and put an end to the anachronistic centralization on the Han model that the Wei dynasty had unsuccessfully attempted to achieve.[35]

Juan Chi was the son of a loyal servant of the founder of the Wei dynasty; he may even have been the descendant of the earliest promoters of the dynasty, since his family was influential in the very region Ts'ao Ts'ao first raised troops. He himself had served the dynasty since 239 when he occupied his first official post. He could perhaps have construed Ssu-ma I's actions in 249 to have been in the best interest of the reigning dynasty: the almost universal condemnation of Ts'ao Shuang and his friends by later historians may, of course, have been justified. But it soon became clear, as we shall see, that Ssu-ma I and his successors were not working for the emperor as loyal subjects. They were working for their own interests and intended (eventually) to set up their own dynasty. Yet Juan Chi remained, throughout his political career, closely associated with the Ssu-ma. A superficial reading of his biography might lead one to believe he was one of their loyal servants, indifferent to the usurpation they were slowly, but ruthlessly, bringing about.[36] He never tells us where his loyalties stood in so many words. How could he, when even the leaders of the Ssu-ma, down to the eve of their actual usurpation, proclaimed themselves loyal to the reigning Wei dynasty? How could he, when even the slightest suggestion of sedition could bring rapid death not only to himself but to his entire family? It was only by satire and innuendo that he could say what was in his heart, and only by serving as little as possible that he could stay loyal to the reigning dynasty in this period of disloyalty and paradox. Any other procedure, any frank outburst or even retirement (as in the case of Hsi K'ang and, later, Hsieh Ling-yün) could be interpreted as hostile to the actual governing force and bring total destruction. The poems we have read are probably satirical, but, in my interpretation at least, can hardly be called seditious. Their criticism of the prodigality of Ts'ao Jui is given, I believe, more in sadness than in ire, but it is neither 'anti-Ts'ao' nor 'pro-Ssu-ma'.

One of the few dated works we have by Juan Chi is a *fu* written sometime after the coup d'état of 249. In it he goes about as far as he ever does towards outright criticism of the men in power. He does so, however, by the most devious of satires. Read superficially, the following *fu* seems far removed from politics, but in the context of his other work and of its date, it seems almost surely satirical. The short preface tells the background succinctly.

The doves

During the Chia-p'ing period [249–254] I acquired a pair of young doves and fed them day after day on millet. Later they were killed by a dog, and I wrote the following *fu* about them:

That good year's bounteous foison
> Was at the period when you vaguely see only the first glimmer-
> ings of universal renewal.[37]

Rare birds, bound by bonds of love,
> Belonging to the species of the singing doves,

5 Swooped among the leafless trees to find a nook in which to bear
> their young,
> Lodging their high tiered nests[38] in a distant pine.

They breathed the cloudy vapors in and out, in harmony with
> natural forces,
> Roaming, one after the other, in the morning light.

Having thus lived idly for ten days, they brought forth their
> young,

10 And admired the fine appearance of their seven fledglings.

First they folded their wings, with their feathers set upright[?],
> But they were caught in the violent autumnal wind:

They were thrown over, with no one to save them,
> And when again they were shaken and fell, there was no one
> to help them.

15 They rose above Mount Huan and wandered here and there[39]
> Yearning to return when they approached their old country-
> side.

They raised their doleful song as they parted
> Saddened that once they left they would no longer perch
> together,

But would flit here and there, forever homeless:

20 How pained [the parents] were for the affliction and fear of
> their weak children!

On whom could they rely to nourish them?
> The brothers could only depend upon one another.

They turned away from the grass of the fields to seek human
> kindness
> And took refuge in a gentleman's quiet room.

25 The food of fragrant millet seemed good to them
> And they found their peace in his unhurried chambers.

When they entwined their necks as they cleaned their striped
> breasts,
> They heightened the overflowing seduction of their florid

beauty.

They set straight their handsome forms to show forth their adorn-
ments,

30   Desiring that their majestic bearing be always just as it should.

For a time they looked up and down and roamed at will,

Seeking love in the present moment.

Why should they yearn to soar in the air?

They wanted to requite the love that was shown to them and
forget the hunter's net.

35   They encountered the furious rage of a mad dog:

It was as if their fragile bodies had received a whip of thorns.

He wanted to destroy them, annihilate them,

And then throw them away and let them disintegrate.

On the surface there seems nothing satirical about this poetic epitaph for a
pair of stray doves that Juan Chi, in his fondness for birds (his poems are full
of references to them) tamed and fed. But there is something peculiarly violent and abrupt about the last lines which makes one look for some hidden
meaning. Is this a satire against Ssu-ma I, lampooned as a 'mad dog' for having
killed Ts'ao Shuang and his brother Ts'ao Hsi? The events of 249 must have
been in everyone's mind and even the slightest allusion would suggest them to
a contemporary reader.

If Juan Chi did indeed want to write a satire, the doves were a good choice,
because white doves are said to be a sign of good government and semi-
miraculous appearances of them occurred at various moments during his own
lifetime.[40] The description of birds who take refuge in a scholar's courtyard
was also a common theme,[41] an allegory of the help a poor scholar-statesman
might receive from a man in power. Line 12 perhaps also contains a direct
reference to the Ssu-ma. The doves 'were caught in the violent autumnal
wind'. The 'autumnal wind' in Chinese is literally a 'metallic wind', a common
epithet, since metal is symbolic of the west and of autumn. But it was also to
be symbolic of the usurping Ssu-ma (Chin) dynasty, since the Wei had chosen
the 'element' earth as their symbol in 237,[42] and, according to the complicated theories of the Five Elements then in vogue, the element of earth would
be overcome by the element of metal.[43] If the doves do indeed symbolize the
Ts'ao family or some of their supporters executed by the Ssu-ma, the 'metallic wind' could symbolize the usurping Ssu-ma. Whatever the inspiration for
this minor work, its subject matter introduces us to the somber, pessimistic
facet of Juan Chi's psychology that we will see again and again.[44]

When Ssu-ma I died in 251, Juan Chi was given the same post of *ts'ung-shih
chung-lang* in the headquarters of his son and successor, Ssu-ma Shih.[45] The
new generalissimo continued in the tradition of his father by eliminating all

the elements in the government that might prove disloyal to him. The climax of his reign came in 254. In that year he killed Li Feng 李 豐 in cold blood with the pommel of his sword during an interview with him,[46] and had other intellectuals who had collaborated with Ts'ao Shuang executed. A few months later he deposed the twenty-year old emperor Ts'ao Fang (the 'Prince of Ch'i') and installed a new emperor, thirteen-year old Ts'ao Mao (the 'Duke of Kao-kuei-hsiang'). These acts were carried out against men who attempted to save the Ts'ao dynasty from the usurpation that was daily becoming more obvious, but Ssu-ma Shih dressed them up with floods of hypocritical tears, and long, solemn, meaningless Confucian sermons on his loyalty to the Ts'ao and to their empire. By 254 his pretensions were clearly understood. When Ts'ao Mao, the new young emperor, arrived in Lo-yang, he alighted from his carriage to bow to the assembled officials who had come to meet him. The officials tried to prevent him, saying that the emperor should not bow before his servants. Ts'ao Mao disregarded them, saying, 'I am another's servant', implying, of course, that he had to obey the orders of Ssu-ma Shih.[47]

The second and, alas, the last dated work by Juan Chi, the *fu* 'Shou-yang Mountain', was written exactly at the time of the deposition of Ts'ao Fang. It is a precious, if ambiguous, clue to his own feelings about the grave political events taking place. Ts'ao Fang was deposed during the ninth and tenth moons of the sixth year of the Chia-p'ing era, that is, roughly speaking, during the month of October, 254. The new emperor, Ts'ao Mao, proclaimed a new era, that of Cheng-yüan, on the second of November. Thus when Juan Chi in his short introduction speaks of the 'first year of Cheng-yüan', we see that he wrote after the deposition of Ts'ao Fang. The title of the poem itself tells us the work is concerned with politics, for Shou-yang Mountain is always associated with two figures from antiquity, the brothers Po I and Shu Ch'i (Elder I and Younger Ch'i), who, after the fall of the Shang dynasty at the very end of the second millenium B.C., refused to serve the new Chou rulers, choosing to 'hide away on Shou-yang Mountain, gathering and eating ferns until they died of hunger'.[48] Confucius praised the attitude of the two brothers,[49] and they are generally considered, by orthodox Confucianists, to be paragons of steadfast and disinterested virtue. The deposition of Ts'ao Fang did not mark the formal end of the Ts'ao dynasty, but it underlined very clearly the (already obvious) dynastic intentions of the house of Ssu-ma. Juan Chi, son of a servant of Ts'ao Ts'ao and himself an official of the dynasty, would be in a position somewhat analogous to that of the two brothers if and when Ssu-ma Shih actually proclaimed a new dynasty. Should he turn to the usurpers, the Ssu-ma, or should he hide himself away on some Shou-yang Mountain and remain faithful to the declining Ts'ao? As will be seen in the Preface to the *fu*, Shou-yang Mountain is described in dramatic juxtaposition with the would-be usurpers' headquarters. The mountain was about five kilometers northeast of the city wall of Lo-yang, so that Juan Chi could probably see it easily from his official office. But it is strange that, as he says in his Preface, he went to the *south* wall enclosing the headquarters compound and turned *north*. This means that he had before him both Ssu-ma Shih's headquarters and in the background, above it, Shou-yang Mountain. On the ideological plane, he had his government office and possible political activity before him, and, looming over behind it, the mountain of retirement from political life. It should perhaps be remarked that the mountain was a famous burial place from antiquity[50] and that it housed the tomb of the first Wei emperor, Ts'ao P'i. The *fu* is thus built around the fundamental tension between a political and social life on the one hand, and a solitary, eremitic life in loyal retirement on the other.

Shou-yang Mountain

In the autumn[51] of the first year of Cheng-yüan [254], when I was still an Adjutant[52] in the generalissimo's[53] headquarters, I walked alone to the south wall and turned north towards Shou-yang Mountain.[54]

Before the end of the year,
    Just at the beginning of a new week [?], the sky was heavily
        overcast.
The wind whirled in crooked gusts;
    The rain spun about and soaked my lapels.
5   Crickets were singing in the eastern chamber
    And the shrike cried in the western wood.
Friendless as the season drew to its close,
    I felt anguished and sick at heart.
I dusted my silken robes to go out of the gate,
10   But my hat strings I left untied,
As I slowly wandered to and fro to cast my thoughts afar,
    Sighing deeply, chanting softly.
I wanted to dress up and leave,
    For the vulgar crowd, a disorderly lot, has laughed at me.
15   Quiet, solitary, I stood alone;
    Truly, I was like a lonesome tree without support.
In my heart I desired only one thing: separation;
    The mob's falsifying attacks on integrity seemed so foul to
        me![55]
Even if I might really fulfil my true self without leaving the world,
20   I should still rather fly away to lead the life of a hermit!
For a moment I raised my head to broaden my view
    And gazed at Shou-yang's crest.

The trees in thick woods there were densely entangled
And gave rise to the confused sound of the soughing wind.

25 Below, it was steep and precipitous, without refuge;
Above, it was clear and open, without support.
The phoenix soars over and does not perch
Where hooting owls crowd and roost together.[56]
Pushed along far away as by the wind
30 The two old men, [Po I and Shu Ch'i[57]], exhausted, there
took their stand.
Truly they lived tortured as in a prison [in Chou]:
How could we, at leisure here, dare to indulge in slander of
them?
Since they rejected [Chou's] good millet and had none,
They could do nothing but gather ferns and accept death.
35 Others turned their backs on Yin [=Shang] and followed Ch'ang
[=King Wen of Chou],
Hastening to leave danger and defeat.
These [two] came forward and did not cooperate [with Chou]:
What is there in their action to praise as 'Good' or 'Just'?

They were reckless of their lives and unhappy;
40 Their principle was to struggle for renown.
Look well into what the preceding generations have said of this:
What is there to admire in all their eloquent discussions?

If they sought for the Way in trivialities,
Why have there been so many words and falsehoods wasted on
them?
45 As for me, I shall guard my soul in pure emptiness:
Why should I talk [of these two] with overflowing commiseration?[58]

The general progress of this poem is easy to follow. Juan Chi begins by describing himself as a solitary figure, misunderstood by a vulgar, back-biting
crowd. The whirling wind is symbolic of calumny; the crickets and the shrike,
of the approach of winter. His robes are silken because he is an official in the
government. His disregard for his untied hat strings shows his disdain for
ordinary social behavior, a disdain we shall see again and again and that has
become part of his historical image. This spurning of society is at the center
of Juan Chi's preoccupations in this *fu*. To avoid criticism from the snickering
crowd, however, he realizes that he must set himself right, 'dress up', if he
wants to leave. His disenchantment with human society is one of the great
themes of his poetry and here reinforces his feelings of loneliness and his desire to leave the world.

All these morose, anti-social thoughts must have occurred to him while he was looking at his government office, for it is only in line 21 that he 'raises his head'. The desire to 'fly away' naturally makes him look up towards the mountains, the traditional home of hermits, but the portrait he paints of them is hardly tempting: his appreciation of mountain landscape is much closer to that of the poet of the 'Chao yin-shih' in the *Ch'u tz'u* than to that of the medieval landscape poets who were to follow in less than a century.[59]

As Juan Chi suggests in lines 41–2, Po I and Shu Ch'i had been a perennial topic of discussion for Chinese thinkers. The mere mention of their name, or of the Shou-yang Mountain, suggested what was perhaps life's greatest moral problem to countless generations of Chinese of the ruling class: should they serve in government or should they, when the men in power were lacking in virtue, hide away in private life and take no part in the direction of state affairs? It is difficult for us to realize the importance of the moral choice involved. Chinese society was, and probably still is, much more 'monolithic' than anything ever known in the West, and a failure to serve in the government meant a failure to serve mankind, a failure to realize one's life as a moral being.

The problem became obsessional in times of strife and inspired a great number of literary works in which the author attempted to justify his decision to avoid or accept political commitment. Shortly before 170, Juan Chi's father's teacher, Ts'ai Yung, in the preface to his own 'Explanation', 'Shih-hui' 釋 誨 , quotes the names of Tung-fang Shuo, Yang Hsiung, Pan Ku and Ts'ui Yin, all men who had written similar self-justifications,[60] and he could have included many, many more. The agonizing dilemma has persisted throughout Chinese history, and as likely as not, the anguished authors include in their essays a discussion of Po I and Shu Ch'i and of their decision to remain aloof from politics after the accession of the Chou to power. Confucius, who himself was unable to serve in government for any length of time, praised the two brothers on numerous occasions, and orthodox thinkers generally echo his praise, as does Juan Chi's own father in a eulogy he wrote of Po I and Shu Ch'i.[61] 'Heretical' writers such as Chuang-tzu[62] or Tung-fang Shuo[63] make fun of them, saying their sacrifice was vainglorious and useless. Other, more syncretic writers such as Ssu-ma Ch'ien in the first biography of the *Shih chi*, present a highly nuanced view of them and show how difficult the problem really was.

Juan Chi's attitude is complex and contradictory, as is often the case with him. First, in line 32, he seems to praise the two ancient figures, or at least to refuse to admit the kind of 'slander' found in *Chuang-tzu* 8. But then, in lines 38 and following, he very much imitates Chuang-tzu, and seems to write off the two brothers' sacrifice as vainglorious and futile. The entire first part of the *fu* (lines 1–30), moreover, is thoroughly in accord with Confucian tradition in its description of a lonely scholar revolted by the world's corruption. We will find this contradiction between traditionalism, 'Confucianism', devotion to ancient social and political values on the one hand, and 'Taoism', rejection of all social values on the other, throughout Juan Chi's works. There is no simple explanation for it, but the author of Juan Chi's funerary stele referred to earlier (see Introduction, note 2) has suggested one reason that seems important in reference to the 'Shou-yang Mountain' *fu*. According to him, Juan Chi 'denigrated Po I and Shu Ch'i's purity so that it would be impossible to praise his own [purity].' That is, by ostensibly making light of Po I and Shu Ch'i's sacrifice, Juan Chi was covering up his own tracks, dissimulating his own 'retirement' within politics, his own attempt at maintaining himself pure in a political situation he could neither openly denounce nor openly extricate himself from. The penultimate line, in which he declares he will 'guard his soul in pure emptiness', suggests a quasi-religious resolution of his dilemma. Such an attitude adds a new dimension to the traditional retirement from politics preached by righteous men in times of corruption: Juan Chi is here a forerunner of a new kind of hermit, a religious recluse.

That current events inspired Juan Chi's meditation seems certain, since he condemns the duplicity of his contemporaries outright, but his attitude towards the events themselves is less clear, and a pentameter poem he wrote on the same theme does little to clarify it. On the contrary, the poem seems to open up an even broader philosophical vista than the *fu*. Like all the other poems by Juan Chi, this one is not dated, but the setting and the very vocabulary show it to be affiliated to the *fu* (Huang Chieh 'suspects' it was written at the same time). The first line imitates the first line of a popular ballad (*yüeh-fu*).[64]

9

As I walked out the Upper Eastern Gate
    I looked off north, towards Shou-yang's crest.
Below were men who gathered ferns;
    Above, a grove of goodly trees.
5   Where can I find good times again?
    Stiff frost has wet my robe's lapels.
Cold winds shake the mounts and hills;
    Somber clouds make the darkness thicken.
The singing goose flies away south
10   As the shrike gives forth a doleful noise.
This blankness comes from the *shang* mode:
    O! What grief and sorrow wound my heart!

The 'Upper Eastern Gate' of line 1 was the northernmost of the three gates in the eastern wall of Lo-yang.[65] It was the closest gate to the Pei-mang Mountains and to their culminating point, Mt Shou-yang, to which Juan Chi turns his gaze. The tacit allusion, immediately understood by all Chinese readers, is to Po I and Shu Ch'i, and line 3, referring to 'fern gatherers', only confirms the already obvious reference to the two martyrs. The 'grove of goodly trees' of line 4 is perhaps an allusion to *Shih chi* 128, p. 11, where an Eden-like forest, free of tigers and wolves, rapacious birds and poisonous snakes, is so named. The following line, literally translated, reads: 'Where is there a favorable time?' It is a strange line and seems to echo (according to Ku Chih), in its grammar as well as in some of its meaning, *Shih ching* 197: 'When Heaven gave me birth / Where was my time (= at which unlucky time?)' (Karlgren's translation). The implication, of course, is that the times are out of joint (Shen Yüeh), but the line's strange grammar seems to make one look for a *place* where the 'times' might be 'good', to look towards the mountain of retirement. But the following lines bring us back to reality: time is not spatial. The frost that wets his lapels and the bad weather show that autumn has arrived. The wild goose, a traditionally heroic bird, has left for the south, but the bird that remains, the 'shrike', is less easy to account for. The word *t'i-ch'üeh* is generally used to name either the cuckoo or some rapacious bird that I have (following *Ch'u tz'u*, p. 32) dubbed 'shrike'. His song is said to be sad and to announce the moment when the flowers lose their odor. The cuckoo, in China as in Europe, sings only in spring, during the mating season, and his 'doleful noise' would be singularly out of place in this very autumnal poem. Huang Chieh says the bird 'sings in the fifth moon (quoting the *Ta Tai li-chi* 2, p. 7b) and then, in autumn, he gives forth his doleful sounds'. The implication is that the bird sings a second, different song in autumn. This bird, in any case, is not the cuckoo who leaves his mating home in summer.

The penultimate line refers to the season in terms of scholastic Five Element theories. These theories, partially discredited among contemporary thinkers, held that there was a correlation between the human and the physical worlds, that the musical modes, for example, each corresponded to one of the seasons, and each of these corresponded to a color. Autumn's musical mode was one beginning on the second degree of the pentatonic scale (*shang* 商), and its color, white. The more traditionally minded of Juan Chi's contemporaries actually believed there was a correspondence between the seasonal rise of the *yin* and the *yang* 'breaths' in the earth and the chromatic pitch pipes that were the basis of the Chinese musical scale. The year was divided into twelve consecutive periods, and at the beginning of each of these one of the 'breaths' in the earth would rise just enough to blow the corresponding pitch pipe.[66] The 'blankness' or 'whiteness' of autumn can thus very concretely be said to 'come from' or at least be consonant with a musical mode, since the very 'breath' of nature was tuned to that mode at the time. Not only is there scholastic, pseudo-scientific, 'proof' for the relation between musical mode and the season, but the season's color itself has a certain basis in fact. On 23 October each year, give or take a day or two, with a regularity that only those who have lived in a climate ruled by the monsoon can believe, hoarfrost falls and covers the earth for the first time in the year.[67] Juan Chi's line is thus both 'pseudo-scientifically' and factually an exact description of autumn and gives an appropriate introduction to the last line of the poem, expressing the heart-breaking sadness the season inspires in him, especially since the *shang* mode is traditionally thought to be eminently sad.

Even the oldest commentator on this poem, Shen Yüeh, who is usually very wary of 'satirical' interpretations, insists upon such an interpretation for this poem. In his commentary to lines 3 and 4 he says: 'Po I and Shu Ch'i would not even eat Chou's millet; how much less would they accept it from unrighteous men'. The Chou conquerors included some of the saints of Confucianism; the 'unrighteous men' he refers to are the Ssu-ma usurpers. The whole poem is thus bathed in the political context that, in part, inspired it. But autumn is its subject, a subject of lamentation in so many poems of the third and fourth centuries,[68] and autumn means the coming of death and destruction. Lines 5 and 11 may make this poem seem as obscure, to the Western reader, as the more purely satirical poems we have just read; but this is not the case, for the Chinese reader, familiar with the philosophy to which we have alluded, can appreciate the poem on its various levels: as a lament for the coming of autumn, the approach of death to the natural world, to the poet, and to the dynasty he serves.

The following short poem, which begins with a first line often used in ballads almost identical to the first line of Poem 9, is not completely intelligible without some satirical hypothesis.

64

At dawn I left the Upper Eastern Gate
    And, from afar, looked off towards Shou-yang's base.
The pines and cypresses were thick and deep
    Where the orioles played together.
5   Roaming about within the Nine Bends
    I hesitate, not knowing where to go,
For when I remember my days gone by
    I become oppressed and think of the Bewitching Lady.

The fact that the Pei-mang chain, and Mt Shou-yang, were used as burial grounds is emphasized in the third line, for 'pines and cypresses' were traditionally grown on funeral mounds. 'Nine Bends' was the name of a canal that was part of the Ku 穀 River as it flowed from before the Upper Eastern Gate towards the southeast and entered the Lo River (*Shui-ching chu* 16, p. 74, which quotes this poem with some variants). We know Juan Chi had a country home not too far from the 'Nine Bends' at a place called, after his family name, 'Juan's Bend' (cf. note 27) and it may have been there that he retired after refusing Chiang Chi in 239. His restless wandering in this region is thus easily accounted for. That the sight of Mt Shou-yang and its tumuli should occasion his restlessness, his indecision, is no longer strange to us either. But what are we to make of the last two lines? Who is the 'Bewitching Lady'? There is no way of knowing with any assurance. Huang Chieh believes the words allude, on a superficial level, to a concubine of the last ruler of the Shang dynasty (to which Po I and Shu Ch'i remained loyal on Mt Shou-yang), and, on a satirical level, to one of the too numerous concubines of Ts'ao Jui. For him, the penultimate line is a reference to Juan Chi's life before he became an official, before 239, during the reign of Ts'ao Jui. He also quotes a long tetrameter poem ascribed to Juan Chi (cf. chapter 3, note 56) which clearly bemoans the evil influence of bewitching women upon dynastic rulers. But Ku Chih believes the poem to be about Ts'ao P'i, whose tomb actually was on Mt Shou-yang and who, a short time before he died, issued an edict ordering some of his concubines to be sent back to their homes after his death (*San-kuo chih chi-chieh* 2, p. 65b). Ku Chih uncharitably adds that this edict shows that 'Ts'ao P'i did not forget about sex (*ch'ing* 情) even a short time before his death'. Chiang Shih-yüeh believes the orioles, *li-huang* 鸝 黃 , in line 4 are a reference to the orioles, *ts'ang-keng* 倉 庚 , in *Shih ching* (156, 4) where they describe a young bride going to her new home. His suggestion is not very convincing, but one would like to see some symbolism in the orioles flying among the funereal trees. Tseng Kuo-fan suspects the whole poem is a fabrication of later men building on the first two lines borrowed, with unfortunate changes, from Poem 9. For him, 'The last three words of the last line are simply incongruous where they are'. Without some sort of satirical interpretation, I think he is right.

Poem 16, like Poem 9, is an example of a poem in which the physical and human worlds are correlated and, according to Ho Cho, it contains, like the 'Shou-yang Mountain fu', a hidden allusion to the events of 254. The scene of this poem is not Lo-yang, but (as in Poems 29 and 31) central Honan, near the capital of the ancient kingdom of Wei and Juan Chi's ancestral home.

16

Back and forth I pace on Lake P'eng's shores,
    Then turn about to look towards Ta-liang.

In the green waters great billows arise;
    The grassy wastelands stretch on and on.
5   Scurrying animals criss-cross in wild disorder;
    Flying birds circle in the air, one after the other.
    Now the stars of the Quail are due south,
    The sun and the moon just face to face.
    The north wind sharpens the bitter cold
10   As cloudy vapors let fall a light frost.
    I am a traveller, and friendless;
    Anguish fills my breast wherever I look.

    'The small man tots up his merits;
    'Constancy is the good man's way.'
15   He does not fear ending his life in hardship –
    And so I sing here, in this stanza!

This poem is again set in autumn, but it does not end on a note of passive mourning: in the last lines Juan Chi opposes the decay and disorder he sees around him in the best and firmest Confucian tradition. The first six lines are the description of a world close to chaos. Ta-liang in line 2, capital of the ancient state of Wei, is, of course, symbolic of Lo-yang, capital of 'modern' Wei. But perhaps Juan Chi evokes Ta-liang for another reason: because it had long since been destroyed. It thus becomes a symbol of decay, intensified by what the poet sees about him in the surrounding countryside: the inanimate and animate objects of nature both seem to be in complete disorder – a stormy lake, empty deserts, and agitated wild beasts. Even the sun and the moon are in conflict, 'face to face'. Lines 7 and 8 seem to be trying to tell us the exact time of the year and add, perhaps, another allusion to the ruin of a dynasty. Line 7 is almost a literal citation of the *Tso chuan*, Hsi 5: 'At the juncture of the ninth and tenth moons, the morning of the day *ping-tzu*, when the sun is in the tail of the Quail and the moon is in Ts'e, *the constellation of the Quail* will be *due south*. It will surely be at *that time* . . . that Chin will annihilate Kuo.'[69] In line 8 Juan Chi contradicts the *Tso chuan*'s date ('at the juncture of the ninth and tenth moons') by saying that the moon is directly facing the sun: it is the fifteenth of the lunar month. The following four lines complete the picture of a friendless wanderer. In the last four lines, however, the tone changes. The quotation from *Hsün-tzu* 17 shows, as Ch'en Tso-ming says, that Juan Chi is not a pure nihilist or high-minded Taoist as he is so often said to have been. Hsün-tzu contrasts the petty man's search for immediate gains with the superior man's 'higher interests'. In the same way, Juan Chi, in the face of the chaos he sees about him, proclaims his refusal to deviate from his constant principles, even though this means that his life will be filled with suffering and hardship.

But why has he set his scene in ancient Ta-liang? Why has he insisted on specifying the exact time of the year, to the very day? We are surely right to look for satirical elements here if anywhere in his work. Ta-liang, capital of the ancient kingdom of Wei, fell to the Ch'in in 225 B.C., with the result that the kingdom (homonym of the Ts'ao-Wei dynasty) disappeared forever. Is there not a suggestion that the modern 'kingdom of Wei' was also about to fall in Juan Chi's own time? Lines 7 and 8 refer only to the time of the year – the fifteenth day of the ninth or tenth lunar month – and not to the year itself. We have already seen that Juan Chi refers cryptically to the 'beginning of a new week' in the autumn of 254 in his 'Mt Shou-yang fu' in which he also evokes similar wretched autumnal weather. Ho Cho (echoed by Ch'en Hang and Chiang Shih-yüeh) has not hesitated to suggest that Juan Chi was referring to events of the same year here and in particular to the moment Ssu-ma Shih sent an official to tell the Empress Dowager that he was going to depose the emperor. According to him, 'Ssu-ma Shih decided his course of action and spoke to the Empress Dowager just exactly at the time the sun and the moon were facing one another'. Unfortunately, the only date we have for these events is the *chia-hsü* day of the ninth lunar month of the sixth year of the Chia-p'ing era: 17 October 254 (*San-kuo chih chi-chieh* 4, p. 26a). This was, however, four days after the full moon. The new emperor mounted the throne on 2 November, the fifth day (not the sixth, as Ho Cho says) of the next lunar month. These general events did occur at the juncture of the two lunar months when, according to the *Tso chuan*, the Quail is at the meridian. Ho Cho's theory is, therefore, plausible, but it is not certain. The deposition of 254 was a crucial event in Juan Chi's life and in the life of every servant of the Wei dynasty, and it may well have moved him to bemoan it in verse. But there were similar events in the years preceding and following that might have done so too. Whatever the allusion is to current events, the poem does not choose sides in the conflict; it is a passionate statement of moral purpose, or a refusal to sacrifice principles even at the risk of living in pain and hardship.

The following poem is again full of enigmatic references that make it seem satirical, and it too ends with a statement of constancy to higher principles.

75

East of Liang there is a fragrant plant
 That has bloomed twice or thrice in a single morning.
How sensuous its appearance, how gorgeous its bewitching shape
 As its splendor shines upon a fallen town!
5 There is nothing in it of a bright and wise man;
 It is, rather, a seducer, a flatterer;
And its frivolity is only a momentary matter:

How can it know the reputation it will have in centuries to come?
The graceful beauty at the side of the road
10   Fears only the setting of the sun and the moon.
How can we see that the Dark and Holy Tree
In the endless distance is, after all, without form?

As Huang Chieh says, and as we have already seen, in Juan Chi's poems
'Liang' should be read as a cryptic reference to the contemporary Wei dynasty.
In the four poems in which the word appears as a proper noun (Poems 16, 29,
31 and this one) such an identification is highly probable. The poem's subject
is a 'fragrant plant', a binomial expression used in the 'Li sao' to describe the
good officials of the past, but here there seems little good about it, except its
outward beauty. The fact that it blooms two or three times in a single morning (*chao* 朝) suggests it satirizes a particular official who has come to the
forefront of political life three times during a single dynasty (*ch'ao* 朝). In
Juan Chi's time there is an added hint of serving three different factions. The
'fallen town' of line 4 is, of course, an allusion to the 'town-toppling' beauty
mentioned in *Shih ching* 264. The following line, too, makes an oblique reference to *Shih ching* 260, 4: 'For he is bright and wise / And thus protects his
person'. The 'fragrant plant' is thus described in the first eight lines as a
flashy, superficially brilliant political figure whose reputation will suffer in
years to come for his lack of seriousness.

The 'graceful beauty' of line 9 is less easy to interpret. Is she, as Huang
Chieh suggests, Juan Chi himself, fearing the imminent fall of the dynasty?
'The side of the road' (as Ku Chih says) implies someone (like Juan Chi himself) not in an important position. The fear of the passage of time is a constant
in the entire series and one could easily imagine Juan Chi describing himself as
fearful of the setting of the sun. But it seems a strange personification for him
to take.[70]

The last two lines, superficially the most cryptic of them all, give the poem
its meaning. *Chuang-tzu* 1 tells of a 'Dark and Holy Thing' (*ming-ling che*
冥 靈 者, diversely interpreted as a tree or as a tortoise) for which 'spring
lasts five hundred years and autumn another five hundred', that is for which
a 'year' lasts one thousand ordinary years. It is thus the opposite of the
'fragrant plant' of line 1. More than this, if one looks further, it is a plant
(again diametrically opposed to the beauteous 'fragrant plant') that, in the
final analysis, is 'without form' of any kind. It is actually something like a
metaphor for the *tao*. *Huai-nan-tzu* 1 says 'that which is without form is the
Great Ancestor of things'. Huang Chieh appropriately quotes the *Han-shih
wai-chuan* 5, 2 (Hightower translation, p. 160): 'Confucius had the heart of a
saint. He moved about in the realm of the Way and of Virtue; he wandered in
the province of the formless.' He should have added the next line: 'He re-

garded human relations in the light of eternal principles', for Juan Chi seems
to be saying something similar here and to be putting 'eternal principles'
above the fawning, flattery, fickleness and infidelity that he saw about him in
the struggle for power in Lo-yang, above even the fear of the passage of time,
a fear he was so prone to himself.

The striking description of the 'fragrant plant' makes one think there was
indeed a model, a man Juan Chi was trying to satirize. Is it necessary to say
there is no way of knowing who it was? Perhaps the best way of showing this
is simply to list the suggestions given so far: Wang K'ai-yün says the model
was Chia Ch'ung 賈 充 and his clique; Huang Chieh says it was Wang Hsiang
王 祥; Ku Chih says it was Cheng Ch'ung 鄭 冲 . This poem, like the preceding one, is quite probably satirical, but, again like the preceding poem, its
deeper meaning is more abstract and teaches, in the final interrogation so
typical of the endings of Juan Chi's poems, the primacy of what is eternal and
unchanging over worldly power and physical beauty.

Poem 11 is again a satirical work, although it too can be interpreted without allusion to particular men or events.

11

Deep flow the waters of the Yang-tzu,
    A maple wood growing along its banks.
Swamp orchids cover the roads
    Where black coursers hurtle past.
5   Gazing afar makes me sad
    And the breath of spring moves my heart.
So many outstanding men in the three regions of Ch'u
    Were led on to debauchery by Chao-yün!
Red flowers shed perfume
10   In Kao-ts'ai where they sported together.
But when I think with pain of the russet sparrows,
    My tears fall at once, and no one can stop them!

The first six lines of the poem are closely adapted from the last lines of the
Envoi of the 'Chao hun' poem of the *Ch'u tz'u* (Hawkes translation, p. 109).
They are descriptions of the lush and sensual land of the south. They are also
more than that. The commentary of the corresponding lines of the 'Chao hun'
by Wang I 王 逸 (second century A.D.), which Juan Chi surely knew, interprets them allegorically. The maple trees are in the right place, along the river
where they can get plenty of water, but the swamp orchids (symbolic of pure
officials) are not where they belong; unpicked for a long period, they have
spread to the roads and clogged them up. They are like fine courtiers who,
languishing in the desert, will not be able to help their sovereign keep from

losing his throne. If the good courtiers are not in their place, what are the 'outstanding men' in the three regions of Ch'u (eastern, western and southern Ch'u; cf. *Shih chi* 129, pp. 23–5) doing? They are being debauched by a nymph, the famous Chao-yün of the 'Kao-t'ang fu' (*Wen hsüan* 19), whose very name has come to mean amorous intercourse in classical texts. They pursue their pleasures in Kao-ts'ai (the present Shang-ts'ai in Honan), formerly part of Ch'u. The evocation of this city recalls a story from the *Chan-kuo ts'e* (Crump translation, No. 219) describing the dissolute life of the nobles in the retinue of King Hsiang of Ch'u. Chuang Hsin attempted to make the king mend his ways by telling him a series of allegories, showing how many un-suspecting animals were destroyed while they were insouciantly disporting themselves. One of these allegories speaks of russet sparrows who happily play among the trees, not knowing a young sportsman is about to shoot them down with his pellets and spring-action bow.

This poem, then, is very clearly a satire against dissolute ways among the nobility. There is no way of knowing exactly whom Juan Chi has in mind and, as usual, there are many theories. The best is probably that of Liu Lü who believes the poem refers to Ts'ao Fang, Prince of Ch'i. Like his step-father and predecessor, Ts'ao Jui, Ts'ao Fang was known for his dissolute life. When he was deposed in 254, Ssu-ma Shih accused him, in an edict signed by the Empress Dowager, of profligacy and of cavorting with singing girls.[71] Many of Ts'ao Fang's associates, moreover, were southerners who had also been ac-cused of profligacy, and could be called 'outstanding men from the three regions of Ch'u'. The shoe fits, but it may very well fit other feet too: Ho Cho, Chiang Shih-yüeh, Ch'en Hang and Tseng Kuo-fan all prefer to see Ts'ao Shuang and Ts'ao Jui as the victims described in the satire. Whatever the cor-rect interpretation may be, in this poem describing the sensuous, sweet-smelling and intoxicating atmosphere of the south, Juan Chi bemoans the fall of carefree debauchees, surprised by some stronger force. In the context of his life, it is difficult to imagine that the object of his compassion was other than the Ts'ao family, slowly being annihilated by the Ssu-ma.

2
TUNG-P'ING

These satirical works show us that Juan Chi was very strongly afflicted by the sudden decline of the Ts'ao-Wei dynasty, and that he meant to keep himself 'pure', away from the opportunists and profiteers. But it is clear from what we know of his appointments in the following years that he was not ready or not able to leave political life. He was knighted 'Marquis within the Passes', *kuan-nei hou* 關 內 侯, in 254 when Ts'ao Mao mounted the throne. This was the lowest of the honorary Wei knighthoods given to men living in the capital ('within the Passes') and usually included no fief.[1] At the same time he was given the semi-honorary post of *san-ch'i ch'ang-shih* 散 騎 常 侍, a high (third grade) 'supplementary' post that required him to supervise the drafting of imperial declarations and to judge the decisions of the important imperial secretariat, *shang shu* 尚 書. He is said not to have liked this latter post, perhaps because it drew him into the very center of political life.[2] Neither of these posts can be considered to be of the first rank, but his receiving them at this time of the consolidation of the Ssu-ma's power shows that he was well looked upon by the ruling clique.[3]

Ssu-ma Shih died on 24 March 255, half a year after having placed Ts'ao Mao on the throne and a little over a week after having broken the revolt of the loyalist Kuan-ch'iu Chien 毋 丘 儉. He was succeeded as generalissimo and de facto ruler by his younger brother, Ssu-ma Chao, who was particularly fond of Juan Chi.[4] He took him into his headquarters as Advisory Adjutant as his father and brother had and, according to the following anecdote, allowed him to indulge an old ambition. The anecdote sounds fanciful, but it is in all probability based upon a grain of truth.

> Juan Chi was by nature aloofly indifferent to the world, giving free vent to his fantasies and taking no pleasure in serving as an official in the government. Ssu-ma Chao loved him dearly and never missed an opportunity to chat and jest with him. He let him have whatever he desired and did not press him to take an official post. Juan Chi once nonchalantly said to him: 'When I was young I travelled to Tung-p'ing and took delight in the local customs: I should like to become governor of

Tung-p'ing.' Ssu-ma Chao was pleased and let him have his way. Juan Chi immediately straddled his donkey and, taking the shortest road, arrived at the commandery. There he destroyed all the walls of the official bureaus, allowing the 'inside' [the governors] and the 'outside' [the governed] to look at one another. Thereafter the edicts were 'clear and tranquil'. After ten days or so he straddled his donkey again and left.[5]

The decidedly Taoist nature of this anecdote ('clear and tranquil' is an allusion to *Lao-tzu* 39) and Juan Chi's unlikely and highly symbolic wall breaking make the whole thing sound a bit suspicious. But we do know that he did travel to Tung-p'ing when young (above, p. 8), and a funeral inscription gives him the title 'Governor of Tung-p'ing' 東 平 相.[6] Even more important, Juan Chi has left two *fu* which describe Tung-p'ing and the region in detail and prove that he had surely been there.

That is really all they prove, however, because even a brief glance at either of the *fu* shows that Juan Chi found no delight whatsoever in the region: both poems are descriptions of unmitigated disgust with everything western Shantung had to offer. The blackness of these works is so unrelieved, and Juan Chi shows himself such a pure misanthrope in them, that I would like to quote them both in full, as precious glimpses of his character and as almost unique examples in *fu* history of diatribes against a region and its population. I will begin with the 'K'ang-fu fu' simply because it is shorter and less complex.

The 'K'ang-fu fu' is called 'Yüan-fu fu' 元 父 賦 in all existing texts. But there is no place known in history with such a name. It is obvious that the variant *k'ang* 亢 [7] is correct, since K'ang-fu 亢 父 was situated in exactly the region described in the poem, about twenty-five kilometers to the south of the present Chi-ning in western Shantung and some ninety kilometers to the south of Tung-p'ing. The poem is a listing of the vices of the region and of its degenerate population and seems to be an artistic demonstration of the theorem of causality suggested in lines 20 and 21 (distant echoes of *Shih chi* 23, p. 23): a bad geographical milieu produces a bad population.[8] The poet continually vibrates between these two poles, describing the region at some length and then relating the evil of the physical geography of the place to the evil of the inhabitants. He punctuates his texts at fairly regular intervals with the phrase 'that is why the people there . . . ', giving a certain rondo-like form to an otherwise rhapsodic piece. K'ang-fu is very definitely located geographically in the last half of the poem where a large number of places are described as being to its north, south, east or west. It and Tung-p'ing are in fact in a low-lying part of Shantung that must have been very swampy indeed in the third century.

K'ang-fu

I once travelled to K'ang-fu, and when I climbed its ramparts I was filled with melancholy. I recorded my feelings in a *fu* that is meant to show that K'ang-fu is not a pleasant place to be.

K'ang-fu is at the very limit of the Nine Provinces,
    A somber ruin left by former dynasties.
That is why its inner and outer walls are low and narrow,
    Rickety, cramped and short.
5   In its fields, filth gradually settles out of the water
    And then mixes together with the wet mud.
A square moat around it
    Is full of dripping waters.
Only vile vegetables grow there,
10   And most of them are indeed inedible.
The land is low and heavy with cold *yin*,
    Its vital breath untempered [by warm *yang*].
The sun does not make his full rounds there
    So that the plants do not mature.
15   That is why the people are obstinate and insincere blockheads,
    Morons impossible to civilize.

The frontiers of the region are cut off and choked up,
    Hemmed in close by deep, water-filled abysses.
The end product [a stupid population] is related to its [geo-
        graphical] origins;
20   The causes are related to their effects,
From former times until today,
    Throughout the ages, year after year.
Chü-yeh [swamp] has stagnated behind [K'ang-fu]
    And the remote Chi River has covered all before it.[9]
25   The irrigation canals have not flowed freely
    So that dirt and slime have accumulated in great quantity.
Unworthy men have flocked here in droves
    So that there are no sages within their rooms.
And therefore the people let themselves go in disorder,
30   Hide in prairies and dwell in swamps,
Living the life of deer,
    With the ambitions of porcupines.
This being the case, they do not plough the earth of their plains,
    And their plantations are few and far between.
35   Pokeweeds and reeds fill the marshes
    Where mosquitoes and gnats afflict the skin.

The difficult passes in the distance are

Chin-hsiang in the west and Kao-p'ing in the east.[10]
The hills there are high and precipitous,
40   The torrents deep and obscure.
Good creatures dwell not there
   Where bears and tigers live.
Therefore the people suffer their bites
   And are themselves like beasts or birds.

45   The passes near at hand are
   Ming-chiu covering the front and Ch'ü-ch'eng, open at the
      back.[11]
Owls swoop there in flocks
   And foxes are without number.
Therefore its people are like wolves or wild dogs in temperament,
50   Strike out at others like lightning [?] and show no kindness.

To the south one looks off toward Ch'un-shen
   And to the east one sees Meng Ch'ang.[12]
One limit of the region is the city on the Hsüeh
   And one frontier is Shan-yang.[13]
55   In the inns and taverns
   Thieves are hidden.
Towards the north, P'ing-lu is near,
   A western border of Ch'i.
There are short cuts to Yen and to Chao
60   Where [the thieves?] may escape to sport at ease.

Therefore the people are secretive and one-sided
   Dissembling and partial.
Full of egotism and deceit,
   Giving themselves over to cruel evilness,
65   They have set up no civilizing ritual or justice,
   Nor are they united in a pure moral transformation.
Former sages have told us
   That there are places that can be enlightened while others re-
      main benighted.[14]
How now, man of Goodness,
70   Could you loiter in this land?

Should this savage attack on an entire region and its inhabitants be called 'Swiftian', or downright pathological? Are there such regions in the world, or, more exactly, are there such thoroughly degenerate people in the world, ungraced by any redeeming characteristics? Or is all this symbolic? Is Juan Chi here writing in a satirical tradition aimed at denouncing a group of politicians rather than the region it ostensibly describes?

In spite of the very great originality of these two *fu*, Juan Chi is not working completely outside any tradition. The very oldest *fu* (or rather proto-*fu*) known, that of Hsün-tzu in the twenty-sixth chapter of his works, contains a passage in which he strongly castigates the people of a region. They are called arrogant and violent and, in the last sentence of the *fu*, Hsün-tzu asks how he could possibly associate with them, just as Juan Chi does in 'K'ang-fu'.[15] The description of geographical regions, moreover, is itself in the oldest and most popular *fu* tradition. The description of the human and physical geography of a region can also be seen in the 'Treatise on geography' of the *Han shu*. The allusion to Shan-yang in line 56, followed by the description of 'thieves hidden in inns', may actually be inspired by the 'Treatise', which tells us that the people of 'Shan-yang were wont to become thieves' (*Han-shu pu-chu* 28B, p. 67a). The descriptions in the 'Treatise', too, are much more pessimistic and unfavourable than those of the great *fu* tradition, and are much closer to Juan Chi's. The popularity of these geographical treatises can be seen in the fact that there are a number of them listed in the 'Treatise on bibliography' in the *Sui shu* as having been written just at this time.[16] The *Sui shu* itself, in its 'Treatise on geography', continues the tradition and, it is interesting to note, says that the people in this part of Shantung, inspired by the lingering influence of the Chou ancestors, the Duke of Chou and Confucius, loved traditional culture, were righteous and imbued with the spirit of antiquity![17] Thus we can see that Juan Chi has combined two traditions in his works: he has adapted the realistic descriptions of the geographical treatises to the *fu* form.

But, to come back to our earlier question, is all this allegorical? Are these impossibly evil people in their unbelievably insalubrious environment the Ssu-ma and their powerful allies in disguise?[18] If they are, it seems to me that they are so well disguised as to be unidentifiable — and thus useless as objects of satire. If this *fu* is satirical, and its violence certainly seems to suggest it is, it is so on a very abstract level and its target must be something more general. It seems impossible that Juan Chi meant this as a satire against some particular group: he has left so few clues and been so categorical in his depiction of evilness in K'ang-fu that we must recognize this work as a general condemnation of human evil. This is, it almost goes without saying, a very un-'Taoist' attitude, all the more so because Juan Chi belabors the men of K'ang-fu for their lack of civilization and their animal-like behavior.[19]

The 'Tung-p'ing fu' is very definitely related to 'K'ang-fu', not only because the regions described are so close to one another (Tung-p'ing is ninety kilometers to the north of K'ang-fu), but because a long section of the poem (lines 45—120) is so similar to it. But 'Tung-p'ing' is a much more obscure poem, more difficult to read and very much more complex. Above all, it is much closer to the tradition of the numerous poems in the *Ch'u tz'u* which

describe the frustrations and mystical escape of disappointed officials. The
first forty-four lines are a very general introduction that have little to do with
Tung-p'ing. Lines 1–22 are a semi-cosmogonical description of the universe.
They are followed (lines 23–44) by the portraits of Taoist cosmonauts, cosmic heroes dear to the heart of Juan Chi, who roam at will in the most inaccessible and the most magical of the haunts of the immortals – the K'un-
lun and the various isles of the blessed in remote corners of the sea – as well
as in the far reaches of space. The actual (very unflattering) description of
Tung-p'ing only occupies lines 45–120. In the succeeding lines, until the refrain, Juan Chi engages in some philosophical speculation in which he seems
to be drawing very tentative and paradoxical conclusions from the contrasts in
the first two parts of his *fu*. He contrasts nature and society, the sincere in
heart and the heartless, and (lines 147–54) shows that certain 'superior'
beings or things are useless in certain milieus: by analogy, he suggests he is too
pure for his surroundings (lines 155–6) and yearns to escape to a mystical
roaming with the immortals. The beginning of the refrain (lines 165–92), in
the shamanistic, *Ch'u tz'u* tradition, describes this roaming and the meeting
with an immortal. But the meeting only shows that he is not of the same kind
as the immortal, and the rest of the poem shows him trying to come to terms
with life here below. My translation is relatively free. The text, as so often in
Juan Chi's lesser known works, is often corrupt. The bracketed question
marks [?] follow the passages that baffle me the most; if I had used them in
all passages of doubtful interpretation, there would be many, many more.

Tung-p'ing

Each of the Nine Provinces has its shape
    And each of the Nine Wildernesses its own features:[20]
Their regions are now high and now low,
    And their creatures all have their own forms.
5   When these regions are open, they communicate with the world,
        But when they are closed, they do not;
When their rivers flow, there is movement,
    But when they are stopped up, the movement will cease.
When the regions are raised up, hills will form;
10   And when they are hollowed out, there will be swamps.
These formations meander on and on
    Until they are surrounded by the Great Sea.
Then they are divided into states and towns
    And markers are set up to delimit them.
15   The four seasons regulate the heavenly bodies;
    The *yin* and the *yang* spread forth their breaths.
These changes bring others in their wake, over and over again,

Giving form and internal life to the things of the world.
Clouds rise and lightning strikes;
20   There is noise and then quiet.
Some find their peace in this,
     But others are bewildered by it [?].

If one looks at the gaping void of winding cliffs
     Or at a road in hidden wild lands
25 Or at a distant, secret region
     Or at a city in an endless desert,
One will see that all these rare and bizarre sights
     Cannot be shown on a map.[21]
And there are universal voyagers,
30   Men of refined and all-embracing natures [?],
Who mount the whirlwind
     And tread the highest floating clouds,
Who let the pure and the impure both go by,
     Who abide good fortune with the bad.
35 These are men like Ling-lun who roamed with the phoenix on the sunny
          slopes of the K'un-lun range,[22]
     Like Tsou-tzu who blew warmth into the shade of Millet Valley,[23]
     Like Po-kao who mounted and descended the heights of Shang-chi,[24]
     Or Hsien-men who roamed the peaks of the Three Mountains.[25]
Above they sported in Hsüan-p'u;[26]
40   Below they roamed in Teng-lin.[27]
The phoenix *feng* sang spontaneously for them
     And the phoenix *luan* soared and danced of its own accord.
There the auspicious grain is bountiful;
     But their millet is not like ours.

45 There is a vile place, reached through side roads,[28]
     Where there are heaps of deer and pigs;
It is not made beautiful by the fair and clean,
     But is the resort of the filthy and impure.
To the west of the place one looks off towards A-chen
50   And can see Ch'i-p'u at the same time,[29]
'Among the mulberries on the P'u'[30]
     Where the dissolute dwelled.
[Here] the Three Chin[31] concocted their alliances
     And Cheng and Wei spread their disorder.
55 The eminent oppressed their followers,
     But it was the followers who remained [?].
That is why violence ran loose within families
     And poisoned hate sprang up between husband and wife.
These people still had boundless desires to do bad:

60   How could it be long before they gave vent to them?
      It was this land that was the center[32]
          When the Liu princes assembled.[33]
      High precipices towered over the city wall
          And the endless river surrounded the houses:
65   The Shu family and its married relations[34]
          Did indeed live upon their banks.
      With its back to the mountains, facing the waters,
          The region was filthy, full of egotism,
      So that in the small quarters and border towns
70   No one would deny the bad things said of it.
      True sentiments were cut off and thinking warped
          So that the inhabitants could gain more and more possessions.
      Their fields were flat lands full of weeds
          And in their husbandry they missed the proper times.
75   They did not plough their fields,
          Nor did they weed.
      So much water collected in the [irrigation] pools
          That it overflowed in great billows and laid the fields low.

      In the east the region faced the Three Ch'i
80   And in the west it touched Tsou and Lu.[35]
      The long road for one thousand *li*
          Received their itinerant merchants
      Who sometimes used force to make [their clients] comply
          And were helped by soldiers.
85   Arrogant menials from small towns
          Lived here.[36]
      The waterways lead, by the quickest route,
          To Lake Tung-t'ing and to the state of Ch'u,
      And they carry [southern] influences [to Tung-p'ing],
90   Directly to it, and to its entire domain.
      Thus they inherited [southern] customs
          And were without rules, without models:
      Not barbarians, they still followed no laws,
          And came to do harm.
95   Thus, in their cooperative ventures, each vaunts his own power;
          They turn away from reason and towards debauchery.
      Extolling the passions and chasing after profit,
          The only thing they respect is excess.
      Their dwelling places are hidden and obstructed,
100   Obscure and dark,
      Built near tombs,
          And surrounded by clandestine rooms.

Therefore, to live in them befuddles the mind;
   To speak of them makes one feel sadness.
105 I fear that only by moving away
   Could one find a place to awaken one's true feelings.
On the outside of the territory the muddy [Yellow] River surrounds its
      ponds
   And the clear Chi washes its frontiers.[37]
To the north there is a range of mountains
110   Steep and dangerous.
So high and pointed are its peaks
   That clouds and lightning strike against them.
The far-reaching wind beats down harshly,
   Mournfully, desolately on the Great Plains.

115 To the south is the wandering Wen, so deep,
   And whose running streamlets become a lake.[38]
The deep forests of flourishing trees
   Have dense foliage intermingled.
Flocks of birds circle in the sky
120   And the animals run across one another's path.
Although the peasants are unfortunate,
   Perhaps nature – the mountains and lakes – could supply what they
      lack.
What the sages of old esteemed
   Was that their government and its doctrine be decorous;
125 What those Dark and True [Taoists] treasured
   Was to be alone and unknown.

I ask a villager to give me his random impressions,
   Then he raises his voice in the returning wind [?].
I look at the weed infested thick woods
130   And turn towards the luxuriant greenness of the Eastern Mountain.[39]
I admire the old hamlet sayings[40]
   And give forth this new poem to solace my feelings.
The stiff frost is, in truth, not yet heavy,
   Why should the cinnabar tree flower again [?].[41]
135 The poet at the Northern Gate lamented in his overflowing grief;
   The poet of the Lesser p'an ode was pained that he alone was true.[42]
The sea gull was upright and straightforward and admired humaneness:
   Why should he, in his pure simplicity, not be able to live as he
      pleased?[43]
The formal beauty of this bird moves one's very aspirations;
140   How much more [is one moved to disgust?] by these heartless men?

Then, with impetuous sincerity, I cast my thoughts afar

And [undecided, as if] floating here and there on a swirling wind,
    want to return [to some valid abode].
The fabulous Ch'in-p'i bird[44] roams on the mountain crests;
    Rising above the flock of inferior birds, it races away.
145 Things that have been transformed and have spirit-like joy [such as the
    Ch'in-p'i]
    Cannot be overtaken by those [like us] who gaze at them from afar.
If you would board a light boat of pine and ride the mountain gorges
    Even though you have no ropes, you can control it by your weight
    alone.
But if you gallop straight ahead on an excellent courser in a narrow
    lane,[45]
150 You will not even be able to reach a lame donkey.
[Riding a horse where a donkey is needed is like] roaming in Yüeh to
    sell ceremonial caps,[46]
    While the first thing to be seen there is that they wear rhinoceros
    horn [head pieces],
Or like carrying embroidered silks to sell to the northern barbarians
    While it is well known that they must wear felt and fur.
155 In the same way I may offer to my sovereign the even temper of pure
    virtue,
    But where in this region could I dwell?

I mean to return to a place of good morals
    And ask Wang-tzu [Ch'iao] to roam with me.[47]
We will rinse our mouth with the pleasantness of jade sap,
160   And drink the pure flow of clear water,
Ceasing only when I have emptied my heart:
    For then what affliction could I keep in my breast?[48]
And I say again [in my Envoi]:[49] How good is the purity of the seasons
    of the year!
    How beautiful the way spring gives way to summer!
165 I confide my thoughts to the whirlwind and ride away upon it,
    Using my body as my carriage.
I gallop along heaven's dividing lines,
    Asking my way from Great Wind.[50]
Black clouds arise in the four directions;
170   Cold rain whirls about and falls.
Suddenly I awaken and lose my way,
    Trampling the void and going on.
The *fu-yao* tree shades the Ho-hsü Mountains;[51]
    Hsien-ch'ih Lake sparkles in Tseng-ch'eng.[52]
175 I rejoice in the brightness as it appears in the morning,
    Delighting in the sun's fiery essence.

I sound the depths from an Empty Boat[53] and put my mind at ease,
    Roaming about, for a time, in the Sea of Purity.
I am attentive to the trustworthy teachings of the Dark Truth
180   And think of the form the Perfect Man puts on:

So variegated that you cannot see the infinite detail;
    When you think of him you judge him more closely the farther away
        you are.
And when he turns his carriage among the irrigation canals in the fields
    It is as if he could reach K'ung-sang.[54]
185 His words overflow and do not cease
    And his mind works continuously without respite.
He assembles books and admonitions to show forth the proscriptions,
    And goes to the bottom of what was difficult to fathom in the multi-
        tude of teachings.
Then he, the Spirit, far, far away in the distance, takes his leave to
    return
190   And I stand in awe of the pair of rings that are at his side.[55]
I sigh that all the birds do not flock together
    And lament that the far distance [where the Spirit has gone?] goes
        on and on without end.

I am moved by how easily weeds grow tall
    And gain the praises of the aides of the emperor.
195 But I fear I will blow away forever, carried off by the wind,
    To live with Chuan-hsü on Mt Fu-yü.[56]
Although my zithers may remain,
    How could the notes of my songs be played again [after my death]?
I think of roaming wildly to see marvels,
200   But what does it avail to rocket on high?
It is confused, dark and chaotic,
    Unbridled, overflowing, unquiet.
I will correct my main errors and change my position,
    Stand up straight in my court robes and set myself right.
205 I will confirm to the rules in my behavior,
    And practice divination on my tortoise shell to examine what my
        actions should be.
When I look off to see how far my carriage will go,
    In truth, it stays near and does not go far.
How could I stay away three years without asking [news of the Court]:
210   Once I leave, I will return nine times!
Looking back at the bright sun as it first arises,
    I rush along the winding hill and correct my appearance.
Now is the time of autumn's whirling winds
    Giving witness that decay must soon follow.

215　I must abandon the extravagant ways of my distant [roamings]
　　　　And become bound to others by eternal pacts [of social intercourse].
　　　I will make the rounds with the shepherd at leisure in Hsiang-ch'eng[57]
　　　　And intone the pure teachings of the ancients.
　　　I shall be wet by the wind and rain:
220　How would I dare to soar on high or roam in an official bureau?
　　　I will furtively and quietly remain true to my integrity,
　　　　Calmly and serenely, to the end of my days.
　　　Why should I care about staying in one place long?
　　　I will change my appearance and go to some different region,
225　And there I will choose some high place to perch
　　　And forever be joyous, happy and calm.[58]

Like the 'Shou-yang Mountain' and the 'K'ang-fu', the basic impetus of the
'Tung-p'ing fu' is probably political, but here Juan Chi places the political
problem in a much broader philosophical framework. In fact he touches on
almost all the issues that are developed more fully in the rest of his works.
The whole poem, it seems to me, is based upon a single underlying contrast, a
tension which springs from the successive descriptions (lines 1–44 and lines
45–120) of two aspects of the world: the natural world and the human world.
The first is the 'primordial' world, the world as it was created or as it is in its
purely natural aspects, a world of cosmic forces inhabited by cosmic heroes.
The second aspect of the world he describes gives the poem its name: it is
Tung-p'ing in all its human squalor. In 'K'ang-fu', Juan Chi tried to show how
an inferior natural environment gave birth to an inferior population; in 'Tung-
p'ing' he places all the blame on the people and actually seems to look upon
nature as something good in itself (lines 121–2). The last hundred or so lines
of the poem attempt to grapple with the problems that this dichotomy presents. They are the most difficult to interpret and the most interesting from
the point of view of Juan Chi's own feelings. The relations between the different couplets are sometimes so difficult to see, however, that I should like
to attempt to interpret them in detail here. At some points the obscurity of
the relations seems to suggest either textual corruption or some ulterior, satirical motive that has escaped me. Or perhaps I have simply not understood.
　　The first two lines of this section, 121 and 122, suggest the main subject:
the relations between nature and man. But they do so on a very concrete and
immediate level, springing directly out of the preceding description of Tung-
p'ing and its inhabitants. I have translated the words *pu-shu* 不 淑 by 'unfortunate', giving the words the traditional meaning they have in *Shih ching* 69.
Literally they mean 'impure, not virtuous' and some of this meaning must be
felt here. The unfortunate ('impure') peasants, unable to eke out a living in
their fields, can turn to the mountains and lakes for game and wild plants. The

next four lines (123–6) seem to change the subject entirely, but I do not think they really do. They contrast the Confucianists' esteem for a formal society, inspired by a clear philosophical doctrine, with the Taoists' search for untrammelled freedom far from any social group. Juan Chi has here raised his problem to a higher philosophical plane, but it remains the same: what should man's relation to nature be? Should he turn away from it and towards human society with the Confucianists, or toward it, with the Taoist saints?

Lines 127–9 bring the problem back to his immediate subject, the inhabitants of Tung-p'ing and the natural world that surrounds them. The last couplet also complicates his contrast, for nature here is sometimes 'weed infested' and sometimes 'luxuriantly green'. The simple dichotomy becomes more complex. So complex, in fact, that in the next line (131) Juan Chi suggests, in an allusion to Chuang-tzu, that these contrasts are not fundamental and that we should attempt to rise above them in assimilating them all, as the Great Man assimilates different doctrines, as nature itself assimilates the contrasts found in it. He here recalls the Taoist principle of the 'equalizing of things' (*ch'i-wu lun*), of the relativity of all our earthly knowledge, one of the most important of Chuang-tzu's doctrines and one that profoundly influenced Juan Chi.

Lines 133 and 134 recall the passage of time, another perennial topic. Lines 135 and 136 seem quite far afield. They evoke two poems of the *Shih ching* in which two misunderstood officials bemoan their fate, accepting their forced inactivity silently. Coming as they do after the evocation of the passage of time, these lines introduce Juan Chi's own anguish, that of a loyal, virtuous man unable to do anything in the corrupt world in which he lives and who sees time running out on him. The four following lines (137–40) are a parallel to the innocence and goodness of these two hapless officials in the natural world. The sea gull sought to serve the pure and good child just as the officials sought to serve a good prince: both were frustrated, the first by evil courtiers, the latter by the boy's father – all 'heartless men'. In this way Juan Chi has come back to his original contrasting of the human and natural, but he subtly has woven his own anguish into the text. In lines 141 and 142 he tries to find a 'place to return', a place with which he can identify, that he can call his own. The truly superior beings, such as the Ch'in-p'i, the lord of the K'un-lun, roam at ease on the highest peaks; they seem to rise above all the differences in the natural and human world and in so doing fulfil themselves. Juan Chi would willingly follow them. But how can the smaller birds hope to follow them? This is a complaint we will hear again and again in his works. The lines that follow (147–54) try to show that, just as the Ch'in-p'i is unapproachable in his own, Olympian realm, so are 'superior' beings and things useless in certain contexts: a small, light boat is needed to shoot the rapids in mountain

torrents, a donkey to navigate tortuous passes, and Chinese garments of great
price are simply useless among the barbarians. The conclusion? Like the sad
officials in the *Shih ching* and like the sea gull, Juan Chi's virtue was not appreciated in 'this region' (Tung-p'ing), he was a courser in a mountain pass,
perhaps even a Ch'in-p'i among . . . chickens. He decides he must leave the
world altogether, seek out the Taoist heroes who roam the cosmos and associate with them in the mystical 'supernatural' world of Nature (lines 157–62).

These last six lines introduce the mystical roaming that is the main subject
of the Envoi. By 'emptying his mind', Juan Chi is ready to meet the Taoist
immortal or Spirit in a mystical voyage reminiscent of similar meetings in the
universal 'shamanistic' tradition in general, and of the 'Yüan yu' in the *Ch'u
tz'u* in particular. This mystical voyage is in fact his way of attempting to resolve the dilemma between nature and society that I said earlier was the inspiration of the poem. By emptying his mind, Juan Chi is able to identify himself with the entire cosmos; by refusing to take sides in any human, partisan,
egotistical enterprise he is able to transcend individual phenomena and identify with Nature itself. This resolution of his dilemma is, however, short lived.
With the departure of the, after all, fearful Spirit (lines 189–90), Juan Chi
begins to realize that he is separated from him by differences too great to
overcome. The Spirit is eternal (line 192) and he is not (lines 193–8), and the
incoherence of the mystical experience itself seems almost distasteful to him
in lines 199–202. From line 203 and to the end of the poem Juan Chi draws
his conclusions. He will not attempt to follow a Taoist life in the heart of
nature, but will return to human society in spite of the unflattering portrait
he has painted of it in Tung-p'ing. He will cling 'furtively' to his virtue, as if
that were the only way he could preserve it in the corruption he sees around
him, and, if necessary, he will leave Tung-p'ing altogether and attempt to find
a 'high place' where he can 'nest'. These last lines, like those of 'Mt Shou-
yang', are vague and seem to suggest some kind of retirement in the midst of
society, the solution he finally accepted in his own life.

I cannot pretend to have understood the 'Tung-p'ing fu' completely. Certain elements (that are perhaps satirical) have escaped me entirely; others I
have probably understood only in part. Some of the obscurity of the work
stems from the tradition in which Juan Chi is writing, the tradition of the
Ch'u tz'u that mixes politics and religion, disappointment with the world and
mystical escapism. To what extent are the religious elements only symbolic?
To what extent is the mystical voyage a simple description of escape from the
inhospitable world of political reality, and to what extent is it a real spiritual
voyage? To what extent does the Perfect Man or Spirit symbolize some political reality (the emperor, the head of the government), and to what extent is
he a spiritual ideal, a Taoist saint whose philosophy and religious regimen

Juan Chi would like to imitate? I believe there is no clear-cut answer to these questions. As we proceed in our study of Juan Chi we will see these dichotomies appear again and again, and be reduced to the same ambiguous reply. The mystical experience itself seems to tempt Juan Chi strongly, but in most instances, as in this poem, he rejects ultimate commitment to it and to the Taoist search for immortality. In any case, the conclusion of the 'Tung-p'ing fu', the return to social life after a period of mystical roaming, symbolizes two aspects of Juan Chi's thought that I consider basic. He was profoundly influenced by Taoist epistemology and metaphysics, by Chuang-tzu's dialectical demonstrations of the relativity of ordinary social values and of the importance of the greatest value, the *tao*, the Absolute; but, paradoxically, he was unwilling to leave society or renounce all belief in social values, and he attempted, throughout a life filled with contradictions, to realise his Taoist aspirations within a Confucian social framework.

Juan Chi became governor of Tung-p'ing because of his friendship with Ssu-ma Chao. There is an anecdote, of doubtful authenticity since it appears only in the *Chin shu* (*Chin-shu chiao-chu* 49, p. 3a), that shows that their relations must have been very close indeed.

> Ssu-ma Chao once tried to marry [his son, Ssu-ma Yen, who was to become] Emperor Wu [the first emperor of the Chin dynasty], to Juan Chi's daughter. Juan Chi got drunk for sixty days so that Ssu-ma Chao could not even talk to him about it, and then Ssu-ma Chao finally desisted.

Since this anecdote cannot be dated, there is no telling whether or not Ssu-ma Yen was already thought of as the 'usurping crown prince' at the time the event it describes took place, but it shows clearly enough that Juan Chi was considered a man powerful enough for the ruler of China to seek an alliance with. His power may not have been purely material; it may have been moral power. His reputation as a serious and as yet uncommitted poet may have been strong enough for Ssu-ma Chao to want to keep him as close as possible to his own side. This anecdote, if it is authentic, shows how important a man Juan Chi was, and how eager he was to avoid ultimate political commitment.

All his posts were in the generalissimos' headquarters and were thus connected with contemporary military life. His last official post, the one by which he is remembered in history, was also a military one, and seems to have been given to him around 256.[59] The following anecdote describing his appointment is permeated by the same alcoholic fumes that helped him avoid the ultimate commitment of becoming the future emperor's father-in-law.

When Juan Chi heard that the post of Colonel in the Infantry, *pu-ping hsiao-wei* 步兵校尉, was vacant, that there was a good quantity of excellent wine in the kitchen, and that the intendant was clever at brewing wine, he sought the post for himself. Then he gave himself over to wine, went on a blind drunk and dropped all the affairs of this world.[60]

Wine plays an important role in Juan Chi's life (but not in his works); still I suspect Juan Chi's activities as Infantry Colonel were not purely alcoholic — whatever our experience to the contrary may be with some of his Western counterparts. Throughout Juan Chi's entire lifetime there were campaigns against the two other kingdoms, against rebels, and especially against northern barbarians. The *pu-ping hsiao-wei* did not have a very high ranking post (it was of the fourth grade), but he was, as we have seen Juan Chi always was, close to the center of government as head of a branch of the imperial guard. The only indication we have that Juan Chi may have indeed done actual campaigning is in one of his poems, if the poem is in fact autobiographical.

61

When I was a lad I learned to fence
    And was so good I'd have beaten Ch'ü-ch'eng.[61]
My brilliant bearing split the clouds in two;
    I outstripped them all, was known far and wide
5   Brandishing my sword at the desert's edge,
    Watering my horses at the wild rim of the world.
How my banners fluttered in the wind!
    How my gongs and drums sang out: 'twas all was heard!

But warfare has made me sad,
10   Filled me with raging sorrow;
For when I think of how I spent my youth
    O! the bitterness I feel, how it gnaws!

I have adopted a pseudo-popular tone in my translation because Juan Chi is writing, as is so often the case, in a *yüeh-fu* tradition. Ts'ao Chih's 'White horses', 'Pai-ma p'ien', is written in the same tradition and might have inspired Juan Chi. Military prowess, in any case, was perhaps a common subject for self-satisfaction (Ts'ao P'i's autobiography talks of almost nothing else) since warfare was incessant, and fencing, in particular, was an integral part of the young official's curriculum.[62] The hero Juan Chi describes is, as usual for him, a cosmic one: his very bearing, his 'air' has such a strong aura or charismatic effect that it 'splits the clouds', and his movements span the entire known world. Different forms of banners, gongs and drums were all traditionally used to signal the attack (drums) or retreat (gongs): banners during the day and drums and gongs at night.[63]

This poem is one of the clearest Juan Chi has written and yet, so intent are his commentators on explaining what is (deliberately, I think) left vague, that they have come up with conflicting interpretations. The poem is obviously one of frustration, of regret for having spent his youth preparing for a profession that he has since learned to dislike. Why does he dislike it? Because 'warfare makes one sad' (a literal, word for word translation of line 9). This much is crystal clear. But some of the critics want to know why warfare has made him sad, and that is where the trouble begins. Chiang Shih-yüeh believes it is because Juan Chi 'only heard the sound of the gongs and drums and actually never did engage in battle. His fencing served no purpose: how could he not be sad and remorseful?' And this interpretation is followed by Ch'en Hang, the scholars of Peking University, and Frodsham and Ch'eng. My own interpretation of the line agrees with that of Ku Chih (he believes the poem to be a satirical one about Ts'ao Chang 曹 彰, who was too successful a warrior and who was poisoned by his brother, the emperor Ts'ao P'i, for his pains), A. Waley, and (probably) Tseng Kuo-fan. Grammatically both interpretations are possible, *tan* 但 having the ambiguity of English 'only': 'I only heard' can mean (*a*) 'all that I heard was', or (*b*) 'all that I did was to hear'. The commentators who opt for the second do so, I think, so they can explain line 9: 'warfare' (or perhaps 'army life') 'makes one sad when one doesn't engage in battle'. This finds a clear (if somewhat far-fetched) explanation for line 8 in the poem, and would also be in harmony with Poems 38 and 39, where warrior heroes are enthusiastically exalted. Tseng Kuo-fan suggests another explanation: 'When Juan Chi rejects, at the end of his life, his youthful desire to establish great deeds by following a military career, he is meditating on the fact that his enemies are not in Wu or Shu [the two enemy kingdoms of Wei], but within the halls [of Lo-yang].' By this he means that the real warfare he should have waged was against the Ssu-ma in Wei. Huang K'an believes that warfare saddened Juan Chi because it showed him that his real desire was to preserve his life (to seek for immortality) and not to throw it away on the field of battle. This interpretation would make the poem similar to Poem 15 in which Juan Chi regrets his early Confucian enthusiasm.

The diversity of these interpretations seems to me to prove one thing: there is no way of knowing exactly why warfare has made Juan Chi sad and filled him with remorse. That is not the subject of the poem. The subject of the poem is the disillusionment he experienced, after having perfected his warlike arts, when he was confronted with war itself, and the poem belongs with other works of its kind in world literature, from Homer to Hemingway. Its force, I believe, lies in the way Juan Chi has contrasted the magnificent youthful dream of 'cloud splitting' glory with mature disillusionment and remorse.

3

ASSASSINATION AND RETREAT

The deposing of the emperor, Ts'ao Fang (called Prince of Ch'i), in 254 was without doubt one of the most important events of the end of the Wei dynasty, but the assassination in 260 of his successor, Ts'ao Mao (called the Duke of Kao-kuei-hsiang), was even more moving to contemporaries and shows us clearly how the brutality of the Ssu-ma rulers towards the reigning dynasty contrasted with the enlightened attitude of Ts'ao P'i toward the last Han ruler. Ts'ao Mao's assassins were later themselves executed by the hypocritical usurpers, but it was clear at the time and later that the assassination was inspired by the Ssu-ma. Poem 65 is a curious lamentation which can best be understood, I believe, as a satire and, although critical opinion differs, it very possibly bemoans the assassination of Ts'ao Mao.

65

When the Prince was fifteen years old
    He roamed at will on the banks of the I and Lo.
His bright face shone with the beauty of spring flowers;
    Clever at dialectics, he remained pure and true.
5   He could not see Fou-ch'iu-kung
    And raise his hand to take leave of his contemporaries.
His frivolity turned easily into confusion;
    By floating hither and thither aimlessly he threw his life away.
[And the crane who was to take him to immortality] flies and flies,
      singing and soaring,
10   Moving its wings in pain difficult to bear.

Juan Chi has combined two stories in this poem. The first is of the Chou Crown Prince Chin in the *I Chou-shu* who was renowned as a subtle dialectician at the age of fifteen and who died young (*I Chou-shu* 9, p. 5b). The second is the story of his homonym, Wang-tzu (i.e. 'Prince') Ch'iao 王 子 喬 , from the *Lieh-hsien chuan*:

> Wang-tzu Ch'iao was Chin 晉 , the Crown Prince of King Ling [reigned 571—545 B.C.] of the Chou dynasty. He liked to play the *sheng* 笙 [a

kind of mouth organ] and could reproduce the song of the phoenix. He roamed between the I and Lo Rivers. A Taoist, Fou-ch'iu-kung, took him up Mt Sung. Later Wang-tzu Ch'iao mounted a white crane and stopped on the top of Mt Kou 緱 for several days. He raised his hands to take leave of his contemporaries and went away.

Juan Chi plays the first story off against the second and insists that the Prince could not have seen Fou-ch'iu-kung since, according to the *I Chou-shu*, he died young, and that the crane prepared for him had to fly off in sadness and alone. On the strictly literal level this poem describes the early death of a playboy, one of Juan Chi's favorite subjects. The playboy, this time, is sympathetic to the reader: he is 'pure and true' and his death leads to 'pain difficult to bear'; but still it is his 'frivolity', his 'floating hither and thither', that has led to his death.

Almost all the critics believe this poem to be a satire. Only Huang K'an believes it to be Juan Chi's lament for the non-existence of immortality; the *Lieh-hsien chuan* story is denied by the *I Chou-shu*. All the others see this as a satire of one of the Wei emperors, each critic, alas, choosing a different emperor. Ho Cho says it is Ts'ao Fang (who died peacefully in 274, many years after the death of Juan Chi); Chiang Shih-yüeh says it is the last emperor of the Wei, Ts'ao Huan (who was deposed after Juan Chi's death); and Ch'en Hang, Huang Chieh and Ku Chih all say it is Ts'ao Mao, who was killed on the orders of Ssu-ma Shih in 260. Only the last, of course, is possible, perhaps even probable. Ts'ao Mao was thirteen years old when he ascended the throne in 254, and thus hardly twenty when he was assassinated in 260. He enjoyed 'visiting the University and asking questions of the Learned Scholars' (*San-kuo chih chi-chieh* 4, p. 40b). And the historian Ch'en Shou sums up his life in a paragraph part of which could serve as an epigram for this poem: 'The Duke of Kao-kuei's [i.e. Ts'ao Mao's] talents and intelligence developed early. He was eager to learn and fond of literature . . . But he was flippant and easily angered, and he himself brought about his great calamity.'[1] But there is absolutely no way of being sure about the butt of the satire. Chu Chia-ch'eng suggests it to be Juan Chi's friend Hsi K'ang and not an emperor at all. He may be right, although the choice of a prince as the subject of the poem suggests a royal personage, and his age, one who died even earlier than Hsi K'ang.

As usual, we do not know what part, if any, Juan Chi played in the assassination of Ts'ao Mao; but we do know he was in relation with a man who played an important role in the preliminaries. On 2 June 260, Ts'ao Mao summoned three trusted councillors (unrelated, in spite of the fact that they bore the same family name), Wang Ch'en 王 沈 , Wang Yeh 王 業 and Wang Ching 王 經 , to tell them he had taken all he could from Ssu-ma Chao and that he was determined to free himself from his influence. Wang Ch'en and Wang Yeh treacherously hurried away to warn Ssu-ma Chao. It was with this same Wang Ch'en (d. 266) and another Ssu-ma partisan, Hsün I 荀 顗 (d. 274),[2] that Juan Chi wrote, at some unknown date, a history of the Wei dynasty.[3] This *Wei shu* 魏 書 is no longer extant, but, according to Liu Chih-chi,[4] it seems to have been shamefully pro-Ssu-ma. Juan Chi's collaboration in the writing of such a document again shows how close his ties to the Ssu-ma were. He is partially exonerated by the fact that the work was finished by Wang Ch'en[5] who may alone have been responsible for the political slanting.

There is another poem, ostensibly concerned with 'immortality', that speaks of a 'Prince' and that might very well be a satire on the assassination of Ts'ao Mao after the failure of his plan for a palace revolution.

> **55**
>
> Men say, 'We want to prolong our years'.
> > But once they have prolonged them, where do they want to go?
> The yellow crane calls 'Tzu-an',
> > But *we* cannot hope to live a thousand autumns!
> 5   I sit alone amidst the mountain crags
> > Sorrowfully thinking of the one I am fond of.
> How fine was the Prince
> > As he went hand in hand so tenderly [with his friends]!
> You can be loved right down to the present instant,
> 10   But some scheme or plot is a moment's matter:
> Give up that affair you plan for tomorrow —
> > You may be cheated by dusk today!

It is all well and good to 'prolong one's years' by practicing Taoist recipes of all sorts, but where does one go to hide once one has achieved them? How can one keep one's 'prolonged years' in our dangerous world? There are two slightly contradictory legends concerning Tzu-an and the yellow crane in line 3 (cf. *Lieh-hsien chuan*, Kaltenmark translation, pp. 183–7). According to one version (*Nan Ch'i shu* 15, p. 4a), Tzu-an was an immortal who rode a yellow crane, flying over the famous 'Yellow Crane Tower', Huang-ho lou, near Wu-han. In the other version (*Shui-ching chu* 29, p. 52) Tzu-an seems to have been an unsuccessful seeker of immortality. After his death 'a yellow crane made his nest in a tree on his tumulus and constantly cried "Tzu-an" '. In later poetry (e.g. Li Po, 'Teng Ching-t'ing shan . . . ', *Li T'ai-po ch'üan-chi* 12, p. 15b, a poem containing several echoes of Juan Chi's works) he is simply considered an immortal, and so it probably is here: lines 3 and 4 insist upon the fact that however clever we may be in 'prolonging our years' we cannot hope for immortality. The rest of the poem explains why, in a single example, that of the 'Prince' ('Wang-tzu', as in Poem 65, but also as in Poem 22 where the reference seems to be to the immortal Wang-tzu Ch'iao). His name suggests that of Wang-tzu Ch'iao, a successful 'prolonger of years', but his goodness, his friendliness and confident love did not help him to endure: where could he go to do that when scheming and plotting are 'a moment's matter'?

All the critics seem agreed that this is a satire, and Ch'en Hang, Tseng Kuo-fan, Huang Chieh and Ku Chih all suggest Ts'ao Mao as the subject, but Huang Chieh tortures line 9 most unconvincingly to make it fit into the circumstances of the palace revolt.

A month or so before his death Juan Chi went farther than he had ever gone previously in participating in political life, and went farther than he had ever gone in committing himself to the Ssu-ma's cause. In the tenth lunar month (November-December) of 263,[6] Ssu-ma Chao was again offered a series of titles and honors that were becoming the traditional prelude to the accession of a new dynasty.

> The Wei court conferred the title of Duke upon Prince Wen of Chin [i.e. Ssu-ma Chao] and prepared the ritual of the Nine Distinctions[7] for him, but Prince Wen firmly refused to accept them. When the highest civil and military officials were about to go to his headquarters to entreat him to accept, the *ssu-k'ung* [Minister of Public Works], Cheng Ch'ung 鄭 冲,[8] hurriedly sent off a messenger to Juan Chi asking him to put the request into writing. Juan Chi, at the time, was in the house of Yüan Hsiao-ni 袁 孝 尼[9] where he had been drunk for two days. They propped him up and he wrote on a wooden tablet. Without looking over it again, he gave it to the messenger. The people of the times thought it was done with a divine brush.[10]

Why was Juan Chi chosen to write this text? As *san-ch'i ch'ang-shih* he was required to furnish texts from time to time, but that is probably not the main reason. We have seen that Juan Chi has tried, on repeated occasions, to avoid commitment; we have seen, and will see again and again, that many of his poems are very noble and elevated meditations on the political scene, showing he had a pure and orthodox Confucian attitude towards the affairs of state. He must have represented, in himself, a moral force that the Ssu-ma were eager to have on their side. But Juan Chi's drunkenness again shows that he was not eager to be there and that it was only in such a state that he could bring himself to write a document that he knew would be the prelude to the outright usurpation of the throne.[11]

The letter itself, 'Letter exhorting the Prince of Chin for Cheng Ch'ung', is short and elegant and is reproduced both in the *Wen hsüan*[12] and in the *Chin shu*.[13] It is a purely formal document that I believe is not worth translating here, since it would require an enormous amount of commentary to explain

its numerous allusions, both to antiquity and to current events, and since it is
easily available in a German translation. But Juan Chi's method of 'exhorting'
Ssu-ma Chao is extremely interesting. He begins by citing three examples from
hoariest antiquity of men who have been honored by their sovereigns. Their
successors include innumerable men of feeble achievement who reaped handsome rewards. How much more should Ssu-ma Chao be honored, since he was
the scion of a family who had for generations helped the Wei house keep the
peace. He had himself aided in the pacifying of the troubled kingdom and
would soon be able to conquer Wu and Shu![14] When he has done that China
will again be unified and peaceful; Great Wei's virtue will be more brilliant
than that of Yao and Shun; and Ssu-ma Chao's achievements will surpass
those of the most famous loyal servants of the house of Chou.

> Then he can go to some azure beach and take leave of Chih-po[15] or
> ascend Chi Mountain and bow to Hsü-yu.[16] Would this not be splendid?
> Then he would be perfectly just, perfectly impartial. Who could be his
> neighbour?[17] What need has he of these earnest, petty refusals?

There are two important things to underline in Juan Chi's letter: he constantly insists that Ssu-ma Chao has been working as a loyal servant of the
house of Wei, and, far from encouraging his dynastic ambitions, he urges him,
when he has achieved the unification of China, to turn away from politics
altogether and lead the life of a hermit. The last paragraph (the one I have
quoted) must almost have sounded bitterly ironic in Lo-yang at the end of
263 where 'even the man in the street knew Ssu-ma Chao's ambitions'. This
was probably as far as Juan Chi could go in preserving both his integrity and
his (and his family's) life, but even so, he has been attacked as having used a
'shameful brush' (*ts'an-pi* 慚筆) not a 'divine brush' (*shen-pi* 神筆) to
write the letter.[18]

There is another satirical *fu* by Juan Chi that will help us understand his
feelings towards politics. As usual, he does not speak out clearly, but disguises
his feelings, this time by ostensibly describing a monkey. The *mi-hou* 獼猴,
the common macaque, lived in northern Chinese forests and had long been
used as entertaining pets or even as 'actors' in monkey shows.[19] Juan Chi in
his *fu* describes one that has been caught and used as a pet by a 'gentleman',
or a 'lord' (*chün-tzu* 君子).

The *fu* is divided almost equally into two parts: the first twenty-seven lines
are a Taoist introduction inspired by Chuang-tzu's doctrine that anything that
is useful is in danger of losing its life. The last thirty-eight lines describe the
sad plight of the monkey, caught and held captive because he is an amusing
pet. The opening lines refer to the 'civilizing' actions of the great culture hero
Yü who, after draining and reclaiming the land, divided China into nine prov-

inces, each of which furnished metal for the founding of cauldrons on which were engraved the various animals of the empire.

The monkey

In ancient times Yü regulated the waters and the land
    And sent I to hunt the animals.[20]
He cleansed the river valleys
    And combed the mountain forests,
5   So that the good and bad spirits could be described on the Nine
        Cauldrons
    And the earth's strange beings be brought together.[21]
That is why the thickly furred fox and the brightly spotted leopard lost
        their skins;[22]
    The long-tailed *tsou-yü*[23] offered up its treasure;
The *k'ua-fu*[24] and *lu-shu*[25] had their down made into clothing for the
        southern barbarians;
10   And the blue horses and those of three dappled colors[26] left their
        herds:
    The lives of all these animals were harmed because of their very
        qualities.

If the bear or wolf roam near the river
    And show their value, they court danger.[27]
The *k'uei* backs into an abyss to let himself go to his heart's content,
15   But, should he raise his thunderous voice, he will . . . [lose] . . . his
        his skin [to make a drum].[28]
If by chance you show yourself but once, albeit in a solitary desert,
    They will follow you out to the most remote, most hidden places in
        the world.
The tiny mouse, fearing pursuit, hides
    In a hole deep down inside a holy mound.[29]
20   If, one day, he is tempted to go out in search of food,
    How could one dig him out to prevent him [from gnawing on the
        horns of the sacrificial bull]?[30]
Truly, if a thing has some use and is desired,
    Though rarely seen, it will be caught.
Thus, those animals that are near at hand cannot count their years,
25   And those that live far away do not live for many.
If they are great, they will be spoken of for ten thousand years;
    If they are insignificant, they will be smiled at for a moment.

And the monkey, one of the least important,
    Still seems to be ranked just below [man].
30   He is physically quite like us, but he is not of our species;
    His form is different, and his [color] impure.

Externally he seems clever and sharp, but he is ruled by no internal
  conscience;
  He has a man's face and a beast's heart.
He is by nature narrow and superficial, and yet he seeks to advance in
  the world:
35   He is like Han Fei-tzu imprisoned in Ch'in.[31]
He mumbles often, raising his eyebrows,
  Seeming, falsely, to utter clever words.
The great numbers behind him were like a protective hedge,
  And yet he cut down the trees and lost his neighbor.[32]
40   When he adjusts his robe and bonnet and wears fine clothing
  He has Prince Hsiang's thought of wanting to return home.[33]
When he gives himself over to his passions and makes side-long glances,
  He has Ch'ang-ch'ing's enticing form.[34]
He lifts up his head, purses his lips and makes faces,
45   Increasing his movements and renewing them again and again.
If you bathe him in warm orchid water, he will be even dirtier;
  He has not Sung Chao's ability to seduce.[35]
He is always laughed at and kept tied up;
  Although he is a close companion he is not treated with warmth.
50   What can he do with his many arts and talents?
  He must remain filthy and keep his ugly countenance.
Of nimble appearance, a lover of tricks,
  Up he jumps to leap about the mountain peaks.
Once . . . he runs away to the east
55   He will be hunted in the central hills,
And when he is bound with ropes to make him obey,
  He turns towards the Western Mountains, moaning long.
He hangs on the rafters to put himself at ease,
  But how can he forget the Teng Forest?[36]
60   He begs his master for his gracious favor,
  And provides him with strange sights to the best of his ability,
For a moment that lasts the whole day:
  Why is he so playful and happy, so proud of himself?
For he will lie down and die in the courtyard
65   While his body and soul forever waste away.

The satirical element in this *fu* is not immediately apparent. 'The monkey'
seems, at first reading, to be very similar to the descriptive *fu* by Wang Yen-
shou 王延壽 (*c.* A.D. 130) called 'Wang-sun fu', 'The ape'.[37] The poem may,
indeed, be interpreted as a pure philosophical parable. The first thirty lines —
almost half the entire length — are of strong Taoist inspiration and describe
the plight of innocent wild animals who are harmed simply because they are
useful. The monkey is no exception and, simply because he is an amusing

creature to watch, he is made a captive pet. However well treated he may be, he remains out of his element and will, to the end of his days, think of his native forest. Juan Chi's repeated use of mythological beasts and place names add another Taoist dimension to the poem: the monkey's longing for the Western Mountain (i.e. K'un-lun, line 57) and Teng Forest (line 59) could be interpreted as the Taoist's longing for eternal life.

But Juan Chi has deliberately compared his monkey with famous courtiers, Han Fei-tzu, Hsiang Yü, Ssu-ma Hsiang-ju and Sung Chao; he certainly seems to expect us to compare him with men of the court. The only other person to have published an opinion on this poem,[38] believes Juan Chi to be satirizing the officials of the 'smaller aristocracy', kept at the beck and call of the 'greater aristocracy'. He believes, moreover, that the monkey symbolizes the meticulous, hypocritical ritualists (cf. line 40) Juan Chi makes fun of in his 'Biography of Master Great Man' and in Poem 67.[39] This seems an unwarranted interpretation to me. There are indeed passages in the poem which imply a distinctly pejorative view of the monkey: he is narrow, superficial, utters 'false clever words', is filthy, etc. But the overall impression is of sympathy for the poor animal and commiseration for his loss of liberty. Although I admit it is dangerous to base an interpretation, even partially, on a passage one does not fully understand, I think the allusion in line 39 is highly important. The monkey, like Han Fei-tzu in Ch'in, is described as being in danger of 'cutting down trees', of losing his life by showing a neighbor he understands his secret dynastic ambitions. Is not the monkey, to a certain extent at least, Juan Chi himself, a captive at the court of the Ssu-ma, dreaming of his liberty and forced to play the fool the live-long day? He draws an unflattering portrait of himself, but there is little reason to believe he thought very highly of the role he had to play throughout his political career. This interpretation may seem far-fetched, but it preserves the ambiguity of the feelings the monkey inspires in us, adds a dimension to the poem that it seems at first glance not to have, and is consonant with what we know of Juan Chi's biography.

During his lifetime his own acquaintances had already remarked that Juan Chi had an 'abstruse and distant' attitude which would help explain the obscurity of the satirical element in this fu and in so many other works. 'Ssu-ma Chao praised Juan Chi as "The most prudent [man in all the empire] ". Whenever one talks with him his words are all abstruse and distant: he never praises or blames anyone.'[40] We will see again and again that Juan Chi's whole approach to life is colored by 'abstruseness and distance', an attempt to abstract himself from the dangers and frustrations of the world he lived in. Juan Chi's friend, the great philosopher Hsi K'ang 嵇 康 (221–262), echoes Ssu-ma Chao on this point: 'Juan Ssu-tsung [i.e. Juan Chi] does not discuss other people's faults. I have always tried without success to model myself after him. He is extremely broad-minded, much more so than other men; he has no quarrel with the creatures of this world.'[41] Hsi K'ang is perhaps speaking more wisely than he knows, for shortly after he wrote the letter this quotation is taken from he was executed, having been denounced as 'un-Confucian' by a man he had slighted.

Juan Chi, on another occasion, proved just how prudent he was by getting drunk rather than talk to Chung Hui 鍾 會 (225–264), the very man who denounced Hsi K'ang: 'Chung Hui often asked Juan Chi about current affairs, trying to get him to implicate himself in some misdemeanor by his approbation or disapproval. Juan Chi was able to escape by getting drunk each time.'[42] There are only two or three cases on record of Juan Chi having recommended men for office: a letter recommending an almost unknown figure named Lu Po 盧 播 to Ssu-ma Chao[43] and the statement attributed to him that Chang Hua 張 華 (232–300) had 'talents worthy to aid a prince'.[44]

There is a poem by Juan Chi that is said by all critics to be aimed against Chung Hui.

25

I draw my sword and look upon the naked blade:
    It is not with swords that wounds of words are made.
My only fear is that some clever tongue
    Might speak of me beside the Three Rivers.

5   The Gushing Fountain leaps from Jade Mountain;
    The sun's Hanging Chariot perches in the Fu-sang tree.
The sun and moon travel one thousand *li*
    And the autumnal wind gives forth fine frost.

The road to power leads to both success and defeat:
10   How, alas, could one follow it for long?

The poem falls naturally into two quatrains and a final couplet. In the first quatrain the phrase 'wounds of words' translates *chùng-shang* 中 傷, a binomial expression which usually means 'to harm by calumny', but it can also mean 'to wound' (*Lieh-tzu* 1, Graham translation, p. 28). Juan Chi might thus be saying that he feels he could not be wounded by the blade of a sword: a clever back-biter is more fearful than a naked blade. The reference to the Three Rivers seems almost designed to make the poem more obscure. It is true that Chung Hui did accompany the Ssu-ma leaders, on two occasions, to the southeast (*San-kuo chih chi-chieh* 28, pp. 46a, 48a), the most traditional of the many locations given to the Three Rivers (*Shu ching*, 'Yü kung', Legge translation, pp. 108–10), but there no longer remains any evidence that it was there that he did his informing.

The second quatrain changes the subject entirely, and describes the passage of time. The 'Gushing Fountain' is named in the *Ch'u tz'u* (Hawkes translation, p. 143, line 15). The Jade Mountain is another name often used to refer to the K'un-lun, the Western Mountains, on the western rim of the world, and the Fu-sang tree, where the ten suns perched, was in the eastern sea.[45] In his 'cosmic' fashion of evoking the universe, Juan Chi uses a geographical description of the passage of the sun and moon from one end of the earth to the other to underline the passage of time, the arrival of autumn, harbinger of winter and death. The words 'fine frost' in line 8 (also used in Poem 16) are a subtle allusion to the poem 'Ch'en Chiang' of the 'Ch'i chien' in the *Ch'u tz'u* (Hawkes translation, p. 124):

> The loyal servant, true of heart, tries to protest,
>> But the sycophant is ever at hand to traduce him.
> The autumn herbs are blooming and ready to fruit,
>> When a fine frost falls on them, descending in the night.

The 'frost' in line 8, like the 'naked blade' in line 1, is an arm that can cut us down. The effect of all these 'weapons' should be felt in the last couplet: on the road of political power we are beset by these natural and political hazards. Huang Chieh glosses the words I have rendered by 'alas' as 'sighing', and says they epitomize the whole poem. According to him the line means: 'Sighing will not help prolong [our lives in this world fraught with danger]'. Ku Chih, less convincingly, believes Juan Chi is forecasting Chung Hui's own unhappy end as a revolutionary against his leader Ssu-ma Chao in 264, some months after the death of Juan Chi. This poem is not one of the most difficult in the series, but the abrupt changes from line to line and from quatrain to quatrain, and the subtle allusions give it the feeling of satire, of hidden, dangerous meanings, and this feeling adds, of course, to the poem's power and attraction.

In another poem Juan Chi seems to bemoan the deaths of men killed while they followed the 'road of power'. It is idle to attempt to attach particular names to the men satirized in the following poem, but its tone suggests men of high rank who were admired by Juan Chi.

62

> At midday I adjust my cap and robe
>> Thinking to receive visitors and guests.
> What manner of men are they?
>> They are as fleeting as the flying dust!

5   They gird their robes with cloudy vapors
      And their speech probes the depths of things metaphysical.
   In an instant they have been rejected:
      When will I see such men again?

Many of Juan Chi's contemporaries, like Juan Chi himself, were fond of
'probing the depths of things metaphysical'. The most famous, both as a philosopher and as a friend of Juan Chi's, was Hsi K'ang, killed by Ssu-ma Chao in
262. Tseng Kuo-fan and Huang K'an have suggested he is one of the men
described; the former adds Sun Teng (see below, pp. 149ff) and the latter
Hsia-hou Hsüan, killed by Ssu-ma Shih in 254 (above, p. 21). These identifi-
cations are, of course, arbitrary, but they probably do present the kind of
man Juan Chi has in mind: brilliant, too brilliant to be anything but 'fleeting',
that is, to be able to last in the dangerous world we live in. Line 4 is probably
not meant pejoratively, but as in the 'Nineteen old poems', poem no. 4, where
a similar line describes the fleetingness of life itself.

   The following poem is again, at least ostensibly, a lament for absent friends,
but it opens out into even wider vistas.

49

   I stroll about where three roads meet
      Sadly yearning for the one I am thinking of.
   How could I see him this morning?
      And yet he seems vaguely to be there!
5   Can tall pines grow in swamps?
      Unhoped for, even until the end of time.
   The high birds brush against heaven as they fly,
      Rising to the clouds and playing happily together there.
   How can there be a man walking alone,
10   Shedding tears, grieving over times gone by?

   There is no real need to invoke current politics or some kind of satire to
understand and appreciate this poem. The absent person or, more vaguely,
the 'object of his thoughts' (line 2), is some ideal, something he vaguely sees
before him but that he realizes cannot be there because the current atmosphere
is inhospitable. The 'three roads' in the first line suggest the poet is faced with
some complicated choice. 'Tall pines' are the symbol for steadfastness, loyalty,
trees that live for centuries and never lose their greenery. But they, like Juan
Chi's ideal, cannot be found growing in unpropitious surroundings (line 5).
High-flying birds are another symbol Juan Chi uses constantly; here we see
how their happiness high above the world contrasts with the swamp-like,
frustrating, sad world in which he lives. How indeed can he (or the persona of
this poem) be 'walking alone' (the term has overtones of 'eccentricity', con-

duct above or against normal rules of behavior[46]) so sadly in this unpropitious world when the happy birds show him a much wiser and happier way of life?

All the commentators (except Huang K'an, whose interpretation depends upon an improbable reading of lines 5 and 6) see this poem in a political setting, and I think they are right, although they often seem to me to go too far in their search for satirical targets. Whether 'the object of his thoughts' is the Wei dynasty (Huang Chieh) or Ts'ao Shuang (Chiang Shih-yüeh), I do not know. But the whole tone of the poem does suggest that Juan Chi's ideal is of a loyal, pure official saddened by what he sees about him. The stalwart pine and high-flying birds both suggest retirement, separation from a corrupt world. I do not believe Tseng Kuo-fan exaggerates too much when he says: 'The last two lines mean that Juan Chi *thinks* as Po I and Shu Ch'i do, but he doesn't *act* as they do.' He is unable to choose any of the roads that offer themselves to him at the beginning of the poem.

Poem 13, like Poem 62, speaks of the dangers of the world of politics, but this time the men who are so foolhardy as to engage themselves in such a hazardous profession are condemned outright.

13

I climb the heights to look down upon the surrounding wild lands,
    And gaze towards the north and the blue mountain slopes.
There singing birds fly over
    The pine and cypress hidden mountain crests.
5   I am moved to tears by this; my heart is filled with bitterness,
    Constantly suffering that poisoned malice is so widespread.
Lord Li grieved for the Eastern Gate,
    And Master Su felt the land within the Three Rivers too narrow for
      him.
If you seek goodness, it will come to you:
10 Why sigh and lament any more?

Juan Chi's ascension is symbolic of the attitude he adopts in the poem: he is going to look upon the world and its problems *de très haut*. He gazes toward the north — the traditional site for cemeteries — and sees the mountains clothed in blue-green pines and cypresses, funereal trees in China as well as in the West. The birds, superior creatures, fly over these peaks and sing, but Juan Chi feels affliction when he sees them, for he knows not only that we cannot transcend death, but that even in the short space of life allotted to us we must live in an atmosphere permeated with back-biting and hatred. This affliction prompts him to evoke the examples of two politicians of antiquity who were killed as victims of 'poisoned malice'.[47] The first, Li Ssu 李 斯

(executed in 208 B.C.), is the well known prime minister of the First Emperor
of the Ch'in dynasty who was executed shortly after the death of his sovereign,
victim of a palace intrigue. Before the execution of his entire family, Li Ssu
'turned back to his second son and said: "I would that we could go out the
Eastern Gate of Shang-ts'ai [his home city in Ch'u] again, leading our brown
dog out to hunt rabbits. If only that could be!" '[48]

Su Ch'in 蘇秦 (said to have lived in the fourth century B.C.), a native of
Lo-yang (the center of the Three Rivers[49]), was an ambitious, sophistic poli-
tician who attempted, according to the fictional stories that grew up around
his name, to form a 'League' or 'Axis' aimed at keeping the powerful western
kingdom of Ch'in from attacking its eastern neighbors. At the end of his life
Li Ssu longed to return to his home town, or even only to its Eastern Gate; at
the beginning of his career (which, like Li Ssu's, ended in execution) Su Ch'in
found even his home provinces too small for him and longed for universal
hegemony. The juxtaposition of these two lines is very powerful. The aged Li
Ssu and young Su Ch'in can be seen, in the context of a meditation on death,
as equally unimportant. They are simply men who have ruined their lives seeking for political glory. Juan Chi applies to them, with irony, a phrase
Confucius applied to the brothers of Shou-yang Mountain, Po I and Shu Ch'i.
When Confucius was asked whether he thought the brothers had any rancor
(since they had given up their principality to die of starvation), he replied:
'They sought for goodness and obtained it. What would they have to be
rancorous about?' (*Lun yü* 7, 14). The implication of this line is that Li Ssu
and Su Ch'in 'got what was coming to them': 'they sought for trouble and got
it', as Tseng Kuo-fan says in his commentary. They plunged themselves into a
life of back-biting, intrigue and ill will and profited from it by dying prematurely. Why sigh and lament for such men, for such a life?

Not all critics agree to this interpretation. The most ancient critic, Shen
Yüeh, does, but he adds fatalistic and deterministic ideas that I do not think
should be read into the poem (since we all die anyhow, the sage knows it is
best to stick to his allotted place in life, etc.). Ch'en Hang, Ho Cho and Huang
Chieh, however, refuse to interpret the penultimate line in this way. For them
'Seek for goodness and it will come to you' can only refer to Po I and Shu
Ch'i, and cannot be used ironically. Juan Chi would thus be suggesting a scale
of values: those who seek after gain die ignominiously; those who seek goodness die gloriously. This is not only not in keeping with Juan Chi's appraisal of
Po I and Shu Ch'i in his *fu* on 'Shou-yang Mountain', it does not do full justice
to the meaning of the beginning of the poem, which introduces a very general
meditation on death, giving no suggestion that some die 'better' than others.
A more general, philosophical interpretation alone can bind the beginning and

end together into a whole. Since death is our common lot we would do better not to hasten it with Machiavellian plots and schemes: those who indulge in them do not deserve our sighs.

In a number of poems on the theme of politics Juan Chi concludes on a note of resignation, saying, or implying, that he wants to leave public life altogether. We know that he did not, in fact, leave public life, but his low rank and constant inebriation amounted to a kind of 'public retirement'. The earliest historians to have studied Juan Chi were struck by this aspect of his life. Sun Sheng 孫 盛 (302–373) wrote: 'After [Juan Chi had served the Ssu-ma for a number of years] court opinion felt that, since he had become famous, he should be elevated. But, because political life in his age was fraught with accidents, Juan Chi occupied his post to receive his emolument and that was all . . .'[50] Tsang Jung-hsü 臧 榮 緒 (415–488) echoes him a century later: 'Juan Chi, at bottom, wanted to save the world, but living as he did at the juncture of the Wei and the Chin dynasties, when political life was fraught with accidents, he gave himself over to constant heavy drinking.'[51]

A number of Juan Chi's poems are in fact descriptions of this attitude (although there is not a single mention of drunkenness in his entire work), or of variations of it. Poem 66, again obscure and satirical, is one of them.

66

One cannot go out farther than the Gate of Coldness,
    Nor can one really float [forever] on the sea.
The sun's rays are no longer visible
    And in this darkness we are alone, without a lord.
5   Holding a melon, I think of Tung-ling:
    Indeed I think it shameful to act like the russet sparrow.
The loss of power is a moment's matter
    When someone will mount your grave wearing his sword.
I mourn for the man in the mulberry grove
10   And my tears run criss-cross down my cheeks.
I shall borrow a mount between the Chien and the Wei,
    Saddle it up and go out roaming.

Although every line in this poem is allusive, most of the allusions are readily understandable. The first two lines are parallel and refer to Ch'ü Yüan and Confucius. The former, towards the end of the poem 'Distant journey' that is ascribed to him (*Ch'u tz'u*, p. 86), describes his coming to the 'Gate of Coldness' 'at the world's far end', usually identified with the North Pole. Confucius, dissatisfied with an immoral world, once suggested he would 'get upon a raft and float about in the sea' (*Lun yü* 5, 7). Both of these figures lived cut off from their sovereigns and preferred to leave the world altogether rather than to remain estranged from them. Juan Chi says that it is impossible to leave the world, either by a mystical leap into heaven or a more prosaic boat ride on the sea. And yet we too are without a lord, without a sun to guide us. What shall Juan Chi do? Shall he retire from government and raise melons, as did the former lord of Tung-ling after the fall of the Ch'in (see Poem 6, below, p. 116)? In any case, the small russet sparrows who pick away at their grain oblivious of the danger they are in (cf. Poem 11, above, p. 32) seem shameful to him. They do not realize how easy it is to lose their position: was not the grave of the powerful Han emperor Wu defiled soon after his death?[52] There seems to be no more loyalty in the world, no one like Ling Ch'e 靈 輒 who, because he had been befriended by Duke Hsüan when he was starving to death in a mulberry wood, helped the duke at the risk of his own life when he later had the opportunity to do so (*Tso chuan*, Hsüan 2, Legge translation, p. 290). Is it not better, in such a world, to renounce all ambitions, and get a good horse, in the best horse-breeding area (*Shih chi* 5, p. 9), for a long roaming? This conclusion, a decision to leave the world, seems to me to be in partial contradiction with the first two lines which speak of the impossibility of 'leaving the world'; instead of a mystical evasion (line 1) or an impossible raft on the Eastern Sea (line 2), Juan Chi suggests a more feasible journey on horseback, not quite out of the world, and not quite in it either.

Ch'en Hang and Huang Chieh are in general agreement with this interpretation, but Ku Chih attempts to turn the poem into a more precise historical satire, saying it describes Wei's usurpation of the Han, rapidly followed by the Ssu-ma's usurpation of the Wei. His reasoning is ingenious, complicated and thoroughly unconvincing.

The short Poem 63 again preaches retirement, and is also obscure and possibly satirical.

63

When you think too much you can set your mind on nothing,
 And when you're lonely your heart fills with sadness.
Let me ramble about, gazing upon hills and lakes;
 My hand on my sword, I will mount a light bark.
5 I want only long leisure
 And will come back here to roam again in later years.

The first line of this poem describes a Hamlet-like state of mind, that of a man who has been hamstrung by his excessive cerebration. The relation between this line and the next may seem unclear, but I believe Juan Chi simply means that the lack of any aim in life makes it impossible for a man to engage in any social activity, and that this solitude brings on loneliness and concomitant melancholy. A recent author[53] has suggested, however, that these two lines contrast, that the word I translate by 'loneliness' should be given the technical sense of 'quietude' found in Taoist texts and in some of Juan Chi's other writings. The two lines would thus be another illustration of the paradox underlying Juan Chi's life, his inability to find satisfaction either in an active ('too much thought') or quietistic life. However you interpret these first two lines, this poem, like the preceding one, shows Juan Chi's desire to leave the world. He gives no reason here, apart from purely psychological and very modern ones ('Nervous strain'?), but his choice of the words 'hills and lakes' might suggest an allusion to a satirical poem in the *Shih ching* (No. 145), and his hand on his sword suggests political concern. The last line again underlines his inability to leave the world of politics for long. This poem is obscure, and its very obscurity adds to the anguish of the first two lines.

In the preceding poems Juan Chi's desire to retire from the world seems ambiguous or slightly obscure or paradoxical. In the following poem it is clear and definitive and quite according to traditional Taoist thinking.

74

How fine were the men of antique times
    Who, indifferent to all, found their peace in poverty.
In later, decadent years the *tao* has crumbled and decayed;
    Our dashing about has made vile dust fill the air.
5   Wasn't Ning-tzu just like this?
    No one is willing to sacrifice himself as in Yang Chu's song.
I'm not made to perch now here, now there;
    It's not like me to wander anxiously about.
How ephemeral are questions of glory and shame!
10   Away I go to taste the truth of the *tao*.
Verily, the truth of the *tao* can please us;
    Purity and cleanliness make the essence and the spirit endure.
Ch'ao and Yu lifted high their integrity
    When they went to the river's edge.

The men of antiquity lived idyllically, in complete harmony with nature, until social reformers destroyed their Eden by organizing them into communities, into unnatural hierarchies that caused them to lose their primitive simplicity. Paradise was lost, and man began earning his bread by the sweat of his brow, dashing about, raising worldly dust. Ning-tzu (whose name was Ning Ch'i 甯 戚) was a poor commoner with political ambitions. His low condition made it difficult for him to bring himself to the attention of the great ruler Huan of Ch'i (685–643 B.C.), so he went to Ch'i as a travelling merchant and attracted the ruler's attention by singing a song and beating upon his ox's horn. Duke Huan was impressed, employed Ning Ch'i (also called Ning Yüeh), and eventually gave him ministerial ranking (*Huai-nan-tzu* 12, p. 194). Ning-tzu was thus typical of men in fallen condition: he could not 'find his peace in poverty'. Yang Chu sang a fatalistic song trying to enlighten his friend Chi Liang's son to the fact that no doctor could cure his father; man is a helpless pawn in the hands of fate. The aim of the song was to teach Chi Liang's son 'to do nothing', to be, like the men of antiquity, 'indifferent to all' (*Lieh-tzu* 6, Graham translation, pp. 128–9). Juan Chi insists that he is not like the men of later times, not like Ning-tzu or Confucius who 'perched now here, now there' (*Lun yü* 14, 24), trying desperately to find a sovereign worthy of (and willing to accept) his aid, and who 'wandered anxiously about' (*Meng-tzu* 3B, 3) during his periods of unemployment. He is not interested in public opinion. He is interested only in the search for the *tao*'s truth. This term, *tao-chen* 道 真 , is an echo of a similar term in *Chuang-tzu* 28 (Legge translation, 2, pp. 153–4), *tao chih chen* 道 之 真. 'The true object of the *tao* is the regulation of the person. Quite subordinate to this is its use in the management of the state and the clan; while the government of the kingdom is but the dust and refuse of it.' Ch'ao-fu ('The old nester') and Hsü-yu ('Laissez-aller') are two hermits of antiquity who have understood this message; they refused to accept the office of ruler when it was offered to them by the emperor Yao, and went to the river to wash the pollution of his request from their ears.[54]

This typically Taoist rejection of the world of politics and social life represents only one pole of Juan Chi's very complex attitude towards social and political life. There is another poem that is at the same time more traditional, more complex and, I think, closer to his own general attitude.

42

The king in his works relies on worthy aides:
  He needs shining heroes to accomplish his great deeds.
Fine and compliant, how peaceful, how good,
  How magnificent the voices that sing the praises of these officers!

5 The *yin* and *yang* sometimes go awry;
  The sun and the moon are inconstant in their brightness;
Heaven now smiles and now frowns:
  Human affairs are full of changes.

Yüan and Chi withdrew to the Southern Peak;
10 Po-yang hid away among the Western Barbarians.
They preserved themselves, meditating on the truth of the *tao*:
  How could they have exalted favor and glory?

Anyone can begin well;
  Few can master their endings.

15 How excellent were the men of antiquity
     Whose aura of purity will shine down the countless generations to
         come!

The first stanza, a pastiche of quotations from the Confucian canon,[55] emphasizes the importance of brilliant statesmen and the glory they enjoy. The second stanza is fatalistic, implying that, when the times are not good, heroic actions are useless. Then it is better to retire, as Tung-yüan kung, Ch'i-li Chi and Lao tzu (whose *tzu* was Po-yang) did. The former fled the disorders at the end of the Ch'in dynasty and refused to serve the Han (*Shih chi* 55, pp. 22–3, 27); Lao-tzu left the declining Chou (*Shih chi* 66, p. 6). Although their actions may seem negative to us, Juan Chi points out here that in troubled times preservation of one's life and integrity is worthy of eternal fame. He may seem to contradict his 'Shou-yang Mountain', but the contradiction is only superficial: in 'Shou-yang Mountain' he blames the two hermits for leaving the world because their flight ended only in death; here he praises hermits for fleeing a world in disorder and preserving their lives. The poem is not purely 'Taoist', for the Taoist does not praise 'the king's works' or his 'shining heroes' as the first stanza does. Juan Chi's position in the poem is in fact complex. The 'men of antiquity' he admires in the penultimate line are not simply those who fled society, but also the 'shining heroes' of the first quatrain. If he himself in his own life seemed to have chosen a kind of retirement within politics, it was because he had no choice. But it is clear from the hints he has given in his satirical poetry and from what we have been able to learn from traditional historians that his underlying attitude was not one of Taoist retirement, but of a frustrated desire to serve his sovereign loyally and courageously in the best possible Confucian tradition.

That is, I think, the message of the three poems in tetrameters usually printed with his 'Yung-huai' poems.[56] These three poems are not easy to interpret and we cannot be sure they are meant to be read as a series (as I have read them). Since no commentary was available to me, I am entirely responsible for my interpretation. I see the poems as a meditation on loyalty to the emperor, who is here called the ancient emperor Shun. Shun's wives, the emperor Yao's daughters, whose mourning for their husband (some sources say they committed suicide by drowning themselves in the Hsiang River) has inspired countless legends and poems, are the central figures of these three poems, both as models of fidelity and as inaccessible ideals of immortality.

   1

Heaven and earth are locked in union
     As their primeval essences alternate.
Light and airy is the sun's *yang* breath;

A mild breeze blows softly about.
5   The clear moon brightens the heavens;
      Sweet dew covers the earth.
The tall pines grow thick and dense,
      And the silvervine is lush and rich.
The grasshopper sings so dolefully;
10   The oriole beats its wings.

This moment has moved me and set me to thinking:
      I stand long, craning my neck in hope and in indecision.
How fine was the emperor's court
      Where I [A-] Heng was an aide!
15   But my talents in the civilian arts are not perfect,
      Nor can I cope with the arts of war.
I'll go down to the rivers Yüan and Hsiang
      To throw my lot in with the Fisherman.
And I shall roam and I shall play,
20   And I shall dwell there, and there I shall stay!

The poem begins with a description (borrowed, in part, from the metaphysical appendix of the *I ching*, the 'Hsi tz'u' (Legge translation, p. 393)) suggesting that nature is at the height of its period of creativity. Line 6 (perhaps a distant echo of *Lao-tzu* 32) suggests further that the world is in perfect harmony. In line 10 the oriole is a symbol of spring (as in *Shih ching* 154 and 156). As if under the influence of the burgeoning activity he feels and sees in the world of nature, Juan Chi too longs to enter into an active occupation and, quite naturally, turns toward the court. There he sees (line 14) a great courtier of antiquity, I Yin (who was also called A-heng; cf. *Shih chi* 3, p. 6), minister of T'ang, the founder of the Shang dynasty. Hsiao Ti-fei (p. 21) believes this is satirical for Ssu-ma Shih, but the surface meaning of the line merely suggests a flourishing capital, full of great opportunities. Juan Chi very uncharacteristically pleads his incapacity to serve and seeks to hide away in the south, near Lake Tung-t'ing and the banks of rivers associated with the early emperor Shun's widows and with the Fisherman Ch'ü Yüan consulted when he was exiled from the court (*Ch'u tz'u*, pp. 90–91).

    2

The moon is bright, the stars few;
      The sky is clear, the air cold.
Flags of cassia, banners of kingfisher feathers,
      Pendant jade insignia of rank, singing phoenix bells on the imperial carriage.
5   I shall wash my hatstrings in the sweet spring water

And garb myself with the fragrant orchid.
I shall follow the Two Daughters
And go down to the rivers Hsiang and Yüan.
Their spirituality is mysterious, their hearing subtle;
10   But who could see their jade-like faces?

How bright are the flowers of spring,
And the leaves of green that harbor shining red!
The days and months are passing,
And I regret the luxuriant flowers!

Line 5 refers to a song the Fisherman sings to Ch'ü Yüan when he comes to consult him (it is also found in *Meng-tzu* 4 A, 8, 2): 'When the Ts'ang-lang's waters are clear, I can wash my hatstrings in them; When the Ts'ang-lang's waters are muddy, I can wash my feet in them.' The meaning is that one should keep away from politics when the political world gets 'dirty'. Juan Chi will wash his hatstrings in a pure spring, far from humanity, and he will wear, like Ch'ü Yüan, the pure orchid in his solitary ramblings through the forest. The 'Two Daughters' (so called in *Shang shu*, 'Yao tien', Legge translation, p. 27) refer to Yao's daughters whom he married to Shun. At the latter's death, unable to follow him to his tomb, they are said to have become the goddesses of the River Hsiang which, like the River Yüan, runs into Lake Tung-t'ing. Line 9 may refer to a passage in *Shan-hai ching* (12, p. 4a), where it is said that *Shun's* two daughters (not Yao's) were possessed of spirituality (*ling* 靈 , as in this poem) that 'shone for one hundred *li* around'. It is precisely their superiority to ordinary mortals that explains line 10. The poet has left the world of politics (first quatrain) to follow the two immortal goddesses, but line 10 tells us that he cannot: they, like the immortal Taoists he will seek out in so many poems, are not easily found. And the last stanza shows that, unless they or some other immortal beings can teach us the art of Long Life, time will rob us of our youth.

3

A fresh wind comes so swiftly blowing,
But the long night seems endless.
I wail and sing; my heart pains me;
I sleep alone, then wake and talk.
5   About to drink, I beat my breast in pain;
Facing my food, I forget to eat.
That there is no herb of forgetfulness in this world
Makes me sigh in sadness.
The singing bird seeks out its mate;
10   The 'East wind' stigmatizes the error of estrangement.

Shun's talents were employed,
 And, as emperor, he commanded compliant and fine officers.
Master Pao felt friendship at first sight
 And enabled Father Chung to aid Duke Huan.

15 I return to the bank to sigh for Shun;
 How could I dare not to yearn for his face?
All my aspirations lead me to imitate these illustrious models:
 It isn't that I desire to enter service.
What is it I hold in my heart?
20 Its fragrance is like the orchid's.

This third poem is by far the most difficult of the three, and its ending gives them their ultimate meaning. Like the other poems and, indeed, most tetrameter poetry in Chinese, it is strongly influenced by the language of the *Shih ching*. Lines 3 and 4 are, in fact, direct quotations (from *Shih ching* 229 and 56) and line 7, reading 諼 for 萱 (as in Poem 2, p. 120, below), refers to some unidentified opiate said to make one 'forget one's cares' in *Shih ching* 62 (a poem of separation). Line 10, finally, refers to two poems, both called 'East wind' (*Shih ching* 35 and 201), which tell the sadness of repudiated wives. This whole ten line introduction thus describes the unhappiness of separation — the separation of the poet from the court, and from the nymphs described in tetrameter Poem 2. The four lines which follow change the subject abruptly and allude to quite opposite sentiments. Shun's mounting the throne (referred to with a term reminiscent of *Shang shu*, 'Yao tien', Legge translation, p. 23) allowed him to employ faithful and harmonious officials (the term, as in Poem 42, above, p. 67, is from *Tso chuan*, Wen 18, Legge translation, p. 282); the friendship between Pao Shu-ya 鮑叔牙 and Kuan Chung 管仲 is proverbial and was indeed what saved the latter from being executed, allowing him to make his master, Duke Huan of Ch'i, hegemon of the Warring States (*Shih chi* 32, p. 18).

These examples of friendly harmony in the social and political world contrast strongly with what the poet sees about him and lead him to his final thoughts. He goes back to the bank (presumably) of the rivers of Shun's widows, the nymphs of the Hsiang and the Yüan, to lament the passing of the sage emperor. Hsiao Ti-fei (p. 16) interprets the last word in line 16 as a proper noun: 'How could I dare not to yearn for Yen (Hui)?' This seems improbable to me (cf. the very similar line in Ts'ao Chih's 'Mei-nü p'ien', 'The beautiful girl': 'Who would not yearn for her fine face?' 誰不希令顏) in spite of the fact that the characters *hsi-yen* 希顏 do sometimes have the meaning 'yearning for Yen Hui' (e.g. *Chin-shu chiao-chu* 82, p. 66). The line recalls line 10 of Poem 2 ('But who could see their jade-like faces?') as line 17 of

Poem 1 recalls line 8 of Poem 2, helping to link the three poems together. The last four lines give the conclusion to this long nocturnal meditation upon political commitment and political disengagement, and, in their veiled, satirical way, go as far as Juan Chi ever goes to present his feelings of loyalty to the ruling house. The 'illustrious models' he speaks of are paragons of loyalty — the loyalty of Yao's daughters to their emperor husband actually led to their divinization. Their attitude, reminiscent of Hindu suttee, is not far removed from that of Po I and Shu Ch'i, who starved to death rather than serve a usurper. The last two lines, which have a kind of musical rhythm typical of the best of tetrameter poetry, are, as so often at the end of Juan Chi's poems, in the form of a question: what indeed is he getting at in his invocation of the great loyalties of the past? What does he cherish in his heart? He cherishes purity, the refined, steadfast purity of the orchid, unsullied by political intrigue or infidelity.

And this, too, is the message of the pentameter poetry we have read up until now. With all their contradictions, hovering among desires to leave the world for ever (Poem 74), or simply wait out the current crisis (Poem 63), or retire during a period of corruption (Poem 42), they give us, finally, the image of a man wholly committed to traditional values, to the defense of his true sovereign. But they show us, too, that he realizes that the Ts'ao have brought on their own ruin (Poems 11, 64, 65 and 66) and can no longer be saved (Poems 9 and 61): he must live alone among intrigue, hypocrisy and danger to the end of his days (Poems 13, 25, 49 and 62).

4
ANTI-RITUALISM

Juan Chi deliberately played a very minor role in politics; he played a very major role in society. To put it more precisely, his social behavior, which shocked and angered many of his contemporaries, is one of the best illustrations we have today of the state of social morality in third-century China. More than that, his figure, as it emerges from the numerous anecdotes told about his very bizarre behavior, has stood throughout history as the symbol of the reaction of the individual against the excesses of Confucian bigotry. But his position is by no means a simple one, as we shall see as we examine the elements that can still be assembled to describe it to us: his family background, his behavior as it appears in anecdotal literature and in a precious contemporary account, and in his own essays and poetry.

Juan Chi's political life shows us that he was a man of means, an important figure in the center of political activity solicited by the highest authorities to join them. His refusal to act only accentuates his potential force, his elevated status in society. What are we to make, then, of the following citation from the *Shih-shuo hsin-yü*? 'Juan Hsien and Juan Chi lived to the south of the road and the other Juan lived to the north of it; the northern Juan were all rich, the southern Juan poor.'[1] I do not believe we should understand this to mean that Juan Chi and his nephew were literally poor. I believe it probably means that they 'lived poorly'; that is, they were indifferent to riches and made no pretense of leading a rich man's life. This is, of course, only my interpretation, but it helps explain the contradiction in the different sources describing Juan Chi's life and it also helps explain similar passages in the dynastic histories.[2] An early author says that only Juan Hsien was 'poor' and prefaces his remarks on the Juan family by the following statements which are, I think, much more to the point: 'The Juan had, for generations, been schooled in Confucianism and "managed well their family affairs".'[3]

Just how rich and powerful they were it is impossible to say today. Their members appear often in the medieval dynastic histories, and if the Sung encyclopedist Cheng Ch'iao 鄭 樵 says they began 'to flourish only in Chin and Sung times',[4] he is probably assimilating the end of the Wei dynasty to the Chin as is often (erroneously) done.[5] It is suggestive, too, that a certain Shih 石 family mentioned in the *Nan shih* changed its name to Juan.[6] But the only concrete reference to the Juan's wealth is the existence of a region called 'Juan's Bend' very close to the southeast corner of Lo-yang (see above, chapter 1, note 27). What we know of Juan Chi's life and the 'traditional Confucianism' of his family suggests that the Juan were members in good standing of the new aristocracy based solely on family membership that appeared at the end of the Han, an aristocracy that was to keep its power for many centuries, for a longer period of time than at any other epoch in later Chinese history.

The conditions that brought about this new phase in the history of Chinese society were, of course, so complex that it would be impossible even to outline them here. But the triumph of this new aristocracy, this 're-feudalization' of society, was accompanied by certain changes in social attitudes that must at least be mentioned, since Juan Chi's role in society was to embody a direct reaction against them. The fall of the Han state brought about a subtle but extremely important change in men's moral life.[7] The family began to usurp more and more of the state's omnipresent authority and social morality began to take on more and more of a familial tinge, especially in respect of the most important virtue of them all, filial piety. Filial piety had been the cornerstone of the Han moral system since the beginning of the dynasty (the posthumous names of the Han emperors, except for the two founders, all begin with the word for filial piety, *hsiao* 孝 , for example). It was considered the cohesive moral force that kept society and the very universe together, the respect one felt for one's progenitors being translated on different levels to the respect of a wife for her husband, of a younger brother for an elder, a subordinate for a superior, a subject for his sovereign, and of the sovereign, 'son of heaven', for his metaphysical father. As the imperial framework weakened and the family took on more and more importance in the state, filial piety gradually became an actual familial virtue, and one's demonstration of filial piety, of actual respect and care for one's parents, became the cardinal virtue of a man's entire existence. What had previously been a moral imperative directed above all towards reverence for one's ancestors, was now extended to one's actual, concrete attitude towards one's parents. The consequences of this change in emphasis were disastrous. In the Latter Han dynasty and throughout the Middle Ages 'filial sons' go to such horrendous extremes of self-sacrifice as to render themselves monstrous, while would-be 'filial sons' attempt to profit from their reputation for filial piety in a world where, with the state deprived of much of its power, moral reputation in a closed, hierarchic society has become the sole criterion to judge and to promote. Stories of filial piety now begin to fill the histories. Self-sacrifice for one's parents becomes a veritable craze where, in many cases, the problem is not whether the filial son is sincere or not, but whether or not he is in his right mind.[8]

We have seen how Juan Chi attempted to remain loyal to his sovereign, how, in his obscure and yet passionate poems, he was strongly attached to the imperial idea, to the maintenance of the legitimacy of the throne. His attitude in society, against ritualistic extremists on the one hand and hypocrites on the other, is consonant with this defense of traditional morality. Although his opposition to reigning attitudes is franker, more positive, and therefore easier to define than his loyalty to the throne, he has assumed a pose of anti-ritualism that at first glance seems paradoxical and contradictory. Part of this pose is probably due to the role he played as a clown to protect himself and his family from execution, but part of it comes from his own character: Juan Chi's moral nature was such that he could only show his disgust with the rampant abuses of traditional morality by a grandiose and violent display of rebellion against them. It was only by the complete negation of reigning ritualism that a man of Juan Chi's stature could express his disdain for its excesses.

He himself states this negative aspect of his work in an anecdote in which he is accused of transgressing the ritual by talking to his sister-in-law,[9] a well known taboo in many societies. 'Juan Chi once saw his sister-in-law as she was returning to her parents' home and he bid her goodbye. Someone censured him for it, and he answered: "The rites were not set up for the likes of me!" '[10] Juan Chi is here setting himself 'beyond the bounds' in true Taoist fashion. He is cultivating his myth as a man who disdains all social restraint. The following two anecdotes have the same meaning, but in them we subtly begin to see that Juan Chi is not really a pure nihilist as far as social ritualism is concerned. The first anecdote is quoted in the main text of the *Shih-shuo hsin-yü*:

> Juan Chi's neighbor was a beautiful woman who tended a bar and sold wine. He and Wang Jung often went to drink with her. When Juan Chi got drunk, he would simply go to sleep beside her. Her husband was, at first, extremely suspicious, but, after investigation, he saw that Juan Chi had no other intentions.[11]

It is difficult for us today to read this anecdote in its proper social setting. Just how far the *droit du seigneur* of the third-century Chinese ruling class extended is hard to say. A famous Latter Han ballad, 'Yü-lin lang' 羽 林 郎 , tells the story of a pseudo-'seigneur' very strongly rebuffed by a married barmaid, but that single poem cannot tell us to what extent Juan Chi is simply following his social prerogatives when he goes to sleep next to the woman. By admiring her beauty and yet respecting her honor, however, Juan Chi shows he may be nihilistic in regard to superficial social proprieties but not by any means in regard to basic human feelings.

A second anecdote quoted in the commentary to the above passage of the *Shih-shuo hsin-yü* shows us even more clearly that Juan Chi's lack of ceremony is not merely indifference to social customs.

> Juan Chi's neighbor was a virgin who was both talented and beautiful, but who died before marrying. Juan Chi was not related to her, nor had he known her before her death, yet he went and cried for her, leaving only after he had given full vent to his grief. He was in everything like this: free and unrestrained.[12]

Here Juan Chi clearly shows he is not indifferent to ritual: he deliberately takes part in the mourning rites for one who was almost a complete stranger to him and the gratuitousness of his participation shows us how much he really appreciated ritual when it remained something that could help us assuage our real, natural grief.

Juan Chi's flouting of social conventions and his feigned indifference to the rites must have shocked most of his contemporaries, but his unorthodox attitude towards that which was 'the constant norm of heaven and the very rightness of earth' (*Hsiao ching* 7), filial piety, was far worse than shocking: it was downright sedition, a crime against the state, against the universe itself. The ritual that separated the sexes and ruled the mourning rites had become only secondary; from the Latter Han dynasty onward, filial piety was the keystone of the whole moral edifice. If Juan Chi was going to show the world where he stood, he must do it with reference to filial piety. The following anecdote, which seems to date from around 255, when Juan Chi entered the service of Ssu-ma Chao, shows him playing the clown, attempting to shock his contemporaries into a more natural and spontaneous understanding of filial piety than the rigid, state-endorsed, profitable virtue it had become. The scene is set at an audience of the then de facto ruler, Ssu-ma Chao.

> An official told of a case in which a son had killed his mother. Juan Chi said: 'Tsk! I could condone his killing his father, but how could he go so far as to kill his mother!' The men present at the meeting were astonished by his reprehensible words. The 'emperor' [i.e. Ssu-ma Chao] asked: 'Do you condone patricide, the greatest crime on earth?' Juan Chi replied: 'Animals know their mother but not their father. A man who kills his father is in the same class as the animals, but a man who kills his mother is inferior even to an animal!' The assembly then assented with pleasure.[13]

The Taoist overtones to this pleasantry are obvious,[14] but to know Juan Chi's own feelings about filial piety we must examine how he reacted at the death of his own mother.

Contemporary emphasis on the virtue of filial piety made the death of a parent a crucial moment in a man's life. On that sad occasion he was required to show to the world, by weeping and fasting, how much he appreciated the gift of life his parents had given him. The old ritual was fairly rigorous in its demands: 'When a parent dies . . . his child should take neither water nor broth, nor should he light a fire [to cook on] for three days. His neighbors should prepare rice gruel for his food and drink.'[15] And he was to eat gruel for three years (actually twenty-five months) after the death of his parent.[16] But Juan Chi's contemporaries greatly exaggerated this already quite rigorous regimen. Ssu-ma Chao's own son, the Prince of Ch'i, at his father's death in 265 when he was nineteen years old, adamantly refused to eat. It was only by coaxing and cajoling that he could be convinced that he should end his fast (*Chin-shu chiao-chu* 39, pp. 15a—16a). And his case is only one in many.

After the depositing of the body in the grave it was customary to make some appropriate remark. Confucius considered Chi Cha's burial of his eldest son a model of ritualistic behavior:

> When the funeral mound was finished Chi Cha bared his left shoulder, circumambulated the tomb three times from left to right while wailing. 'It is destiny that his flesh and bones return to the earth, but may there be nowhere his soul does not reach, may there be nowhere his soul does not reach!'[17]

Many of these actions are magical, designed originally to protect the living from the dead man's dangerous ghost or to assure the protection of his powerful virtue, *te* 德, for his descendant.[18] But by Juan Chi's time they had lost their original meaning to become, often, pure formalism.

The crucial moment for Juan Chi occurred in 256,[19] at the death of his mother, the only parent he knew, since his father died when he was two years old. There are a number of anecdotes describing his reactions during the mourning period, and all of them clearly point up the contradiction between his ostensible anti-ritualism and his true filial piety, his profound feeling of what the rites really stood for. We first see him at the very moment of burial:

> When Juan Chi was about to bury his mother he steamed a fat suckling pig and drank two dippers full of wine. And then, when he was to take his final leave of her, he said simply: 'Misery!' He could only wail once, and that once was enough to make him spit blood. He wasted away for a long time.[20]

Another source tries to tell us how Juan Chi reacted before the burial of his mother, at the very moment she died. If I translate it here, it is primarily to show how suspicious we must be of these anecdotes, how easy it was for over-eager historians to embroider on these events and render them a little livelier, a little more 'interesting' or 'typical'.

> When Juan Chi's mother was about to die, he was in the midst of a game
> of chess [*wei-ch'i*] as if nothing were the matter. His opponent beseeched
> him to stop, but Juan Chi would not hear of it and insisted on staying
> until they had finished their game. When it was over he drank three
> dippers of wine, wailed once, spit out several spoonfuls of blood and
> wasted away for a long time.[21]

This is not only 'un-ritualistic' behavior; it is monstrous behavior. To have
drunk wine and eaten meat before his mother's funeral can be tolerated, and
even condoned (as we shall see), but to have sat calmly playing chess (more
exactly, the ancient game known today in Japan and the West as *go*) while his
mother was dying, is inhuman. Little is known of the author of the source
that quotes this anecdote,[22] and his book is one of the eighteen Chin histories
that were replaced in 646 by the publication of the *Chin shu* and subsequently
lost.[23] The great historian Liu Chih-chi 劉 知 幾 (661–721) has shown how
contradictory these anecdotes are, saying that they include attitudes of those
who disliked Juan Chi (they condemn him as an anti-ritualist) and those who
admired him (they praise him as profoundly filial). Liu Chih-chi therefore
accepted neither anecdote and discounted both as historical material.[24] I will
not attempt to prove the historicity of the first of these two anecdotes; all I
can say is that I believe it is consistent with what we know of Juan Chi's
character and thought. He *was* contradictory; he *was* (superficially) an anti-
ritualist; and he *was* profoundly filial. The second anecdote seems spurious to
me not because it is contradictory but because it is so completely inhuman. It
does serve to remind us, however, how tenuous the historical value of all these
anecdotes is.

The aim of the other anecdotes concerning Juan Chi's mourning for his
mother is to resolve this contradiction, to explain how a truly filial son could
so flout convention during his mourning. First we see him receive the visit of a
young man named P'ei K'ai 裴 楷 (237?–291?) who was to become an
important statesman when the Ssu-ma had founded their new dynasty.

> P'ei K'ai was famous when he was young, and had a bright and intelli-
> gent air about him. When Juan Chi was in mourning for his mother,
> nineteen year old P'ei K'ai[25] went to pay a condolence call on him. Juan
> Chi then left his position of mourning,[26] his mind quite calm. He came
> up chanting and singing with all his might, as if there were no one
> present. P'ei K'ai did not change his expression because of this and his
> movements were as they had been before. He quickly gave full vent to
> his feelings and cried alone. When he had finished crying he retired,
> maintaining unchanged his imposing countenance and his movements.[27]
>   Someone asked P'ei K'ai: 'In all condolence calls the host cries and
> the guest then acts in accordance with the ritual. Since Juan Chi did not

cry, why did you?' P'ei K'ai answered: 'Juan Chi is a man "beyond the bounds"; that is why he does not respect the ritual regulations. Men like myself live within accepted customs; that is why we live according to the rules of good breeding.' The men of the times admired them both as having attained perfection.[28]

P'ei K'ai's explanation of Juan Chi's peculiar conduct belongs to a category of brilliant philosophical conversations called 'pure talk', *ch'ing-t'an*, that flourished in the third and fourth centuries. By calling Juan Chi a man 'beyond the bounds' he evokes an incident in *Chuang-tzu* very similar to his own visit to Juan Chi. In chapter 6 of the *Chuang-tzu*, an apocryphal Confucius is asked to explain the conduct of some Taoists who mourn for a lost friend by singing a song and who greet 'with unaltered expressions' a Confucian disciple come to pay a condolence call. Confucius tells his disciple that these are 'Men who roam beyond the bounds . . . in the undifferentiated breath of heaven and earth' and that there can be no common ground between himself, 'a man who roams within the bounds', and these superior beings (*Chuang-tzu* 6, Legge translation, 1, p. 251). P'ei K'ai is thus cleverly pointing to a parallel between antiquity and his own day at the same time as he explains away Juan Chi's unceremonious behavior as being the behavior of a Taoist, detached from the passions of the world.

Not all of his contemporaries were so tolerant, however. One of them, Ho Tseng 何 曾, actually tried to get Juan Chi punished for his bad manners. Ho Tseng was a ritualist 'feared by the men of the court for the rigor with which he enforced the moral law' (*Chin-shu chiao-chu* 33, p. 16a). He was also an intimate partisan of the Ssu-ma and instrumental in deposing Ts'ao Fang (*ibid.*, p. 13b). The following anecdote shows him in action:

> When Juan Chi was in mourning for his mother he attended a gathering at Ssu-ma Chao's taking both wine and meat. The Governor of the Capital Province, *ssu-li* 司 隸, Ho Tseng,[29] was also at the gathering and said: 'Our illustrious Lord is now, just at this moment, engaged in governing the empire by means of the virtue of filial piety. And yet Juan Chi, in heavy mourning, drinks wine and eats meat quite openly at my Lord's table. He should be exiled beyond the seas to preserve the orthodoxy of our morality!' Ssu-ma Chao replied: 'See how Juan Chi is wasting away! How is it you cannot commiserate with him? "When a man is sick," moreover, it is quite definitely according to the ritual "to drink wine and eat meat"!'[30] Juan Chi ate and drank without a halt, without changing his expression.[31]

Ho Tseng's words are extremely ominous: if Juan Chi had been convicted of unfilial conduct he could have been executed, not merely exiled. Ssu-ma

Chao's defence of him shows that he considered Juan Chi's mourning to be perfectly sincere and even pathetic. He has no need to invoke Taoist parallels here to excuse his eccentric favorite; he shows that Juan Chi was at bottom profoundly filial and, in his bizarre fashion, profoundly orthodox. His opinion thus contrasts with P'ei K'ai's, that Juan Chi was a man 'beyond the bounds', and again emphasizes the contradictory nature of Juan Chi's attitudes: he was a Taoist indifferent to all human suffering; he was a filial son profoundly affected by the death of his mother. Part of the contradiction can be explained away by saying that Juan Chi was 'playing the Taoist' to hide from public life. But the deeper reasons behind his 'Taoism' have already been alluded to: the anti-ritualism of Chuang-tzu helped him tear away the stiff, inhuman façade of contemporary Confucianism, and allowed him to show his filial piety in a more natural way.

It seems clear that, during his lifetime, and certainly afterwards, it was the 'Taoist' element in him that captured most men's imaginations. Neither can there be any doubt that he intended them to look upon him as a (harmless) Taoist eccentric. The following anecdote shows him cultivating his myth, scaring away the very man who later convinced the filial orphan of Ssu-ma Chao that he should not starve himself after his father's death:

> During Juan Chi's mourning period Hsi Hsi 嵇 喜, Hsi K'ang's elder brother . . . went to pay him a condolence call. Juan Chi had the knack of showing the pupils of his eyes [normally] or only the whites, and when he met commonplace men he showed only the whites. Juan Chi did not cry when Hsi Hsi came [as he should have when receiving a condolence call], and showed only the whites of his eyes. Hsi Hsi, not at all pleased, retired. When Hsi K'ang heard about it, he went to visit Juan Chi with a present of wine and his zither under his arm. They thereupon became good friends.[32]

Juan Chi's manipulation of his eyeballs is famous in Chinese tradition and later poets like to refer to friends or enemies respectively as 'men to whom one shows the pupils or the whites of one's eyes' in allusion to this anecdote. Just exactly how Juan Chi managed his little trick must remain (fortunately) one of history's minor secrets. He probably had the knack of rolling his eyeballs in such a way that the pupils disappeared entirely under his eyelids. Mrs Gamp (in *Martin Chuzzlewit*) could boast of similar ocular dexterity, and Shakespeare is probably referring to something resembling Juan Chi's 'white eyes' when he speaks of 'wall-eyed wrath or staring rage' (*King John* IV, iii, 49). Whatever Juan Chi did do, it was probably quite hideous, and admirably suited to scaring away importunate callers without compromising himself politically. It was also an excellent method of proving himself 'a man beyond the bounds'; the grotesqueness of the act, coupled with the uncommon muscular agility to which it gave witness, prove that Juan Chi is akin to the surrealistic immortals with green hair, or red eyes, or furry skin, that abound in Taoist hagiography. And it was precisely this kind of grotesqueness that appealed to Hsi K'ang, himself a seeker of immortality. When Juan Chi saw him arrive with his pot of wine and his zither he knew at once he was a kindred spirit, since no man 'within the bounds' would dream of making music or drinking with a recently bereaved gentleman.

If this anecdote is authentic it marks the beginning of a friendship that has had great resonance in Chinese history. Hsi K'ang's philosophy and Juan Chi's poetry are the greatest achievements in mid-third-century Chinese intellectual life and their stature as literary men, together with their unorthodox behavior, have made them both symbols of a kind of free-thinking rare in Chinese history. They are, moreover, the two key figures in a group, real or imaginary, of free-living intellectuals whose collective fame outshines even their own: the Seven Sages of the Bamboo Grove: Juan Chi, Hsi K'ang, Hsiang Hsiu, Shan T'ao, Wang Jung, Juan Hsien and Liu Ling. These Seven Sages are said, but only in works that date from at least a century after the fact, to have gathered at Hsi K'ang's country estate in the foothills of the T'ai-hang range, some eight kilometers from White Deer Mountain, Pai-lu shan 白 鹿 山 (*Shui-ching chu* 9, p. 59). There they are said to have drunk together, and discussed philosophy and literature in a bamboo grove belonging to the estate. There are all sorts of reasons for believing that these meetings were imagined by later historians who lived at a time when such landscape-viewing gatherings were beginning to become popular and traditionalistic scholars were seeking 'ancient' antecedents for them,[33] but there can be no doubt that their existence, real or imaginary, corresponds to a current of third-century thought that the Chinese like to call 'spontaneity' or 'naturalism' (*tzu-jan* 自 然). Some scholars have even seen the 'naturalists' as a group of thinkers and politicians leagued together north of the Yellow River against the conservative Confucianists in Lo-yang. The latter, partisans of the 'Doctrine of Names', *ming-chiao* 名 教 , supported the usurpation by the Ssu-ma family of the Ts'ao 'naturalists'.[34] But actually the individual Seven Sages' political and even intellectual allegiance is hard to pin down with any precision;[35] even Juan Chi's 'naturalism' differs profoundly from Hsi K'ang's, as I will try to show.

Whatever one's misgivings about the actual existence of the Seven Sages or about their collective philosophy, they became very famous by the end of the fourth century when essays about them appear. The discovery in 1960, near Nanking, of a tomb dating from around that time in which their effigies are depicted in bas-relief on bricks along the walls, shows how very popular they were — so highly esteemed that a man chose to have them as companions in the afterworld![36] And their celebrity has hardly diminished throughout the Far East down to the present day.

The strongest argument in favor of the actual existence of the Seven Sages as a group is the fact that they all seem to have known one another and that they mention one another in some of their works. Juan Chi never speaks of any of the others in his works (he seldom refers to current events at all), but Hsi K'ang has written ten short phrases describing Juan Chi that are a precious corroboration by a contemporary, in an authentic work, of the anecdotes we have been discussing. I have already quoted part of this passage (p. 59), but here is Hsi K'ang's entire description:

> Juan Chi does not discuss other peoples' faults. I have always tried without success to model myself after him. He is extremely broad-minded, much more so than other men; he has no quarrel with the creatures of this world. His only fault is that he drinks too much, to such an extent that he has been reprimanded for it by ritually minded gentlemen who hate him as if he were their enemy. Fortunately the Generalissimo [i.e. Ssu-ma Chao] has protected him.[37]

There is one other contemporary account of Juan Chi's social behavior, another letter, this time addressed directly to Juan Chi by an otherwise unknown personage named Fu I 伏 羲 . The letter appears only in Yen K'o-chün's *Ch'üan San-kuo wen* 53,[38] but since there is an answer to it by Juan Chi in his works and since both letters are very much in the style of the period, there is little reason to doubt their authenticity. The Fu family, from Lang-yeh (southeastern Shantung), was a very famous scholarly family until the end of the Latter Han dynasty when, in 214, Ts'ao Ts'ao had hundreds of its members, including the reigning empress, executed together. Whether or not Fu I was from the same family (the family name is a rare one), his letter sounds indeed as if it had been written by a conservative member of the Establishment from an aristocratic family of long lineage.

The letter is well written and not lacking in common sense. But it is very long and its arguments can easily be told in résumé. I will quote only enough of it to give the reader an idea of Fu I's criticisms and then give those parts directly concerned with Juan Chi's character in full. The very beginning of the letter gives the gist of the main argument:

> I have heard that the only way we can achieve merit or accomplish fine deeds is to base our conduct on the Saints and Sages; the only way we can rejoice in our integrity and develop our nature is to be moved by the desire for glory and fame. Should we reject the Saints and turn away from the Sages, we will be unable to escape from well-meaning medioc-

rity; should we pass over glory and rise above fame, we must unavoidably remain miserable and dishonored.

For Fu I, desire for fame and glory is one of the constants of history and of human nature; men have different abilities, different interests, different aims, but they all go in the same direction, toward universal recognition, towards fame and glory. But the only way we can attain lasting glory is by conforming to the immemorial social laws and rituals handed down to us by the founders of Chinese culture, the Confucian Saints and Sages. There are no exceptions to this rule. Only men without talent say they are indifferent to fame – and then attempt to achieve it by showing off, going against the rites, behaving strangely: 'They laugh as loudly as they can, and then stare the whole day long.' (The allusion to men like Juan Chi is obvious: his youthful silence in the presence of Wang Ch'ang, his 'white eyes' for commonplace visitors.) These men would do better to admit their mediocrity and fall into line. In that way at least they will not be left entirely behind and lose all chance of participating in the government.

Only after thus exposing his basic tenets does Fu I address Juan Chi himself directly. We see at once that he does not know him intimately for he quotes other men's opinions of him. These are contradictory. Some say he is brilliant, but lacks practical political acumen; others say he is mediocre and attempts to hide his mediocrity by keeping aloof and mysterious. Fu I then recapitulates his main arguments, applying them to Juan Chi in order to show how contradictory he is. If Juan Chi, like all other human beings, is bent on distinguishing himself, one must imagine that his retirement has some hidden aim: he is biding his time to build up his fame before seizing the proper moment to carry out his ambitions. Or, if he is really indifferent to fame and simply wants to enjoy himself, he should be living a life of pure hedonism. But a cursory glance at his way of living shows he has neither famous guests at his gate nor rich meals and voluptuous bed partners in his chambers. This is madness, and worse than madness for, if it becomes common practice, it will lead to the disintegration of the empire and a period of revolts and wars.

But just how does Juan Chi live? Fu I gives a little sketch of his actions that supplements what we have read in the anecdotes:

> I hear that you roar with indignation and anguish, sobbing pathetically, pouring out tears. Or that at times you strike your belly and laugh loudly, rolling up your eyes, gazing on high. You are by nature domineering and go against the world; you've set your target against the wind and ignore all others as if there were no one else alive.

But this kind of alienation from society can only end in madness. Fu I preaches a 'reasonable' philosophy, telling Juan Chi to analyze his sentiments more clearly and not to carry on when he has no ostensible reason to do so.

Fu I then, in a few phrases, describes another aspect of Juan Chi, one that is only hinted at in the anecdotes and that is mentioned briefly at the beginning of his biography in *Chin shu* 49. 'Juan Chi,' it says there, 'would shut himself in his room to read for months on end without putting his nose out the door.'

> There are also judgements circulating about you that say you are of a refined nature and well versed in the things of antiquity, that you apply yourself with assiduity to the study of letters, that your books accumulate until they fill your rooms, and that you read them all [well into the night] by taper light. Your eyes are filled with the finery of righteousness; your mouth sated with the adornments of the Way. Lowering your head you chant; raising it you sigh: as far as the technique of the thing is concerned you could be a pure Confucian!

But of course Juan Chi is not, in his behavior at least, a 'pure Confucian'. Since he ignored all the Confucian rituals and ceremonies, his actions are quite inconsistent with his learning.

In the very middle of his letter, Fu I abruptly begins a new subject: the Taoists. He knows Juan Chi's strange behavior belongs to a tradition and he sets about to disprove the sources of that tradition. He makes short work of it. Chuang Chou (i.e. Chuang-tzu), Huai-nan-tzu, Tung-fang Shuo and all the others say that since they can 'cast their spirits to the ends of the world' and feel 'at east in the cosmos', they have no need to live in the world of men:

> Life, indeed, according to them, is a painful corvée. But they don't kill themselves as they should if they would carry out their own arguments to their logical conclusion. They say property is a filthy bond, but they don't throw away theirs and become laughing stocks. Thus we can see that, filled with dissatisfaction over what they cannot obtain, they hypocritically pretend to be 'without desires' and 'liberated'.

Nevertheless these men were outstanding; it was only because their contemporary conditions were so benighted that they hid themselves away. But Juan Chi is not at all in the same class. And here Fu I underlines the contradiction that we have already seen in the 'Shou-yang Mountain fu' and in his political life: Juan Chi 'does not want to flee the world, and he does not attempt to enter the world'. He is neither a great Taoist hermit, nor a great statesman. He is like a beautiful, untamable horse, one that could not be given away.

The Taoists were right to flee a benighted world, but Juan Chi has no such excuse. The Wei dynasty is flourishing and urgently needs men to re-unify the empire. Fu I says that Juan Chi is the kind of man needed, one whose talents as a strategist could bring peace to the world and glory to himself. (This is another indication that Juan Chi had been engaged in some kind of military activity.) He is obviously a brilliant man: why does he hide his intelligence? Intelligence is not something that is depleted when it is used. Juan Chi should use his and engage in worldly actions to prove himself to those who doubt his qualities. Fu I ends his letter by asking Juan Chi to explain himself so that he, Fu I, can explain him to the rest of the world.

If my hypothesis is correct that Juan Chi did not leave the world because by so doing he would expose himself to the suspicion of sedition, and that he did not engage in it because he was against the usurpation of the throne by the Ssu-ma, he obviously could not answer Fu I's letter truthfully. Even if, as I believe is the case, he was, at bottom, in agreement with much of Fu I's philosophy, he could hardly admit it. And, of course, he does not in his response. His 'Answer to Fu I's letter' is couched in purely Taoist terms and was certainly not meant to enlighten anyone about his motives. It is a flamboyant statement of Chuang-tzu's mystical theory of the incomprehensibility of true or absolute greatness to the purely rational mind. Fu I is treated as an inferior intelligence incapable of understanding Juan Chi's mystical aims. He is shown, in other words, the 'whites of Juan Chi's eyes'.

An answer to Fu I

The reception of your letter and the perusal of its contents have put me in a mind to send you an answer.

Now, not even the fastest wings can visit the heights of the nine-fold blue skies, nor can the darkest fins fathom the depths of the Four Seas. How much less can the unfeathered [and unfinned] species talk about them! A dark cloud, too, has no fixed form; the winged dragon has no constant manner: the former will sometimes pass over in the morning and be rolled up at night, its transformations taking place with great rapidity; the latter will sometimes hide in the mud or fly in the sky, descending in the morning and rising in the evening. When they spread themselves out, the Eight Directions do not suffice to contain them; when they squeeze themselves together, they can move with ease in no place at all.[39] But this cannot be seen by a blind man or understood by a tiny insect; great and distant things cannot be examined by men of limited powers; divine changes and spiritual transformations cannot be investigated by men with small capacities. How can you, Sir, in your petty way, endeavor to seek my conception of the Truth?

Men's powers cannot be considered equal and their tastes differ: the phoenix *luan* leaps into the Milky Way to dance and to move its wings, but the dove and quail[40] are happy to swoop above the brushwood forest; the hornless dragon floats to the Eight Shores[41] to wash his scales, but the gregarious turtle enjoys himself in puddles along the road. Thus we each follow our own preferences in our affections to procure our joy; if you stick to your own [taste] and criticize another's you will never be able to see all tastes as quite relative and equal [as a truly great man does].

Now, when a man sets up his aims in life, he should spread his net wide to catch the world; how could he complacently march into the net himself? It is he who should set himself up as an example to serve as a frame of reference to the vulgar crowd: how could he idly cut down his own natural gifts to conform to a label that they would give him? And if by chance the moment is not propitious to his designs, if the secret springs of destiny do not conform, then he must let his spirit leap up, he must raise high his will and leave far behind the world as he transcends it. Then he can let his spiritual energy [?] run wild on the outer rim of the Realm of Mystery; he can lift up his marvellous ambitions beyond the limits of heaven and earth, soaring upon rays of light, swooping up and down, mounting chaotically into the heights. Relaxed, he moves together with the transformations of the Way; rambling at ease, he glides along with the sun and the moon. When he encounters fame or renown, he equates them with any other transformation in the world's vicissitudes. He goes above that which has nothing above it and below that which has nothing below it. He dwells in no room and leaves through no gate, equating all the movements of the ten thousand things, following the contractions and swellings of the Six Breaths of the universe.[42] He holds together at the Great Pole all the strings of the Somber Net [? in which the world is enmeshed][43] and caresses the star 'Celestial One' in the chaotic wastes of space. The swirling grime of our world cannot follow in his wake, nor can its flying dust besmirch his purity. He has only left his corporeal body here with us: how could you hope to examine his spirit?

In spite of the fact that, [as you say], there are no professsions that cannot be heard of, no plans that cannot be told, surely it is not strange to say that intelligence has its limits? Just look, Sir, where your desires lead you: you would boast of having money to keep a city-toppling beauty, and then you seek after piddling business affairs; you establish heaven-reaching rituals, and then compare men using superficial social labels. You fatigue your precious body to enslave others, and then harbor the fetid filth such labor produces in your system to hasten your death. You are like a man sunk in a puddle formed in an ox's hoofprint who is indignant because heaven's river, the Milky Way, has no end! To hold these base attitudes is shameful; to engage in these acts is pathetic!

I believe in a transcendent plan of action and have faith in a great Way that is vast and secret. To plod with slow and cramped step along the common road, with no way to cast my thoughts afar, simply makes me melancholy.

A chronic illness has weakened my spirits these last days and I have not been able to put forth many forceful teachings.

Juan Chi

To a Western reader this exchange of letters may seem to be the discussion between two medieval philosophers, the first a partisan of the *via activa* and the second of the *via meditativa*. But the difference between the two protagonists' philosophical positions is much subtler, so much so that I am not sure there is any difference at all. Fu I has admitted the existence and perhaps even the validity in times of turmoil of the *via meditativa*; he accuses Juan Chi of following it only half-heartedly, not leaving the world and not entering it. And Juan Chi himself, although he refuses to admit that a Great Man will diminish himself in any way to act in society, as Fu I would have him, gives as his first aim the conquest of the world: 'he spreads his net wide to catch the world'. It is only 'if, by chance, the moment is not propitious to his designs, if the secret springs of destiny do not conform', that he leaves the world of men to transcend it in the spirit. Juan Chi's ultimate answer to Fu I is really no answer at all; it is simply a brutal declaration of his opponent's stupidity. The brutality of the answer is perhaps tempered by the extraordinary brilliance of the style, by the high-flown mysticism, borrowed from Chuang-tzu but hardly less striking than his. The style is so brilliant, indeed, the prose seems so intensely sincere, that we are left with an uneasy feeling of not knowing exactly where Juan Chi's true aspirations lie. If his 'Taoism' is secondary, as I have been contending, if it is in great part a role he has assumed so that he could escape real political commitment, it is also an important component of what must be called his 'metaphysical anguish'. Like other creative thinkers of his period (Wang Pi in particular), Taoist metaphysics, the idea of an Absolute underlying the relativity of the world as we know it, fascinated him. It provided a metaphysical basis for his thinking that ancient Confucianism could not give him; it helped him express the desire for 'absolute greatness' that (as we shall see) haunted him. The result is an uneasy amalgam of the two basically conflicting philosophical attitudes: Juan Chi seeks to 'save the world' as a Confucian saint, while at the same time he tries to rise above it as a Taoist hero.

Juan Chi has evaded Fu I's question with great prudence, using the method described by Ssu-ma Chao himself: 'Ssu-ma Chao praised Juan Chi as the most prudent man in the empire: whenever you talk with him, his words are abstract and distant; he never praises or blames anyone.'[44] It is indeed by 'abstract and distant' words that he has answered Fu I here.

5

CONFUCIAN ESSAYS AND A STRANGE UNDERSTANDING OF CHUANG-TZU

It is clear from his poems and, especially, two prose essays that Juan Chi was not only the anti-social Taoist he would have us believe in his letter to Fu I and in his drunken clowning. The clearest statement of his 'Confucianism' is to be found in his 'Yüeh lun' 樂 論, 'Essay on music'. His point of view in this essay is so traditionalistic, so far from the common image of his character and philosophy, that it has been suggested that the essay, as we have it, is incomplete or perhaps even a forgery.[1] Yet it is, in fact, with the 'Yung-huai shih', the best authenticated work we have of his, since it is quoted by a contemporary, Hsia-hou Hsüan 夏 侯 玄 (209–254), and criticized by him. It can even be dated as having been written earlier than 254 (the date of Hsia-hou Hsüan's execution), but we do not know how much earlier and, since Juan Chi was forty-four years old in 254, it cannot with any assurance be discounted as a youthful work. The essay is very clearly written, but it is fairly long and, since 'it does no more than transmit Confucianist theories',[2] I have decided not to translate it here in its entirety.[3]

The main problem to be discussed in the essay is a purely traditional one and is stated at the outset by an otherwise unknown 'Liu-tzu' 劉 子 . The early portion of Juan Chi's answer to Liu-tzu really contains all the elements that will be developed in greater detail in the rest of the 'Essay on music'. Here is the beginning of the essay.

> Liu-tzu asked the following question: 'Confucius has said, "There is nothing better than the rites to guarantee the safety of the ruling class and the good order of the people; and there is nothing better than music to change the customs of a people or to alter its habits."[4] Now, it is indeed by the rites that men are separated from women, that the relations between fathers and sons are perfected, that the sovereign and his ministers find their stations, and that the common people are kept in peace. As an instrument of government, nothing comes before the rites and, thus, indeed, "There is nothing better than the rites to guarantee the safety of the ruling class and the good order of the people". But what use to government are the sounds made by metal and stone, silk and

bamboo, bells and drums, and tubes and strings, or the gestures made with the shield and battle-ax, plumes and oxtails, the evolutions and movements of the dance? And what harm would their absence bring to civilization? Why then did he say, "There is nothing better than music to change the customs of a people or alter its habits"?'

Master Juan answered: Your question is indeed well put! When Confucius wrote on this subject in the past he only touched on the main points; he did not present a general outline of it. I will do this for you now, and let you fill in the details for yourself.

Now, music is part and parcel of the very structure of the universe and of the beings that inhabit it. When music is in accord with this structure and assimilates this nature, then it will be harmonious; but when it departs from them both, it will be discordant. When the Saints of old invented music, they made it to be in conformity with the structure of the universe and to bring to perfection the natures of the beings that inhabit it. Thus they determined the instruments belonging to each of the eight directions of the universe so that they might correspond with the sounds of the eight winds pushed abroad by the alternation of the *yin* and the *yang*;[5] they adjusted the musical tube *huang-chung*, the tube of central harmony,[6] and thereby opened up the affections of all living beings.

Since [music is thus intimately related to all natural and human phenomena], when the musical scale is well tuned, the *yin* and the *yang* will be harmonious; when the instruments are in tune, all beings will remain true to their species. Men and women will not change their places; the sovereign and his ministers will not infringe upon one another's position. Within the Four Seas, all will have the same outlook; the Nine Provinces will all fall into step. When music is played at the round hill, heavenly spirits will descend; when it is played at the square mound, earthly spirits will arise.[7] When heaven and earth thus unite their virtues, all beings will be concordant in their lives. Punishments and rewards will not be used and the people will be peaceful of themselves.

The male and female principles of the universe move easily and simply:[8] refined music, too, is uncomplicated; the Way and its Virtue are level and plain:[9] the five notes of music, too, are insipid. Refined music is uncomplicated, and so the *yin* and the *yang* communicate naturally; it is insipid, and so all beings are naturally joyous. Daily they grow in unconscious goodness and achieve their moral transformation; their customs and habits change and alter, and they are all united in this same joy-music.[10] This is the natural Way; this was music at its beginnings.

Juan Chi has done much more than simply answer Liu-tzu's question; he has sketched in a whole theory of the universe, a theory of the relations between man and the cosmos. He has done so, however, on strictly traditional lines, reciting the scholastic theories that had been codified long before, and that can be read in more detail in a great variety of ancient and Han works.[11] The theory is not without interest, or even beauty. The imaginative correspondences between the tones of the musical scale, the winds, the seasons, the affections and so on, are very evocative and we have, at one time or another and in one form or another, parallels in other cultures. But what is striking here in this essay by Juan Chi, the man who said, 'The rites were not made for men like me,' is the great place made for music as the accompaniment of ritual, as the regulator of the social relations of which he was ostensibly so contemptuous in his life.

I have translated only the first eighth of the essay, but in it Juan Chi has stated the main theme he is only going to develop afterwards. Once he has stated the scholastic theory of music's influence upon the universe he broaches a corollary that only good music, music of the Saints, rules it well, and it is this idea that he develops right to the end. He has already told us, in a few phrases, what this music was like; it was 'uncomplicated' and 'insipid', and its simplicity unified the empire and kept society stable and (unlike Taoist theories) strictly hierarchical. But the Saints disappeared, for a time, from the face of the earth, and the simple, unified civilization they had invented disappeared with them. Men began to use their individual intelligences and passions to control their lives. Men in the south, in Ch'u, heroic by nature, wrote military music; those in the central state of Cheng, inclined towards debauchery, wrote licentious music. And these works awoke strong emotions in their auditors, emotions that separated fathers from sons, rulers and ruled, destroyed family ritual and ruined agriculture. Then new Saints arose to impose once again a kind of refined music, dignified, measured and ceremonious, so that each class of society, 'in descending degree from top to bottom, to the very common people, could hear it. Those who sang, sang the praises of the virtue of the former kings; those who danced, repeated the gestures of the former kings . . . ', and in this way assimilated into their very souls the unifying harmony of the sage kings of old. And since this music was strictly measured in tone, in rhythm and as to the instruments that played it, and since the choreography that accompanied it was strictly regulated, it inspired the people as a whole with a sense of unity and individuals with a sense of their place in society. 'Inferiors did not yearn for the music of their superiors; sovereigns did not covet the wives of their ministers. There were no quarrels between superiors and inferiors: loyalty and duty reached a degree of perfection.'

But once again this saintly music was discarded. The emperor Ai of the Han dynasty (reigned 6 B.C.–A.D. 1) was the culprit, and his misdeed let loose the worst kind of licentiousness inspired by unorthodox music. What was needed was a saint who could produce a new 'orthodox music', for this music was not something composed once for all. Its beauty and powers did not depend on its author or its name: ' . . . its name might change, but not its basic pitch.[12] Thus one may examine music with a man who has understood the transformations of the Way, but a man who attaches himself to the sounds of the instruments is not worthy to discuss the musical scale.' This cryptic sentence is based upon a passage in the *Li chi* (Couvreur, vol. 2, p. 50) which attempts to show that the true musical connoisseur is interested in the 'sounds' of music only as very minor stepping stones leading to an understanding of the 'notes' (or 'instruments' or 'airs'), and these only to understand 'music' 樂 itself. It is clear from the context in the *Li chi* that this 'music', thanks to its relation with ritual and its intrinsic value, gives the man who understands it the key to perfect knowledge of the Way of government. The actual sounds of music are (*dixit* the *Li chi*) on a *bestial* level of understanding; the sage appreciates music abstractly in its cosmological and political context. Saintly music's 'insipidity' and lack of 'complexity' are thus essential qualities: they give the music an ascetic quality, make it purifying for the listener. As a proof of the truth of his theories, Juan Chi quotes the famous passages on music ascribed to Shun and his music master, K'uei, in the *Shang shu* that are so concise as to be fairly obscure,[13] and interprets them as being the description of this 'insipid' and 'abstract' music. And the final proof, the ultimate canonic reference, is of course to Confucius: 'When Confucius was in Ch'i he heard [Shun's music named] "Shao" and for three months did not recognize the taste of meat' (*Lun yü* 7, 13). This famous passage is generally taken to mean that Confucius was so impressed by the ancient ritual music that he forgot all else, not even noticing what he was eating. But Juan Chi wants to give it a more precise meaning: 'Supreme music[14] [such as Confucius heard] makes a man to be without desires, with his heart calm and his breath-soul settled, so that meat has no taste for him. Thus the music of the Saints is harmonious, and nothing more.' In the earlier part of his essay Juan Chi simply retells the scholastic theories of the interrelation of music and morality, music and the cosmos. But he ends in a slightly more original vein. By insisting upon saintly music's ascetic quality he absolves it from the accusation that Lao-tzu had levelled against it when he said (*Lao-tzu* 11), 'The five notes deafen the ear'. Juan Chi also goes against tradition in another way. It was a commonplace in ancient writings on music that good music, especially music written for the zither (*ch'in*), Juan Chi's own instrument, was necessarily 'sad', *pei* 悲 , or, one should probably translate, 'moving'. *Ch'in* playing which did not move one to tears was somehow inferior.[15] But towards the end of his 'Essay on music',

Juan Chi tries to show how 'music' that stirs the emotions, and thus saddens the mind, cannot be identified with 'joy'.[16] He reverts for a moment to Han scholasticism to add: 'When [after the decay of saintly music,] there is no longer any music-joy in the world it will indeed be difficult for the *yin* and *yang* to be harmonious and for catastrophes not to occur.' But the very end of the essay is again devoted to the 'demonstration' that 'music-joy' cannot be sad and still be 'music-joy'.

Juan Chi's essay thus presents two main arguments. First, he insists upon the importance of music in the functioning of the cosmos, relying on scholastic theories. If these theories were universally accepted in the third century in China, we might simply 'suspend our disbelief' and accept them for the sake of the argument. But these theories were very seriously criticized during Juan Chi's lifetime, and had been doubted for centuries. Hsia-hou Hsüan, who was just a year older than Juan Chi, disposes of them as well, I think, as could be done today. He begins by quoting a sentence from the beginning and one from the end of Juan Chi's essay, both of which I have translated above:

> Master Juan says: 'When the musical scale is well tuned, the *yin* and the *yang* will be harmonious; when instruments are in tune, all beings will remain true to their species.' 'When there is no longer any music in the world, it will indeed be difficult for the *yin* and *yang* to be harmonious and for catastrophes not to occur.' This is to say that musical scales and notes not only transform men and other beings, but that they are also capable of harmonizing the *yin* and the *yang* and keeping away catastrophes. Now, heaven and earth have their fixed positions; the strong [*yang*] and the weak [*yin*] influence one another.[17] There are periods of waxing and waning. When, during Yao's reign, there were nine years of rain, he was saddened by his people's suffering from famine; when, during T'ang's reign, there were seven years of drought, he wanted to move his altars. How could this have been caused by the scales being out of harmony or the notes not being complete? These things are all natural phenomena and are not brought on by human actions.[18]

The second argument Juan Chi presents, that 'sad' music is not music, or, to put it more coherently, that ideal music calms, unites and rejoices, is less easy to discuss because, on one level, it amounts to a matter of definition, and on another, it belongs to a very hazy and impressionistic appreciation of the effects music has on a listener. Two people seldom agree on the precise emotional 'content' of a particular piece of music. His position recalls, vaguely, his friend Hsi K'ang's. In his extraordinary essay 'On the non-emotional character of music', 'Sheng wu ai-le lun' 聲 無 哀 樂 論 , Hsi K'ang, too, seems to be defending music from Lao-tzu's strictures and to be pushing music's unemotional quality to the point of absurdity; but he does these things in a much more original and philosophical way, and has no recourse to traditional scholastic theories. He defends the thesis that no music, in itself, has emotional content – no music, not just perfect or saintly music; any emotion we feel comes from ourselves. The most he will say is that some music is irritating, because of its tempo or from some other purely objective, technical reasons, and, for the same reasons, some music is calming and unifies the mind, preparing it for meditation.[19] His conclusion resembles Juan Chi's description of 'insipid' saintly music, but his bold and brilliant dismissal of scholastic theories places his essay far above Juan Chi's in the history of Chinese philosophy.

If the 'Essay on music' is not great philosophy, is it perhaps a commentary on contemporary politics? On a certain level I believe it is, but it can hardly be called 'satire'. Juan Chi's constant preoccupation throughout the essay with uniformity of doctrine, with conformity to a single way of thinking, his emotional denunciation of individualism, of 'ministers infringing upon sovereigns', of regionalism, of separation of any kind as the root of all evil, seem to me to show he is in fact writing (as is his wont) a very personal, passionate essay against the usurpatory abuses of his time. And this personal commitment explains the extreme, totalitarian insistence against any kind of individualism; in his absolute devotion to the throne and to the imperial idea, Juan Chi blasts away against any kind of deviation from the Way of the Saints as reprehensible subversion. This insistence upon uniformity and centralized authority reminds us, too, of Ts'ao Ts'ao's attempt to rebuild a strong, centralized authority on the Han model. The Ssu-ma, on the contrary, seemed ready to allow a 'refeudalization' of China, giving more and more power to the great clans.

The essay ends strangely, in its denunciation of 'sad' music that is not 'music-joy', with references to two political figures who followed 'sadness' and ended badly: the second son of the First Emperor of the Ch'in dynasty, who mounted the throne after the assassination of his elder brother, and Li Ssu, the First Emperor's Prime Minister who was one of the persons responsible for the assassination. The ending certainly should be read against the background of current events, and gives a certain appropriateness to the essay as a whole: present-day society was no longer united, uniformly ranged around the emperor, and it consequently lacked harmony and the 'joy' only true 'music-joy' could give it.

The second essay in which Juan Chi shows himself clearly attached to Confucian social philosophy is called 'Understanding the *I ching*', 'T'ung *I* lun' 通 易 論. The essay on the *I ching* is as obscure and difficult as the essay on music is clear and easy to read. This obscurity and difficulty does not come from any profound or complicated philosophy, nor is it, I believe, the sign of hidden satirical intentions. It is simply that Juan Chi has decided to talk about the *I ching* in its own terms and give his essay the enigmatic form of that classic and its appendices, while quoting constantly from them.

The essay begins (lines 1–61: I have numbered the Chinese phrases from beginning to end and called them 'lines') with an introduction describing the origin of the *I ching* under the legendary sovereign P'ao (or Fu) Hsi. Juan Chi, following the account in the third appendix, 'Hsi-tz'u', shows how P'ao Hsi, to organize and promote the well-being of the empire, described the mechanism of the universe in the sixty-four hexagrams that make up the work. It is by following these hexagrams and the laws of the universe they describe that the early kings were able to rule and preserve China in its ideal state.

The longest section of the essay (lines 62–298), modelled on the appendix called 'Hsü kua',[20] is also the most difficult and consists, almost entirely, of cryptic commentaries on the sixty-four hexagrams presented in the traditional order but often without naming them directly, only hinting at their identity by using lines from the hexagram in the discussion. The section, like the *I ching* itself, is cut into two parts after the thirtieth hexagram where Juan Chi has added a fairly long (lines 132–67) general commentary similar to the introduction. After the end of this section (line 298), Juan Chi discusses (lines 299–348) the eight trigrams in imitation of the appendix 'Shuo kua', and then (lines 349–412) analyzes five individual hexagrams somewhat in the manner of the 'explanations' (*t'uan* 彖) attributed to King Wen. The next eighty-eight lines of the essay define some of the prominent terms in the *I ching* ('dragon', 'former kings', *chün-tzu*), and the end of the essay (lines 502–561) is composed of general comments on the underlying philosophy of the work.

The whole essay, from one end to the other, seems to be inspired by two main, interrelated motives: first, to preach Confucian morality, the role of the sovereign, the acceptance of one's place in the hierarchy, loyal service to one's lord, etc.; secondly, to accomodate one's self in the world in the most advantageous way by examining present and future conditions as they appear in the sixty-four hexagrams. These two are related because the hexagrams prescribe purely Confucian reactions as the solutions to the world's problems. A few quotations will suffice to give the general impression of the work. First, here is the beginning, after the introduction, of the section which passes in review the sixty-four hexagrams (lines 50–77). (The numbers in square brackets refer to the numbers of the hexagrams in the traditional order, the words between quotation marks are quoted from the *I ching*, under the hexagram in question, and the words beginning with capital letters are names of hexagrams.)

The *I* is a book that draws [its wisdom] from the entire cosmos, follows the movements of the *yin* and *yang* and examines the very sources of prosperity and decay: it takes things out of obscurity and brings them into light. Thus when, in the first line of Ch'ien [1], it says, 'The dragon is hidden and not used', it means that the great man's virtue is stored away and is not manifested, that he is hidden and has not yet succeeded. He must bide his time and then rise up, follow the transformations of the world and then come forth. It is only after Heaven [1] and Earth [2] have taken their places that things Sprout [3] and Grow [4]. Waiting [5], we bide our time; when in Conflict [6] we establish justice; our Armies [7] assemble multitudes; and Union [8] keeps the people peaceful. Thus 'the former kings set up the myriad states, remained affectionately related with their vassals' and led their hearts. They repeatedly provided for them [?], Restrained [9] and controlled them. Thus the 'upper and lower' [10?] were in perfect harmony. 'The Way of heaven and earth was created, helping all that was in conformity with heaven and earth and aiding the people' [11] to follow its truth.

With the *I ching* in one hand and Juan Chi's essay in the other the above text loses much of its obscurity. The same is true of the section that describes the eight trigrams, but this section is further complicated by Juan Chi's mixing in of Five Elements theories and attempts at explaining the distribution of the eight trigrams among the eight cardinal directions. It is in this section that he comes closest to the Han tradition of *I ching* scholarship. In the rest of the essay Juan Chi's explanations are closer to Wang Pi's anti-scholastic revolution than to the numerological, superstitious and unphilosophical explanations of their Han predecessors. His interpretations differ from Wang Pi's in that they are less abstract; they translate the *I ching*'s images directly into political or social philosophy, instead of attempting, as Wang Pi does, to see more basic human or even metaphysical problems in them. For Wang Pi, a hexagram is often the description of a play of forces (symbolized by the *yin* and *yang*) that govern a certain, changeable human condition; for Juan Chi it describes a certain state of affairs in the (usually) political world.

There is a good example of this contrast between the two authors in the next section of Juan Chi's essay, in which he discusses individual hexagrams. The first hexagram he discusses, 'Ta kuo' (no. 28, 'Great excesses'), is also discussed by Wang Pi as one of the eleven hexagrams he takes up at the end of his *Chou-i lüeh-li* 周 易 畧 例 . Juan Chi simply says:

What is 'Ta kuo'? The beam has no support. 'The great [= *yang* lines] are in excess' [䷛ quotation from the *t'uan*]. The former kings ruled

the world in this wise: punishments were set up, but none transgressed;
the penalties were clear, but never applied.

Juan Chi's 'explanation', aside from the fact that it seems to have little to do
with the text of the hexagram, is not in the tradition of the Han scholiasts:
there is no reference to astrology or numerology and the divinatory aspects of
the hexagram are completely lost. His version of the *I ching* hexagram is
purely philosophical, but it is a rather trite and traditionalistic (Legalistic)
philosophy. Wang Pi sticks much closer to the form of the hexagram (two
outer *yin* lines enclose four *yang* lines) in order to describe 'a world in which
the beam is weak'. This particular situation is described in abstract terms and
the relationships between the various lines of the hexagram are exploited to
show the interactions possible and necessary under such conditions. His abstract approach opens the door to an extremely complex and subtle philosophy
of man's place under various changing vital conditions and makes Juan Chi's
exegesis look quite pedestrian. Most of the latter's comments in this section
are purely political and are possibly in part satirical. Hexagram 62 'Hsiao kuo',
'Small excesses', for example, is described (lines 382—3) by: 'transgressing rank
and overcoming superiors harms orthodoxy and puts one's person in danger'.

But satire against the usurping Ssu-ma and their supporters, if such it is, is
without doubt secondary. Juan Chi's main interest, as in the essay on music,
is moral and Confucianist. This is especially clear in the last two sections of
the essay, where he defines particular terms and sums up. This is what he has
to say about the term *chün-tzu* 君 子 , 'the superior man' (lines 469—86).
(The bracketed numbers again refer to the hexagrams whose *I ching* commentaries are quoted in the text.)

> What is a 'superior man'? He is a man who aids a saintly [ruler] and
> defends his [heaven-given] mandate [to reign], who upholds [orthodox]
> doctrine and makes clear the law, who looks into the combination of
> events before he acts, who serves another [i.e. the ruler] according to
> the Way. He relies on orthodox virtue to help him discriminate what is
> just; he investigates that which is going towards decay to preserve him-
> self. Thus he 'regulates the empire' [3] to adjust that which is [too]
> full; he 'acts resolutely' [4] to promote justice; he 'eats and drinks' [5]
> to await the proper time; and he 'discriminates' the right and wrong of a
> matter before he 'starts an affair' [6]. And he does all this to glorify
> 'the former kings' enfeoffing of their vassal kingdoms' [8] and to aid
> the saint [ruler's] divine ambition. When he sees a danger, he thinks of
> the difficulty [it could engender] ; when he meditates on a catastrophe,
> it is to prepare for defence against it. He classifies 'things and puts them
> in their place' [64], prudent and respectful of the inchoate beginnings
> [of the affairs in this world] . . .

Nothing here but traditional philosophy: the superior man is perfectly, entirely devoted to his sovereign, and his main purpose in life is to aid him and guide him along the Way traced out by the Saints of antiquity.

The very last section (lines 501ff), put into the mouth of the 'superior man', as are many epigrams in the *I ching* itself and in other ancient texts, gives, in résumé, an idea of what this Way was, and how we can practice it with the aid of the *I ching*. The text is very concise and often alludes elliptically to ideas developed more fully in the *I ching*. Moreover, Juan Chi throughout is writing on two levels. On one level he is speaking in technical terms about the *I ching*: when he says '*yin*' or 'soft' he means a broken line; on another level he is writing about aspects of the real world. Two translations of parts of this essay would be necessary to bring out the double resonances implied in the terminology. To avoid being too obscure I have decided to paraphrase some parts of the end of the essay rather than translate them literally and to ignore, in the main, the purely technical aspect of the text.

The first paragraph (lines 501–19), full of echoes of the 'Hsi tz'u', describe the universe as it appears in the *I ching* and as it functions in reality. The description of basic universal unity and order is followed by a description of the differentiation of the natures, *hsing* 性, and passions, *ch'ing* 情, of the beings of the world, into contrasting forces, *yin* and *yang*, hard and soft. This division, in turn, leads to the development of attraction and repulsion among the beings (love and hate) and then to feelings of profit and loss and of repentance (all these are terms commonly used in the *I ching*). The trigrams and the divination instruments help us to interpret these contrasting forces and to find our way in their midst. More than this (lines 520–22), the Saints in the *I ching* 'have posited the virtues of goodness and justice, *jen* 仁 and *i* 義, to help keep human nature in its rightful place, and it is when goodness and virtue are complied with that good and bad fortune can be decided'. Juan Chi implies a great deal in these few cryptic lines: that goodness and righteousness, the cardinal virtues of Confucianism, have been established as a restraint upon emotions resulting from the interplay of perfectly natural forces, and that obedience to these virtues influences the allotment of good and bad fortune. The first of these implications is absolutely un-Taoist; the second quite in disagreement with common experience.

Juan Chi seems conscious of the latter and he develops the idea up until the end of the essay, carefully explaining just how virtue is rewarded. The establishment of goodness and righteousness is part of the whole hierarchical system that the Saints have set up (lines 523–40), distinguishing different ranks, different temperaments (*yin* and *yang*, hard and soft): those who prudently follow the saintly prescriptions (in their lives, in their reading and usage of the *I ching*) will succeed; the others will fail. Even when appearances seem

to say the contrary, those who 'go against and seek outside the saintly hierarchy [in society, in the *I ching*] will surely end badly, even though they may
[seem] to find good fortune, while those who know them and hold to them
firmly will surely succeed, even though they may be reduced to the last
extremity'. These contradictions, these apparent, superficial defeats of virtue
and triumphs of evil teach the adept of the *I ching* that 'quietude is the basis
of virtue and egotistic violence the origin of evil'. One must learn to wait
things out quietly, to observe the prescriptions stoically, in spite of appearances, for 'to proceed ahead is to begin to return; to end completely is to project a beginning: what has not yet arrived cannot be destroyed, but what has
already been used cannot go any further'. These semi-paradoxes are basic to
an understanding of the *I ching* which teaches a philosophy of waiting,
patience, seizing the right moment.

The next lines (lines 541–9) illustrate the preceding ideas with an example
from history. 'How is it,' asks Juan Chi, 'that Chou 紂 [the last, wicked
emperor of the Shang dynasty], who was in fact a very ordinary man, was
graced with the title of emperor, while the Chou 周 clan [the founders of a
new dynasty], who presented their offerings to their divine ancestors on the
Western Mountain, were grudged the rank of a small marquisate? The former
had been given the virtue of a plebeian, the latter that of a ruler, and yet their
[real] rank was not yet distinguished.' The miscarriage of justice is flagrant.
Juan Chi's answer: this state of affairs existed 'because the Way of heaven had
not yet worked its way to its dénouement and because the goodness of the
one and the evil of the other were not yet perfectly developed'. This historical
example quoted, Juan Chi reiterates his plea for stoicism and quietism: since,
as history shows, virtue ultimately is triumphant, 'those who understand the
Way of heaven do not desire [to act against it]; those who see deeply into
human virtue do not grieve'. And the result of all this, very much in the same
vein as the essay on music, is social harmony, described just before the very
end of the essay: 'Those who are in high position do not oppress those who
are lower than they are; the humble do not transgress against the honored:
one cannot go against the Way, nor oppose virtue. Thus the Saint stands alone
and is not melancholy; the masses are greatly benefitted [42, reading 大 for 不].
The Way will be with you when you interpret [the *I ching*]; it can be used
without end. Thus it can be seen that one succeeds with the *I ching*.'

The obscurity and imprecision, the plays on words and on the names of the
hexagrams, should not blind us to the fact that this is a very serious, almost a
passionate essay. Juan Chi seems to be pouring forth his profound faith in
Confucian morality and in its embodiment in the philosophy of the *I ching*.[21]
This should not surprise us. His whole political and social life was spent following an 'extreme prudence' typical of the adept of the *I ching*. The fact that

he was able to preserve himself and his family in very dangerous circumstances, without sacrificing his integrity, shows that, in his case at least, the system worked.

There is another essay by Juan Chi that touches on some of these same problems. It is a more original essay and therefore more difficult to interpret, but its basic philosophy is really very close to that of the essays on music and on the *I ching*. The essay I am referring to is called 'Ta Chuang lun' 達 莊 論 , 'On understanding Chuang-tzu', and seems, at first glance, to be a Taoist tirade against Confucianism. On closer study, however, it will be seen to be a much more complicated work and, if it hardly earns the title of 'philosopher' for Juan Chi, it shows him attempting a kind of eclectic synthesis of traditional Confucianism and Taoist metaphysics that makes him an interesting figure in third-century thought. The essay will definitely repay closer study than is generally given it.[22]

The text of the essay is in a poor state[23] and many passages are not completely comprehensible, but the general outline and the tendency of the thought are clear enough. Juan Chi has chosen a form intermediate between the philosophical essay and the *fu*; he seems unable to express himself otherwise than as an artist, moulding his thoughts into poetic medium.[24] He begins by describing a kind of Taoist hero, an immortal, universal man, so perfectly identified with the cosmos as to be indifferent to all changes in time and space. Line 19 introduces a group of Confucianists who have come to argue with him. The description of the Confucianists is satirical and biting. One of their members finally gets up enough courage to speak for the group (line 35) and, after attempting to show that he, too, is a great man, and after outlining in a few words the essence of Confucianist doctrine (lines 57–66), he finally comes to the point in lines 67–9, where he sums up Chuang-tzu's theory of the relativity of all things and suggests that these ideas can only be held by a sophist (lines 70–71).[25]

Juan Chi's spokesman, who is not Chuang-tzu and is named only 'Master', *hsien-sheng* 先 生 , does not necessarily represent Juan Chi himself, but I believe he comes very close to it. He is presented dramatically, playing the zither in a state of mystical or semi-mystical exaltation, much as Juan Chi himself is described in the *Chin shu* (below, p. 137), and in any case reminiscent of the philosopher described at the beginning of the second chapter of *Chuang-tzu*, the chapter that inspires this whole essay. The beginning of his speech reminds us of Juan Chi's answer to Fu I: he tells his listeners that they must broaden their horizon, see things from a universal point of view, meet Chuang-tzu on his own level, if they hope to understand him. In lines 57–69, the Confucianist had contrasted his philosophy with Chuang-tzu's by showing it to be a philosophy that has norms of good and bad, encourages production, profit, high position and life itself, while Chuang-tzu's preaches a kind of monism that equates everything with some 'unity' that would do away with all the distinctions the Confucianists treasure and that they believe keep the world in peace. The Master has not told his listeners that their theories are false; he says only that they must modify their viewpoint to see things in a higher perspective.

Beginning with line 95, and for the next fifty lines, the Master attempts to explain Chuang-tzu's metaphysical monism by something that is really quite different from it: traditional theories of cosmogony that see the world as a combination of 'elements' or 'forces' that collaborate harmoniously together, and that vaguely adumbrate some kind of ancient atomistic theory, taking *ch'i* 氣 , primeval 'breath', *pneuma*, as the basic building block. He alerts us to his originality in the very first line (95) by using the word 'spontaneity', *tzu-jan* 自 然 . This word itself does not play an important role in Chuang-tzu's philosophy, although the idea of 'spontaneity' or 'naturalness' is of course an important element in all Taoist thought. The Master's use of the term here, moreover, at the very beginning of his peroration, and as the First Mover of his cosmogony, shows not only that it has become a key term, but that it can no longer simply mean 'naturalness' or 'spontaneity' — it has become a power of its own, not simply the description of a state of being. The term appears as an absolute of some sort in *Lao-tzu* 25,[26] but it achieves its finest philosophical development in the commentary to the *Chuang-tzu* by Kuo Hsiang 郭 象 (d. 312), and I believe Juan Chi is here writing in the same philosophical tradition. 'Spontaneity' here means 'of itself': heaven and earth are born 'of themselves'. They are not the manifold manifestation of a single, absolute Unity (the *tao*); they are simply themselves, of themselves, spontaneously. This negation of the *tao* or this assimilation of the absolute to the pluralism of 'things as they are' at one blow destroys the metaphysical monism of ancient Taoism, and gives a quasi-metaphysical sanction to the world as it is, to 'things as they are'. What then becomes of Chuang-tzu's relativism, the main theme of the second chapter of his work, of the idea that the things of this world have only relative reality compared with the absolute, with eternity or infinity? That is what the Master is going to show us. The first ten lines are fairly opaque and their opaqueness comes, I believe, from the fact that 'spontaneity' is not really a replacement for the absolute *tao*: we can 'understand', paradoxically at least, that the multiplicity of this world disappears in the face of the absolute *tao*; in the face of 'spontaneity', 'limitless' though it may be, one hesitates.

The lines that follow show all the difference between Chuang-tzu's metaphysical argument and the Master's. The latter has described not the relativity of the manifold world, but its integrated harmony (lines 105–10, 129–32) and basic, atomistic identity in 'breath' (lines 111–28). The conclusion (lines 144–7) is almost word for word from *Chuang-tzu* 5, but where *Chuang-tzu* reads: 'the ten thousand beings are all one', Juan Chi has: 'the ten thousand beings are of one body'. The difference would perhaps be of no importance in another context[27] (Chinese philosophical terminology is notoriously imprecise), but here it is highly revealing: the ten thousand beings that make up the universe are not melted mystically into a Unity; they are considered as being part of a single, integrated organism. The next section (lines 148–72) presents Chuang-tzu's theory of the relativity of all in this world accurately but ends again with a 'paradox' that sounds like Chuang-tzu but really is quite different: the 'beard' and 'eye-brows' are not blurred into an undifferentiated Unity, as they would be in Chuang-tzu's thought; they are simply raised to a higher degree of abstraction as 'hairs' of the body.

The next section is one of the most difficult to follow. The Master seems to be contrasting Confucianism with Chuang-tzu's philosophy, to the favor of the latter, but the actual terms seem, in most cases, very objective. Confucianism is said to be a doctrine that assigns a 'lot', *fen* 分 , to each being;[28] the *Chuang-tzu* is very modestly described as some ideas that Chuang-tzu wanted to develop. One gets the impression of an objective analysis of the two doctrines: Confucianism is shown to be a social canon; Chuang-tzu's philosophy, the personal ideas of a single thinker.[29] The lines that follow seem definitely to praise the 'large view' of Chuang-tzu, but they are followed immediately by a long development in which it is not really the cosmic point of view of Chuang-tzu that is preached, but the necessity for integration within a whole, a point of view equally as applicable in orthodox Confucianist philosophy as in Taoism, or perhaps even more applicable. At any rate the following lines (194–206) develop the idea of the importance of integration and harmony in an organism, and lines 207–24 give the illustration of ideal harmony in the case of the Perfect Men of legend, showing how their 'global' view led them to equanimity and long life.

These ideas are developed in the next sections. Lines 225 and following again put the emphasis upon seeing oneself as part of a whole and go forward toward a philosophy of the renunciation of desire, a philosophy related both to Taoism and to the *I ching* that preaches retreat, retirement, an attempt at integration through restraint and abdication; in the case of the contrary, in the case of men who assert themselves and quarrel, the principle of spontaneity disappears and the world falls into disorder (lines 250ff). Numerous historical examples are invoked of disasters brought about by self-assertion and one-sided action. The harm caused by them seems more Confucianist than

Taoist, in particular the separation of fathers and sons, rulers and ruled (lines 257–8) and the diminishing of loyalty and sincerity (line 287), cardinal Confucian virtues that are usually treated with derision in *Chuang-tzu*.

Beginning with line 290, using a method he has used in the essay on music, Juan Chi (or the Master) traces the decay of the world from primeval innocence, when 'each thing was in its place' (line 308), to the disruption brought about by heterodox thinkers and sophists of all kinds. Chuang-tzu, in any case, did not write his book to take part in this contention (lines 363–4): he wrote simply to divert himself and filled his book with metaphors and fictions. It can be seen in other writers (Mo-tzu, Chan-tzu) that the ideal method of teaching is one of laissez-faire, not coercion. The implication is that Chuang-tzu, too, preached his laissez-faire philosophy as a kind of mental hygiene, to free the mind so that it could grapple with more important things, the affairs of state! This whole section is very similar, in its decrying of philosophical dissension, to the essay on music.[30]

Towards the very end of his essay the Master finally gives us his opinion of Chuang-tzu's book, and it is hardly a flattering one: his book is 'not worth talking about'! (Juan Chi again denigrates Chuang-tzu in Poem 38: below, p. 219.) His book is, moreover, uninformed in the cosmogony developed later in Taoist 'religion'.[31] It is good for its philosophy of laissez-faire psychosomatic hygiene which makes it possible 'to adhere to loyalty and sincerity and to keep the upper and lower classes in peace' (lines 388–9) – again two Confucianist sentiments. The Master castigates his interlocutors for their insincerity, and the essay ends with the pitiful image of the Confucianists in humiliated and shameful retreat.

The importance of this essay is two-fold. It represents Juan Chi's most elaborate attempt at re-animating post-Han Confucianism with Taoist metaphysics and it shows us, at the same time, how his profound disillusionment with the disloyalties and corruption of contemporary Confucianists made him yearn for some kind of 'wholeness' and 'unity' in which all mankind would work together in a single, integrated organism. Chuang-tzu and Taoist philosophy are of course omnipresent in this work, but only as a 'method', a superior way of looking at the world from a more sophisticated, metaphysical plane. They are not here seen as destroyers of ancient Confucianism but as a method of reforming it, of infusing a kind of 'spontaneity' and cosmic awareness in what had become a vitiated and narrowed political dogma. This is the true 'understanding of Chuang-tzu', according to Juan Chi; aside from this, 'his book is not worth talking about'!

On understanding Chuang-tzu

When Jupiter is in the mansion called *mao*, or when it is in the mansion

called *ch'en*,[32] when all things in nature begin to sprout, or when, in the
5   months of late autumn, the nights are long, the Master wanders about
here and there, roaming against the wind. He goes off along the bank of
the Red River[33] and comes back by climbing the slope of the Hidden
Hill,[34] gazing down the road to Ch'ü-yüan,[35] looking back towards the
10   vast provinces [he has just visited]. He stops in a vague stupor and rests
in forgetfulness, not realizing why he had previously been moving or
15   why he remains still now. He sighs and feels joyless, sadly returning to
the state of plain simplicity. It is noon and he is idle, leaning against his
backrest and strumming his zither.
20   Some dilettantes of the official class who had heard about him got
together and composed a text in which they set forth some doubts that
had been constantly nagging them. Then they peered into their mirrors
to put their ornaments straight and, gnashing their teeth and leading one
another on, they followed off, one after the other, according to their
25   age, walking in strict ranks, staring with their eyes fixed on high.
Tramping in the footsteps left by the one who went before, they trod
up the stairs [leading to his reception hall], hurrying their pace, in best
30   ritual fashion, hands on breast, elbows outspread, and slightly leaning
forward.[36] They sat down shoulder to shoulder, made a respectful bow
with their sleeves and then drew themselves to a straight, upright position. But they hesitated to approach, none daring to take the first place.
35   Then one man among them, who was their brave hero, with angry
eye and all his muscles tensed, spoke out in a loud voice: 'I was born
after the time of T'ang and Yü[37] and grew up in the generations succeeding Wen and Wu.[38] I amused myself during the heyday of Kings
40   Ch'eng and K'ang[39] and am at the height of my powers under our present sovereigns.[40] I am learned in the doctrine of the Six Books of the
Canon and practiced in the relics of our scholarly lore. I have, for a very
45   long time, dressed in silken robes, worn flying feathers in my cap, let
my swallow-tailed skirt hang down to my toes and raised up the pair of
water-birds [embroidered on my sleeves[41]], and still I have never heard
50   that, in its essentials, the Supreme Way differs in any fashion from this
[orthodox Confucianism as I practice it]. Great men have praised it;
small men have accepted it: I would like to hear your Supreme Doctrine
in order to dispel my doubts.'
56   The Master asked: 'Just what are these doubts?'
His guest: 'The Way of heaven is to honor life; the Way of earth, to
honor steadfastness. The saint cultivates these two in order to establish
60   his fame. Good and bad fortune are both allotted; what is right and
what is wrong have their unchanging laws. We work for profit and
65   esteem power, hate death and treasure life. That is how peace comes to
the empire and great deeds are achieved. But now Chuang Chou has
equated good and bad fortune and said that life and death are the same;

70   he takes heaven and earth to be but a single entity and the ten thousand species to be a single category.[42] Is this not a case of seeking confusion in order to pervert the truth, and then thinking oneself sincere?'

75   Then the Master strummed his zither in a nonchalant manner, heaved a long, sad sigh; looked down and smiled faintly; looked up and let his gaze wander; and breathing his spirit in and out, [shaman-like] he retold what he saw:

80   There once was a man who wanted to look off from the top of Lang Peak.[43] He furnished himself with formal attire[44] and mounted the magnificent courser Hua-liu.[45] He got as far as the foot of the K'un-lun Mountains, and he died there, never to return again to his home. Formal attire is the kind of ornaments that we commonly wear, and Hua-liu the kind of horse that one ordinarily mounts: neither of them can be

85   used to fly up to the top of Tseng-ch'eng or to roam about in Hsüan-p'u![46] The rays of the Torch Dragon,[47] moreover, would not shine in a single hall, nor would the mouth of Mount Chung speak in a small

90   room.[48] Now, I will try to topple the giddy heights [I have been speaking from] and stop up the limitless torrents [of my arguments — I will try to come down to your level]. I will tell you the reasoning you must follow: but will you be able to understand and grasp a bit of it?

95   Heaven and earth were created in spontaneity; the ten thousand beings were created in heaven and earth. Spontaneity has nothing outside it[49] and therefore heaven and earth take their names from it: heaven and earth have something within them; therefore the ten thou-

100   sand beings can be produced there. Facing the limitlessness of the one, who would say there were differences in it? And facing the interior of the other, who would say there were dissimilarities in it?[50]

105   The earth inundates the dryness [of heaven]; heaven opposes [earth's] dampness.[51] The moon rises in the east; and the sun sets in the

110   west. Thus there is a following of one thing by another, a separation and then a unification. That which rises is called *yang*; that which falls is called *yin*. On earth we speak of veined patterns; in heaven we called

115   them striped.[52] What is steamed we call rain; what is scattered, wind; what is flaming hot we call fire; what is frozen, ice; what takes form we

120   call stone; what forms images, stars.[53] The beginning we call morning; the end, night. When [water] pierces through, we call it a river; when it revolves, we call it a whirlpool. [Earth] that is flat we call land; when

125   piled up, mountains. Men and women are of the same rank,[54] moun-tains and marshes of the same vital breath.[55] Thunder and wind do not

130   strike against one another; water and fire do not lessen one another. Heaven and earth unite their virtues; the sun and the moon harmonize their rays. When all is spontaneously part of one single body, then the

135   ten thousand beings of creation will all follow their normal develop-ment: their going in [to death] will be called 'becoming obscure'; their

coming out [into life], 'becoming bright'. This [whole process is no
more than] the rise and fall of a single vital breath, transformed but not
harmed. Thus [since they, too, are transformations of a single breath],
heavy overcast weather, thunder and lightning are not different phenom-
140 ena; heaven, earth, the sun and the moon are not dissimilar things. That
is why [Chuang-tzu] says: 'When we look at things as they differ,
145 then the liver and gall, Ch'u and Yüeh [all differ]; but when we look
upon them as similar, then the ten thousand beings are all of the same
body.[56]

Man is born between heaven and earth and puts on his bodily form
150 spontaneously. His person is an accumulation of *yin* and *yang* vital
breaths; his nature is the true nature of the Five Elements;[57] his passions
the changing desires of his roaming soul; and his spirit that by which he
drives through heaven and earth.[58] From the point of view of birth, all
things are long lived; if we reason from the point of view of death, all
155 things die young. From the point of view of smallness, all the ten thousand beings are small; looked at from greatness, all the ten thousand
160 beings are great. A child who dies is long lived; P'eng-tsu [= Methuselah]
165 died young. Autumn down is great; Mount T'ai is small.[59] In this way,
life and death can be considered to be of the same species; right and
wrong in the same category. Should we want to separate them, we may
170 say 'beard' and 'eye-brows' are different names; should we want to consider them together, they are both hairs of the body.

The words of the Six Books of the Canon[60] preach the doctrine of
175 the allotted position [each of us is to occupy in the world], while
Chuang Chou's *dicta* develop his ideas to the highest point. When you
look upon something from the point of view of greatness, then as far as
180 you go you reach no end; when you reason from smallness, then things
have their limitations. Now, to keep [the people] in groups of five or
ten[61] or to examine the names of those who are to the left or to the
185 right[62] is to believe in a partial, one-sided doctrine; but those who follow
spontaneity and who assimilate their own nature to that of the very
heaven and earth believe talk that is distant and vast. The ears and the
eyes are both organs with their own names and places allotted to them.
190 They occupy their organic place and do not, in order to separate themselves from the hands or the feet, split themselves off the torso. But
195 dilettantes of this later age do not look into the root of the matter.
They all say 'I, and that is all there is to it: what have I to do with
others?' They harm their lives and their natures and actually become
200 their own enemies, cutting off their own members without feeling the
pain. The eyes see pleasing forms but do not attend to what the ear
hears; the ear listens to what it likes, paying no attention to what the
heart is thinking; and the heart rushes headlong after its desires, making
205 no attempt to bring peace to one's nature. That is how diseases take

hold and the will to live becomes exhausted; misfortunes and disorders arise and the ten thousand beings are gravely damaged.

210   The Perfect Man maintains his tranquillity both in regard to life and to death. Because he is tranquil in regard to life, his passions do not lead him into confusion; because he is tranquil in regard to death, his spirit does not leave him. That is why he can transform himself with the *yin* and *yang* and not change, follow the mutations of heaven and earth and not move. As far as his life is concerned, he lives out his natural longevity; and when he comes to die, he follows what is fitting. His

215   heart and vital breath are calm and well regulated, without diminishing or waning. It was in this way that Kuang-ch'eng-tzu lived on Mount K'ung-t'ung and was able to enter the Gate of the Unending;[63] that Hsüan-yüan climbed the K'un-lun Mountains and left the root of his

220   black pearl there.[64] Thus it is that those who hide themselves find it easy to remain alive, but those who turn away from what is fundamental find it hard to endure for ever.

225   If Feng-i[65] had not met Jo of the [Northern] Sea, he would not have known he himself was so small.[66] If Yün-chiang had not lost to Hung-meng, he would have had no way of realizing his own pettiness.[67] These examples show us that those who say that they themselves are right will

230   not become illustrious and that those who set themselves up under their own power will not be firmly established; those who preserve what they have will have something to rely on; those who keep what they do not have will have nothing to hold on to.[68] The moon wanes before it

235   waxes; when the sun rises, it is [only] to sink [again]. It does not remain long in Hsien Lake above Yang Valley, for it will soon sink, as its Hanging Chariot sets.[69] Thus [the cyclical order in nature] shows that those who search for gain, lose, as do those who compete in order to shine with intelligence; those who have no desires are sufficient unto

240   themselves; those who are empty receive fullness.[70]

Now, it is the Way of spontaneity for the mountains to be calm and

245   the valleys deep; the fulfilment of a sage, to obtain this Way and remain upright. But those who put their intelligence and cleverness into action will be harmed by external things, while those who make clear what is right and what is wrong put their persons in danger. Those who adorn themselves to show forth their purity, are confused about life; those

250   who fear death and glorify life lose their completeness. In these cases the principle of spontaneity cannot operate: heaven and earth do not communicate[71] and the sun and moon fight in their courses: morning and evening no longer come at their proper times and there is no longer

255   any division between night and day. Men become contentious in their hurrying after profit, scrambling about against one another in all directions. Fathers and sons are no longer united; rulers and their subjects fall apart. Then, one who repeatedly speaks, seeking [the reputation of

260 being] faithful, is [really no more] sincere than [the man who stayed] under the bridge.[72] One who would restrain himself for others, is practicing goodness beyond the outer wall [?]. A man who would make

265 secret his strangulation is a son who would ruin his house.[73] Men who would cut stomachs or slice flesh are officials who would disrupt the state [?]. Those who sparkle in the choicest flowers and garb themselves in dewy vapors are men who would benight the world.[74] Those who

270 would tread upon frost and dew or cover themselves with the dust and mud of this world[75] are covetous and avaricious men.[76] Those who purify themselves to chastize the world and who cultivate their persons

275 to show [others'] impurities are no different from vile calumniators. Those who constantly measure right and wrong, and turn away from solid substance to run after artificial arts, are the equal of misleaders. Those who, in truth, speak against beauty and joy to give themselves the

280 appearance of being 'sincere', and wear pearls and jades to throw themselves into fire and water, end like Chieh and Chou.[77] To eat lentils,

285 ferns, live with hunger and die is the way Yen [Yüan] and [Po] I ended.[78] Thus, when the road to fame and profit opens, true loyalty and sincerity diminish; when words defining right and wrong appear, the purity and solidity of men's passions are smelted away.

290 But the extreme perfection of the Way is muddled[79] into unity, undivided; being uniformly made into one body, gain and loss are unheard

295 of. Fu-hsi knotted cords; Shen-nung taught how to work the land:[80] those who went against [their teachings] died; those who followed them lived.[81] They had no way of knowing that avariciousness was punishable

300 or that integrity was worthy of fame. When the essence of the Supreme Virtue is all pervasive and that is all, when the Great Equality[82] is pure and firm and does not have a double standard, when all are pure and

305 tranquil, calm and solitary, empty and waiting, when 'good' and 'bad' are not distinguished, 'right' and 'wrong' are not fought over: then the ten thousand beings will return to their places and confirm to their true feelings.

310 After the Confucianists and the Mohists, the Sophists arose side by side;[83] good and bad fortune attached themselves to things; the heart was filled with thoughts of gain and loss. Followers were assembled,

315 cliques formed and dialecticians encroached upon one another's theories. In the past, heroes of the great Ch'i and knights of the Three Chin[84] looked at one another in anger and made a show of their courage, provoking separation [of primitive unity]. They all believed it was diffi-

320 cult to reach a hundred years of age, that the sun and the moon might stumble for them at any moment. So they all surrounded themselves with great numbers of attendants, splendid robes, beautiful pearls and

325 jades and elegant curtains and wall coverings. In the outside world they flattered their lords and masters; at home they cheated their fathers and

elder brothers. They exalted their talents and knowledge and ran about
competing in the world whenever they could. Families were harmed
330 because of their 'clever' sons; states disappeared because of their 'tal-
ented' officials. Thus they did not reach the end of their naturally
allotted years and they cut themselves off completely from what should
have bound them to the morals of the world.[85]

333
[11 lines deleted because of textual corruption]
343

Now the separation of words is talk that destroys the Way; and the
345 twisting of arguments is the beginning of the ruin of Virtue. A divided
vital breath means sickness for a single body; a man of divided loyalties
is a catastrophe for all of creation. In this same way, those who dress up
in fine clothing and politely bow by placing their hands on the cross-bar
350 of their carriages go cut off from the mass of men.[86] Those whose
thoughts dwell on success and failure seek enemies while sitting still.
Those who rise above impediments and attack difficulties are men of
the Chao family [?] and those who lift up mountains to fill up the sea
355 are men of Yen and Ch'u. Chuang Chou, seeing things were in this state,
related the wonders of the Way and its Virtue and revealed the bases of
360 non-activity. He expanded his descriptions with metaphors and developed them with fictions. [That was the way] he diverted his non-active
mind a little and [that] he roamed at ease during his lifetime. How
could he have hoped to have his work [posted on] the gate of Hsien-
yang[87] or argue with the scholars at Chi-hsia?[88]
365 A man good at getting close to people leads them, and that is all: he
never opposes them in any way. Thus Kung-meng Chi-tzu wore embroidered robes when he saw [Mo-tzu], and Mo-tzu, [who was against
370 such luxuries] did not attack him.[89] Kung-tzu Mou of Chung-shan had
his heart set on entering the service of Wei, but Chan-tzu [the Taoist
who was against state service] did not repress him.[90] Conform to the
way they have come and to the way they are going. Follow and respect
them: make them reside in their own position; open them and develop
375 them: make them be at ease with themselves.
380 But Chuang Chou's book is not even worth talking about! He has
still never heard of the discussions on the Great Origin [of the universe]
nor of the subtle words of mystical Antiquity![91] He can only [teach
us] how we can prevent ourselves from being harmed by the things in
this world and vitalize our body; when no damage is done by external
385 things, our spirit will be purified. And when our body and spirit are
both [intact] within us, then the Way and its Virtue will be complete;
men will not depart from loyalty and sincerity and the upper and lower
[classes in society] will be in peace. But you, my guests, use modern
390 language while cleaving to antiquity; your theories are the same [as

those of the ancients] but your ideas differ. You keep your basic [corrupt ideas] within your heart and they have no relation whatsoever to what comes out of your mouths!

Upon this the disciples, shaking and shivering like the wind or waves,
395 looked at one another with startled eyes. They retreated *en masse*, tripping and stumbling as they went. They looked at [the Master] from afar and then later realized, thanks to this [meeting], how untruthful they
400 were. They lost their vital breath and were filled with shame at their weakness and vileness.

6

SOCIETY AND SOLITUDE

The text of the 'Ta Chuang lun' is very corrupt and the essay is accordingly difficult to interpret. But there are a number of poems that touch upon Juan Chi's attitudes towards society and, as usual, it is to them that we must turn to learn his 'innermost feelings'. Two of the poems are concerned directly with Confucianism, or, more exactly, with two types of Confucianists; the others describe the excesses that harm men in high positions, the infidelity inherent in human relations and, finally, the solitude Juan Chi feels in a socially unacceptable world.

The two poems dealing with Confucianism may seem, at first glance, to show Juan Chi as a Taoist at heart, a man who ultimately denies the validity of ceremonial and hierarchy, but, like all his poems, they are subtler than they seem at first reading.

67

The great Confucianists rely upon rules and regulations;
    Their very clothing is cut according to constant standards.
They arrange the honored and humble in a fixed order,
    And regulate everyone and everything according to the law.
5   They adorn themselves and adjust their expressions,
        As they bend in two like musical stones, holding on to their insignia
           of rank.
In their reception room they set out water,
    While their private quarters overflow with the finest grains.
In public they encourage chatter of virtue and purity.
10   But, at home, they put an end to all that is sweet-smelling.
Even when they speak without restraint, from their hearts,
    They still talk about the doctrines of the Way and of Righteousness.
O! Their self-abasing scraping, their ritualistic gesturing,
    All their posing sickens me to the core!

My translation 'the great Confucianists' in line 1 is based upon a supposed allusion (reading 鴻 for 洪) to Yang Hsiung, 'Yü-lieh fu' (*Wen hsüan* 8, p.

23; von Zach, vol. 1, p. 123). If one simply translated the two characters as if there was no allusion intended (as does Yoshikawa), the line would read: 'To enrich life one needs rules and regulations'. This would attenuate or remove entirely the satirical tone I have given to the first five lines. Line 5 contains an echo of *Lun yü* 8, 4; and there is perhaps an ironic echo of *Li chi*, 'Li yün' (Couvreur, vol. 1, p. 505), in lines 7–8: ' . . . there is water in the private quarters, . . . wine made from grain in the reception rooms . . . '. There are other echoes and near-allusions to Confucian texts, giving the poem a strong flavor of canonic ritualism.

At first reading the poem looks like a typical Taoist anti-Confucianist diatribe, the kind one encounters so frequently in the *Chuang-tzu*. But only at first reading. Chuang-tzu demolishes his Confucian whipping boys on purely philosophical grounds, showing how petty their ritualism and formalism are in the face of the immensity of the universe and eternity. Juan Chi does nothing of the kind here: his criticism of the 'great Confucianists' is made on personal grounds, within the scope of Confucianism itself. He is not criticizing because they are Confucianists, but because they are corrupt, hypocritical Confucianists. Even more important, when Chuang-tzu finishes with his Confucianist opponents, he roars with laughter. Such is obviously not the case here. Only a profound Confucianist could write such a satire, for only a 'believer' could be so grieved at the misbehavior of his fellow believers.

The interpretation of the second poem about Confucianists is even more delicate.

60

The Confucianist knows the Six Books of the Canon thoroughly,
    And so strong is his resolution that he cannot be opposed.
He would not move if it meant straying from the ritual,
    Nor dare to talk if it were to say something against the model of the ancients.
5   When thirsty he drinks from a pure spring's stream;
    When hungry he makes a single bamboo dish of food do for two meals.
He has nothing to sacrifice at the seasons of the year
    And his clothing makes him constantly suffer from the cold.
With his feet half out of his shoes he chants the 'South wind';
10   In his hemp-padded gown he smiles at the elegant carriages.
He believes in the Way and holds fast to the Books of Poetry and History;
    He would not accept a single meal unjustly given.
With what burning enthusiasm men write words of praise and blame!
    They make Lao-tzu heave a long sigh!

Like the preceding, this poem is again stuffed with allusions to Confucian texts. Line 3 recalls *Lun yü* 12, 1. Line 4 recalls *Hsiao ching* 4: 'Do not dare to speak if your words are not the model words of the former kings.' Line 6 recalls *Lun yü*, 6, 9, and *Li chi*, 'Ju hsing', Couvreur, vol. 2, p. 606. There is a variant 甘 for 芋 which would make the line read: 'When hungry he is happy with a single bamboo dish of food', but cf. Poem 69, line 6 (below, p. 114). Lines 7–10 all refer to an anecdote which appears in *Chuang-tzu* 28, Legge translation, 2, pp. 157–9, and in *Han-shih wai-chuan* 1, 9, Hightower translation, pp. 19–21. Yüan Hsien, a poor but honest disciple of Confucius, shames Tzu-kung whose riches had obscured the true meaning of virtue and righteousness for him. The 'South wind' is a song attributed to the saintly emperor Shun. Line 12 refers to *Li chi*, 'T'an kung', Couvreur, vol. 1, p. 250: a beggar, if he is a righteous man, would starve rather than accept food given to him in an improper manner.

The poem has been variously interpreted as a scathing denunciation of Confucianism (Frodsham and Ch'eng), a denigration of Confucianism's narrow system of values (Fukunaga 1958, p. 156), an objective statement of Taoist and Confucianist points of view (Shen Te-ch'ien), and an appreciation of a true Confucianist's sincerity (Yoshikawa). It is the ambiguity of the last two lines that explains this difference of opinion. 'Words of praise and blame' translates a term often used in reference to the Confucian annal *Ch'un ch'iu*. Confucius is said to have used 'words of praise and blame' in a hidden, satirical way to criticize the actions of the men in his history (cf., for example, *Han shu* 30, p. 1715). The term is thus usually used in reference to Confucianists, and it is possible to interpret the line as referring to the poor Confucian scholar (as does Fang Tung-shu). The line would then have to read: 'With what burning enthusiasm *he* writes words of praise and blame.' Lao-tzu's sigh in the last line remains, in any case, ambiguous, and it is most probably wrong to attempt to explain the ambiguity away. He sighs because he knows it is futile to grade anything: relativity is the only reality in the world as we know it (*Lao-tzu* 2, quoted by Chiang Shih-yüeh). He knows, too, that the quarrels among philosophers and philosophies are characteristic of a world fallen from antique grace (*Chuang-tzu* 11, Legge translation, 1, pp. 295–9, quoted by Huang Chieh). But, it seems to me that, strictly within the context of this poem, Lao-tzu is sighing for the futility of grading a man or placing him in one or another philosophical camp, when he sees the fine character of one who is supposed to be his 'enemy'. The whole 'conflict' between Confucianism and Taoism melts away in the presence of this exemplary scholar whose poverty, indifference to wealth and general integrity would be ornaments to any faction.

Is Juan Chi 'really placing the Confucianist above Lao-tzu' (Chu Chia-ch'eng) in this poem? It almost seems so; his sigh seems one of pure admiration. Comparison of the relative merits of the two philosophies, and in particular of their two founders, Lao-tzu and Confucius, was a favorite topic of contemporary thinkers.[1] The prose essays of Juan Chi we have read incline me strongly to believe he was at heart a Confucianist, as were almost all his contemporaries, or at least those in active life. We have a short phrase attributed to Juan Chi in a Taoist text by an otherwise unknown T'ang writer, Lu Hsi-sheng 陸 希 聲 that says as much. The text is the preface to the *Taote chen-ching chuan* 道 德 真 經 傳 and is found in the Tao tsang.[2] In it Lu Hsi-sheng attempts to show that Lao-tzu and Confucius are both Saints, complementary equals in the history of Chinese thought: the first taught the fundamentals, the essentials, *chih* 質 , the second, the learned qualities necessary to a civilized man, *wen* 文 . Lao-tzu was in fact a complete philosopher, as great a Saint as any who ever lived. And yet Wang Pi, in a celebrated conversation (*Shih-shuo hsin-yü* A, (Section 4) pp. 60b–61a), said that Confucius, the true Saint, was able to identify completely with the *tao*, while Lao-tzu was not yet able to do so. 'That is why', adds Lu Hsi-sheng, 'Juan Chi called [Lao-tzu] "a superior sage, a man who came in the second rank after Saint [Confucius]"'. His opinion seems to be the same as Wang Pi's.' Juan Chi's own writings on Lao-tzu and Confucius (all found in *T'ai-p'ing yü-lan* 1, pp. 4b, 6a, and 7a) are all so fragmentary as to be useless to reconstruct his thought about them. In one of the fragments, an essay entitled 'On understanding Lao-tzu', 'T'ung Lao lun' 通 老 論, he speaks of 'the Saint', presumably Lao-tzu, and in his 'Eulogy of Confucius', 'K'ung-tzu lei' 孔 子 誄, he presents Confucius as the great master of metaphysics and cosmogony, praising him as a scholar of those very subjects Chuang-tzu (in the 'Ta Chuang lun') 'knew nothing about'. In the 'T'ung Lao lun', again, he equates the *tao* of Lao-tzu with the *t'ai-chi* of the *I ching* and the *yüan* 元 of the *Ch'un-ch'iu*. As usual, Juan Chi's attitude is complex, and he shares a penchant for syncretism with his contemporaries, picking and choosing among the philosophical attitudes of his forerunners. But, as this poem and so much of what we have read until now testify, his attitude towards Confucius and his philosophy was far from being unconditionally hostile.

The following five poems, each in its own way, are concerned with society and, again each in its own way, preach against the excesses of social life. All of these poems are pessimistic and look upon social life as something evil or even fundamentally impossible.

69

We know it's easy to meet men,
    But to keep them as friends — that alone is truly hard!

A perilous road it is, full of suspicions and doubts,
  Where one should not seek for bright pearls.
5 *He* wants to take part in the Great Banquet;
  I want to skip every other meal.
One wants to diminish and the other to augment: the result is bitter
    grudges;
  There are words of anger, and then − what is there left to say?

This is an extremely original poem, not only for its time, but in Chinese
poetry in general. And it is original in spite of the fact that friendship is one
of the most hackneyed themes of Chinese poetry, for no other poet has ever
treated the theme on such an abstract level. The poem is completely pessimistic and can hardly (one hopes) be taken as the last word on friendship. It
is only one aspect of it, the one Juan Chi must have seen most clearly on his
day, and one, also, that is still with us. Two of the lines are ambiguous. The
'bright pearl' of line 4 seems to be, as elsewhere in Juan Chi's poems (59, 72),
a symbol of great material wealth (Yoshikawa). Friendship is thus tacitly
compared to a perilous road where it is premature (the Chinese literally says
'cannot yet be sought for') to consider exchanging objects of great value. But
the line is not completely clear in the context. Tseng Kuo-fan believes there is
an allusion to Tsou Yang 鄒 陽 , 'Yü-chung shang shu tzu-ming', *Wen hsüan*
39, p. 12b, a letter in which the author attempts to justify himself before his
sovereign who does not appreciate his true worth. According to the letter, if
you throw a shining pearl 'into a group of men on the road in the dark, they
will all put their hand on their sword and cast furtive glances at one another'.
But Huang Chieh opposes this interpretation, seeing the 'bright pearl' as a
symbol for 'virtue' (?). The Great Banquet in line 5 is a sacrifice theoretically
made only by sovereigns and including a bull, a ram and a pig. It is also mentioned in *Lao-tzu* 20 as an image of popular enjoyment. If one friend desires
to lead a life of riches and the other desires a modest condition or even
poverty, then there will be (line 7) *sun i* 損 益 , a compound rich in meaning,
with echoes in at least three books of the Canon. In the *I ching*, *sun*, 'diminishing', is a highly considered virtue (as we have seen in the essay on that text
by Juan Chi). By 'diminishing' one assures oneself that, as the wheel of fortune moves, one will augment, whereas conscious 'augmentation' only leads
to subsequent diminishing. Tseng Kuo-fan, however, interprets the words
differently: 'Diminish his superfluity to augment my insufficiency'. This does
not seem to be particularly in keeping with the rest of the poem, since 'I' does
not desire any 'augmentation'.
    Ch'en Tso-ming and Wang K'ai-yün see the poem as political satire aimed
against Ssu-ma I. The former suggests Juan Chi is expressing his desire to
remain a loyal subject and condemning Ssu-ma I's desire to usurp the throne

('enjoy the Great Banquet'), while the latter sees Ts'ao Jui and Ssu-ma I as the protagonists. Huang Chieh opposes this interpretation, but it does have the merit of underlining the fact that Juan Chi is here contrasting two basic attitudes towards life, an attitude of sage-like retirement and one of brash and unwise opportunism, of pleasure-seeking and dissipation. This is the contrast that underlies all of the five poems I have gathered together in this group.

The following poem is a particularly clear example.

59

There was an old man on the river bank,
 A basket-weaver who threw away a bright pearl.
He enjoyed his meals of pigweed and peas
 And took delight in his humble grass hut.
5 Not for him the life of fast-living playboys
 Who gallop along in light carriages pulled by fine steeds!
They are born, one morning, beside some fashionable square,
 But by evening they are buried, tucked away in some by-lane.
Their joyous laughter does not last their revelry:
10 It is but an instant before they groan.

When I look at these two or three men
 My pent-up anger begins to subside!

The 'fashionable square' in line 7 is, literally, a 'crossroads'. Only the rich and mighty could build their houses directly on the main thoroughfares; all others had to live within the small wards into which the medieval Chinese city was divided. The 'by-lane', *heng-shu* 横 術 , of the succeeding line is less easy to understand. The term appears three times in Juan Chi's works (in the 'Tung-p'ing fu', above, p. 4, and in Poem 73, below, p. 185) and also in *Han shu* (*pu-chu* 63, p. 21a) where its meaning is not clear. My translation fits all the contexts and respects the basic meaning of the two characters that make up the term.

The poem takes its theme from the story from *Chuang-tzu* 32 (Legge translation, 2, pp. 211–12) hinted at in the first four lines. A poor weaver of rushes advises his son to destroy an extremely precious pearl he had found in the depths of a pool. He realized that such a gem must belong to a fierce black dragon who would certainly take vengeance on the violator of his treasure. By contrasting this wise, modest old man with the fast-living high officials of his day, Juan Chi is again following Chuang-tzu's anecdote, for it, too, was addressed to a man tempted by political glory, a man who had just received ten carriages from the king of Sung. Chuang-tzu warns the man that the king of Sung is fiercer than any black dragon and that his gift would have fierce consequences, meaning, of course, entanglement in political life. Juan Chi here merely puts these two ways of life in opposition: rural obscurity, delight in simplicity and security on the one hand, and urban excesses and danger on the other. I have preserved the hyperbole of lines 7 and 8; common in Chinese, it may seem a bit strange in English to express the shortness of life as being 'born in the morning and dead in the evening'.

The last two lines present some difficulties. Do they refer only to the short-lived officials, and do the words 'two or three' echo *Shih ching* 58 and mean men who have changed their allegiance 'two or three times'? This would give the poem a satirical flavor and suggest that Juan Chi's satisfaction in the last line is a bit grim, happy to see these fickle men reach an early death as the Psalmist is happy 'to take their little ones and dash them against the stones'. I do not believe so, although such an interpretation is perfectly possible. It seems better to me to understand the 'two or three men' as refer- ring to all the men mentioned in the poem: the rush-weaver and the high officials. Juan Chi's satisfaction comes from his observation of the contrast between these two types of men and the outcome of their lives. Both inter- pretations are possible (and not entirely contradictory), but I like to think mine binds the poem together better. Chiang Shih-yüeh, Ch'en Tso-ming and Tseng Kuo-fan all think the poem satirizes two-faced intriguers and they are probably right: the sudden deaths of the 'fast-living playboys' certainly suggests they did not die naturally.

The dangers of public life are again contrasted with the joys of a bucolic life of poverty in the next poem.

6

Long ago I heard of Tung-ling's melons
    Growing close outside the Blue-green Gate.
In field upon field they crowd down to the cross-paths,
    Large and small, like babes and their mothers holding fast to one
        another.
5   So bright were their five colors sparkling in the morning sun
    That fine guests from the four corners gathered there.
Oil in a lamp burns itself away:
    Great wealth brings on calamity.
One can live out one's life in plain cloth clothing:
10   Favor and emoluments cannot be relied upon.

This poem is based upon a biography briefly told in *Shih chi* 53, p. 9: 'Shao P'ing 邵 平 had been Marquis of Tung-ling 東 陵 under the Ch'in. When the Ch'in were defeated he was made a commoner. He was poor and raised melons east of the city walls of Ch'ang-an. Since his melons were good, the people of the times called them "Tung-ling melons" after the name of

his former fief.' Lines 3 and 4 are extremely difficult to translate. There are
three variants (軡 for 吟 , 拘 for 鉤 , and, in the *Shui-ching chu* 18, p. 109,
拒 for 距), and it is possible there might be some slight textual corruption.
The seven translators and commentaries (in Japanese, German, English and
Chinese) I have consulted differ widely. I believe (with the Peking editors)
that the main idea behind the lines is that there is a bountiful crop of melons
in Tung-ling's broad fields. There is an allusion in line 7 to *Chuang-tzu* 4
(Legge translation, 1, p. 222), in which we are warned not to 'shine too
brightly', for intelligence is a dangerous thing and can destroy the man who
uses it (since it leads to high position) as the oil in a lamp destroys itself when
producing light. It should perhaps be emphasized for the modern Western
reader, used to a more pluralistic society, that Shao P'ing, by refusing to
remain Marquis of Tung-ling or to re-enter service under the new dynasty, by
agreeing to wear 'plain cloth clothing' (i.e. by becoming a commoner), is cutting himself off from all social life that really counted in ancient China; any
prosperity or notoriety or 'fine guests' his melons might have procured him
were strictly second best.

Although it seems clear that Juan Chi is contrasting Tung-ling's secure and
happy life as a commoner with the dangers a man in public life must face,
two critics, at least, Ch'iu Kuang-t'ing and Wu Ch'i, believe the poem describes
the dangers of Tung-ling's prosperous existence. Both insist upon the fact that
in troubled times one must hide oneself to be able to survive and Tung-ling
has stayed close to the capital walls. Their interpretations are untenable. As
Huang Chieh says, they fail to take into account the penultimate lines: however prosperous he may have become, the former Lord of Tung-ling was now
definitely a commoner. But these critics do well to draw attention to the fact
that Tung-ling set himself up in the shadow of the capital, for I believe that is
one of the reasons Juan Chi was attracted to his biography (he refers to him
again in Poem 66). Was not his own life, spent in low-ranking positions, but in
the center of court activities, similar to Tung-ling's? Tung-ling did not serve
two dynasties, the Ch'in and then the Han; Juan Chi did not want to serve the
Wei and the 'proto-Chin'. The poem is thus on the one hand satirical, and on
the other, taking its moral from the allusion to Chuang-tzu in line 7, a warning
against excessive wealth and high position.

The following poem is similarly on the dividing line between social and
political criticism.

8

How fresh and bright the sun is sinking in the west,
   Its last rays shining on my robe!
A whirling wind puffs against my four walls,

As the cold birds huddle together and support one another.
5 The chou-chou still hold [one another's] feathers in their beaks [to
    enable them to drink]
And the ch'iung-ch'iung, too, thinks of his hunger [knowing his
    friend will help him assuage it].
Why then do the men in power,
    Bent in two like musical stones, forget the point to which they
    should return?
Why boast so idly of glory and renown
10 And bring on withering, and sadness to the heart?
It is better to flit with swallows and wrens
    And not to follow the Yellow Crane in its flight.
The Yellow Crane roams to the ends of the earth;
    Once in mid-flight, how could one return?

The doublet *cho-cho* 杓 杓 ('fresh and bright') usually describes the beauty of spring flowers (as in poem 12, line 4, or *Shih ching* 6): the setting of a 'fresh and bright' sun makes one wonder if Juan Chi is referring to the deposing or assassination of one of the young emperors, or, in a more general way, to the premature demise of the Wei dynasty. The whirling winds, a symbol of calumny, add to the satirical atmosphere. The cold birds who huddle together in the next line give the main theme of the poem: we must keep low and hidden and help one another to ride out the winter storm that is going to overtake us. The evocation of the two bizarre beasts in lines 5 and 6 is meant also to underline the fact that even they know how to take care of themselves and help one another in an inhospitable world. The chou-chou appears in *Han Fei-tzu* 8, section 23, Liao, vol. 1, p. 245, and in a fragment from *Chuang-tzu* found in *T'ai-p'ing yü-lan* 928, p. 1b. He has a heavy head and a forked tail; his head is so heavy that, were he to try to drink unaided in the river, he would topple over into it. So he seeks a mate to hold his feathers in his beak and allow him to drink without toppling over. The ch'iung-ch'iung appears in very ancient texts (e.g. *Shan-hai ching* 8, pp. 4b–5a) as a horse-like animal, very rapid, but unable to procure its own food. He is fed by an animal called a ch'üeh 廢 who is unable to run. In case of danger, he mounts on the ch'iung-ch'iung's back and they speed away (cf. *Lü-shih ch'un-ch'iu* 15, p. 172). The change from this strange animal world to the 'men in power' in line 7 is masterly, for they too are represented in a strange position, bent in two. But do these grotesque actions bring them 'home' (*kuei* 婦), do they help them keep safe in a hostile world? On the contrary, their actions seem only aimed at bringing empty glory. How much better for them to remain hidden among the humble than to attempt to follow some overly ambitious career in the benighted atmosphere that will follow the setting of the sun. The key word is 'to return', *kuei* (used twice as a rhyme word in the poem, in lines 8 and 14): the birds and animals know how to return to their nests and dens at night; by remaining humble we too can return to our rightful places, near our legal sovereign (?), in some humble station in life (?). Heroic action might make such a 'return' impossible.

The Chinese commentators again seem to be fairly equally divided as to the reference of the last lines: does Juan Chi refer to himself or to the 'men in power' of line 7? The complete lack of unanimity suggests that it is perhaps improper to attempt a solution. Juan Chi here, as so often, is perhaps speaking abstractly and in the context of this particular poem: in the cold winter darkness that is falling about us, we must learn to lie low and not attempt any outstanding actions. The Yellow Crane is a bird associated with Taoist immortals (cf. Poem 55) and, in general, with a kind of heroic grandeur that obsessed Juan Chi and which appears again and again in his poetry (cf. Poem 43) and in his 'Taoist' prose essays. If we take his warning not to follow the Yellow Crane at its face value, for himself as well as for the men in power, then this poem will be in contradiction with much of his work (and especially Poems 21 and 43). This should not surprise us in this most contradictory of poets, especially since this contradiction springs from those of his own life; he, too, stayed close to the swallows and wrens and did not attempt to follow the Yellow Crane in its flight.

The next poem is an even clearer demonstration of Juan Chi's dislike of riches and excesses in living, and in its last lines it adumbrates a subject we will study in greater detail in the following chapter.

72

On the highway they gallop along in fine carriages;
    On a long stream they ride in light boats.
How could this be in accord with our spontaneous nature?
    It is the road to power that leads them on.
5   High renown befuddles the will;
    Heavy profit saddens the heart.
They cause intimate friends to turn against one another,
    And flesh and blood to treat one another as enemies.

I want all the more to destroy my pearls and jade
10   To enable me to rise up [to heaven] and wander aimlessly about.

The first four lines of this poem sound strangely modern, like someone complaining of the speed on modern highways. The roads and waterways in the first two lines reinforce the image latent in the cliché 'the road to power'. This kind of excessive speeding, so contrary to our natures, is inspired by our desire for power. And it is 'power' that must be avoided if we are to keep from perverting our minds and sentiments and alienating our best friends and relatives. By avoiding these worldly 'roads' – the highway, the main waterways and the 'road to power' – by destroying our material riches, our pearls and jade (echo of *Chuang-tzu* 10, Legge translation, 1, p. 286), we can attain to a kind of spiritual apotheosis which is, indeed, *the* Road, the *tao*. But we will come back to Juan Chi's mysticism in the next chapter.

The poems we have just read show us that Juan Chi did not reject society out of hand, but that he rejected its excesses. His criticism of the ills of society seems even more profoundly felt and more categorical in the next poems I have grouped together; these have infidelity in social relations as their theme. I have grouped these poems and, in general, all his works dealing with society, as if they represented an evolution towards misanthropy, a more and more violent and profound turning away from the social values put forth in the essays on music and on the *I ching*. But of course there is no way of knowing the chronological order of his poems or the evolution of his thought. My aim is to give some semblance of order to the body of his thought, and is not to suggest, even hypothetically, that Juan Chi followed an evolution similar to my arbitrary grouping together of his poems.

The first two poems sing of fidelity and infidelity in love. The first of the two is heavily allusive and difficult to understand without a commentary.

2

The two nymphs roamed along the river bank,
    Playfully dancing along with the breeze.
Chiao-fu tucked their girdles' gems in his tunic;
    How young and beautiful they were, and smelled so sweetly!
5   How soft and tender they were together, how joyful their love:
    They would not forget one another for a thousand years!
Theirs was beauty that would destroy a city or seduce the men in Hsia-ts'ai,
    Loveliness that binds itself to one's innermost heart!
Such intense feelings give rise to sad thoughts,
10   And one plants the herb of forgetfulness near the orchid chamber.
For whom, [now], should she wash and oil [her hair]?
    She would have rain, and grudges the morning sun!
Why must relations as strong as metal or stone
    Be afflicted, one day, with the pain of parting?

The first three lines of the poem allude to a story in the *Lieh-hsien chuan* (Kaltenmark translation, pp. 96–101); Chiao-fu of Cheng meets two nymphs who give him their belt jewels. This gift is perhaps symbolic of a marriage contract, but they separate and he realizes that both the jewels and the nymphs have disappeared. Line 7 contains two allusions to descriptions of feminine beauty that would seduce an entire city, *Shih ching* 264 and 'Teng-t'u-tzu hao-se fu' attributed to Sung Yü in *Wen hsüan* 19, p. 10a. If we read the poem simply for what it says and do not look for hidden allusions, it is a lament for estranged lovers. The first eight lines describe the beauty of the ladies (in polygamous China lovers are not necessarily counted in pairs), and the tenderness of the affection the lovers shared. The next four lines are all echoes of Poem 62 of the *Shih ching* which describes the sorrow of a wife separated from her husband. Although the poem does not say so in so many words, it is clear that the lovers of the beginning of the poem have become separated, and the last two lines bemoan this separation on an abstract level. The lack of any explicit reason for the separation of the lovers seems to make the separation spring from the very strength of their emotion and adds to the force of the last lines: all human affection seems destined to be frustrated.

But the critics are not agreed as to the meaning of the poem. Shen Yüeh separates the last two lines from the rest of the work and makes them refer to another category of affection or fidelity, perhaps because the term 'relations as strong as metal or stone' appears in *Han shu* 34, p. 1874, as a description of fidelity in the world of politics. He interprets the poem in the following way: 'Youth and beauty will not be forgotten for a thousand years, while relations as enduring as metal or stone are lightly severed in a day. [As Confucius said in *Lun yü* 9, 18:] "I have not yet seen a man who loved virtue as he loved sexual desire".' To accept this interpretation, lines 9–12 must, I presume, be understood as a proof of wifely constancy: if Chiao-fu could love the nymphs so passionately and the woman in the *Shih ching* her husband so faithfully, why must pacts between men of action or friends be so lightly broken? Suzuki Torao interprets, as I have, the poem at its face value, but feels obliged to carry the original story of the two nymphs and Chiao-fu throughout the entire poem. It is Chiao-fu who is here unfaithful and the two nymphs who mourn his absence in lines 9–12. Suzuki feels, however, that the construction of the poem is 'confused' and not like Juan Chi's other works. The juxtaposition of lines 1–8 and 9–12 and the almost helter-skelter sequence of the lines of the poem seem to me, too, to be slightly chaotic. Perhaps the loose relation between the lines heightens the feeling of the chaos of passionate love and passionate longing and is, in a way, a structural embodiment of the pessimistic cry against ineluctable separation in the last lines: the very lines of the poem seem not to hang together. Other critics see the poem as a satire against the Ssu-ma: how could they pretend to be loyal, faithful and even affectionate servants of the Ts'ao and then one day break relations by turning upon them as they did towards the end of Juan Chi's life?

The following poem also takes infidelity as its theme, but is so disconnected, the lines following one another in such a disjointed way, that it certainly seems to have some satirical background.

20

Yang Chu cried at the fork in the road;
    Mo-tzu was saddened when the silk was dyed.
Once there are deferential bowings and long separations,
    It is hard to meet with those who have flown away.
5   Not only can amorous feelings be [inconstant] like this;
    Our very existence is subject to the same [inconstancy].
Mournful decay is what saddens man,
    But calamity is inexorable!
The woman from Chao seduced Chung-shan;
10   Her softness and humility made her cheated all the more.
Ah! Man on the road,
    How are you able to keep going?

The first two lines allude to two famous philosophers of antiquity, Yang Chu and Mo Ti. The former was dismayed at how easy it was for a disciple to 'take the wrong path', like a lost sheep, and, by a false interpretation of a master's philosophy, stray away from the Great Path, the *tao* (*Lieh-tzu* 8, Graham translation, p. 176). Mo-tzu sighed to think that a man was influenced so strongly by his teachers: he was like raw silk which could be dyed any color (*Mo-tzu* 3, Mei Yi-pao translation, p. 9). The two ideas are only superficially similar, but they are yoked together in *Huai-nan-tzu* 17, p. 302, much as they are here, to show how inconstant human nature is, how easily and irrevocably it can be misled or deliberately change its allegiance. This human inconstancy is examined in the lines that follow, first as the result of separations, then in the cooling of love, and finally our entire existence is seen as something inconstant in itself. The words translated as 'existence' are actually a binomial expression, *ts'un-wang* 存 亡, 'existence and disappearance' (of life, a state, thing).[3] The movement of ideas binding together these eight lines is anything but clear, and the allusion to 'the woman of Chao' that follows is inaccurate. It would seem that Juan Chi wants to allude to the story in *Chan-kuo ts'e* (Crump translation, No. 454) in which a princess of Chao is married to the king of Tai (a kingdom north of Chung-shan). Her younger brother, king of Chao, taking advantage of his sister's marriage, killed his new son-in-law during a drinking party and annexed his territory. The appalled widow committed suicide when she heard the news of her brother's perfidy and her husband's murder. Her sad life certainly is a story of 'softness and humility cheated all the more' and could very well be adduced as an example of inconstancy. But she did not seduce Chung-shan: she was married to the king of Tai.

My translation and interpretation do not satisfy me, but the interpretations offered by the commentators seem even weaker to me. Huang Chieh says line 3 refers to the process of abdication practiced by Shun who peacefully ceded his throne to Yü, a process that was altered by the founders of the Shang and Chou dynasties who used armies and warfare to found their thrones. He would read the line as: '[The process of] deferential bowing [= abdication] has long been separated from us.' And he continues his (to my mind) very arbitrary interpretation, line by line, making the poem a description of violent usurpation with obvious relevance to Juan Chi's own times. Ch'en Tso-ming also emphasizes the relation between the Ssu-ma's 'deferential bowing' and 'compliance' (line 5) which led to their usurpation. Ku Chih sees the poem as a veiled description of the reasons for the decline of Wei's power. Only Tseng Kuo-fan treats the poem more abstractly as the description of inconstancy, but for him, too, the words *ts'un-wang*, 'existence and death', refer to the fall of a state. Po Chü-i begins a poem entitled 'To Master T'ang' (*Ch'üan T'ang-shih* 424, p. 4663) with the lines 'Chia I cried over contemporary affairs;/Juan Chi cried over the fork in the road'. He is of course alluding to this poem and (the context in his own poem makes it abundantly clear) he interprets Juan Chi's tears to be, like Chia I's, 'over contemporary affairs'. This poem is one of many whose veiled references to contemporary politics make complete understanding impossible.

However we interpret them, Poems 2 and 20 speak of infidelity in one form or another – a lover's or a subject's infidelity. The following poem, ostensibly at least, seems diametrically opposed to them, and sings of eternal affection between, strangely enough, the catamites of two ancient kings, the lords of An-ling and Lung-yang (the latter's name has become synonymous with sodomy).

12

Long ago, when in the flower of their youth,
    An-ling and Lung-yang
Were as young and fresh as delicate peach blossoms
    Shining forth with a tender light.
5   Their happiness was like the spring,
    And when they bowed they were [severe] as the frost of autumn.
Their sidelong glances were charged with seductive charm
    And their very words and smiles gave forth perfume.
Hand in hand they shared their happy love
10   And at night they used the same clothing.

They wanted to be a pair of birds in flight,
　　Uniting their wings, soaring about together on high.
In red and blue they wrote their shining promise:
　　'We shall not forget one another for all eternity!'

Ch'an 纏 , lord of An-ling (locality which seems to have been near the present Yen-ch'eng in southern Honan), was the favorite of the king of Ch'u. Warned by the sophist Chiang I 江　乙 that when his beauty faded his influence over the king would fade too, An-ling, choosing a propitious moment, swore he would follow his sovereign even in death and as a result was awarded his fief. The story is told in *Chan-kuo ts'e* (Crump translation, No. 181) and *Shuo yüan* 13 (pp. 17a–18a of the Han Wei tsung-shu edition). The two versions are very similar, but the *Chan-kuo ts'e* sets the scene in the reign of King Hsüan 宣 (369–340 B.C.) while the *Shuo yüan* specifically names King Kung 恭 (reigned 492–462 B.C.). The lord of Lung-yang, like the lord of An-ling, seems to appear in only one anecdote. Fishing in a boat with his sovereign, presumably King An-hsi 安　釐 of Wei (reigned 275–243 B.C.), he begins to cry when he catches a great number of fish, because, as he explains to the king, he likens himself to the fish he will have to throw back: there are many beautiful men in the kingdom; when the king tires of him, he, too, will be 'thrown back'. The king promulgates an edict saying: 'He who dares say "beautiful man" will be executed, with all his family.' (*Chan-kuo ts'e*, Crump translation, No. 376.)

The poem does not present many problems in translation. There is an allusion in line 10 to *Shih ching* 133, a poem singing of comradely devotion, but the *Yü-t'ai hsin-yung* version of this poem has a variant for 'clothing': 'coverlet and skirts'. Suzuki Torao has an ingenious suggestion for lines 5 and 6: 'They make us happy, as if they were the spring/And we bow before them like grass withered by the frost'. But what are we to make of the poem as a whole? On the literal level, as Suzuki says, it is a song celebrating homosexuality. And, as he doesn't say, it is the only poem in the entire series to celebrate a lasting personal relationship. Suzuki goes even further and introduces, quite gratuitously, the first person in line 9, suggesting the poet himself wants to cavort with the two pretty boys.[4]

None of the other commentators presents a straightforward interpretation of this poem, and I believe they are right. Wu Ch'i says the poem takes it impact (*miao* 妙) from the first two words: 'Long ago'. Juan Chi is criticizing the effeminate courtiers of his day who will change loyalty to their ruler without hesitation and are not as constant as the courtier-catamites of yore. This is clever, perhaps too clever. It seems better to me simply to take this poem as ironic, as a satire of the two-faced courtiers he saw about him, not necessarily of the Ssu-ma rulers themselves, as many critics would have it, but of all the inconstant politicians eager to swear allegiance 'for ever' to anyone in power.[5]

It must be admitted that Juan Chi does not refer directly to An-ling's and Lung-yang's relations with their sovereigns, but (anachronistically) to their relations with one another. On the surface, Suzuki Torao is undoubtedly right in stating that this poem is the celebration of a homosexual relation. But in the context of Juan Chi's poetry and in the context of Chinese tradition, such an interpretation seems highly improbable to me. Juan Chi's poems of friendship, of social relations in general, aside from this single poem, are all uniformly negative; An-ling and Lung-yang were given fiefs and were courtiers: the influence of sexual partners, of either sex, in government was always condemned in China. It is hard for me to believe that this poem is not satirical, that it is not, like the following poem, a veiled condemnation of some contemporary figures.

56

Our heaven-given destiny exalts or humbles us;
    Failure or success come in their own time.
Beautiful, vicious flatterers,
    Seeking their advantage, come to cheat.
5   Ingratitude ruins charity
    And only makes the slanderers snicker.
The pied wagtails sing amidst the clouds
    And fly and fly without end.
How could they know that crooked men
10   Would one day be unable to hold on?

Like so many satirical poems, the clearest thing about this one is that it is unclear. Let us try, before invoking possible hidden allusion, to see what the bare words can tell us. The first two lines place the whole poem in a fatalistic atmosphere and suggest that our acts are sometimes incapable of protecting us from the inexorable laws of destiny. The 'beautiful flatterers' in line 3 are the subject of the poem. They flatter and cheat, and their ingratitude (reading 悳 for 惠 in line 5 with Huang Chieh) destroys whatever charity (or imperial favor) they have been given for their pains, making the giver a subject of derision by slanderers. But they should be careful: although they may blithely fly without pause like the happy wagtails (*motacilla chinensis*) they will be cut down in their iniquity and in their unawareness one day. But the poem is not really clear. It is also possible to consider the pied wagtails to be symbols of the innocent victims of the flatterers, in which case the last word in the poem should be translated 'depended on'.

The very generality of the poem seems to suggest some allusion to a particular case, for we know that all flatterers and ungrateful opportunists are not always caught. Chiang Shih-yüeh, Huang Chieh and Ku Chih all think Juan Chi is referring to the men who brought about the assassination of the Duke of Kao-kuei-hsiang in 260. Their explanations differ in detail, but they all feel the poem does not refer to a single individual. Ku Chih, for example, thinks the ungrateful flatterers are Wang Ch'en 王 沈 and Wang Yeh 王 業, both of whom had been befriended by the young emperor and yet hurried to tell Ssu-ma Chao of his plans to throw off the Ssu-ma's influence by a palace revolution. He also thinks the last lines refer to the brothers Ch'eng Ts'ui 成 倅 and Ch'eng Chi 成 濟 who, egged on by the future imperial father-in-law of Ssu-ma Yen, Chia Ch'ung 賈 充, assassinated the emperor during his pathetic 'revolt',[6] and were then executed by Ssu-ma Chao to save appearances. He appeals to the fact that the pied wagtail appears in *Shih ching* 164 as a symbol of brotherly cooperation and that the two brothers were shot down on the roof of their house hurling imprecations ('singing in the clouds'! Cf. *Wei-shih ch'un-ch'iu*, quoted in *San-kuo chih chi-chieh* 4, p. 60b). But the pied wagtail appears again in *Shih ching* 196 where it symbolizes ceaseless activity, as it does in a work by a man whose life and work resemble Juan Chi's strongly, Tung-fan Shuo ('Ta k'o-nan', in *Wen hsüan* 45, p. 4b), so that Juan Chi may simply be trying to underline the flatterers' industry.

There may well be allusions to contemporary events in this obscure poem, but it seems impossible to see clearly today just what they were. What is clearer is that this is a poem describing the downfall of cheating, ungrateful flatterers who have returned evil for good.

This is also the theme of Poem 51, another poem difficult to translate but whose general meaning is quite clear.

51

A constant heart falls from grace;
    Imposing virtue loses its proper place.
How can we cultivate good words [when they will be mistaken]?
    Well-meaning favors are not easy to bestow.
5   Do you not see the swallows flying south
    With their wings moving unevenly?
Kao-tzu said the new poems were 'grudging';
    Ch'ü Yüan was grieved by his separation [from his sovereign].
Why was Mr Chaos
10   Quickly and Suddenly destroyed in body and form?

The first four lines set, in general terms, the meaning of the examples which follow: goodness is seldom recompensed in this world. The following

lines give illustrations of this general statement. Lines 5 and 6 are a near
citation of *Shih ching* 28, a poem traditionally thought to have been the
lament for a virtuous woman who has been repudiated through no fault of her
own (her son had been killed by his half-brother). On a more immediate level,
the image of the swallows' wings moving out of phase can be taken as symbolic of the lack of harmony in human social relations. Kao-tzu (in *Meng-tzu*
6B, 3) thought a poem (*Shih ching* 197) in which a son bemoans the fact that
he has been unjustly deprived of his position so that his father might satisfy
the desires of one of his concubines was a poem of 'grudging'. Loyal Ch'ü
Yüan (called by his title, *san-lü* 三 閭, in the poem) was dismissed by his
sovereign after having been slandered by another official. He then wrote his
famous long poem, 'Li sao', whose title, according to one interpretation,
means 'sorrows of separation'. The last two lines refer to an anecdote in
Chuang-tzu 8. Two mythological figures, emperors of the northern and
southern oceans, Quick and Suddenly, want to repay their host, Chaos, for his
repeated hospitality by drilling into him the seven orifices that allow ordinary
men to see, hear, eat and smell, and which he lacks. 'Every day they drilled
another orifice, and, after seven days, Chaos died.' The fourth of the allusions
thus opens on to pure Taoist philosophy: since it is so difficult to bestow
favors, since it seems impossible to see one's goodness recompensed, perhaps
it is better to keep to oneself, recapture a state of 'chaotic' existence in which
one neither sees nor hears, eats nor smells; one simply floats along parallel to
the other beings without conflicting with them in any way.

Of course Juan Chi's poem is much subtler than my heavy-handed exegesis;
he only suggests the four examples of unrequited goodness and draws no conclusions. But, although the poem is not difficult to interpret, most of the
critics still see it as a political satire. Tseng Kuo-fan says the first four lines
show the Ssu-ma repaying the Ts'ao with evil for their kindness, and the last
two the horrors they could commit. Huang Chieh basically agrees with him,
but interprets (most unconvincingly) each line in such a way as to make it
the echo of some event in the history of Ssu-ma/Ts'ao relations. Ku Chih disagrees with both Tseng Kuo-fan and Huang Chieh and says the first eight lines
refer to Ts'ao Chih and his unfortunate relations with his brother, the first
Wei emperor, Ts'ao P'i, and only the last two lines refer to the Ssu-ma's defeat
of the Ts'ao. The problems evoked in the poems, loyalty, imperial favor,
official recognition for good acts, can of course be seen as problems in political life, but nothing in the poem authorizes us to assign them to criticism of
this or that political camp.

This poem thus presents a thoroughly pessimistic view of organized human
society as it existed since antiquity and ends by opening out on a suggestion
of Taoist anarchy. The following poem is consonant with it, and searches for

the roots of this social incompatibility more deeply in the human psyche itself.

30

I urge on my carriage and go out of the gate:
    My aim is to travel afar.
But where could I go in my travels?
    I will reject boasting and fame.
5   And when I am empty of boasting and fame,
    All I shall want is to suit my inner feelings.

An unlined curtain can cover the brilliant sun;
    A high terrace cuts one off from low sounds;
Vicious slander causes acquaintances to part;
10   Floating clouds can darken the day.

There are pleasant and beautiful persons who would share their clothing
    with you,
    And beauties whose single glance could overthrow a city;
But their willingness is only temporary,
    And the flower of their youth does not bloom twice:
15   The early morn suddenly becomes evening
    And we no longer see the form we loved.

A yellow bird is flying off to the southeast:
    I confide my words to it, bidding my friends adieu.

The main difficulty with this poem is to see the relation between its parts, its fundamental unity. Perhaps the best way to show this is by a prose summary. Juan Chi says he intends to take a long voyage, and the abruptly decides that in reality he has nowhere to go in the physical world; he would do better to see to his soul, to give up worldly aims and 'suit' his 'inner feelings'. But can he really let his 'inner feelings' shine forth as long as they are in danger of being troubled by social critique and inconstant love? Slander separates friends (lines 7–10); time destroys affections based upon passion (lines 11–16). In both cases one is frustrated and one's 'inner feelings' are perturbed. Better to remain solitary, to take leave of one's friends, than to remain prey to the turmoil and insincerity social life engenders.

    Why does he send a 'yellow bird' to the 'southeast'? Huang Chieh believes there is an allusion to *Shih ching* 187 whose traditional title is 'Yellow bird' and whose verses describe a man yearning to leave the corrupt state in which he is living in order to return home. He prefers to interpret the word I have rendered 'bid adieu', *hsieh* 謝 , as 'speak with', furthering the idea of returning home rather than leaving all one's friends. Juan Chi's home was in Wei-shih which is indeed to the southeast of Lo-yang so that it is possible that he is thinking of his friends at home here, as he seems to be in similar lines in the following poem translated, no. 36. But it is possible, too, that he is simply echoing ballad technique, giving a direction which has no particular symbolic meaning. This poem is not a simple political satire, as Chiang Shih-yüeh would have it, bemoaning the death of the Duke of Kao-kuei-hsiang; it seems to me to be much more a personal, philosophical and religious meditation. It can thus be seen as the summing up and the conclusion of those criticisms of society we have already read: it turns away from fame, social relations and passions and suggests, as the 'Shou-yang Mountain fu' did, a turning inward, an almost mystical search for the 'inner feelings'. Huang Chieh's perfectly valid translation of the word *hsieh* as 'speak with' suggests a flight from politics to a simple life with one's friends at home, an idea much more congenial to the Chinese mind. But Juan Chi's rupture with society was more absolute as the following poems will show us.

The poems I have grouped together in this section seem to be the logical conclusion to Juan Chi's disillusionment with social life. They contain other elements, of course, but their main purport is to describe his solitude. Poem 36 seems obscurely to continue the meditation begun in Poem 30.

36

Who says it is difficult to cope with the affairs of this world?
    One can live out one's life roaming at ease!
A flowering tree hides the view near my hall;
    Endlessly, distantly, I meditate on that which has no form.
5   Wandering in perplexity, I think of my dear friends,
    As, suddenly, it becomes dark again.

I will confide my words to a bird flying east;
    That will help me calm my feelings.

The words 'roaming at ease' in line 2 form the title of the first chapter of *Chuang-tzu* and are rich in connotations, suggesting a Taoist life of 'inactivity' (*wu-wei*), of mystical roamings in the *tao*. Line 4 seems to corroborate this interpretation, for it describes a meditation on 'that which has no form' which, in some Taoist texts (e.g. *Huai-nan-tzu* 1, pp. 10–11), is an epithet of the *tao* or at least of the inchoate universe which, according to Taoist cosmogony, preceded the world as we know it. Thus 'that which has no form' is also 'that which precedes form', i.e. the future, the as yet formless 'shape of things to come'. The 'flowering tree' in line 3 that cuts off his view may be the inspiration for his meditation: it is a symbol of the evanescence of our floating life and its very 'beauty of form' could suggest 'that which is without form'. Juan Chi's meditation, then, can be considered as an ambiguous searching out of the truth somewhere between Taoist mysticism and the examination of the as yet formless 'forms' of the future as practiced by the adepts of the *I ching*. And darkness suddenly falls as he thinks of his friends, and, presumably, their place in the future scheme of things. The suddenness of the coming of darkness underlined in the poem suggests some sudden catastrophe or the rapid coming on of death. By sending his words (this poem as a warning?) to the east (and his friends at home?) he says he can calm his troubled heart. The carefree beginning is really ironic: it is not easy to cope with the affairs of this world (cf. Poem 33, line 7); and the comfort he feels at the end of the poem is quite relative. The whole poem thus becomes a kind of ironic commentary on the Taoist statement that begins it: the meditation on the imminent tragedy, the rapid passing of time bringing darkness and death all point to how difficult indeed are the affairs of this world, and the homeward-flying bird is a desperate apotheosis, a rising above the human condition (as at the end of Poems 30 and 32) to attain some haven of peace and permanence.

Poem 37, in any case, which follows the preceding in the traditional order and may form a 'pair' with it (as in the case of Poems 33 and 34), shows us how passionately he felt his isolation from his friends, how impossible it was for him to attain to Taoist 'indifference' or ataraxia.

37

This is the best season,
    And the drizzling rain has sprinkled the dust.
I look down the road for the one I am thinking of,
    Who at dusk has still not come.
5   When human passions are moved to torment
    And mount like roaring waves, how can they be pushed back?
I brush away my tears, and keep my sadness and pain within:
    To whom could I tell my bitter, bitter feelings?

The words 'best season' have the overtones of 'mating season' (*Shih ching* 14, commentary) and imply meetings between friends or lovers, or, as always in Chinese, between an official and his sovereign. Juan Chi's friend does not come, and the violence of his disappointment makes us search for some explanation; but Juan Chi cannot give it to us: he can share his bitterness with no one.

Poems 33 and 34 seem clearly to be a 'pair' of poems since they have very similar, and very striking, beginnings. But, like the two poems we have just read, they are still separate works, each with its own differing 'atmosphere' and quite separate conclusion.

33

A day, and then another night;
  A night, and then another morning.
My face changes from what it was
  As my vital spirits wear themselves away.
5 My breast is filled with scalding fire
  As I am touched again and again by the world's vicissitudes.
The business of life presents endless complications
  And all our wise plans, alas, cannot suffice to cope.
I only fear that in a trice
10 My soul's breath will swirl away with the wind:
To the end of my days I shall tread on thin ice
  And no one will know that my heart is on fire.

In the first four lines we see time wearing away the poet's life. Lines 5 and 6 add a new element: the anguish brought by the vicissitudes of a changing world, the world of 'transformations' described in the *I ching*. The 'scalding fire' in line 5 suggests great danger or hardships, something akin to 'going through fire and water' in English. This whole business of living in the world seems to defy our mental powers, and Juan Chi can only live out his life in anguish and fear of sudden catastrophe. The penultimate line echoes the last lines of *Shih ching* 195 and 196. The fire in the poet's heart in the last line is neither heartburn nor passion; it is a scorching, scarring anguish, burning away at his psychosomatic equilibrium. The whole poem, as Huang Chieh points out, illustrates Juan Chi's 'extreme prudence', since he doesn't give the slightest hint of the actual reasons for his anguish. Han Yü has echoed the very striking first two lines of this poem in an avowed imitation (*Han Ch'ang-li chi* 7, p. 85 of the Kuo-hsüeh chi-pen ts'ung-shu edition).

Poem 33 is not, strictly speaking, a poem of solitude, but its 'sister poem', no. 34, is. The first four lines of the poem show clearly that it is related to no. 33, but it develops differently.

34

A day and then another morning;
  An evening and then another dawn.
My appearance changes from what it was
  As my vital spirits ebb and ripple away.
5 I have such affliction as I raise my cup,
  Thinking of my friends of days gone by,
That I face my wine unable to speak,
  Sorely grieved as bitterness fills my breast.
I should like to plow the sunny side of the eastern fields,
10 But who would keep true to himself with me?

> This sadness and pain are only a momentary matter,
>   But high deeds would wound my frail body.
> Where shall I practice being now crooked, now straight?
>   I will take dragons and snakes as my neighbors!

The anguish of Poem 33 persists in the first four lines of this poem, but it soon gives way to loneliness, to the regret that there are no friends left who are willing to keep their integrity by leaving the life of politics and returning to the soil with him. (He echoes his own letter to Chiang Chi with his reference to 'plowing the eastern fields' in line 9.) There is a subtle hint of the purges of the Ssu-ma here, since Juan Chi's bitterness (line 8) was probably not caused by his friends' natural deaths. He must take himself in hand, however, for he realizes he can do nothing about it: any attempt at 'high deeds' (line 12) would be suicide. The traditional meaning (in the *Shu ching* and *Hsün-tzu*, for example) of 'crooked and straight' in the penultimate line is 'good and bad', but Tseng Kuo-fan, followed by Huang Chieh and Ku Chih, all prefer to see it as describing the movement of the snakes and dragons in the last line and as echoing the line of the 'Hsi tz'u' (*I ching*, Legge translation, pp. 389–90; cf. *Han shu* 87A, p. 3515) describing the movement of the inchworm. Juan Chi is asking: 'How can one be alternately straight and crooked, alternately hide and appear, as the dragons and snakes do when they hibernate in winter [and then appear again in spring]?' He would like to live a life of bucolic peace, but the intense solitude of such an existence (lines 9–10), together with the danger involved (lines 11–12), leave him with the only other solution possible: a life of snake-like hiding in the tradition of the adepts of the *I ching*. But the context of the poem shows he accepts this alternative only out of despair, not out of cold calculation.

Solitude is a theme of the next poem and it, like the two preceding poems, is animated by the thought of the passage of time.

7

> This summer's blazing heat
>   Will be about to leave in one month's time.
> Green leaves hang on the fragrant trees;
>   Blue clouds move themselves sinuously through the sky.
> 5   The four seasons alternate again and again,
>   As the sun and the moon rush headlong, one after the other.
> I pace back and forth in my empty room,
>   Pained to the heart that I have no friend!
> How I should like to look upon everlasting happiness [with him]
> 10   And see the sorrow of parting nevermore!

Almost all the Chinese commentators would have us believe the subject of this poem is the change in dynasty that was to take place shortly after Juan Chi's death: he is said to be lamenting the passing of the Wei. This may be true, but it is very important not to let this secondary meaning obscure the basic, literal images of the poem for us. These images are all of movement and of departure; only in line 3 do we feel a momentary halt in the stilly poised green leaves, hanging precariously motionless in the heat of the summer. Lines 3 and 4, as Wu Ch'i judiciously remarks, are the only lines in all the 'Yung-huai' poems that seem peaceful and happy, and even they serve only to set off the despair of the last lines. Summer's parting, the movement of the clouds, of the seasons, of the sun and the moon, seem reflected in Juan Chi's anguished pacing back and forth. And when he formulates his wish in the last lines he seems to want to oblige us to read it in the framework of the entire poem since he, rather strangely, uses two verbs for 'to see' (he wants to 'look upon' eternal happiness and not 'to see' the sorrow), reminding us of the strong visual images of the earlier part of the poem. His plea is not merely against 'taking leave' of his family, his (non-existent) friends, or of his dynasty, but also, on a quasi-metaphysical level, against the passage of the sun and the moon, of the seasons and of time itself.

In Poem 14 time is again a main theme, and the poem is flooded with the feeling of solitude.

14

Autumn is here with its foretaste of cool air;
    Crickets are singing on my bed curtains.
These things fill my breast with deep anxiety
    And painfully clog my heart with gloom.
5   So many words that cannot be told,
    Overflowing phrases that no one can hear!
A light wind blows upon my sleeve of gauze;
    The bright moon shines forth its pure brilliance.
The morning cock is singing in some tall tree:
10   I order my carriage to set forth on the voyage home.

This is a very delicate poem, a poem that contains lines of passionate intensity, sandwiched (so to speak) between cool and subtle descriptions of early autumnal (i.e. by traditional Chinese reckoning, August) natural scenery. The passion of the middle lines (3–6) seems to spring naturally from the coming of autumn, harbinger of winter and death, but the repetition in lines 5 and 6 (resembling the first two lines in Poems 33 and 34) is ambiguous. On the one hand the lines echo the song of the crickets, and on the other they point up Juan Chi's solitude, his lack of some friend with whom he could share his premonitions and innermost anxieties. According to Wu Ch'i, the song (*ming*

鳴) of the crickets, as well as the song (*ming*) of the cock are both slightly ominous or at least irregular. In poetic tradition, influenced by *Shih ching* 154, 'In the tenth month the cricket is under the bed'. This poem is placed in the first month of autumn, the seventh lunar month of the Chinese year. The cock, too, crows at sunrise, not in bright moonlight. These unseasonable natural phenomena show, according to Wu Ch'i, that Juan Chi was writing as an adept of the *I ching* here, as a man who could see the secret springs (*chi* 幾) of great events at their infinitesimal origins. Under these conditions it is no wonder that he calls his carriage to take him 'home', wherever that may be — the mountain forests and eremitic retirement according to Lü Yen-chi and Tseng Kuo-fan, or more simply, to his ancestral home to weather out the coming winter with his family.

The last poem I would like to discuss in this chapter is also the most severe in its absolute solitude.

17

> I sit alone in my empty hall:
>> With whom would I rejoice?
> I go out of the gate, down to the great road,
>> And see no moving carriage or horse.
> 5 I climb the heights and gaze at the Nine Provinces,
>> That, far, far in the distance, divide the empty plains.
> A lone bird flies to the northwest,
>> While a stray beast goes off to the southeast.
> At the close of day I think of my dear friend:
> 10 Talking with him would have brought relief.

As Wu Ch'i points out in his sensitive remarks on this poem, Juan Chi has here 'exhausted his feelings' of solitude. He sees no one in his hall, no guests ('carriages and horses' often symbolize guests) in the main road, no one, nothing in the entire empire that he seems to see stretching out before him. This is 'abstract and distant' talk indeed! He has raised his loneliness to metaphysical proportions and shows himself here to be absolutely alone in the entire universe. The solitary animals that seem to rush off, in opposite directions, to the ends of the earth, only serve to accentuate this universal emptiness. There is no necessity to follow Ho Cho, Ch'en Hang and Ku Chih and see them as symbols of loyalists fleeing to Wu (which was to the southeast of Wei) and Shu (which was *not* to the northwest).

The sadness in these poems of solitude shows how profoundly attached Juan Chi was to social life, and his essays show how profoundly attached he was to the traditional Confucianism that regulated it. But his behavior in society, his drunkenness, his anti-ritualism were too striking not to have been misinterpreted in later ages.

> At the end of the Wei, Juan Chi was a man given to wine and was reckless of all his actions. He would bare his head, let loose his hair and sit naked with his legs spread out. Later idle young aristocrats such as Juan Chan 阮瞻, Wang Ch'eng 王澄, Hsieh K'un 謝鯤, Hu-wu Fu-chih 胡毋輔之[7] and their like all took Juan Chi as their spiritual ancestor and said they had obtained the Root of the Great Way. They threw away their bonnets, took off their clothes and showed forth their ugliness like any animal. The more extreme were called 'Universal', and the less, 'Enlightened'.[8]

About this same time, that is some thirty years or so after Juan Chi's death, Chang Han 張翰 (272–328), because he 'let himself go indiscriminately', was called the 'Infantry [Colonel, i.e. Juan Chi] of the Lower Yangtze Basin':[9] 'He preferred a cup of wine *right now* to posthumous fame.'[10] The Seven Sages of the Bamboo Grove, and Juan Chi in particular, became the examples of dissipation, free living and general immorality: 'Look at Juan Chi's conduct and you will understand the cause of the decay of ritual doctrine.'[11] The great historians of the seventeenth and eighteenth centuries attributed the fall of the ancient morality to the Seven Sages[12] or to Hsi K'ang and Juan Chi[13] much as Gibbon attributed the fall of Rome to the introverted, religiously oriented Christians. Not all critics were as damning. Tai K'uei 戴逵, who died in 395, sharply distinguished between the flaming youth of the Yüan-k'ang era (291–300), 'who cocked their caps because they had no virtue', and the Seven Sages, 'who knit their brows because they were [truly] in pain' (*Chin-shu chiao-chu* 94, p. 44b). Tai K'uei was by no means a 'libertine' himself; on the contrary, he is said to have been a rigorous ritualist and 'to believe profoundly that "to let oneself go" was to be immoral'. Although he never served in government himself and lived his life out in retirement, he was distinctly averse to those who, for religious (immortality-seeking) or other reasons did not aid their sovereigns. He defends the Seven Sages because, according to him, they understood the true meaning of traditional morality, not only its outer trappings (*Chin-shu chiao-chu* 94, p. 44a).

Juan Chi himself seems to have realized the danger of carousing for carousing's sake when he forbade his son to imitate his libertine ways: '[Juan Chi's son,] Juan Hun 阮渾 (*tzu* Chang-ch'eng 長成), had his father's air and demeanor. He too wanted to play the 'Enlightened'. Juan Chi said to him: "[Your cousin] Juan Hsien is already part of our group: it's just not for you!" '[14] I believe Juan Chi refused to let his son partake in his anti-ritualistic activities because he felt he was too young to understand the profound political, social and philosophical reasons behind his own behavior, much as Tai K'uei says the generation following Juan Hsien could not understand the Seven Sages' anguish.

And well might they not understand them! As we have seen in the anecdotes and in his own works in this chapter, Juan Chi's attitudes towards traditional ritualism and society are extremely complex, and colored, as every aspect of his life seems to have been colored, by the political climate at the end of the Wei dynasty. He posed as an anti-ritualist, as a type of 'Taoist' 'beyond the pale', living an untrammelled life of 'spontaneity'. But when we read the anecdotes told of him, of his mourning for his mother in particular, we see that under his apparent indifference to ritual and to its contemporary keystone, filial piety, he was extremely, profoundly filial, indifferent to the superficial, ossified trappings of ritual, but sensitive to its inner reality. He answers the Confucian traditionalist Fu I with a mystical tirade inspired by Chuang-tzu, but when he puts his own ideas on ritual and society on paper, in the essays on music and on the *I ching*, they are thoroughly orthodox, and when he devotes an entire essay to Chuang-tzu, he treats him almost with disdain, and denatures his philosophy without any qualms. His poetry, without doubt the most intimate of his works, again shows us his ambivalent attitude towards Confucianism, castigating outright a corrupt Confucianist, making Lao-tzu sigh over a simple, poor and honest Confucian scholar. But in the poems dealing with friendship, with attitudes towards social living, towards human infidelity, we begin to see the basic reasons behind his contradictory nature, behind his rejection of the very ritual he really held to be the only bulwark against anarchy and universal discord: his complete disillusionment with society as he actually saw it about him. He describes an ideal human society based upon traditional ritual and philosophy on the one hand, and bemoans the fact that buman beings are incorrigibly unfaithful towards one another, to the extent that it is better either to leave society altogether or to resign oneself to complete solitude within it. Shall we explain away the illogicality or, to put it more charitably, the 'idealism' of this position by arbitrarily positing dates for all these undated works? The idealistic 'Confucianistic' essays would be youthful works; the disillusionment with society products of his maturity. There is a poem (but only one, no. 15) that supports this hypothesis; but it must remain a hypothesis for lack of more ample evidence.[15] I prefer to think that Juan Chi held on, in one way or another, to his youthful idealism throughout his life, although the terrible disillusionment of maturity, and of the tragedies at the end of the Wei, tempered it and forced him, in his solitude, to look more and more into himself to see if he could achieve some kind of ideal, some kind of personal realization within his own soul.

7

THE IMMORTAL WOMAN

We have seen Juan Chi in politics and in society. It is time now to look at him at home, to study his mystical tendencies, religious aspirations and his attitude towards Taoist immortality.

In the *Chin shu* 49, unfortunately the only source to record it, we read the following:

> Juan Chi was an excellent performer on the zither. When he was satisfied [with what he had played] he would suddenly forget his physical being. Many of his contemporaries called him stupid, but his elder cousin, Juan Wen-yeh,[1] constantly admired him, thinking Juan Chi surpassed him. Thereafter all thought Juan Chi exceptional.[2]

Although, in the original Chinese, the relation between Juan Chi's zither and his 'forgetting his physical being' is not made explicit, the relation between mystical rapture and zither (*ch'in*) playing is well attested,[3] and, as we will see in a moment, Juan Chi himself has a semi-mystical view of music as something 'beyond sound'. But, whether or not his 'forgetting his physical being' is the result of his music, it is highly significant. It can only be interpreted, in this context, as some kind of mystical experience, and the 'stupidity' Juan Chi was accused of may very well be some sort of *docta ignorantia* familiar to mystics from *Lao-tzu* 20 to Nicholas of Cusa.[4] The fact that Juan Chi himself has experienced this kind of extra-corporeal rapture gives added interest to the mystical passages in his works that we might otherwise imagine to be formal citations of *Chuang-tzu* or of the *Ch'u tz'u*. On the contrary, his whole view of man and the world seems to be colored by this mystical bent, which he shares, incidentally, with a great number of his contemporaries — on both sides of the Old World.

One of the most 'mystical' of his works is a curious *fu* called 'Purifying the thoughts', 'Ch'ing-ssu fu' 清 思 賦 . As in so many of his works, Juan Chi has here taken a perfectly traditional theme and given it a new meaning. 'Purifying the thoughts' belongs to a literary tradition reaching back to the 'Shen-nü fu' attributed to the shadowy pre-Han figure Sung Yü[5] and reanimated when Juan Chi was thirteen years old by Ts'ao Chih in his 'Lo-shen fu'.[6] These two *fu* take as their subject the meeting of a mortal man and a nymph and are, in the main, the description of the extraordinary beauties of the nymph in question. In both cases the nymph remains chaste and the poets end by extolling her (and their own) virtue and forebearance. The title of Juan Chi's *fu*, moreover, shows it to be in a sub-tradition stemming from this main branch, a sub-tradition in which the poet (from Chang Heng onwards) attempts to 'still his passions' or 'quiet his desires' after having been exposed to the view of some particularly beautiful member of the opposite sex.[7]

Most of the works belonging to this tradition, and especially to this sub-tradition, slavishly follow their archetypes, producing what are in fact only slight variations on a theme. Even as great a poet as T'ao Yüan-ming, writing a century or so after Juan Chi, has felt obliged to cleave very close to the line of tradition in his *fu*, 'Stilling the passions'.[8] Juan Chi's originality is all the more striking when read against this very close-knit tradition: although in the central, and longest, part of his poem (lines 42–142) he stays fairly close to the descriptions in earlier works, the forty-line introduction, the short ending, and the whole meaning of the work are quite original.

The opening lines alert us immediately to the fact that this is no ordinary *fu* to 'still the passions': they are the statement of some mystical or semi-mystical theory of super-sensorial beauty. The lines that follow are often obscure, but right up to the end of this forty-line introduction Juan Chi seems to be trying to prove the existence of this beauty 'beyond form or sound' by quoting ancient examples of it, and to describe the state of mind we must be in in order to perceive it. He preaches a kind of quietism dear to the Taoists and to mystics the world over. There are many unintelligible lines in this section and surely as many or more textual corruptions, but the general message is clear: it is only through renouncing our passions that we can achieve true bliss.

The next, and longest, section is a reverse proof of this theory. True to the tradition of this kind of *fu*, Juan Chi describes his meeting with an absolutely bewitching female spirit or 'immortal', who is also an accomplished musician. Her appeal is to both the eye and the ear, and she thus falls short on both counts of the super-sensorial criterion of our poet. It is in this middle section that Juan Chi is most traditional, following the narratives of the 'Shen-nü' and the 'Lo-shen' *fu* very closely. The nymph, or immortal or whatever she is, is beautifully described, first as a sublime musician, zitherist and singer, then as a prospective lover. Finally she gradually disappears, fading away like a cloud as she goes back into heaven. After her disappearance Juan Chi, in the last fifteen lines of the poem (155–70), turns against the inconsistent spirits and welcomes human sages. But his return to common humanity is only

temporary: his aspirations lead him to a mystical flight out of the universe
entirely.

Purifying the thoughts

[I]
I believe that
The form that can be seen
Does not constitute sensuous beauty;
That the note that can be heard
5   Does not constitute excellent music.[9]

In ancient times the Yellow Emperor attained apotheosis as an immortal
        on the top of Mount Ching[10]
      And performed the 'Hsien-ch'ih' music on the crest of the Southern
        [Mountain].[11]
So spirit-like was the music's subtlety
      That neither K'uei[12] nor [Po-]ya[13] could hear it clearly.
10   Nü-wa shone brilliantly on the shores of the Eastern Sea
      And fluttered about on the side of Hung-hsi.[14]
The woods and stones dropped
      And the jewelled terrace did not shine forth its light [?].[15]

Thus it is only in things that are subtle, marvellous and invisible
15   Or quiet, lonely and inaudible
That one can gaze at grace, beauty and purity.
Therefore when the bright sun sends forth its rays
The Empress Li[16] does not walk out and show herself,[17]
And when the bells and drums roar clamorously
20   Yen-tzu does not raise up his voice [to sing].[18]
It is when one's [mind] is pure, empty, and limitless
That spiritual beings assemble before one;
When it whirls about in the incoherent [*tao*]
That it penetrates mysteries and plumbs the obscure;
25   When your heart is of ice and your nature of jade
Then, bright and pure, your thought will prolong itself.

When you are calm and quiet and without passions
      Your ambitions will be at ease and your affections suited;
And when your innermost thoughts are harmonious
30   You will be satisfied wherever you go.
The cold wind travels through the grain

      . . .   .

When the baby in Shen was sad, his mother returned;
    When the wild goose in Wu was doleful, an image was produced.[19]
35   In these cases the emotion was so strong it reached to the spirits;

How could it be so impetuous and not befuddle one?
When your ambitions desire nothing, your spirit will be upright;
    When your heart is not agitated, you will be naturally sincere.
When you firmly hold to the One, your internal condition will be perfectly in order;
40   If you are able to stop here and now, you will not be thrown over.[20]
And as clear dawn changes into late night
    You will be able to point to the sun's place of setting with lasting peace of mind.[21]
Now that the sun has set
    And black night has barred the gate,
45   The moon's charioteer adjusts the reins
    And a pure breeze blows through the air.
The light curtains flutter again and again
    As the flowered matting lies quiet and still.
The clams chant softly;[22]
50   The crickets sing slowly.
I look off towards the towering heights of the Southern Mountain
    And back towards the dark, dark greenery of the Northern Wood.
Jupiter[23] has sunk behind the back chambers;
    The bright moon shines on the front garden.
55   Lacking sleep, I stretch out,
    When suddenly I am aroused and excited!

[II]
How can my long-lasting spirit follow quietude
    When there is something attracting it elsewhere?
My desires flow wildly and make me change my meditation;
60   My heart is fiercely shaken and fills with passion.
It is as if someone had come and could be touched,
    As if the person had gone away and yet had not left!
My heart becomes confused and loses all sense of order;
    My feelings run wild and are impossible to control.
65   My faculties of perception are unable to tell whether this is real:
    It must indeed have been like this at Yün-meng![24]
I am stunned by the extraordinary way she uses her marvellous voice
    And gaze upon her surpassing beauty here before me.
She begins to play upon her zither from Cinnabar Mountain[25]
70   And I hear, in her music, the jagged crests of the exalted mountains.
    She begins slowly, making only the slightest sound.
Quietly, cleverly her feelings meander here and there.
    Then she summons forth a cloud to provide breath [for her song]
Which becomes stirring, shattering:
75   Her voice flies up to the heights and swells abroad.

It is as if one climbed the K'un-lun and looked out upon the Western
    Sea!
[Her voice] soars over the vague and obscure distances,
So that one is unable to measure how far it goes.

[Moved by her music] my heart wells forth endlessly;
80   My thoughts go far, far, without reaching half way,
Like Teng-lin who died at the Great Swamp
    Or Ch'in-p'i who was saddened at the Jewelled Bank.[26]
Wandering back and forth undecidedly,
    Meandering in the immense spaces,
85   I roam in P'ing Garden and look off afar[27]
    And ride [in a boat] with a bright flag on the River Hsiu.[28]
My thoughts are long and severe so they can reach forever [?].
    They clean the great expanses of the flat highway;
I follow the road far to arrive straight away;
90   Open the gates to the women's quarters and enter the inner door.
How admirable her beauty as she whirls in her play,
    As she leans on the east wind and glows radiantly!
She has bathed and cleansed herself in the depths of the Wei;[29]
    Her body is pure and immaculate.
95   She covers her face with white jade [powder?],
    And she wears red cloud-mist as her garment,
Picked out with the sparkling essence of the Nine Splendors[30]
    And with Yao-kuang[31] giving forth a pale light in her girdle.
How her clothes flash and sparkle in their varied hues,
100   A crowd of colors all harmonious together!
How they glimmer and shine,
    Mixed in variegated profusion!
She was like Morning Cloud united [with the rain],
    Like the interdependent transformations [of the *yin* and *yang*]![32]

105 I'll have Ch'ang-i[33] go first to tell her of my love
    And order the River nymphs to return together with her here to me.
She walks with ease and steps forth alone,
    Casting sidelong glances towards the pillars on either side as she
        ascends the staircase,
Shaking her [jewels] from Gem Valley[34] and her singing jades,
110   Chanting the wandering [notes] of the tune 'Ling-yang'.[35]
She treads in the highest spheres of dissolving [cloud-mist?],
    Stepping on the slight remains of scattering [fog?].
She slips out of her An-chao [?] red slippers,
    Moves on to the bed matting and gathers together the curtains.
115 She explains why she has come into this chamber
    When a sudden wind warms us up.

Her perfume emanates from her and is wafted abroad;
    Her alluring face shines forth her beauty.
Her pure words are intimate and [fragrant] as orchids,
120   Her phrases pleasing and always proper.
We give ourselves over to this meeting of our spirits
    And we float together on the remaining rays of the sun and the
        moon.
I can avail myself of the subtlest particles of her pure breath,
    And enjoy the perfection of all her beauties for my own ends![36]
125 I want to tell her I love her now, tonight,
    But I still ask myself whether it is right or not.[37]
I am bathed in her perfume exhaled by the night
    And try to leave for a short time, but always return to her.
I look at her with joyful love, but am not calm;
130   Before I have said all, my heart is oppressed.
Alas! That I could lean upon the clouds,
    Spread my wings and fly away with her!

I would leave the narrow confines of my central hall,
    Giving up home life.
135 The curtains [at home] would be spread out, but not used;
    The back rests and mats set up, but not touched.
I would [rather] ride on the trailing mist of a cloud carriage,
    And mount a chariot pulled by Hsia-hou's two dragons.[38]
I would break [a branch] from the cinnabar tree to shade me from the
    sun
140   And raise a mushroom parasol of three layers,[39]
Flying and flying, careening to one side and the other,
    Wildly soaring in all directions, far in the distance!

I gaze at the morning mist spread out
    That looks like the [immortal] beauty harboring sadness.
145 Its variegated colors mix together and form a pattern,
    Then suddenly scatter without leaving a trace.
It is as if she were about to speak and then does not;
    Her mood again changing, she floats about in the air.
As if her hair were let down and not arranged,
150   Her ornaments dispersed, and her body dissolved,
She casts a sidelong glance as she leaves:
    In her heart she would like to come to me, but she is [already] far.

[III]
Before she disappears completely she seems a riot of beauty,
    Finer than the formal order of the constellations of heaven!
155 Then the vast expanses become clouded over

And I suddenly no longer recognize my old home.
I go to the Yellow Creature's[40] high pavilion,
    As the Thunder Master rumbles and the rain falls.[41]
I shall welcome outstanding wise men and elders
160   And whip Li-lun[42] and Ying-ku,[43]
Destroy phantoms, break the spirits,
    And climb, by the most direct road, to where my aspirations lie.
I will let my feelings expand throughout the entire universe:
    Who will say I look back in doubt?
165 I will leap up beyond all, and, galloping away,
    Reach the Pole Star and go out beyond it.
Grasping heaven's dividing lines and showing them, [proving I have
      indeed left the world],
    I will look down upon the North Pole and then leave forever.
Once the things of this world no longer bind my heart,
170 How could a single woman be worth my thoughts?

The three parts into which I have divided the *fu* are fairly clear. The first describes the philosophical background, the importance of the renunciation of desires, the superiority of the super-sensuous over all that can be perceived by the senses; the second, an encounter with a beautiful immortal during which all the poet's senses are violently brought into play; and finally, the departure of the immortal and the poet's renunciation of the world and his mystical ascension to, presumably, some union with the absolute. But it must be admitted that the actual significance of the 'immortal' (if such she is) is not all that clear. As we shall see in the next poem and in a later group devoted to 'immortals' in general, Juan Chi's attitude towards immortals is one of yearning and admiration. The last section, too, is abrupt and contains many difficult lines, of doubtful interpretation (159–61 especially).

The whole *fu* is an extraordinary document, if I have interpreted it rightly. The idea of 'renouncing the senses', of turning away from worldly pleasures, is a fairly common one in Taoist literature, in both *Lao-tzu* and in *Chuang-tzu*: only by such a renunciation can a man maintain his 'microcosmic integrity' and not be torn apart by conflicting attractions. But the early philosophers (Confucian as well as Taoist) never suggested as complete a renunciation of the passions as Juan Chi seems to express here. Celibacy, for example, is unknown, and is even considered harmful by later Taoist thinkers. In earlier *fu* on the subject of 'stilling the passions', moreover, the poets attempt to forget about their ladies because they are inaccessible for one reason or another; but Juan Chi is placing the 'purification of his thoughts' at the center of his work. He is attempting to attain a spiritual purity in which all passion, including sexual passion, is absent. Nor is it question here of a simple mystical escape from a hostile world, a theme exploited with great artistry centuries before Juan Chi's time in the *Ch'u tz'u*. Here the mystical purgation is at the center of the poem, and the poem thus becomes a truly religious one, one in which mystical philosophy is made the true theme, not simply a *pis aller* for political commitment; the poet shows himself, albeit in a rudimentary way, at grips with the psychological problems purgation poses. Is it too far-fetched to recall that Juan Chi was, in the last years of his life, the contemporary of the Egyptian Saint Anthony, born in 251?

In Poem 19 Juan Chi again describes a meeting with a bewitching immortal and he does so in terms inspired by poems in the 'Shen-nü fu' tradition. But the poem is very different from the 'Ch'ing-ssu fu' and brings us back to the unresolved ambiguities of Juan Chi's thought.

19

There is a beauteous person in the western regions
    Glistening white as the bright sun's rays.
The robes she wears are of thin silk gauze
    And from her girdle hang crescents of jade on either side.
5   Her adorned face shines forth enticing loveliness,
    As, following the breeze, she leaves a subtle fragrance.
She climbs the heights to look towards the one she loves,
    Raising her sleeve [to shade her] from the sun.
Placing her face among the clouds,
10   She waves her sleeves and rises, soaring in the void.
Then swirling about in chaotic space
    She casts a sidelong glance back toward me.
How I love her, and yet we never united!
    Conversing with her would cause me such pain!

While the 'Ch'ing-ssu fu' ends positively on a note of mystical exaltation, this poem ends, like so many of the poems in the series, on a note of frustration, of sadness of which the cause is not immediately apparent. Why would conversation with this ideally beautiful person provoke such pain in Juan Chi's breast? Is it because he knows he can never 'unite with her'? Read simply for what it says, Juan Chi's pain seems to be the pain of someone who finds it impossible to attain to an ideal that he sees beckoning before him. What is the ideal? What does the immortal woman represent? Is she again a female temptress who would destroy his psychological equilibrium, as in the 'Ch'ing-ssu fu', or is she some truly good and desirable aim? There is no way of knowing and the poem must be read as a poem of frustration, of refusal or inability to unite with what he loves.

As suggestive a poem as this has of course inspired the commentators to seek for concrete explanations of Juan Chi's frustrations, to define the symbolism of the immortal more precisely. The fact that they are in complete disagreement as to what she represents seems to me to prove, or at least to imply, that they are wrong to attempt any precise identification. Most of them (Liu Lü, Chu Chia-ch'eng, Fang Tung-shu) point out that the first line echoes *Shih ching* 38, a poem about a 'western beauty' thought to refer to a saintly king of the Western Chou. Juan Chi's complex love and desire and pain in the last two lines would thus be his chagrin at being unable to serve a saintly ruler. Chiang Shih-yüeh and Wu Ju-lun, on the contrary, think she represents the Ssu-ma beckoning from their exalted position to Juan Chi who refused to 'unite' with them and who suffers at the state of the world. Huang Chieh feels that lines 8 and 12 contain some hidden allusion which he believes to be to Ts'ao Shuang. When the latter took over the regency (line 8), he summoned Juan Chi as an adjutant (line 12), but Juan Chi refused (cf. above, p. 16). Do not these contradictory explanations, each making good points, none completely satisfactory, suggest that there is no key to this poem? Juan Chi imagines some ineffable happiness which approaches him, beckons to him and leaves him filled with complex feelings of love and pain. This abstract interpretation gives the poem an almost romantic tinge that is not really out of keeping with Juan Chi's solitary, anguished personality. That his ideal does after all have political overtones does not necessarily rob it entirely of more abstract significance.

Although he has not said so in so many words, Juan Chi's idealized ladies are immortals — every aspect of his descriptions shows that this is true. The sadness he feels because he is not able to unite with them is, on one level, sadness for his own mortality. The authors of what I suppose must still be called the 'standard history' of Chinese poetry say that 'when we read any of the eighty-odd poems by Juan Chi we can see that his sadness comes from the fact that all things and beings within the cosmos are "impermanent" '.[44] To a great extent this is true, perhaps even truer in his poetry than in that of any other Chinese poet, in spite of the fact that most Chinese poets are obsessed with the passage of time and that late second- and third-century poets seem particularly anguished about it. I have grouped together the following four poems because I think their main theme is impermanence, but I might well have included many more.

Poem 27 describes a mortal counterpart of the immortal beauty in the 'Ch'ing-ssu fu' and in Poem 19. The opening lines seem to set the scene, somewhat in the style of the opening lines of some of the songs in the *Shih ching*. We are placed in the center of the empire, in the fashionable capital, and near the traditionally 'lascivious' state of Cheng.

27

Chou and Cheng meet at the center of the world
    And their roads go out towards the central provinces.
There lives a captivating, elegant beauty,
    Radiant and at the height of her charms.
5   Her black hair gives radiance to her rosy face,
    And there is splendor in her sidelong glances.
I dream of receiving just one of her town-toppling looks;
    A seductive glance would make me so proud!
I would like to roam with her in the third month of spring,
10   But the morning sun will suddenly stumble and fall.
How quickly decay sets in!
    We would part, and then what would we do?

Again frustration is the result of Juan Chi's ardent desires; he can no more achieve some kind of lasting, happy relation with this bewitching mortal than with the immortals of the previous poems. It is in fact precisely her mortality, and the fragility of her youthful beauty that disappoint him: their relation cannot be the lasting one he is so eager to achieve. The whole poem is a kind of reverse *carpe diem*, bemoaning the rapid passage of time. Chiang Shih-yüeh and Ch'en Tso-ming both think Juan Chi is speaking allegorically and bemoaning his inability to serve the waning Wei dynasty. This interpretation only renders Juan Chi's anguish at the passage of time more complex; it does not by any means explain it away.

The passage of time and the human mortality it brings with it are familiar themes in the philosophy of Chuang-tzu. In the following poem, Juan Chi draws a Chuang-tzu-like conclusion from his realization that time makes all our actions only relatively important.

52

The ten suns rise from Yang Valley
    And, checking their pace, gallop a myriad miles.
They cross the heavens, shine on the Four Seas,
    And in a twinkling plunge beyond the bank of the River Meng.
5   Who would say they blazed for long
    Or that they were slow to travel and then to sink?
Those who have passed on did not live for long;
    They, too, have gone under the brambles and thorns.
A thousand years are like a single morning,
10   The time for one small meal and all is finished.
How useless to argue and fight
    Over what is right and wrong or what leads to gain or loss!

> As soon as you count your profits and see that your schemes can only
>   go so far
> You'll be able to put an end to your feelings of grief

According to Chinese mythology the sun rose in the easternmost Yang (variant, T'ang 湯) Valley and set at the western rim of the world, beyond the banks of the Meng. There were ten suns, one for each day of the week (cf. *Shan-hai ching* 9, pp. 3ab). In line 2 the words translated 'checking their pace', *mi-chieh* 弭 節 , recall the 'Li sao' (*Ch'u tz'u*, p. 28) where Ch'ü Yüan has the sun's charioteer, Hsi Ho, 'check his pace'. This is a paradox in the context here. Perhaps Juan Chi is trying to suggest that the slow movement of the sun across the sky as we see it is only apparent: the sun is actually propelled by the inexorable, hurtling power of rapidly passing time.[45] In line 8, the suggestion is that the untended graves of those dead for a long time become covered with brambles and thorns (cf. Huan T'an, *Hsin lun, Ch'üan Hou Han wen* 15, p. 11a).

In a crude résumé of this poem one could say the first ten lines preach temporal relativism, and the last four draw the conclusion: since our life is really very short, all our ambitions, all our gain and profit, will lead us only to the grave. The realization of this truth should bring peace and contentment with one's fate. The third character in the last line, *chü* 遽 , is, however, ambiguous; it can make the line a question, which would give the following translation for the last two lines:

> Count your profits and you'll know your schemes can only go so far:
> How then will you be able to put an end to feelings of grief?

The overall lesson of the poem is the same: time robs us of all our worldly ambitions. The realization of this truth can give you (in the two lines of conclusion) Taoist peace, or it can drive you to the depths of despair. Perhaps the ambiguity is intentional and Juan Chi is trying to show us that Taoist 'indifference' or *ataraxia* is really only another kind of despair.

Even Ch'en Hang (echoed by Wang K'ai-yün), who seems interested in Juan Chi's poems only insofar as they can be interpreted as political satires, is forced to see this poem as satire on a very abstract level indeed. He suggests it preaches that all must come to an end, the Han who preceded the Wei, and then, in the not too distant future, the Chin who were soon the follow the Wei. This kind of allusion hunting reduces the sport to an absurdity and shows that we are right to treat some of the poems, at least, quite independently of current events.

The meditation on the vanity of worldly ambitions is carried on into the next poem, which follows the poem just translated in the traditional order.

53

Nature has a fixed pattern:
   The Way of life and death is inconstant.
However clever you may be,
   This Great Law will never change its course.
5   Why then does the fawning sycophant,
   Full of presumption, flush with pride?
He rides in a fine carriage, spurs on his good horse,
   Or leans against his backrest, facing a sumptuous meal.
The clothing he wears is of thin silk gauze
10   And he has an apartment for his idle moments on a hidden terrace.
Can't he see the flowers at evening
   Whose petals, one by one, flutter to the side of the road?

This poem is, obviously, a satire against the two-faced, sybaritic officials at
the Wei court. The carriage, horse, backrest, fine clothing and 'country house'
are all perquisites of high and favored officials, much as dachas are meted out
to special personalities in the Soviet Union today. But the role of these officials
in the poem is to show how useless all their glory is in the larger context of
our mortality.

The following poem is devoted entirely to the description of the shortness
of life, this time in the animal and vegetable kingdoms.

71

The hibiscus flowers shine on the grave mounds,
   Twinkling with radiant color.
But when the bright sun drops into the forest,
   Petal by petal they will flutter to the side of the road.
5   The cricket chants in doorways and windows;
   The cicada sings amongst brambles and thorns.
The mayfly plays for only three mornings,
   Swarms of them preening their wings.
For whom do they display their fine coats,
10   Bobbing up and down as they rub themselves clean?
How long is their lifetime
   That each, in his way, exerts himself with such passionate energy?

This pessimistic attitude owes much to the writings of Chuang-tzu. But this
does not mean Juan Chi is simply repeating a time-honored theme: his obsession with the passage of time appears so often in his poems and with such
deeply felt anguish that it can only be considered one of the most pervasive
and one of the most important elements in his life and work.

8

THE PURSUIT OF IMMORTALITY

Obsessed as Juan Chi was with the passage of time, it is not surprising that there are more poems in the series devoted to the theme of immortality than to any other single subject. Whatever his final verdict was on the existence of immortals themselves, the subject obviously interested him enormously. He was not the only Chinese of his class to be interested in the subject. Immortality seeking became extraordinarily widespread at the end of the Han dynasty and probably reached its height of popularity in the third and fourth centuries, precisely during Juan Chi's own lifetime. His friend Hsi K'ang was one of the large number of contemporaries to make the pursuit of immortality his life work. In the case of Juan Chi, however, aside from the numerous poems that treat the subject, we have only one reference linking him with immortality seekers, a reference to his visit to a rather nebulous figure named Sun Teng 孫 登. We do not know when this visit took place, nor where (the sources conflict), but the accounts given are extremely interesting, and not only accord very well with what we know about Juan Chi's character and philosophical attitudes, but contradict, to a certain degree, the popular image that has grown up around him.

Since he is mentioned in a poem by Hsi K'ang ('Yu-fen shih'), Sun Teng is surely not entirely mythical. If the number of sources that contain his biography (quoted in *Chin-shu chiao-chu* 94, pp. 2a–3b) is any guide, he must indeed have been a very well known figure. I would like to quote the first part of his biography as it is given in the *Chin shu* (a good digest of earlier fragmentary sources) because it will give us some idea of what Juan Chi had in mind when he talks about 'immortals'.

> Sun Teng, whose *tzu* was Kung-ho, was a man of Kung 共 in Chi 汲 commandery.[1] He was homeless, but stayed in the mountains in the north of the commandery where he lived in a cavern in the earth that he had made for himself. In summer he wove grasses to wear as a shirt and in winter he let his hair down to cover himself. He liked to read the *I ching* and played a one-stringed zither.[2]

All those who saw him felt friendly towards him and took pleasure in his company. There was not an ounce of hatred or anger in him. He was once thrown into the water to arouse his anger, but he just came out and broke into an enormous guffaw.

From time to time he would wander among men and some of the householders he passed would set out food and clothing for him, none of which he would keep: when he had taken his leave he threw them all away.[3]

Once when he went to the mountains at I-yang[4] he was seen by some charcoal burners who knew he was not an ordinary man. But when they talked to him, he did not answer. Wen-ti [Ssu-ma Chao] heard about it and sent Juan Chi to investigate.[5]

Ssu-ma Chao became generalissimo in 255 so that Juan Chi's visit should probably be dated sometime later. In the *Chin shu* account, moreover, after Juan Chi visits Sun Teng, Hsi K'ang is said to have gone to see him. It seems that Hsi K'ang's visit (said to have lasted three years) took place from 258 to 260;[6] if this is the case, Juan Chi's should probably be dated around 257.[7] The *Chin shu* places the encounter in the mountains of I-yang, as does the *Shui-ching chu*,[8] but other sources[9] say it took place in the Su-men Mountain, near Sun Teng's usual haunts. There is no way of knowing which version is correct (if either).[10] The *Shih-shuo hsin-yü*'s account is the most complete:[11]

Infantry [Colonel] Juan's whistling[12] could be heard for hundreds of paces.

A True Man[13] unexpectedly appeared in the Su-men Mountain[14] and the woodcutters all told stories about him. Juan Chi went to have a look. He saw him crouched down, his arms about his knees, on the edge of a precipice. Juan Chi climbed the mountain, came up to him, and then sat down facing him with his legs spread out fan-wise.[15] He expatiated upon the whole of antiquity, beginning with the most ancient period, for which he exposed the Mysterious and Solitary Way of the Yellow Emperor and the Divine Husbandman,[16] and going down to an examination of the excellencies of the flourishing virtue of the Three Dynasties.[17] When he asked the True Man's opinions about it, the latter remained fiercely silent. Juan Chi went at it again, this time describing that which is beyond activity,[18] the art of perching the spirit and controlling the breath,[19] to see what the True Man would say about it. But he remained unchanged: his glassy stare hadn't budged an inch. Juan Chi then faced him and whistled for quite some time. Finally the True Man smiled and said: 'You may do that again.' Juan Chi whistled again, until he had whistled himself out, and then he retired to about halfway down the mountainside. There he heard a flowing[20] sound that seemed to be produced by several sections of flutes and drums, and the wooded valley carried on its echo. When he turned around to see what it was he saw it was the man he had just left, whistling.[21]

Whether or not the True Man was Sun Teng or an anonymous 'Master of Su-men Mountain', as Juan Chi calls him in his 'Biography of Master Great Man', is relatively unimportant: the True Man is obviously a Taoist sage, and if he is not an immortal, he is very much like one. Juan Chi has not gone to see him to become his disciple, as Hsi K'ang was to do with Sun Teng; he has gone more or less as a tourist, and a very scholarly tourist at that. He has heard of his reputation and he wants to try him out. He begins with historical chitchat, and finds that bores his host. He then changes to philosophy, to Taoist philosophy if we accept the Sung edition's text, to both Confucianism and Taoism if we accept the variant. Still no effect. As a last recourse he tries *hsiao* 嘯 , which I have translated as 'whistling'.

Like so many Chinese terms, *hsiao* has a distracting range of meanings, clustered around the basic idea of 'producing sound through puckered lips', from the lion's roar to a man's whistling, passing through vocalization, chanting or wailing. All these meanings are well attested, althouth I believe 'whistling' and 'vocalizing' seem most appropriate here. I have chosen the former for the following reasons: the *Sun Teng pieh-chuan* (quoted in *T'ai-p'ing yü-lan* 392, p. 4b) describes Juan Chi's *ch'ang-hsiao* 長 嘯 as *liao-ts'ao* 嘹 嘈 , a term descriptive of the sound of the flute; the text of the *Shih-shuo hsin-yü* itself compares Sun Teng's *hsiao* to the sound of 'flutes and drums'; and, finally, because of some remarks by Feng Yen 封 演 who in his *Feng-shih wen-chien chi* 封 氏 聞 見 記 (*c.* 800) discusses, under the rubric 'Ch'ang-hsiao', a work called 'Hsiao chih' 嘯 旨 , written by a certain Sun Kuang 孫 廣 in 765, and makes direct reference to Juan Chi's and Sun Teng's talents in this art. Sun Kuang cryptically defines *hsiao* as sound produced by '[breath] striking against the tip of the tongue' [氣] 激 于 舌 端, says it is a method of communicating with the spirits and achieving immortality, and gives a genealogy of those who learned the art, beginning with T'ai-shang lao-chün 太 上 老 君 and ending with Sun Teng and Juan Chi (Juan Chi is said to have only learned 'a small part of it, and after him it was no longer heard of').[22] This does not tell us just what kind of sound was produced. The translator of the 'Hsiao chih' as it is found in the *T'ang-tai ts'ung-shu* says (erroneously, I think) the term meant to 'chant poetry',[23] which, whatever sound it specifies, precludes whistling. But Feng Yen, towards the end of his article, remarks on the fact that the kind of *hsiao* practiced during his time differed from old usage. In his time, he says, 'the mouth was opened and the tongue curled', and the lips were neither contracted nor moved, as they were in earlier times, according to Cheng Hsüan (127–200) and Ch'eng-kung Sui 成 公 綏 (231–

273) whom he quotes.[24] These 'proofs' are not definitive, but they seem to show that, at Juan Chi's time at least, *hsiao* had the meaning 'to whistle', perhaps combined with the meaning 'to chant, wail'.[25]

Whatever *hsiao* did signify, the important thing to note is that it was an unintellectual art, probably a fairly strange kind of sound that is divorced from speech and reason. Sun Teng was not interested in history, in the examples of the ancient saints and sages, and he has gone well beyond the philosophies of action and inaction, mystical exercises and breath control. He is interested in something beyond philosophy and out of history, in something ineffable and yet of this world. Like the Ch'an masters of the T'ang dynasty who, with their eructations and physical blows, resemble him so much, he knows that the Truth is beyond words, and when Juan Chi whistles Sun Teng sees that he is not merely a pedant, but also an adept of an art that imitates nature, that he is able to control his breath so as to make it resemble the very breath of heaven (*Chuang-tzu* 2). And when Juan Chi descends the mountain, Sun Teng shows him what a real True Man can do, what a man who has identified himself with no partial philosophy, no historical figures, with nothing less than Nature herself, can do: his whistling is the very breath of Nature, Wordsworth's 'among the solitary hills, low breathings . . . '.

One of the most interesting things about this famous meeting between Juan Chi and Sun Teng is that it presents the former first as a traditional scholar, and only afterwards as a Taoist whistler. This description comes closer, I think, to the complex truth about Juan Chi than the portraits made of him as a pure nihilist, an unceremonial clown or an untrammelled Taoist adept. But immortality-seeking Taoism did play an important role in his life, as we shall see now, in reading the poems that take the immortals as their theme.

These poems represent over one quarter of all the 'Yung-huai' series. A superficial reading might suggest that Juan Chi'a main preoccupation in them was really the pursuit of immortality, that like so many other educated men on both sides of the ancient world in the third century A.D., he was turning wholeheartedly to religion as a way of escaping from the pain of daily life. As usual, such a straightforward, uncomplicated interpretation of his works would fail to do complete justice to them. The cult of the immortals and the search for immortality did, I believe, play a role in China somewhat similar to the role played by the numerous religions that invaded the Mediterranean world at the end of antiquity. Appearing relatively late in the history of Chinese thought, probably no earlier than the third century B.C.,[26] the search for immortals and for immortality became extremely widespread at the end of the Han, as archaeological reports from China show us over and over again, and immortals appear, with increasing regularity, in the literature that preceded and followed Juan Chi. He must have been aware of this popularity and, I believe, more than aware of it: he was tempted by the pursuit of immortality, profoundly attracted by the mystical bliss that the immortals enjoyed far from the world of men. But in the majority of his poems on immortals and immortality, he is using them more as allegorical symbols than as expressions of his 'innermost thoughts'. In so doing he is following contemporary and traditional usage. However important immortality-seeking had become, the majority of the Chinese intellectuals, then as now, did not really believe in it, and when they refer to it in their poems, as they so often do, it is usually to express their distaste for the real world, their unbearable sadness in the face of the injustice or misery they see about them. There are exceptions (Hsi K'ang being the most famous), but in most of the works of contemporary poets (including the greatest of them all, the Ts'ao family, Ts'ao Ts'ao, Ts'ao P'i and Ts'ao Chih) the evocation of the immortals serves an allegorical purpose.[27] In the majority of Juan Chi's poems on immortals, then, we must be alert to allegory. But there is a small number where the allegory seems not to account for everything in the poem, where the search for the immortals, or at least for some mystical bliss such as they enjoy, seems to be real and not allegorical, and the pathetic poems describing his doubts about the existence of immortals seem to me to be, paradoxically, a proof that they were not simply allegorical figures to him: does one put into doubt the existence of a figure that one deliberately and gratuitously chooses as allegorical?[28]

I have arranged these poems into three groups, the first group in this chapter and the two following in the next chapter. In the first group (ten poems) the immortals play an allegorical role most clearly; in the next (four poems) Juan Chi seems to be describing the kind of permanent bliss the immortals enjoy for its own sake; and in the last group (nine poems) he expresses his doubts and his attempts to find some substitute for immortality. In the first group he seems to be evoking the immortals and their haunts as some kind of ideal never-never land where he could escape from the ravages of time (and politics).

The first poem in the first group is one of the most anguished in the entire series.

24

My grief is so deep it has fettered my will;
    I live in anguish, as if constantly frightened:
Before my pleasures have ended
    The red sun will fall headlong in the west.
5   The crickets are at my window,
      And the cicada cries in the courtyard.

My own passions have not yet found their peace:
   Who would say he knew my true heart?
I would like to be a bird among the clouds
10   And, when a thousand miles away, give one cry of pain!
The three magic mushrooms spread over the Isle of Ying;
   A distant roaming there can give long life.

The crickets in line 5 are the harbingers of autumn (*Shih ching* 154); the cicada in line 6, the symbol of ephemeral life (*Chuang-tzu* 1, Legge translation, p. 166). The 'three magic mushrooms' (perhaps some kind of hallucinogenic mushroom or mushrooms) are variously enumerated (*Pao-p'u-tzu* 11, 'Immortals' medicines', alone gives two different series), but they all seem to give immortality ('rising to heaven in broad daylight', *Pao-p'u-tzu* 11, p. 47) or at least a 'longevity of one thousand years' (*ibid.*). The Isle of Ying is one of the three islands inhabited by immortals in the Eastern Sea (*Shih chi* 6, p. 40). 'Distant roaming' (line 12) is the title of a poem in the *Ch'u tz'u* describing a mystical journey to heaven.

Although the poem should of course be read against the background of contemporary politics, it is not simply a cry of anguish for a falling dynasty, as Chiang Shih-yüeh would have it, or the doleful plea of a distant courtier to his unhearing sovereign, as Ch'en Tso-ming believes. It may be both, but what it actually says is even more complicated. In the first six lines Juan Chi's anguish seems to come from his perception of the all too rapid passage of time. But in lines 7 and 8 the poem becomes more complicated. Huang Chieh and Ch'en Tso-ming (if I read his commentary correctly) interpret line 7 as: 'I have no bosom friend'. *Hsiang-hao* 相 好 means, literally, 'to like one another', and often has the meaning of 'friend, intimate'. But Juan Chi places the word *wei* 未 before the two characters, meaning that they must be read as adverb and verb: literally 'my heart (seat of the intelligence) and my entrails (seat of the passions) do not like one another'. For some unknown reason he is at war with himself: his intelligence tells him one thing, his affections another. Shall we attempt to describe his inner conflict more precisely? To say, for example, that his intelligence (heart) says to join the Ssu-ma and his entrails (affections — what we would call his 'heart'!) tell him to sacrifice himself for his sovereign? But the very next line (line 8) seems to tell us not to indulge in this kind of analysis. His anguish is unfathomable and he seems to yearn for some kind of apotheosis, some way of leaving the world, of transcending it, its temporality and his own inner conflicts, whatever these latter may be. The last two couplets are of course a reference to an apotheosis as an immortal (often spoken of as winged creatures), but his doleful cry shows us his flight from the world is not a blissful rising up to the immortals' paradise, but an allegorical quitting of an unbearable world.

In the following poem it is again the perception of the passage of time that seems to drive the poet to flee from the world.

3

A path forms under good trees,
 Under the peach and plum of the eastern orchard.
But the winds of autumn will blow upon flying bean leaves,
 And that is when decay sets in.
5 The brightest flowers become haggard and thin;
 Brambles and thorns grow in the hall.
Whip up your horse and leave!
 Go up to the foot of the Western Mountains!
One cannot even preserve oneself;
10 How much less can one cherish one's wife and children?
Stiff frost covers the grass in the plain:
 The twilight of the year draws to its close.

The commentators (Li Shan, Liu Lü, Ch'en Hang and others) believe this to be a lament for the impossible political conditions in Wei China. The Western Mountain is another name for Mt Shou-yang, where Po I and Shu Ch'i found refuge so as not to serve the usurping Chou dynasty. The first two lines, moreover, seem clearly to refer to an often quoted metaphor which compares good officials to peach and plum trees: 'The peach and plum do not talk, yet a path forms under them', made by people coming to see their flowers and gather their fruits (*Han shu* 54, p. 2469). The good, sincere and loyal official, according to this interpretation of the poem, must be aware that the dynasty is falling and that to avoid serving a new one he must flee to the Western Mountain and await death in eremitic retirement.

The Western Mountain, however, can also be understood as the K'un-lun, since they are, indeed, the 'westernmost' mountains in the empire. Juan Chi himself unmistakably uses the term in this way in Poem 82 when he speaks of '. . . plants of the Western Mountains/Pearly tree coral and cinnabar grain'. This gives the poem a completely new facet of meaning: the succession of seasons described (spring and summer in lines 1 and 2, autumn in lines 3–6, winter in the last two lines) makes us feel the passage of time and the approach of old age and death. The escape to the Western Mountains is to the land of Hsi-wang-mu and of the immortals where one may attempt to achieve long life, for in our world no one is safe. Line 10 may also contain an allusion to a phrase attributed to Emperor Wu of the Han dynasty. When the latter was informed of the legendary Yellow Emperor's apotheosis to the land of the immortals accompanied by seventy of his retinue, Emperor Wu exclaimed: 'In truth, if I could do as the Yellow Emperor did, I should leave my wives and children as easily as I take off my slippers!' (*Shih chi* 28, p. 66). But the order of the lines in the poem suggests that Juan Chi's withdrawal is again allegorical. If the last couplet had been placed after line 6, we might feel his escape to the Western Mountain was successful; placed as it is, the poem makes us feel that all is lost and that night is upon us.

The very similar Poem 57, with its reference to Jade Mountain in the penultimate line, supports a reading of the Western Mountain as the K'un-lun in Poem 3.

57

A violent wind shakes the surrounding wilds;
    Gyrating clouds cast the corners of my hall into shadow.
For whom are the bed curtains prepared,
    And who will lean against the backrest and staff?
5   One does not have to be a brilliant sage
    To see [the sun has already set] in the hedges!
The men of the world are so deaf, so short-sighted:
    Where do they think they are going, in their blindness?
I will fly here and there with the wind,
10   Far, far away from my old home,
Leaving my banners below Jade Mountain,
    Rejecting both shame and renown.

The first two lines of this poem may have political overtones, suggesting calumny and changing allegiances, but they also simply suggest a spell of bad weather, a forewarning of the dark months of the year and of the annual 'death' of nature. The backrests and staff are used more particularly by old people. Backrests were the equivalent of armchairs in chairless pre-Sung China (and in traditional Japan). They, staves and bed curtains were all given to older officials by the emperor as presents of esteem (cf. for example *Hou Han-shu chi-chieh* 37, p. 1331). Line 6 speaks only of 'mulberries and elms'. These trees were both used as hedges and have become a set phrase for 'old age', i.e. that epoch of life when 'the sun, just about to set, is still in the hedges'.[29] In line 11, Jade Mountain is the abode of the queen of the immortals, Hsi-wang-mu (*Shan-hai ching* 2, pp. 19ab).[30] The whole poem thus describes a flight from politics, and more precisely from aging in the world of politics. The last line preaches an indifference to political life that perhaps contains an echo of Confucius (*Lun yü* 15, 24). The sentiment is, basically, Taoist, but it is typical of Juan Chi to use two terms consecrated by Confucius: his 'rejection of praise and blame' is perhaps inspired by a purely orthodox Confucian desire to avoid commitment to a corrupt or usurping government.

Wang K'ai-yün and Huang Chieh both think Juan Chi is talking about the fall of the Wei. The former thinks he is retroactively stigmatizing Ts'ao Shuang's and Ho Yen's 'blindness' and the latter (more convincingly) the great officials who accept Wei's gifts without realizing the state is about to fall. Chiang Shih-yüeh sees the poem as a satire against Cheng Ch'ung 鄭 冲 (d. 271), a high official who had served both the Wei and the Chin and who received imperial gifts, including a backrest, staff and bed curtains, from the Chin rulers in 270 (*Chin-shu chiao-chu* 33, p. 10ab). But Juan Chi died seven years before Cheng Ch'ung received these gifts! Chiang Shih-yüeh's anachronism should remind us how perilous these attempts at identification are. The first two lines of the poem alert us to satirical intent, and the escape to Jade Mountain may be an allegorical way of simply escaping from the world. On one level, his leaving behind his banners and his rejection of shame and renown can be read as a joyous Taoist renunciation of worldly glory; but on a deeper level it is also a pathetic retreat from a corrupt and inhospitable world.

In the following short poem Juan Chi again turns to the immortals to escape from the rigors of time and politics.

50

The cold dew hardens into frost;
    The flowering grasses turn to straw.
Who would call a sage wise?
    How can one bear to understand [this truth]?
5   Let us ride on the clouds and summon Sung and Ch'iao,
    And breathe in and out for ever!

Line 2 perhaps echoes the 'Li sao' (*Ch'u tz'u*, p. 32): 'Why have the fragrant flowers of days gone by/Changed into worthless mugwort?' Why have the good courtiers of yore all given way to today's mediocrities? But the line also means just what it says: the frosts of autumn kill summer's grasses. Again it is the passage of time that the sage must recognize if he hopes 'to be able to stay for long' (*I ching*, 'Hsi tz'u', Legge translation, p. 349). The only solution is apotheosis as an immortal: Sung is Ch'ih Sung-tzu and Ch'iao, Wang-tzu Ch'iao. Breathing exercises formed a very important part of Taoist regimen. 'Breath' being the basic vital constituent of our bodies, breath control and breathing exercises could bring immortality and completely replace more ordinary nourishment.

In the preceding poem and in those that follow the theme of time becomes almost obsessional; political concern is almost always present, but it is attenuated in many of the poems which follow, raising Juan Chi's preoccupation with the theme to an almost metaphysical level: time becomes an abstract force, carrying away all before it.

4

The Heavenly Horses are bred in the northwest,
　　But, from of old, they follow the eastern road.
Since time itself has no stop
　　How could we keep riches and honors for ever?
5　　The pure dew covers the swamp orchids;
　　Stiff frost wets the prairie grass.
What in the morning is lovely youth,
　　In the evening becomes hateful old age.
Who but Wang-tzu Chin
10　　Could keep his beauty for ever?

'Heavenly Horses', *t'ien-ma* 天 馬, were a breed of Central Asian horses that were imported from Ta-yüan (now in the Central Asian Uzbek Republic of the Soviet Union), what was then called the 'Western antipodes', *hsi-chi* 西 極.[31] They are the subject of a song dated 101 B.C. written in commemoration of the execution of the king of Ta-yüan by the general Li Kuang-li (*Han shu* 22, pp. 1060–61) and the sending of some three thousand of these excellent, 'blood-sweating' horses to the Han court. By his wording, it is clear that Juan Chi has the Han poem in mind here.

But just what is the place of these 'Heavenly Horses' in Juan Chi's poem? They are the symbol of the unexpected changes in our lives, animals who are transported against their will from one end of the world to the other. 'How much faster does the change from rich to poor come, or from noble to base!', as Shen Yüeh puts it. The horses' journey thus symbolizes all the other changes described in the poem: the dew of spring which changes to frost in autumn, youthful beauty which changes to ugly old age. Three of the couplets in the poem are contrasting: the northwest and the east of lines 1–2, the dew and the frost (spring and autumn) in lines 5–6, morning and evening in lines 7–8. The word in line 3 I have translated as 'time' is actually 'spring and autumn', another contrast. The whole poem is thus made up of very strong spatial and temporal contrasts which infuse the poem with the tremendous sense of change that threatens our life.

If the poem is satirical, it is so on only the most abstract level, that is, by its emphasis on change, it hints at the imminent fall of the Wei dynasty. Ch'en Hang believes that the arrival of the Heavenly Horses from distant Central Asia symbolizes the long laid plans of the Ssu-ma (he of course mentions the fact that the second character of the family name 'Ssu-ma' means 'horse'). Ku Chih, however, believes the poem describes, in hidden allegory, the sad life of Fang, the Prince of Ch'i (Ts'ao Fang). His attempt to prove this (in which he links together this poem with Poems 5 and 10) verges on parody.

The following poem, although longer and more complicated, is again concerned almost exclusively with the passage of time.

32

The brightness of morning reaches its height but once,
And then the brilliant sun suddenly darkens in the west.
How fast it leaves here!
Is autumn already upon us?
5   Man's life is like dust or dew:
The Way of Heaven stays for ever far, far away.
When Ching of Ch'i climbed the mountain
His tears fell in floods down his cheeks.
When Saint Confucius stood near the long stream
10   He lamented that [time] passed as quickly as the floating [waves].
I cannot reach those who have gone,
Nor can I detain those yet to come.
I would like to climb T'ai-hua Mountain
And roam about its crest with Sung-tzu.
15   The Old Fisherman understood the sorrows of this world:
He rode with the current, floating in his light skiff.

In line 8 Duke Ching of Ch'i (died 490 B.C.) is shown as a man anguished at the thought of death, crying at the distant view of his capital from the top of Mount Niu when he thought he must soon die and leave it (cf. *Yen-tzu ch'un-ch'iu* 1, p. 24, 7, p. 178). There are two allusions in line 9. The first is to *Lun yü* 9, 16. The translation of this passage of the *Lun yü* is contested. The interpretation of Sun Ch'o (late fourth century), the closest in time to Juan Chi, would give: 'When the Master was on the bank of a river he said: "[The years] pass like this, not ceasing night or day".' The second allusion is to the *fu* by Lady Pan in *Han shu* 97B, p. 3987: 'Man lives in only one generation and then passes away suddenly as if floating by.' Lines 11 and 12 are a near citation from the *Ch'u tz'u*, 'Yüan yu' (Hawkes translation, p. 81): 'Those who have gone before I should never see;/And those yet to come I could never know of.' T'ai-hua Mountain in line 13 is Hua-shan, the sacred mountain of the west in Shensi, one of the most famous and beautiful of the Chinese mountains. 'Sung-tzu' in line 13 is the immortal Ch'ih Sung-tzu and the 'Old Fisherman' in line 15 is the hero of a short piece in the *Ch'u tz'u* that bears his name (Hawkes translation, pp. 90–91). He preaches compromise or retirement in troubled times.

The 'suddenness' and rapid 'flow' of time is again the ostensible main subject of this recondite poem, made up of familiar quotations and allusions. But there is surely an under-current of politics here as well. The slight change in the quotation from the 'Yüan yu' in line 12 – 'detaining' those who come instead of 'hearing' of them -- could again be interpreted as a satire aimed against the usurpers. Both Fang Tung-shu and Wang K'ai-yün interpret the poem as a satire, and the last couplet suggests they are right. Ch'ih Sung-tzu is probably allegorical here, symbolic of the flight from active political commitment (as in *Han-shu* 40, p. 2037). And yet, even if we interpret the work as satirical, the passage of time remains an extremely important aspect of it, and when Juan Chi roams with Sung-tzu or floats in the Fisherman's skiff, he seems to be vanquishing time as well as withdrawing from the rigors of politics.

Poem 35 continues this same meditation on, perhaps, a more abstract plane: there is no Old Fisherman telling us to leave the world only in troubled times. This poem states categorically in the very first lines that the world *is* trouble!

35

Oh! How confusing is the business of this world,
    And how little time man has to cope with it all!
Our years of vigor are carried off so fast:
    Early dew awaiting the morning sun!
5   I would like to seize Hsi Ho's reins in my hands
    So that the bright sun would no longer move its rays.
But the road to the Heavenly Steps is cut off,
    And there is no bridge to the distant Sky River.
I will wash my hair on the shores of Yang Valley,
10   Roam afar on the slopes of Mount K'un,
Climb upon the immortals' rocky mountains
    And gather the fragrance of the orchids in autumn.
Why should I fight in the world of our times?
    In the Summit of Summits one can soar without end!

Hsi Ho in line 5 is the sun's charioteer (cf. H. Maspero in *Journal asiatique* 204 (1924), pp. 29–37). The first usage of the term 'Heavenly Steps', *t'ien-chieh* 天 階, seems to be in Chang Heng's 'Tung-ching fu' (*Wen hsüan* 3, p. 32b) where it means 'the imperial throne'. Later usage gives it a more literal, astronomical meaning, as Juan Chi obviously does here. But there is always the possibility of a double meaning. The 'Sky River' is, more literally, the 'Cloudy Han', that is, the Milky Way. In lines 9 and 10, the sun rises in the east, in Yang Valley (*Shu ching*, 'Yao tien', Legge translation, p. 18), and sets beyond the K'un-lun, in the far west. The 'Summit of Summits', or 'Great Summit', *t'ai-chi* 太 極, is an important philosophical term appearing in the *I ching* ('Hsi tz'u', Legge translation, p. 548) signifying the Absolute which contains both the *yin* and the *yang* and is the ultimate ontological entity from which the manifold beings take their existence.

The poem is constructed almost exactly like a sonnet in which each quatrain states a philosophical position or, more modestly, a point of view, and the final couplet sums up and chooses. The first quatrain thus presents a pessimistic view of the 'world of affairs' and the realization that the passage of time is robbing us of our youth and vigor. The second quatrain bemoans the fact that we are earthbound, unable to rise into heaven and, by some epoch-making heroic action similar to that of the mythical heroes of the *Shan-hai ching*, stop the sun and, concomitantly, the passage of time. The third quatrain is the alternative to the second: since such heroic action is impossible, let us attempt to prolong our life like the immortals, by some distant roaming in their magic mountains. The final couplet sums up: secular, temporal, worldly life is not worth the battle; a mystical flight into the Absolute[32] is the best solution.

Chiang Shih-yüeh, Ch'en Tso-ming and Ch'en Hang all feel that Juan Chi's desire to stop the sun in his journey is a way of 'extending the Wei dynasty's reign'. The ambiguity of the term 'Heavenly Steps', of course, underlines this aspect of the poem. But it no more authorizes us to consider the work as a political satire than the mystical wording of the last line authorizes us to state categorically that Juan Chi has decided to devote his life to spiritual meditation. His heroic actions and evocation of the immortals may simply be an allegorical renunciation of worldly life in the tradition of the *Ch'u tz'u*.

Poem 10, while it ends by making allusion to the immortals and their arts, is mainly concerned with another theme we have seen often in Juan Chi's poetry: youthful prodigality.

10

There are many strange dances in the Northern Quarter
    And subtle sounds on the banks of the P'u,
Where frivolous, idle playboys
    Drift along with the tide of prevailing fashion.
5   They take the short cuts and follow narrow roads,
    Striving hard as they haste to debauchery.
How could they see Wang-tzu Ch'iao
    Riding the clouds, circling above Teng Forest?
Only the art of prolonging life
10   Can calm my heart!

The last, wicked emperor of the Shang, Chou, is said (*Shih chi* 3, p. 26) to have 'had his music master Chüan compose new lascivious music, dances for the Northern Quarter and beguiling [?] airs.' Just what the 'Northern Quarter' was originally is not clear. R. des Rotours (*Courtisanes chinoises à la fin des T'ang* (Paris, 1968), pp. 49–50) associates it with a place spoken of in *Shih chi* 28, p. 14. In the *Wen hsüan* it is spoken of as a type or title of music, or, as here, as a place where such music was played. In T'ang Ch'ang-an it was the name of the gay quarter. Line 2 contains an allusion to the kind of music played in the country near the P'u River, Shantung, said to have had a corrupting influence. It was 'music that would doom a state'; cf. *Li chi* 17 ('Yüeh chi'), Couvreur vol. 2, p. 49; *Han Fei-tzu* 3, p. 43. The 'short cuts' and 'narrow roads' in line 5 contrast, of course, with the true Way of the saints, the *tao*. The Teng Forest of line 8 was formed from the staff of K'ua-fu who threw it there before he died of thirst in his race with the sun (*Shan-hai ching* 8, p. 2b).

This poem again looks like a satire against the flaming youth of third-century Lo-yang, although it may even be a personal reminiscence of Juan Chi's own early dissipation. The poet contrasts the ephemeral frivolity of the youthful playboys with the eternity of the immortals, his 'only consolation'. His choice of the Teng Forest as a background for Wang-tzu Ch'iao's aerial loopings is particularly interesting. Teng Forest is a monument to a man who attempted to win a race with the sun, that is, in Juan Chi's own imagery (Poem 35), with time: Wang-tzu Ch'iao transcends the Forest and he transcends Time, the Time that the frivolous youths are so energetically killing.

The critics differ only in their understanding of to whom line 7 refers. Li Shan and Chiang Shih-yüeh make it a general statement meaning, in effect: 'Wang-tzu Ch'iao cannot be seen/ . . . /But his method of prolonging life exists/And it can comfort my heart.' Wu Ju-lun says the last four lines have to be reversed: 'Only the arts of prolonging life/Could comfort me/But I cannot see Wang-tzu Ch'iao/Flying above Teng Forest.' He is thus expressing doubts about the existence of immortality. Ho Cho and Wu Ch'i have still another interpretation, believing Wang-tzu Ch'iao symbolizes a kind of studious and serious Confucianist (cf. Poem 65) that the young and frivolous blades in the first six lines could not hope to 'see'. It is the ambiguity of the Chinese language that permits these contrasting interpretations. The last four lines should probably be understood without definite pronouns ('How could *one* see . . . ') and leave the reader in doubt: 'Under the conditions described in the first six lines, how could Wang-tzu Ch'iao be seen . . . Only the art of prolonging life could comfort my heart.' (The last pronoun is explicit, but could be read in the plural.) Whatever interpretation one gives to the poem, Juan Chi is here contrasting worldly dissipation to a life in retreat from the world; he accords a strong priority to the 'art of prolonging life' and this is important, whether one interprets the poem on the allegorical level ('I am so disgusted with the world that only retreat from it can comfort me') or takes it for what it actually says.

The last two poems in this group are again on the borderline between allegory and true concern with the search for immortality.

15

Years ago, in my early teens,
   My aims were lofty, my loves the Books of the Canon.
I wore coarse clothing, but my ideals were precious:
   I tried to vie with Yen and Min.
5 I opened my window to look out at the surrounding land,
   Climbed the heights and gazed towards those I was thinking of.
Tumuli covered the hill crests:
   Ten thousand generations sharing a single moment!
After a thousand autumns, ten thousand years,
10   Where had their glory gone?
It was then I understood Hsien-men-tzu
   And now, sobbing, I mock myself dolefully.

The words 'in my early teens' (literally, 'thirteen or fourteen') in line 1, associated with the word 'aims' in line 2, make one think immediately of *Lun yü* 2, 4, where Confucius says: 'When I was fourteen my aim was to study.' The next line is almost word for word from *Lao-tzu* 70: 'The Saint wears coarse cloth clothing and carries jade within his breast.' Yen and Min are Yen Hui and Min Sun (Min Tzu-ch'ien), two of Confucius's most esteemed disciples. They seem to be 'those' he 'was thinking of' in line 6, according to Huang Chieh. Hsien-men-tzu in the penultimate line is a Taoist immortal, perhaps the earliest to appear in a historical work (*Shih chi* 6, p. 45). His name means 'Master Tomb-door' (cf. *Shih chi* 6, p. 69) and the penultimate line could be read: 'It was then I understood the Master of the Tomb-door'. (There are many variants, the most important being *ling* 令 for 今 in the last line.) There are two words indicating time in the poem, in the first line ('years ago') and in the last line ('now', if we refuse the variant). The tense of the intermediate lines is left vague. If we keep the past tense until the penultimate line (with Frodsham and Ch'eng), we must believe his 'understanding' of Hsien-men-tzu, occasioned by his view of the tomb-clad hills, occurred when he was thirteen or fourteen; if, on the contrary, we begin the present tense earlier (in line 5 with von Zach or in line 7 with Watson, for example), this 'understanding' can be considered to be taking place at the writing of the poem or only a short time earlier. Poetically, there are advantages and disadvantages to either alternative, but it should be stressed that the Chinese leaves the tense undetermined.

The poem has been understood as a 'conversion' to immortality-seeking Taoism (Frodsham and Ch'eng, Ho Ch'i-min). According to this interpretation, the view of the tombs that seem to contain all of Time gathered up in a single moment (line 8), reminds the poet that worldly glory is transient and not, as the Confucianists believe, 'imperishable'. This realization makes the poet understand what Hsien-men-tzu, a Taoist immortality-seeker, was actually getting at, and he finds he can only laugh at his youthful *naïveté*.

But there is another, quite different, view of the meaning of the poem. The difference arises from the interpretation of the role of the Taoist immortal in it. Ho Cho (followed by von Zach and Chang Chih-yüeh, p. 81) and Wu Ch'i believe that Hsien-men-tzu is evoked allegorically, as the symbol of a man seeking to flee a corrupt world. 'Upon the advent of the cruel Ch'in dynasty,' says Ho Cho, Hsien-men-tzu 'only put on the spurious guise of immortality seeking' so that he could flee the world. For Wu Ch'i 'the true sense of the poem is in the word "vie" put after [in the Chinese] Yen and Min' (i.e. he really does want to be a perfect Confucianist).

I believe both these positions are unsatisfactory; they both fail to take into account aspects of the poem. The critics who see it as pure political satire must ignore the striking lines 7—10. Juan Chi insists upon the fact that his meditation is on an almost metaphysical level, on the meaning of Time itself, not on the vicissitudes of a passing dynasty. Those who see the poem as a religious conversion fail to take into account the subtleties of the very rich last line. The words all three translators render 'out loud', *'laut'*, *chiao-chiao* 嗷 嗷, is an onomatopoetic doublet, that is to say, the translator's despair. The only way to attempt to find some vague approximation of what the author may have meant when he used one of these doublets is to look into the contexts in which other authors have used it. Most (and above all *Chuang-tzu* 18, Legge translation, 2, p. 5) use it to describe 'the sound of crying'. Hsieh Ling-yün uses it to describe 'the sound of apes screaming in the night' 嗷 嗷 夜 猿 啼, and Ts'ao Chih 'the sound of a bird searching for its flock' 嗷 嗷 鳴索羣. 'Out loud' is a meaning created for Juan Chi's line; it satisfies no other context of the doublet I have seen, and I don't believe it can simply mean 'out loud' in the line. It must carry with it a nuance (at least) of sadness. The word translated 'laugh', *ch'ih* 嗤, too, is 'laugh' only in the sense of to laugh at someone, to scorn or ridicule: it is not a mystical Taoist guffaw, or a hearty, self-satisfied chuckle at what an idiot he had been when he was young and naïve. The sadness of his 'laughter' casts a shadow on the entire poem, makes us realize that this is no ordinary 'religious conversion', no joyful acceptance of a new way of life. It shows that Juan Chi had failed to resolve his 'contradictions', that his realization of man's mortality has made him see how shallow his youthful enthusiasms were, but it has perhaps not replaced them entirely. Sadness and unresolved contradictions are the hallmarks of

Juan Chi's final couplets, as a syncretic view of Confucian ethics and Taoist metaphisics is the hallmark of his philosophy. Thus neither of the two views of this poem seem to do it full justice: Hsien-men-tzu does not represent simply a man who has fled society to escape a cruel government, nor does he signify an unqualified acceptance of immortality-seeking Taoism by the poet.

The following poem seems to contradict a good deal of what I have just said and to present Juan Chi as a real Taoist convert. But we must again look more closely into what is in fact a very subtle poem.

40

When the Great Origin gave birth to the Two Aspects
    And the Four Symbols set in motion the celestial sphere,
The shining sun spread forth its warming essence
    And the pale moon let fall its luminous rays.
5   The sundial's shadow follows the bright revolutions [of the heavens]
          over and over again,
    But how frail, alas, is the life of man!
It seems to flit by, like dust carried off by the wind,
    Or to disappear suddenly, like rainbow vapors drying in the sun.
What I would like is to prolong my years:
10   Glory and honors do not impress me one whit!
An-ch'i walked on the road to heaven;
    Sung-tzu lived apart from the world.
How can I get wings to soar into the sky,
    To veer about, mounting the cloud banks?
15   Oh! Confucius, what was your aim?
    What would you do among the wild men of the east?

The cosmogony of the first two lines is inspired by the *I ching* ('Hsi t'zu', Legge translation, p. 373): ' . . . the Summit of Summits (*t'ai-chi* 太 極) . . . produces the Two Aspects: the Two Aspects produce the Four Symbols'. The 'Great Origin' is another epithet for the Summit of Summits, the cosmos in the state of primeval unity. The 'Two Aspects' are the first cosmogonic differentiation of this unity, either heaven and earth or the *yin* and the *yang* (or both). The 'Four Symbols' are a later hypostasis, usually defined as the four seasons. An-ch'i and (Ch'ih) Sung-tzu are immortals (cf. *Lieh-hsien chuan*, Kaltenmark translation, pp. 115–18, 35–42). The terms used in the evocation of Confucius in the penultimate line allude to his eulogy pronounced by Duke Ai (*Tso chuan*, Ai 16, Legge translation, p. 846).

The development of the poem, until the last two lines, is very clear. The first eight lines show, by using ancient ideas of cosmology (and of the movements of the spheres), how man's life, subject to the regular movements of the sun, is of short duration, and the next six ask how one can become an immortal to escape from death. Line 10 states that the poet is indifferent to worldly glory, that he only seeks for Taoist immortality.

But what is the meaning of the last two lines? The allusion is to the following conversation of Confucius (*Lun yü* 9, 13):

> The Master wanted to live among the nine tribes of the eastern barbarians. Someone said: 'They are rough; how could you do such a thing?' The Master said: 'If a Sage dwelt among them they would not be rough.'

The usual explanation of this conversation puts it in relation to *Lun yü* 5, 6, in which Confucius says he is going to get on a raft and float on the sea because his doctrine is not practiced in China (Juan Chi alludes to this conversation in Poem 66). If Confucius wants to live among the eastern barbarians, then, it is not to civilize them by his presence, but to escape from the bad governments in China. Juan Chi is asking Confucius why he wants to leave China, why he has chosen such an uncomfortable and, especially, unrewarding method of escaping tyranny when he could be 'prolonging his years'. By bringing in Confucius and his desire to leave the world in these last two lines, Juan Chi is in fact enriching his poem with a whole new set of resonances: immortality seeking, by analogy, becomes another method for leaving an oppressive government, and, at the same time, becomes less simply the search for long life. The whole poem takes on a satirical air and the ostensible incomprehension of Confucius's motives becomes, in reality, something quite different. Wu Ju-lun has said, about this poem: 'Juan Chi's desire to seek immortality is the same as Confucius's desire to live among the barbarians. The last two lines seem to scold Confucius, but, in fact, in them Juan Chi expresses his commiseration for him.' For Wu Ju-lun, Juan Chi's 'scolding' of Confucius is ironic, and profoundly pathetic, and the whole poem becomes a veiled plea for the renunciation of a corrupt world.

The poem is an extremely interesting one from the point of view of intellectual history. Whether Juan Chi's basic idea is allegorical or straightforward, the fact that he pities Confucius for not attempting to 'prolong his years' is significant. 'Prolonging one's years' meant searching for immortality, attempting to attain to the state of Taoist bliss that is really a form of mystical experience; it was the closest thing third-century Chinese intellectuals had to a religious conversion. Whether or not Juan Chi himself took the leap into a religious life, into a religious renunciation of the world, is not the question here. The very fact that he asked Confucius why he did not is an exciting one in Chinese intellectual history.

9

MYSTICISM

In the following group of poems Juan Chi comes as close as he ever does to writing pure religious poetry. In the previous chapters we read a number of poems that preach against excess, against too much money, too much power, against too much high living. Here (with the exception of the last poem) we see this dislike of excess carried over into religious philosophy; the poems preach renunciation of worldly pursuits to attain to mystical aims. The first poem, as Fang Tung-shu says, seems to be a set of unrelated couplets and quatrains until it is analysed.

76

How can we study the art of high-speed driving
    When [even] Tung-yeh [Chi] lay exhausted at the side of the road?
The line goes deep, the fishes sink deeper in the gulf;
    When the arrow is threaded, the birds soar higher.
5   I shall float away in my light boat
    Gliding along where nothing can be seen.
Mutual aid in fact helps no one:
    Let's reject and forget one another [like the fish] in the lakes and
        streams!
It is difficult for me to make my face urbane and seductive:
10   My constant aim is a well composed countenance.
[Ch'ih] Sung-[tzu] and [Wang-tzu] Ch'iao know how to prolong their
        years:
    In their state of mystical vagueness, verily, they go on without end!

Ch'iu-chia, in the first line, is glossed as the 'art of chariot driving' in a fragment from *Chuang-tzu* reproduced by Li Shan in *Wen hsüan* 6, p. 21a, and more exactly by Yen Shih-ku in *Han shu* 22, p. 1048, as 'driving horses so they leap up, as if they were flying'. The story of the disciple who could not learn to drive from his master for three years, but who dreamt of the method himself told fragmentarily in the *Chuang-tzu* citation, is told entirely in the *Lü-shih ch'un-ch'iu* 24, p. 314. Tung-yeh Chi 東野稷, in the second line, an expert charioteer, drove his horses too fast and exhausted them; cf. *Chuang-tzu* 19, Legge translation, 2, p. 23, and *Han-shih wai-chuan* 2, Hightower translation, pp. 49–51. Line 3 refers to the practice of threading arrows used in hunting fowl. The cords threaded in the arrow shafts were meant to become entangled in the fowl's wings and cause it to fall. Lines 2 to 8 are inspired by *Chuang-tzu* 6, but line 7 presents some difficulties. The words I have translated by 'mutual aid', *ch'ui-hsü* 吹 噓, have two other meanings: 'to breathe out' (or perhaps 'huff and puff') and 'to recommend for promotion to a higher authority'. The following line refers to *Chuang-tzu* 6, Legge translation, p. 242: 'When the springs dry up, the fish collect on dry land and spit upon one another to keep wet, and dampen one another with their slime. It would be better for them to forget one another in the rivers and lakes.' The words translated 'mutual aid' thus may keep some of their original 'huff and puff' meaning, but to change one of the characters, as Huang Chieh suggests, so that it will mean 'to spit', would make the allusion to *Chuang-tzu* more explicit, but it would also deprive the words of their supplementary resonances. The 'state of mystical vagueness' in the last line translates the words *huang-hu* 恍 惚 used in *Lao-tzu* 21 as an epithet for the *tao*.

The first ten lines of this poem are relatively clear; the last two, irremediably and, I think, deliberately obscure. Lines 1 and 2 set the tone: excessively fast driving (and living) can lead only to exhaustion. The remedy? Hide, like the animals in lines 3 and 4; retire, like the hermit in lines 5 and 6. Juan Chi will keep away from society (lines 7–8) where one must be well-dressed and charming (line 9); he will cultivate a non-committal, bland, enigmatic, 'extremely prudent' persona and hide behind it (line 10). The last two lines seem to describe the result of this hiding, this disappearance into the bosom of nature: the achievement of some kind of immortality which would allow one, once one has purged oneself of worldly ambitions, to go on, like Wang-tzu Ch'iao and Ch'ih Sung-tzu, in a vague mystical oneness with nature, without end. But these last two lines need not be read as the result of the preceding verses; they perhaps describe still another, superior and contrasting state, one to which the previous lines lead, but which are reserved for an élite.

I believe the following extremely difficult poem similarly presents the mystical experience as a way out, an escape from an inhospitable world.

70

If we are sad, it is because we have emotions;
    If we had no emotions, neither would we have any sadness.
As long as no nets ensnare us
    What need have we for myriad-acred domains?
5   A swirling wind brushes against the highest regions of the air;

The rainbow vapors attract [the rays] that dry them out.
My heart has become ashes and lodges in a withered dwelling-place;
Why, then, should I look back towards human shapes?
At last I am able to forget my difficulties:
10   But will I know how silently to leave my self behind?

This poem is so difficult, and the other extended commentaries of Huang Chieh and Suzuki Shūji differ so much from my own that I believe a line by line explication is in order. Line 2 is the translation of a variant given in the *Shih chi* 詩 紀. The other texts read, rather lamely, 'If we had no sadness, neither would we have any thoughts'. The first two lines show the poem's main concern: the sloughing off of the emotions to attain to a state of indifference to sadness and pain. Lines 3 and 4 are clichés: the important thing is freedom. If one is not ensnared in the world, one has no need for great wealth (cf. Poems 6, 59 and 72): freedom is all. Huang Chieh and Suzuki Shūji, however, both believe line 4 means 'What need have you [to escape] to the frontiers, a myriad miles away?' Freedom is still all, in this interpretation, but it puts the lines on a much more purely political level: the escape is not from the dangers of property and high position, but from actual political danger. The next two lines are very difficult to interpret. They do refer to political danger, I believe, but only in a vague and general way. The lines continue to preach retreat, withdrawal from worldly life: the 'swirling wind' is the inconstant official, seen now close to the sovereign, in the 'highest reaches of the air'. And whatever political good fortune ('rainbow vapors') one could find will be short lived, as if summoning their own downfall (cf. Poem 40, lines 7–8). Here Huang Chieh, followed again by Suzuki Shūji, also reads a political message, but they ungrammatically, and without taking the very similar line of Poem 40 into account, translate line 6 as reading 'rainbow vapors wander back and forth before the sun as it rises', and take the line as symbolizing evil officials beclouding the mind of their sovereign. Suzuki Shūji sees an allusion to the passing of the Wei here. These four lines, then, preach against riches (lines 3–4) and honors or high position (lines 5–6). The next two lines (7–8) come back to the mystical preoccupations of the first two lines; renunciation of these two main motive forces in a man's life will leave one indifferent to all, with a heart like ashes lodged in a withered body (a common description in *Chuang-tzu* of a man seized by a mystical rapture – cf. especially *Chuang-tzu* 2, Legge translation, 1, p. 176). Juan Chi does not say withered 'body', but 'dwelling place', or 'house'. Suzuki Shūji believes we must translate a world of tranquility, where all activity has stopped, where no form of sadness can catch his eye.

The last two lines are the most difficult of all. I have attempted to translate as literally as possible, and believe they show Juan Chi again doubting himself and ending with a question as he so often does. Paraphrased, the lines (with the actual words in italics) could read: 'Having accomplished the purgation suggested in the preceding lines, *for the first time I am able to forget my difficulties*, my pains and worries in society. But am I really capable of putting this new-found freedom from worry into practice? *How can I know how* to live out this mystical state in the real world, know how *silently to leave my self*, my superficial being, my aspirations, my loyalties, my social humanity, *behind*, as the immortals do, and soar in the infinite?' The question is, of course, a crucial one, and a rhetorical one requiring a negative answer: 'You will never know how to "leave your self behind", because you are too attached to the world.' Huang Chieh is worried a great deal by the contradictory nature of these two lines. He suggests we reverse them, and read the word *yen* 焉 not as a question word (the meaning it has in its nineteen occurrences in Juan Chi's poetry), but as meaning 'thereupon': 'When I know how silently to leave myself behind, I will at last be able to forget my difficulties.' The suggestion is that Juan Chi desires to remain silent and hidden in an inhospitable world. Suzuki Shūji disagrees, but translates: 'Now I realize that "forgetting myself" is truly difficult;/How can one really know how silently to forget oneself?' And he puts this last line in relation with the historical anecdotes and citations which show that Juan Chi was 'the most prudent man in the empire' (above, pp. 58–9), insisting that it shows his contradictory nature, that secretly within himself he did not feel capable of remaining silent. The poem is, according to Suzuki Shūji, the outstanding example in the whole series of a poem showing contradictory emotions.

Perhaps the most important thing to note among the divergences of these three interpretations is that both Huang Chieh and Suzuki Shūji pass over the mystical aspects of this poem and attempt to read it almost solely as a plea to leave the world or to describe, satirically, the political situation in it. I believe they are wrong, but the only 'proof' I can put forward is that their interpretations require strange, ungrammatical emendations that mine does not require. This is even more true in the case of the next poem.

77

In the space of a sigh we rush on toward old age,
    And in our striving there is constant pain.
And like the river's wildly rolling billows,
    From a common origin we flow in divergent streams.
5   But the hundred years of our lives would hardly seem long
      Were it not for the hatred and hostility we suffer!
Who are those who are hostile and hate us?

Our very ears and eyes put one another to shame.
What we hear and what we see are as different as the barbarians of the
　　east and west:
10　　Our own emotions oppress us.
I will summon the man of mystical understanding
　　And go away, forever roaming at ease.

Lines 3 and 4 literally translated would read: 'I stand near the river and consider the rolling billows excessive;/From a common origin they flow in divergent streams.' There are perhaps distant echoes in line 4 of *Lun yü* 9, 16, where Confucius, 'standing by a stream', remarks on the unceasing passage of time (in one interpretation), and in line 5 of *Lao-tzu* 1 where the 'undifferentiated' (*wu* 無) and the 'differentiated' (*yu* 有) are said to have 'a common origin, but to bear divergent names'. The implication is that we, like the billows, also have a common origin – presumably the *tao*, or, more simply, birth, childhood. Like the rapidly flowing stream, our life, too, would hardly seem long if it were not for the 'divergent streams' in humanity harming one another. This is of course one of the great themes in Juan Chi's poetry which abounds in poems on infidelity, 'poisoned malice', hatred and back-biting. But here he raises the problem to a very abstract level and seeks the origin of this hostility in our own senses. Lines 7 and 8 are extremely difficult to understand. They seem to me to be a question followed by an answer: our ears and our eyes are our enemies. I believe the reference is to mystical Taoist philosophy which mistrusts the senses. In *Lao-tzu* 12, for example: 'The five colors blind man's eye; the five notes deafen man's ear . . . That is why the Saint cares for the belly and not for the ear' (Duyvendak's translation). And Chuang-tzu's 'men beyond the bounds' 'leave behind the ears and eyes' (*Chuang-tzu* 6, Legge translation, 1, p. 252; cf. Poem 28, line 17). But why do the ears and eyes 'put one another to shame'? Perhaps the answer is in the following line 9: the world is so varied, there are so many 'sounds and colors' (= 'what we hear and what we see') in the world, that we can only be confused by the contradictions; our senses can only shame one another by their inability to cope with the infinite multiplicity of information the world offers them. Our emotions oppress us, narrow us, make us unable to see reality, cause us to break off, in 'divergent streams', from our origin. Better to call the men of 'mystical understanding' (*Lao-tzu* 15) and leave the world for a return to the *tao*.

My interpretation does not really please me. Chinese poetry is seldom so abstract and the personification of our senses as our 'enemies' is very uncommon. But the two other interpretations of this poem please me even less. Here is Tseng Kuo-fan's:

This poem says that death is not what saddens us, only the fear that we will die before our term, oppressed by some one who had been our close friend in our youth [line 4]. 'From a common origin we flow in divergent streams', means that men who had been fond of one another in youth find different interests in middle age. Those who are hostile and hate us are no other than the close friends of our youth. Men we have seen and heard morning and night, one day develop new interests and while they are talking and laughing, at the very moment they are looking at you, you have already become [as far apart as if you were] barbarians of the east and west.

Tseng Kuo-fan has not given us his interpretation of individual lines (especially lines 7 and 8), but Yoshikawa Kōjirō does. In line 3 he translates *hsien* 羨 as 'envy' or 'covet': 'Near the river I envy the rolling billows'. This brings the line closer to a famous adage which begins with the same words ('It is better to go home and make a net than to stand near the river coveting the fish'), but makes it difficult to understand the following line. Lines 7 and 8 he does not treat as question and answer: 'Who are those who are hostile and hate us? /Their very ears and eyes are ashamed [of the acts they see and hear them do].' And the following line becomes: 'Their voice and expression [when talking to someone] are as far [from their true feelings] as the barbarians of the east and west'. These interpretations make this poem one of disillusionment with social life and refuse to see it as one dealing with mystical experience. They are perhaps right, and it is presumptuous of me to suggest they are not, but I cannot help feeling my own interpretation sticks closer to the text and to what Juan Chi really meant.

Poem 68, in any case, is an abstract one, perhaps the most purely mystical one Juan Chi wrote. The first four words are taken word for word from the *Shan-hai ching.*

68

In the north I look towards the Valley of Dryness and Darkness;
    In the west I go to roam in Shao-jen.
I look back afar, gazing towards the Heavenly Ford:
    The very vastness of it makes my heart rejoice!
5   How gaudy is the Gate of Life and Death:
    Once I have roamed there, I will never seek it out again.
If perchance I meet the falcon
    I will mount him to fly out of the Southern Forest.
Then, vastly and expansively, when in the Pole Star
10   I will quickly let myself go in wild disorder,
Resting and feasting in the City of Purity:
    I will transcend the world! And who would prevent me?

Kan-mei 乾 眛 , 'Dryness and Darkness', is said to be in the east (Kuo P'u's commentary to *Shan-hai ching* 4, p. 1a). It, like the elsewhere unattested Shao-jen in the next line, is probably a mythological place name, although Huang Chieh reads the words *shao-jen* 少 任 as meaning 'unendurable', and Ku Chih, with his inimitable linguistic sleight of hand, equates 'Shao-jen' with the name of the region of the Western Chou capital, Shao-nan 召 南 . The Heavenly Ford is mentioned in the 'Li sao' of the *Ch'u tz'u* (Hawkes translation, p. 33); it seems to be a star in the middle of the Milky Way. The 'City of Purity' in line 11 is mentioned in the 'Yüan yu' of the *Ch'u tz'u* (Hawkes translation, p. 84).

As all the commentators point out, Juan Chi is here writing in the vein of the mystical 'Yüan yu', 'Distant roaming', attributed to Ch'ü Yüan, especially in the last four lines. His 'distant roaming' is described in the very first two lines in typical fashion for him (carried to its highest point in the 'Biography of Master Great Man') as being a voyage to everywhere at once: the two places mentioned seem to be in the east and in the west. The next lines complete the universality of the voyage for it leads to the heights of the heavens. The next four lines present difficulties. The term the 'Gate of Life and Death' is attested nowhere else. I believe we must accept it at its face meaning: in lines 5 and 6 Juan Chi is saying he is going to transcend the temporal world, the world of living and dying. The meaning of the falcon in line 7 is even more difficult. There is a poem in the *Shih ching*, no. 132, that bears the name 'the falcon'. The first two lines read: 'Swift is the falcon,/Dense the northern wood.' The poem describes either a woman pining away for her lord or, according to others, loyal civil servants complaining they are being neglected by their sovereign. Perhaps here, too, we should read the poem at its face value: Juan Chi is simply imitating the immortals who mount fabulous birds to carry them away on their long, mystical roamings.

In the last four lines Juan Chi reaches the summit of his mystical ascension, the Pole Star being the center and regulator of the universe, sometimes a symbol of the *tao* itself (e.g. *Huai-nan-tzu* 8, p. 117). But again, as so often in these poems dealing with immortality, the last line is a question, a rhetorical question indeed, but still one that contains a note of pathos, of uncertainty.

The Chinese commentators, Huang Chieh, Ku Chih and Huang K'an, all believe this poem is written in imitation of the 'Yüan yu' ascribed to Ch'ü Yüan. But Huang Chieh and Chiang Shih-yüeh also think it contains a satirical element. They both believe Juan Chi is referring to the palaces of Ch'in Shih huang-ti in the terms 'Heavenly Ford'; the 'Gate of Life and Death' becomes the 'Gate of the Life and Death [of dynasties]'; and the 'falcon' is interpreted allegorically as friends of the usurpers by reference to the *Shih ching*: he comes out of the 'north [= the emperor's] wood' while Juan Chi goes out of the 'south wood', showing he is parting company with them. The reference to Ch'ü Yüan is undeniable, and Juan Chi may well have chosen the 'falcon' to suggest the absence of his true sovereign and to give a hint of why he is leaving the world, but that, it seems to me, is as far as one should go in 'satirizing' this poem: it is above all the description of a 'mystical roaming' or, more exactly, of the desire to roam 'transcending the world'.

The four poems I have grouped together at the beginning of this chapter are the most purely mystical in the series, but it can be seen at once that even in them political overtones abound. I do not believe that the presence of these overtones is sufficient reason to consider the poems as uniquely satirical or allegorical. Juan Chi's 'mysticism' (if such it was) was colored by his life in politics, by his concern for the dying Wei dynasty, as was every other facet of his thinking. Two of these four poems (76 and 77) conclude simply by leaving society and the other two conclude with questions, seeming to doubt Juan Chi's own ability to achieve true mystical detachment from the world. There is little doubt in my mind that Juan Chi did not find in mysticism and in the pursuit of immortality the ideal he so passionately longed for. Yet I believe his interest in them was more than simply 'allegorical': he really did look toward these religious aims as something that might calm his anguish. If, as we shall see in the following poems whose main theme is the immortals themselves, he ultimately doubts of the existence of the immortals or of immortality, the *tone* of the poems we have read, and of those we will now read, is the proof, tenuous though it may seem, that he felt a deep and fervent attraction to the ideal of Taoist immortality.

The first of the poems dealing with the immortals is the most 'objective', the least sceptical, but even it, in the penultimate line, contains a word that, accepted at its face value, throws the whole poem into an interrogative cast.

23

Mount Yeh lies in the southeast
    And the River Fen flows from its southern slope.
Six dragons there draw a chariot of breath
    Whose cloud canopy covers the Law of Heaven.
5   Four or five immortals there
    Play and sport, and take their ease in an orchid chamber.
Their repose is all pure and harmonious;
    Their respiration becomes dew and frost.
They bathe in the Cinnabar Depths
10   And then sparkle like the rays of the sun and the moon.
How can one reach their Divine Tower in peace
    And swim about with them in the air, soaring in the heights?

The main inspiration for this poem is the description in *Chuang-tzu* 1 (Legge translation, pp. 170–72) of the immortals (or immortal) on Ku-yeh Mountain:

> There are spirits who live on distant Ku-yeh Mountain whose skin is [as pure and white as] ice or snow and who are as delicate and graceful as a virgin. They eat none of the five grains, but breathe in the wind and drink the dew, ride on cloud vapors, drive flying dragons and roam beyond the Four Seas. When they concentrate their spiritual energies, they preserve all beings from disease and assure that there is a plentiful harvest every year . . . [If Yao] had gone to distant Ku-yeh Mountain, to the sunny side of the River Fen, and seen the four men, he would have dropped the affairs of state at once [?].

I have taken some liberties with the traditional interpretation of this text, translating as Juan Chi seems to have understood it (most authorities do not believe 'these four men' in the last line refer to the 'spirits' or 'spirit' of Ku-yeh Mountain). The geography of this story in Chuang-tzu is confused and ultimately without interest, since the figures depicted seem to be meant as allegorical. The River Fen is in Shansi (northwest of Lo-yang); Ku-yeh Mountain is sometimes located there (*Shan-hai ching* 4, p. 5a), but it is usually said to be on an island in the Northern Sea (*ibid*. 12, p. 4b). Juan Chi's location of it in the southeast seems almost wilful — unless he is mechanically copying the *Shan-hai ching* 4, which begins in the east and works its way south throughout the chapter. The 'six dragons' of line 3 are perhaps an allusion to the beginning of the *I ching* (Legge translation, p. 213). The 'Law of Heaven' in line 4 is the natural law by which the emperor governs the empire; it is also (reading 囶 or 罡 for 綱) the Pole Star. The fact that it is 'covered' here (variant, 'cut off' 切) implies that the immortals live 'beyond the bounds' not only of human laws and customs, but of natural or temporal transformations. The 'orchid chamber' in line 6 usually refers to the women's quarters, reminding us that Taoist immortals were by no means celibate, but practiced the 'bedroom arts' to maintain the proper equilibrium of their *yin* and *yang* elements. 'Cinnabar', *tan* 丹 , in line 9 is perhaps a mistake for *kan* 甘 , 'sweet'. According to *Shan-hai ching* 15, p. 5a, it was in the Sweet Depths that Hsi Ho bathed the sun. If it is a mistake, T'ao Yüan-ming makes a similar mistake in his 'Tu *Shan-hai ching*' where he says the sun is bathed in Cinnabar Lake. Juan Chi himself again uses the term 'Cinnabar Depths' in the 'Biography of Master Great Man' (below, chapter 10, note 39). 'Divine Tower', *ling-t'ai* 靈 臺, a tower built by King Wen of the Chou, is the title of *Shih ching* 242 and is used in *Chuang-tzu* 23 (Legge translation, 2, p. 83) as a metaphor for the

mind. King Wen's tower gave its name to an astronomical observatory built
near the capital beginning with the Han dynasty.

The first ten lines are clear enough, but the penultimate line is very obscure.
Chiang Shih-yüeh, Huang Chieh and Ku Chih all read the first character as *k'ai*
愷 , a perfectly legitimate emendation, which would make the line read something like: 'Happy and peaceful, with penetrating minds', or 'Happy and
peaceful, they penetrate the Divine Tower'. My own reading preserves the
interrogative meaning of *ch'i* 豈 and makes the poem one of the large number
that end on a question. As we shall see in the next poems, Juan Chi's attitude
towards immortals was one of doubt and scepticism, much more in keeping
with an interrogation in line 11 than with a simple affirmative sentence. In
making the last couplet interrogative, he is again expressing, if not doubt
about the actual existence of these fabulous creatures, at least doubt about
being able to reach them.

The first four lines of Poem 78 echo Poem 23 very closely, but the last six
express very new ideas.

> **78**
>
> Long ago there were divine immortals,
> > Those who lived on the slopes of Mount Yeh.
> They mounted the clouds and drove flying dragons,
> > Practiced respiration and nibbled jade flowers.
> 5 That they can be heard of, but cannot be seen,
> > Makes me sigh and groan with pent up passion.
> Pained that I am not of their kind,
> > I feel sadness and bitterness well up within me.
> 'I study that which is here below, and reach toward that which is on
> > high.'
> 10 Time rushes by in headlong confusion: what shall I do?

This poem tells us of Juan Chi's doubts about being able to achieve immortality himself, but it also tells us of his desire to be able to do so: lines 6–8
are all entirely devoted to declarations of passionate longing. His scepticism,
too, is here really more scepticism of his own ability than of the existence of
the immortals. The whole poem, indeed, should be interpreted as showing
Juan Chi's profound longing for immortality. The penultimate line, quoted
from Confucius, takes on a pathetic, highly suggestive meaning in the context. In *Lun yü* 14, 37, Confucius is asked by one of his disciples what he
meant when he said 'Alas! there is no one who knows me!' This, of course, is
one of the themes of the *Lun yü*, that Confucius has had to live out his life in
obscure retirement, unable to find a Prince wise enough to use him as a min-

ister. The Master explains himself in the following words: 'I bear no grudge against Heaven and do not blame men. I study that which is here below and reach to that which is on high. Is it not Heaven that knows me?' Some of this original Confucian meaning carries over into Juan Chi's poem; he, too, is lamenting his obscurity, his inability to find a true Prince. But the main function of the line is in relation to what precedes and follows it in the poem itself. He seems to be using the line somewhat ironically, as if he were saying that his lowly studies (Confucian or Taoist) should permit him to ascend to some immortal heaven, but they do not. The line is thus extremely suggestive and shows Juan Chi torn between his conflicting desires, Confucian and Taoist, this-worldly and other-worldly. And the last line, with its ambiguous adverbial *hu-hu* 惚. 惚., shows that these conflicts were not resolved, that Juan Chi felt himself 'confused' and 'pressed for time' (the two meanings of *hu-hu*), not knowing what to do.

Tseng Kuo-fan and Wang K'ai-yün imply that Juan Chi is here lamenting the precariousness of his political life, unable to leave the world (as an immortal), and working obscurely within it 'known only by Heaven'. But can the immortals be explained away as purely allegorical symbols of retreat? Can the passion in lines 6—8 be simply ignored?

In Poem 80 Juan Chi's scepticism concerning immortals is clearly pronounced.

80

   I go out the gate and look toward the beautiful person;
      But how would the beautiful person be here?
   On the Three Mountains I summon [Ch'ih] Sung[-tzu] and [Wang-tzu]
      Ch'iao;
      But who could hope to see them, even till the end of time?
5   Our life has its limit
      And, bitterly though we may sigh, we cannot know how long it will
      last.
   How suddenly the morning sun goes down,
      As it keeps moving, moving, we know not where!
   Do you not see the grass in late autumn?
10   Now is the time of its destruction.

The 'beautiful person' of the first two lines is probably related to the beautiful immortal woman we met in Poem 19, an ideal figure who represents Juan Chi's highest aspirations. The whole poem tells only of his frustration, of the inexorable passage of time and the coming of death, of the impossibility of meeting such a person here in this world.

Almost without exception, the Chinese commentators see this poem as a political satire, either as a general lament for the passing of the Wei dynasty (Chiang Shih-yüeh) or as a hidden lament for the death of Ts'ao Shuang and his followers in 249 (Huang Chieh and Ku Chih). This interpretation seems to rely upon the fact that Ts'ao Shuang's father, Ts'ao Chen 曹真, is called a 'beautiful person', *chia-jen* 佳人 , as in lines 1 and 2 (*Wei-shih ch'un-ch'iu*, quoted in *San-kuo chih chi-chieh* 9, p. 36b). In line 5, moreover, the words I have rendered as 'limit' and whose usual meaning is 'length', have a special meaning of 'political arts', of knowing 'the long and the short' of a matter. Thus the line may be read 'our life depends upon political arts', as Ts'ao Shuang's did. It is of course possible to read the poem in this way, but it seems needlessly complicated and does not really take lines 3 and 4 into account.

The scepticism of this poem appears again in the next, in which the world's transformations seem to carry away all in their wake. But the poem ends on a question, and with hope.

> 22
>
> Hsia-hou rode in a divine chariot;
>   K'ua-fu made the Teng Forest.
> Life changes into death as the world transforms itself;
>   [Even] the sun and the moon now float [in the heavens], now sink
>   [below the horizon].
> 5   The phoenix sang their notes both high and low,
>   And Ling-lun played their song.
> Wang-tzu [Ch'iao] liked the pipes of Pan:
>   Generation after generation has gone looking for him.
> Who says he cannot be seen?
> 10   Blue Bird! Enlighten my heart!

The first two lines describe two mythological figures. Hsia-hou Ch'i 夏后啓 (or K'ai 開) is a mythological emperor who rode a chariot pulled by two dragons and ascended three times to heaven where he obtained certain musical compositions or ballets (*Shan-hai ching* 7, pp. 1ab; 16, pp. 7b–8a). K'ua-fu raced the sun until it was about to set and then became so thirsty that he drank the Yellow River and the Wei River dry. Still thirsty, he went towards the Great Swamp but died of thirst on the way. He threw away his staff which was metamorphosed into the Teng Forest (*Shan-hai ching* 8, p. 26; M. Granet, *Danses et légendes*, pp. 361ff). Ling-lun, in line 6, an official in the employ of the mythical Yellow Emperor, is said to have accorded his twelve tone scale to the chant of the male and female phoenix (*Lü-shih ch'un-ch'iu* 5, pp. 51–2). According to the *Lieh-hsien chuan* (Kaltenmark translation, p. 109), Wang-tzu Ch'iao (line 7) 'liked to play the song of the phoenix on the *sheng*', a mouth organ which was assembled in the shape of a phoenix. According to the *Shuo-wen chieh-tzu*, the pipes of Pan (*hsiao* 簫), too, were assembled so the tubes resembled the wings of the phoenix. In the last line, the three Blue Birds with red heads and black eyes were said to be in attendance upon Hsi-wang-mu (*Shan-hai ching* 16, p. 3b; 12, p. 1a). There is a variant for the penultimate line in Li Shan's commentary to *Wen hsüan* 31, p. 13a: 雖 言 不 可 知 'Although you say he cannot be known'.

   The first two lines of this poem are contrasting: Hsia-hou ch'i was successful in his trips to Heaven; K'ua-fu failed in his race with the sun. The ascension of the former and the metamorphosis of the latter's staff symbolize the infinite variety of transformations that take place in the universe. These are described more directly in the following two lines about the transformations of life and death and the rising and setting of the sun and moon, themselves symbols of the passage of time. The relation of the following lines to the preceding is tenuous. I believe Ling-lun is evoked because he was able to analyse the phoenix's song and understand the transformations of the universe in that way. His twelve pipes correspond to the changes in the world's annual cycle, each pipe corresponding to a particular lunar month. Wang-tzu Ch'iao, an immortal well atuned to the transformation, also played music related to the phoenix's song. This understanding of the cosmic music has made countless generations of men vainly search for the immortal to hear his music and attain to his understanding of the transformations of the world and then transcend them. The last two lines are wishful thinking imbued, as usual, with sadness: he asks the mythological messengers of a Taoist divinity to show the immortal to him so that he can see one who has risen above the transformations of the world and thus perhaps become immortal himself.

   Huang Chieh, followed by Ku Chih, has a very abstract and philosophical interpretation of the poem. According to him the subject of the poem is the *tao*. Quoting Kuo P'u's rationalizing and philosophical commentary on the *Shan-hai ching* 8, p. 2b, he says that K'ua-fu is only the name given to a spirit, the kind of being who has so assimilated himself to the universe that he is identified with it. When the *Shan-hai ching* says that he is transformed into the Teng Forest, it is only speaking metaphorically: actually K'ua-fu's metamorphosis is metaphysical and unfathomable, like the changes of the *tao* itself. The *tao* is impalpable, inaudible, and yet men, not realizing the symbolic and purely philosophical nature of these mythological figures, seek out the music of the phoenix played by Ling-lun and that of Wang-tzu Ch'iao as if *it* were the *tao*! But, according to Huang Chieh, Juan Chi is saying: 'The *tao* can be seen: men cannot see Hsi-wang-mu, and her Blue Birds see her; men cannot see the *tao*, but I can see it!' The *tao* is present, immanent, in all the transformations described in the poem. But this seems contradictory; Huang

Chieh is asking us to believe that Juan Chi has spent the first eight lines of his poem showing the metaphysical nature of the old myths only to end by asking to receive a sign from them himself!

Huang K'an's commentary is somewhat closer to my own:

> The transformations of the physical world are difficult to fathom completely. Even the light of the sun and the moon disappears from time to time. Thus nothing that is endowed with a body and the breath of life can exist for long. Ling-lun and Wang-tzu [Ch'iao] have gone and later generations have searched for them, but who has been able to see them? When he asks the Blue Bird to enlighten his heart, he is only idly dreaming!

Whichever interpretation one finally chooses (and they are not entirely incompatible), the important thing to notice is that Juan Chi is asking for a *sign*, a visit from an immortal animal, to show him immortality (or the *tao*) exists. Whether or not we take the last line as ironic, or as whimsical, or as wishful thinking, it shows Juan Chi making a religious response (as opposed to a scientific or a philosophical one) to his request for enlightenment in line 9. He is asking for a revelation.

In Poem 41 we learn that he had not received the revelation he so desired; in it Juan Chi states his fundamental scepticism concerning the immortals.

41

The Net of Heaven stretches out over the lands in every direction;
   Wings are folded and not outspread.
Like a crowd of transients, we bob up and down on the waves [of
      fortune],
   Drifting about like wild ducks.
5   Our life has no fixed limit:
   The unforeseen may happen day or night.

The immortals are firm in their resolution to prolong their years:
   They nourish their wills in the void.
Whirling about between the sun and the clouds
10   They keep far from the way of the world.
They treasure neither glory nor fame,
   Nor do the senses provide them pleasure.

Those who went to gather herbs never returned,
   Which is not in accord with the accounts of the divine immortals.
15   This has so oppressed me and filled me with doubt
   That I have been hesitant for a long time.

The 'Net of Heaven' in the first line is probably a reference to *Lao-tzu* 73:

'Heaven's net is broad and, although its mesh is wide, nothing escapes it.' But the term is also used in a less philosophical sense as 'the emperor's net' with which he enrols superior talents into his service (e.g. Ts'ao Chih, 'Letter to Yang Te-tsu', *Wen hsüan* 42, p. 12b). The image of man as a floating water fowl bobbing up and down on the waves of destiny, amorally floating with the current, first appears in the 'Pu chü' of the *Ch'u tz'u* (Hawkes translation, p. 89, line 19). The first six lines are thus a description of man's uneasy place in the moral and political world; attempting to ride the waves of fortune, he is still subject to the unforeseen accidents of destiny. The six lines following contrast life in the world to the life led by Taoist immortals, their absolute liberty being symbolized by the fact that they are far above the 'Net of Heaven' and are able to 'spread their wings' at will. Lines 11 and 12 could be treated as general statements or in the first person (with Fang Tung-shu and Poem 40, line 10) referring to Juan Chi's own indifference to worldly life.

The first twelve lines, then, present the contrast between a courtier's life of virtual imprisonment and the freedom and ease of the immortals who enjoy themselves far from the dangers of the world. But lines 13 and 14 show us that Juan Chi did not really believe in the existence of the immortals. Line 13 (according to Huang Chieh) refers to the unsuccessful missions sent, in the third century B.C., to the Three Islands of the immortals off the coast of Shantung to seek for immortals or immortality-inducing medicine (*Shih chi* 28, pp. 24–7): the failure of the mission to return is proof that the accounts written about the 'divine immortals' were false. Juan Chi's feeling of oppression and his hesitation in the last lines must be read in the context of the entire poem. He would seek to liberate himself from the life of an en-slaved courtier by following the regimen that would lead to immortality if only he could believe immortality possible. His scepticism makes it impossible for him to take the leap. But this scepticism is by no means the 'proof' that his references to the immortals in his poetry are allegorical or satirical. Para-doxically, this scepticism, as it is described in this poem, accompanied by real anguish, shows that his interest in the immortals was an interest in them for what they really were in themselves. If the desire to pursue immortality enunciated so often in his poems were no more than a poetic way of saying he wanted to retire from the world, what possible reason could he have for stating that immortality was, after all, a myth?

This concern for immortals as such, and not merely as an allegory for with-drawal, is again apparent in Poem 81.

81

There were immortals long ago
    Named Hsien-men, Sung and Ch'iao,

Who rose lightly in the bright sunlight,
　　Climbing far on high to nibble the cloudy vapors.
5　Man would like his life to last forever,
　　But thinks one hundred years are long.
　　The bright sun will set in Yü Valley
　　And a night will come followed by no morn.
　　Isn't it better to leave behind the things of this world
10　　And mount in brightness, swirling about with the wind?

Hsien-men, Sung and Ch'iao in line 2 are of course the famous immortals, Hsien-men-tzu, Ch'ih Sung-tzu and Wang-tzu Ch'iao, so often evoked by Juan Chi. The 'bright sunlight' in line 2 translates *chiu-yang* 九 陽, 'nine-fold sunshine', a term which first appears in the 'Yüan yu' (*Ch'u tz'u*, p. 83) where it is glossed as 'the limit of heaven and earth' 天 地 之 涯, but in a work of Chung-ch'ang T'ung it is glossed simply as 'the sun' (*Hou Han-shu chi-chieh* 39, p. 1772). I wonder if it has a meaning here somewhat similar to line 9 in Poem 41, where the immortals are said to 'whirl about between the sun and the clouds'. The only other Yü Valley 隅 谷 (or 嵎 谷) occurs in *Lieh-tzu* (*chi-shih* 5, p. 101), glossed as Yü-yüan 虞 淵 , 'where the sun sets',[1] as it does here.

The first two quatrains contrast the life of the immortals with that of man. The last couplet, slightly ambiguous as usual, does not exactly reject the latter for the former. It suggests that we give up the things of the world, if only for an 'ascension in brightness' (*teng-ming* 登 明, unattested elsewhere). This must be a kind of mystical roaming not unlike the immortals'. Juan Chi seems to be asking us to accept the mystical aspect of their regimen even if we cannot accept the possibility of actually achieving their corporeal or spiritual immortality. This is not to say that Juan Chi is simply imitating the ancient Taoists here, rejecting all but the philosophical aspects of Taoism. This is a religious poem, not a philosophical one, concerned with man's mortality, and it treats the mystical experience as something good in itself, which is never done by Chuang-tzu and Lao-tzu. The emphasis is quite different.

The total lack of satirical elements seems to have discouraged the Chinese commentators who give only rudimentary glosses on difficult words. I believe the very existence of poems, like this one, without any possible satire, shows that Juan Chi was interested in the immortals not simply as symbols of withdrawal, but as the embodiment of a mystical ideal. This poem shows us, too, that, even if he did doubt of the physical reality of immortals (Poem 41), their mystical rapture still tempted him.

Juan Chi again suggests mystical escape in the following long, complicated poem in which his 'medieval' and 'religious' attitude is particularly striking.

28

The Jo tree shines upon the Western Sea;
  The Fu-sang shades Ying-chou.
The sun and the moon travel across their heavenly road
  Giving lightness and darkness in unequal portions.
5 Success and failure come in their own time:
  How could one hope to seek for gain
Or imitate those [worldly] lads on the road
  Who roam so happily together, hand in hand?
And yet, who would say that the *yin* and *yang* in their transformations
10 Bring only failure and never success?
The Scarlet Turtle leaps in the Gushing Fountain
  And flies by night past Wu-chou.
In a second it can move through the universe
  And twice embrace the Four Seas' flow!
15 But a man bound to the arena of fame and profit
  Is like a nag and a courser attached to the same pole.
It is so much better to leave behind the senses
  And to ascend to distant heights, far from sadness and sorrow!

The Jo tree is a mythical tree on the western rim of the world in which the
ten suns set (*Shan-hai ching* 17, p. 7a) and the Fu-sang another mythical tree
on the eastern rim of the world from which the ten suns rise (*Shan-hai ching*
9, pp. 3ab). Ying-chou is one of the Three Islands of the immortals in the
Eastern Sea (*Shih chi* 6, p. 40). The words for Scarlet Turtle, *chu-pieh*, are
written with varying characters and interpreted accordingly. The *Shan-hai
ching* 4, p. 4a, writes 珠 鼈 and says it is an aquatic animal that has the form
of a piece of dried meat with eyes and six legs containing pearls; *Lü-shih
ch'un-ch'iu* 14, p. 142, uses the same characters as this poem and also describes
it as an aquatic animal with six legs. The *Lü-shih ch'un-ch'iu, loc. cit.*, and the
Shan-hai ching 2, p. 15b, say a fish called the *yao* 鰩 'flies by night from the
Western to the Eastern Seas'. Lines 13–14 echo *Chuang-tzu* 11 (Legge translation, 1, pp. 294–5), but Chuang-tzu is referring to 'the mind of man' and
not some mythological flying fish.
  The course of the sun and moon across the sky, from one end of the earth
to the other, giving off their 'unequal portions' of light, suggests a fatalistic,
determined universe in which success and failure are given out, too, in 'unequal portions'. Because of this fatalism it is idle to attempt to join in the
worldly scramble for riches and honors. But lines 9 and 10 suggest all is not
ruled by fate: if one understands thoroughly the various transformations
brought about by the alternation of the *yin* and the *yang*, one will know there
are certain anomalies, certain 'supernatural' phenomena that give us some hope

that we may escape from ordinary fate. Are there not stories of strange turtles leaping from some fountain (in the far west) and flying by night to the very Eastern Sea? In Poem 25 (p. 59 above) Juan Chi uses the same term, 'Gushing Fountain', which he places in Jade Mountain in the K'un-lun. Wu-chou is otherwise unattested, but is probably in the east (since the state of Wu was on the eastern seaboard). In any case the human mind is capable of such an extra-ordinary universal voyage, as Chuang-tzu has said. But a man who would bind himself to the world of mundane things, who will occupy himself only with fame and profit, will be unable to lift his mind up and let it soar in the void. He will be (the image is almost Platonic) like a pair of unequal horses tied to the same pole: one capable of extended flight throughout the universe, the other plodding along in the rut of worldly passions.

The contrast of these two unequal animals announces one of the themes of Juan Chi's poetry that we have not yet treated, his desperate search for great-ness and his spurning of mediocrity. But the most interesting element in this poem is Juan Chi's evocation of a strange turtle capable of flying from one end of the world to the other in a twinkling. He seems to need this super-natural sanction, this miracle within nature to prove that we can conquer fate and rise above mundane existence. His 'mysticism' here is really twofold: a 'medieval' belief in supernatural beings, on the one hand, that is directly related (lines 11–14) to the cosmic flight of the human mind, on the other. The method suggested for this *Erhebung* is again an echo of Chuang-tzu's description of the saints (*Chuang-tzu* 6, Legge translation, 1, p. 252): one must 'leave behind the senses' (literally 'the ears and eyes') if one will rise up to a sphere 'beyond sadness and sorrow'. The Chinese commentators find no direct satire here. Even Ch'en Hang gives a very abstract interpretation, saying Juan Chi is preaching optimism: in the continuous evolution of the transform-ations of the universe, after decline there must be ascension. Tseng Kuo-fan says Juan Chi is writing in the tradition of the 'Yüan yu', comparing his own retreat from the world with the scarlet turtle's voyage. These interpretations simply do not go far enough: Juan Chi's retreat from the world is also a retreat from the 'senses'; it has a philosophical and religious dimension they refuse to acknowledge.

10

THE GREAT MAN

The 'Essay on music' showed Juan Chi attempting to describe a world united in musically inspired virtue; his 'Understanding the *I ching*' attempted to describe the psychological and metaphysical origin of that, mainly Confucian, virtue. But his other works, his *fu* and his poems, for the most part, show us only a world deprived of virtue of any kind – of love, of truth, of lasting joy – and a world deprived of its legitimate sovereign, without whom it was impossible for orthodox Confucianists to imagine any kind of orderly society. We have seen how Juan Chi turned inwards in his poetry; how, having described the political and social iniquity he saw in the world, he turned toward the search for some kind of permanence or absolute value within the world or outside it. The search included, as we have just seen, mysticism and the search for the immortals, but does not seem to have been successful. In this next section of poems I have included those concerned with the great hero and his problems. Juan Chi seems to have centered his anguish and his desires around a great mythical giant, a figure who comes directly from the works of Chuang-tzu, and whose absolute freedom and absolute greatness intoxicated him.

Just how we are to interpret the Great Man and define the role he actually plays in Juan Chi's works, remain problems. He seems to be a purely imaginary hero, a kind of hero of mystical escape. But his importance as the crystallization of Juan Chi's conscious and unconscious yearnings seems to me to be undeniable. In the following poem we see a Great Man being metamorphosed into a great winged creature, first cousin to the immortals who are often shown in such a guise (cf. M. Kaltenmark, *Le Lie-sien tchouan*, pp. 12 ff).

73

On the side road there is a man both rare and strange
    Whose carriage is pulled by fine brown coursers.
At dawn he rises from the wilds of the Isle of Ying
    And at evening he stops in the Luminous Rays.
5   Twice he brushes against the ends of the world
    As up he flies, carried by his own wings.

[185]

He has put away the things of this world:
How could he let them tear at his heart?
And once he has left he will never come back,
10   But he will still be looked for in a thousand years.

With Huang Chieh, I believe this is the description of a Great Man. The meaning of the words 'side road' in line 1 is uncertain, as in Poem 59 (above, p. 115). The Great Man's journey is, as we shall soon see in the 'Biography of Master Great Man', from one legendary site to another. The Isle of Ying is one of the Three Islands of the Immortals in the Eastern Sea (as in Poem 24), and the Luminous Rays some fairy place on the 'southern peak of the eastern pole' according to Wang I's note to *Ch'u tz'u*, 'Chiu huai', 'T'ung lu' (Hawkes translation, p. 143, line 14). This would make the hero's journey take place entirely on the eastern rim of the world. Or are we to understand that he has twice crossed the surface of the earth, from east to west and back again to the east? This is suggested in the following line (line 5), an echo of *Chuang-tzu* 11, Legge translation, 1, pp. 294–5. Chiang Shih-yüeh identifies the term 'Luminous Rays' with the Han palace built by Emperor Wu to search for immortality in Ch'ang-an in 107 B.C. (*Han shu* 6, p. 202), which would place it more or less in the 'west'. But the whole context of the line suggests an allusion to the *Ch'u tz'u*. In the 'Yüan yu' (*Ch'u tz'u*, p. 83, line 39) there is an allusion to a 'Cinnabar Hill' which Wang I says is the 'Luminous Rays', home of the winged immortals. Our hero, too, is winged (or is it his horses that are winged?) and, like the immortals, he has no use for the world, although the world will not forget him for a thousand years.

Both Tseng Kuo-fan and Ku Chih take the poem to be a political satire, in particular against Chung Hui. The opening part of the poem could, indeed, suggest the portrait of a 'self-made man', rising in the 'wilds', reaching a palace and soaring up to the firmament 'on his own wings'. But (aside from the fact that Chung Hui, the son of Chung Yu, was hardly a self-made man) these interpretations require more ingenuity than this relatively straightforward poem can support. It is more important to consider just what kind of creature this winged hero can be. The near quotation from *Chuang-tzu* in line 5 really refers to the mind of man; it is the mind which 'in a twinkling twice brushes against the farthest confines of the universe, the Four Seas'. Juan Chi's use of the quotation here, and his sceptical attitude toward immortals expressed in Poem 41, should alert us to the possibility that his great winged hero is in fact only a hero of the imagination, one who has so liberated himself from the prejudices of ordinary, gregarious humanity, that he can *imagine* himself to be identified with the universe and omnipresent within it.

The key to understanding the great hero in Chinese Taoist thinking is

alluded to in line 7: 'He has put away the things of this world.' The Taoist
hero is a hero precisely because he is sublimely indifferent to the things of this
world. The Christian saint, by loving his fellow men with perfect and infinite
love, achieves a kind of communion with them, and transcends them by knowing God. The Taoist hero achieves a similar kind of exaltation by doing just
the contrary. His absolute indifference to all creatures of this world as individuals allows him to accept them all without distinction and achieve a kind
of communion with the entire universe. Juan Chi was profoundly influenced
by this Taoist ideal; it appears again and again in his work and must be seen to
represent one of the most powerful poles of attraction of his genius.

The theme of the sublimely indifferent Great Man is a venerable one in
Chinese literature. Aside from the philosophical treatment of it in *Chuang-tzu*,
it appears again and again in the *Ch'u tz'u* and in Han *fu*. Juan Chi's development of the theme in his 'Ta-jen hsien-sheng chuan', 'Biography of Master
Great Man', owes a great deal to his models[1] and, like them, combines philosophical and religious elements. But, in spite of borrowings from tradition, it
is very much a personal work, one of Juan Chi's most original. Although it is
called a 'biography', *chuan* 傳 , it is formally closest to the tradition of the
great *fu* of the Han dynasty. The prototype of these *fu*, the 'Li sao' itself, and
many of its imitations, are poems that are in fact the expression of their
authors' melancholy inspired by failure in the political world. Their failure
and the consequent disgust with the world make them want to quit social life
altogether and seek peace among the immortals in heaven or in some exotic
land of exile. Juan Chi has deliberately, I think, ignored this aspect of the tradition in his portrait of the Great Man: he has placed him in an abstract,
philosophical light, at grips with metaphysical, not political, problems. Like
many of the Han *fu*, however, the work is built around a series of questions
and answers, a series of debates between personages holding different philosophical viewpoints. An introduction presents Master Great Man who, because
Juan Chi says 'he once resided on Mount Su-men', is often considered to be
Sun Teng, the hermit he is said to have met around 257 and who lived on
Mount Su-men.[2] The question is purely academic because it is clear that Juan
Chi's hero is in great part, if not entirely, imaginary. He is, to a certain extent
at least, inspired by a figure in the religious Taoist tradition that has only
recently been mentioned in connection with Juan Chi, by the figure of 'Lao-
tzu' transformed into a popular messianic saviour who is, like Juan Chi's
Master Great Man, identified with the very *tao* itself.[3] This deified Lao-tzu
played an important role in the tremendous popular uprisings at the end of
the Han. A number of rebel leaders said they were 'transformations' of the
divine Lao-tzu who would bring Great Peace (*t'ai-p'ing*) to the empire when
their time came. At the end of his 'Biography', Juan Chi invokes his Great Man

very much as a believer would invoke his saviour, but we must be careful not to exaggerate the overall importance of the influence of popular religion in this work. Juan Chi's hero is much more the protagonist of philosophical views than he is a religious deity; the influence is there, conscious or unconscious, but Juan Chi is still writing in a literary, artistic tradition, not as a propagandist for a popular religion.

The Great Man has three interlocutors in all: a Confucianist, a hermit and a woodgatherer. Each poses his questions, which amount to a statement of his particular philosophical position, and to each the Great Man answers, showing the relativity of that position and its ultimate meaninglessness in the face of eternity and infinity, in the face of the absolute *tao*. His exchange of views with the Confucianist is by far the most famous part of the biography, and the one that is the most familiar to us already, being very close to the exchange of letters between Juan Chi and Fu I and to the argument in the 'On understanding Chuang-tzu'.

The Confucianist case of the perfect gentleman establishing immortal fame and worldly honors is stated (lines 39–92) and the Great Man answers by giving the Taoist relativistic view of things, this time beginning with a cosmogony and an early history of the world that is both original and puzzling. It is easy to see why Juan Chi uses the argument: Confucianism takes the solidity and stability of the natural world for granted; ceremonial genuflections and ritualistic choreographies lose their charm when 'the heavens moved with the earth; the mountains crashed down and the rivers rose up' (lines 113–14). But where in Chinese tradition does this cataclysmic view of the world's origin come from? There is perhaps an influence of *Lao-tzu* 25 ('There was something in a state of fusion before heaven and earth were formed'), but we are in the presence here of some further development of ancient Taoist beliefs, things Chuang-tzu, as Juan Chi says in 'On understanding Chuang-tzu', knew nothing about (above, p. 108); things that, under the influence of Buddhism, were to become part of later religious Taoist tradition.[4] The rest of the arguments against the Confucianists are more obviously grounded in Chuang-tzu's philosophy and are fairly easy to understand. Even the most famous and most often quoted passage comparing the Confucianist gentleman to a louse in a pair of drawers (lines 133–46) is probably inspired by a passage in *Chuang-tzu* 24 (Legge translation, 2, p. 109) in which a certain category of men are compared to lice on a pig. The most interesting part of this whole section, aside from the superb, mordant rhetoric, is the description of the Great Man himself. Here again we see a development of Chuang-tzu's philosophy: the latter's 'Perfect Man' or 'True Man' is, so to speak, 'made flesh'; he is described in detail, as embodying the attributes of the *tao*, as presenting, within himself, a microcosm of the universe, as being himself coeval and identical with the universe. Chuang-tzu's symbol becomes something like a living being, more god-like than human, perhaps, but something different from a symbol.

The description of the Great Man is followed (lines 178ff) by the description of the Golden Age, a favorite topic in Taoist literature. Juan Chi's treatment, however, is very original; so original, indeed, as to be considered the first declaration of utopian anarchism in Chinese history.[5] So strong is the idea of the state in Chinese mentality, so strongly are the Chinese convinced of the necessity of government in civilized society, that not even the 'uncivilized' Taoists had dared to imagine a stateless or at least a ruler-less society. Juan Chi, in these few sentences ('For then there was no ruler . . . '), shows how much he had been revolted by contemporary political life, how radically he rejected, in this essay, the Confucianism he underwrites so ardently in so many other works. Far from marking this as a work of satirical exaggeration, a playful slap at the bigoted Confucianists of his day, the extremeness of his condemnation shows how heart-felt it was, how absolutely serious he is.

The hermit the Great Man next meets is an important figure in Chinese history. We have already seen him on Mt Shou-yang in the persons of Po I and Shu Ch'i; here we see him as a slightly misanthropic purist, contrasting his own goodness with the cruelty and mediocrity he sees in the world of men (lines 290ff). The Great Man makes quick work of him, showing him how egotistic he is and how his constant judgement of others is really very far from the Great Man's all-encompassing indifference. The woodgatherer he next meets is more interesting for the Great Man (indeed the three interlocutors are presented in ascending order, each one superior to the preceding), and it is the woodgatherer's relativistic philosophy that inspires him to his most ecstatic verse. The woodgatherer, who ends his exposition with a long pentameter song, has understood enough to raise himself above mediocrity; he has understood the fact that all in the world is subject to time, that nothing lasts, poverty no more than riches and honors. The Great Man thus feels he can develop his thought more freely before this moderately enlightened man and he allows himself to speak in verse, using *Ch'u tz'u*-like lines of varied length with fairly frequent changes in rhyme, handling this very free prosody with great effectiveness.

His cosmic meanderings are depicted in extraordinary verse, a kind of headlong rhetoric that has, I think, had no parallel in English until some recent psychedelic verse. It closely follows its models in the *Ch'u tz'u*, especially the 'Yüan yu', but its tone and aim are different: the Great Man's ecstatic 'distant voyage' is a mystical hymn to absolute freedom, the description of the human spirit freed from all worldly impediments, all purely human or even metaphysical barriers. And this 'human spirit' is not a disembodied 'soul' (an idea foreign to Juan Chi's contemporaries); it includes the whole man in a sub-limated, exalted state that does not seem to exclude sexual ecstasy (lines 519–30). The state described is typical of the mystical experience, provoked in part perhaps by the 'rare mushrooms' (line 554), but it is understood here as the embodiment of absolute freedom and perfect joy. And at the height of his ecstasy (lines 566–72) the Great Man breaks forth into a strange philos-ophy, a hierarchy of hypostases of what we might call 'being', but what for the Chinese must be described more vaguely as 'spheres of value' or 'approaches to the absolute': season, year, Heaven, the *tao*, and spirit, which is the 'root of spontaneity'. In this series of ascending value, 'spirit' transcends the *tao* and underlies 'spontaneity'.

This is a strange philosophy indeed! It is not meant to be examined too closely, I believe; it is an emotional outburst at one of the high points of this emotional poem, and it would be tendentious to attempt to build a philos-ophy on these short, cryptic phrases, for they are almost unique in Juan Chi's works. But the relegation of the *tao* to a position inferior to 'spontaneity' and 'spirit' is surely very striking and is again an indication that Juan Chi has been influenced by both contemporary philosophy and religion. 'Spirit', *shen* 神 , plays an extremely important role in religious Taoism, being the word used for 'god' as well as for the 'spirits' that reside in the body. And 'spontaneity' is, in fact, the concept that replaces the *tao* in the philosophy of Kuo Hsiang (and Hsiang Hsiu?). In this philosophy, which distorts ancient Taoism into a kind of fatalistic paean to the social status quo, 'spontaneity', *tzu-jan* 自 然 , is the force which rules the world. It is taken to mean 'things (or beings) as they are of themselves', as they passively accept the vicissitudes of life (including their social position). This distortion of Taoism allows Kuo Hsiang to produce a new kind of philosophy in which a Confucianist ethic is under-pinned by pseudo-Taoist metaphysics. The enterprise is interesting in the light of Juan Chi's own syncretic use of both Confucian and Taoist philosophies, and his exaltation of 'spontaneity' in this passage.[6] But I do not believe Juan Chi was actually a partisan of this opportunistic philosophy. For him (as for his friend Hsi K'ang) 'spontaneity' seems to have meant something closer to what we mean by the word freedom: a natural use of one's emotions without the constraint of outworn social taboos. We saw this aspect of Juan Chi's character in chapter 4: his untraditional behavior during his mourning for his mother and his other infringements of ritual conduct. But we also saw the other side of his ostensible anti-ritualism: his sincere filial piety and, in the 'Essay on music' and some of the poems, his yearning for an ideal social order. In this 'Biography' he seems to be entirely anarchic, anti-social, totally indif-ferent to all. Thus, even if we cannot state that Juan Chi is indeed a precursor of Kuo Hsiang, his use of the idea of 'spontaneity' here and in the essay 'On

understanding Chuang-tzu' (above p. 100) and his syncretic tendencies all
point to his writing in the same intellectual climate.

The Great Man's answer to the woodgatherer's song (lines 451 ff) represents almost one half of the entire 'Biography'. It is a headlong dithyramb
to liberty, to the freedom enjoyed by a Taoist hero whose indifference to the
world leaves him totally disengaged. This freedom is described mainly as a
kind of ubiquity or at least an ability to roam at will throughout the entire
universe. Beginning in line 512 and until line 536 we see him in a meeting
with immortal ladies, somewhat in the style of the meeting described in the *fu*
'Purifying the thoughts'. The terms are obscure, but his relations seem to be of
a polygamous nature, with a Jade Woman (line 525) and a Beauty (line 526).
But he does not remain in their presence very long. His domain is in the
mystical heights, uniting all that exists into the ineffable One, above good and
evil, near the chaotic unity that preceded the differentiated world as we know
it. And, in lines 665–75, we see again the cataclysmic portrait of the end of
the world (adumbrated in the 'song', lines 456–61), which is probably drawn
to show the fragility of all temporal and material things and the sublime indifference of the Great Man to them.

In line 676 we meet a new hero, the True Man, who was mentioned briefly
in line 320; he is described first in heptameter lines (lines 676–83) and then in
trimeter lines (to line 714). 'True Man' is one of Chuang-tzu's favorite epithets
for the Taoist hero (cf., in particular, *Chuang-tzu* 6, Legge translation, 1, pp.
237–42), but just what he is doing here is hard to determine. Is the 'I' in line
671 Master Great Man or the narrator? Is the 'True Man' simply another epithet for Master Great Man? Or is he an even more exalted personage in the
hierarchy of Taoist heroes?[7] Perhaps it is useless to ask; perhaps these last
paragraphs, and the truly apocalyptic invocation of the savior-like True Man,
are simply the highest point in an emotional outburst, an irrepressible declaration by Juan Chi of his mystical ideal.

The 'Biography of Master Great Man' is a work of mystical escape, an
attempt to realize, in the mind, the greatness, the permanence, the freedom,
the purity that Juan Chi was so frustratingly unable to realize in his life in the
real world. His infinite pain at the corruption of his fellow men can be
assuaged only by imagining himself absolutely alone. This is a work of self-
release, but it is not written in a playful spirit, nor should it be interpreted
simply as an attempt at verbal pyrotechnics whose aim was to throw dust in
the eyes of the followers of the Ssu-ma so that they would put him down in
their books as a harmless Taoist.[8] There may well be some of that attitude in
Juan Chi's answer to Fu I; there is little here. The tone of the whole last part
of the work shows that Juan Chi was speaking from the heart.[9] The apocalyptic spirit of lines 664–75 and then the paean to the True Man in lines 676–714

are unknown in earlier Chinese literature and simply cannot be written off as
a satirical game. The 'Biography of Master Great Man' begins with mordant
satire against 'vulgar' Confucianists and contains humorous elements; but it is,
on the whole, a serious work, a great work, half *fu*, half prose, in an original
form into which Juan Chi has poured his spiritual aspirations. He has
attempted to sublimate his frustrations with the real world by losing himself
in an ecstatic vision, and so powerful is his yearning that he has introduced
religious elements never before seen in China in writers of his class and learning. His Great Man has become a kind of savior, an ideal figure of absolute
goodness and greatness that seems almost to have become an obsession to
him.[10]

The Biography of Master Great Man

I suppose Master Great Man is old. I know neither his family name nor
his polite appellation [*tzu*]. But his description of the beginning of the
5   universe and his remarks on the affairs of Shen-nung and the Yellow
Emperor are brilliant. No one knows how long he has lived. Since he
once resided on Mount Su-men, some people call him by that name.
10   From time to time he nourishes his nature and prolongs his longevity,
glowing with a radiance equal to that of Nature's own. He sees the acts
of Yao and Shun as if they were in the palm of his hand! Ten thousand
15   leagues are to him no more than a pace, and a thousand years, one morning; his movements take him nowhere, and his sojourns are in no place.
All he seeks is the great *tao*: he has no temporary residences. The Master,
by responding to the vicissitudes of the world, remains in harmony with
them: the universe is his home. Should the conditions of fortune and
20   the world be unfavorable, he stays apart, leading a solitary existence,
feeling that it is enough to be able to evolve with the whole of creation.
And so he silently seeks out the *tao* and its virtue and has no dealings
25   with the world of men. The self-satisfied criticize him; the ignorant
think him strange: neither recognize the spirit-like subtleties of his
transformations. But the Master does not change his calling because of
worldly criticism or wonder.
The Master believes that the central area [in which China is located]
occupies a position in the universe not even equivalent to the space
30   occupied by a fly or a mosquito stuck in a curtain. And so he pays no
attention to it and lets his thoughts stretch out endlessly to foreign
places and strange regions, roams about enjoying the sights, unseen by
35   the world, going back and forth, ending nowhere. He left his book on
Mount Su-men before he went away – no one in the world knows
where.
Someone gave a letter to Master Great Man which reads: 'Among the
things honored in the world, nothing is more honored than a gentleman.

40   In his dress a gentleman wears prescribed colors; his facial expressions
      follow prescribed forms; his words obey prescribed rules; his conduct is
      according to prescribed models. When standing [in the presence of a
45   superior] he bends in two like the musical stone, his hands folded
      before him as if he were holding a drum. His periods of activity and
      repose are measured; his pace in walking conforms to a musical beat.
      When he advances or when he retreats, in all his relations with others,
50   everything is done according to rule. His heart seems filled with ice, so
      tremulous he is, so nervous. He restrains himself, cultivates his conduct
      and is each day more prudent than the preceding. He would choose the
55   very ground he walked on, and only be afraid of committing some error.
      He recites the instructions left to us by the Duke of Chou and Confucius
      and sighs over the *tao* and the virtue of Yao and Shun. He cultivates
60   only the [Confucian] law; disciplines himself only with ritual. His hands
      hold the symbols of his rank and his feet toe the line of orthodoxy. In
      his conduct he wants to be a model to the present world; in his speech
65   he wants to set up eternal standards. In his youth he is praised in his
      native place and when he grows up his fame spreads throughout the
      entire nation. At best he desires to become one of the three highest
      officers in the central government, or, at least, to become the governor
      of a province. Thus he clasps his gold and jade, dangles his patterned
70   silk bands, enjoys honored position and is granted fiefs. He spreads his
      fame down to later generations and pits his merits against the past. He
      humbly serves his sovereign and governs the flock of the common
75   people. When he retires he manages his own family and instructs his
      wife and children. He performs divination to build a propitious residence
      and plans to procure a myriad celestial favors for it, to keep catastrophes
80   far away and good fortune near, to keep his family and descendants
      eternally secure. This is truly the highest achievement of a gentleman,
      the kind of praiseworthy conduct that has not changed from ancient
      times until our own. But now, Master, you let your hair down and live
      in the middle of the great ocean, far from these gentlemen. I fear the
85   world will sigh over you and criticize you. Your conduct is laughed at
      by the world and you have no way of achieving success: this indeed can
90   be called shame and disgrace! You dwell in difficult conditions and your
      conduct is laughed at by the men of the world: I cannot believe that the
      Master can accept such a fate!'
          Thereupon Master Great Man sighed in a relaxed way and sent him
      the following answer, using the clouds [to carry his message]: 'What
95   can all that you have said mean? Now, a Great Man is of the same
      essence as Creation and was born with the universe itself. He freely
100   floated in the world, reaching perfection with the *tao*. In accord with
      the successive transformations that take place he disperses himself or
      gathers himself together: he does not keep a constant form. The

divisions of the universe are all within him so that his free and easy
understanding penetrates all without. The [true idea of] the eternity
105 and stability of the universe is not something that the men of the world
can approach. I am going to explain it to you. In the past, at one time
the heavens were below and the earth was above; they turned over time
110 and again, and had not yet reached a stable condition. How [if you had
been living then] could you not have lost your "rules" and "models"?
How then could you have counted them as "prescribed"? When the
heavens moved with the earth, the mountains crashed down and the
115 rivers rose up, the clouds dispersed and the lightning broke apart; the six
directions lost their order; how then could you have been able to
"choose the very ground you walk on" or "make your pace in walking
conform to a musical beat"? Formerly the living fought for existence;
120 the creatures died of worry; men's limbs were not obedient; their bodies
turned to dust. [They were like trees] whose roots were pulled out and
branches cut off; all lost their place. How then could you "restrain your-
125 self and cultivate your conduct", "bent in two like a musical stone" "as
if holding a drum"?

'Li Mu lost his life in spite of his merit;[11] Po Tsung was loyal, and his
family was killed off:[12] if entry into official life to seek for profit [thus]
leads to loss of life, and working for titles and awards leads to the exter-
130 mination of one's family, how then are you able to "clasp your gold and
jades" in myriads and myriads and respectfully "serve your sovereign"
and still able to keep your wife and children alive? Can it be that you
have never seen a louse in a pair of drawers? When he runs away into a
135 deep seam or hides in some broken wadding, he thinks he has found a
"propitious residence". In his movements he dares not leave the seam's
edge nor part from the crotch of the drawers, and thinks he is "toeing
the orthodox line" that way. When he is hungry he bites his man and
140 thinks he can eat forever. But when, [in the event of a great fire] there
are hills of flame and streams of fire, when towns are charred and cities
destroyed, then the lice, trapped where they are, die in their pair of
drawers. What difference is there in your gentleman's living in his small
145 area and a louse in a pair of drawers? How sad it is that he thinks he can
"keep catastrophes far away and good fortune near" and "[his family
and descendants] eternally secure"![13]

'Look, too, at the Sun Crow[14] who roams beyond the dust of the
150 world, and at the wrens who play among the weeds and grasses: there
can certainly be no contact between the small [wrens] and the great
[Sun Crow]; how could you ever imagine that your gentleman had
heard of me? And again, in recent times the Hsia were defeated by the
155 Shang;[15] the Chou were banished by the Liu [Han]:[16] Keng[17] and Po[18]
became ruins; Feng-hao[19] became a mound. In the length of time it
would take a Perfect Man to come and look, one dynasty had succeeded

another; before their residence was established, others had taken their
160 place. From whom, then, would you "receive" an eternal "fief"? That
is why the Lordly Man lives without taking up a dwelling, is orderly
165 without "cultivating" himself. The sun and the moon are his rule; the
yin and the *yang* his measure. How could he have feelings of regret for
the world or be bound to any single period in time? He comes on a
170 cloud from the east and rides the wind that blows from the west. With
the *yin* he keeps his femininity, and with the *yang* his masculinity. His
175 ambitions are satisfied, his wishes fulfilled so that he is never exhausted
by exterior things. Why, then, should he not be able to succeed by himself? Why should "he fear the laughter of the world"?

'In the past, when heaven and earth divided and the ten thousand
things were all born together, the great among them kept their natures
180 tranquil, and the small kept their forms calm. The *yin* stored up their
vital breath, and the *yang* gave forth their vital essence. There was no
fleeing from harm, no fighting for profit. What was put aside was not
185 lost; what was stored up did not become surfeit. Those who died did
not die young; those who lived did not become old. Good fortune procured nothing; bad fortune brought no calamity. Each followed his fate
190 and preserved himself with measure. The bright did not win because of
their knowledge; the ignorant were not overcome because of their
195 stupidity. The weak were not cowed by oppression, nor did the strong
prevail by their force. For then there was no ruler, and all beings were
peaceful; no officials, and all affairs were well ordered. Men preserved
their persons and cultivated their natures, not deviating from their norm.
200 Only because it was so were they able to live to great ages. But now
when you make music you get sounds in disorder; when you indulge in
205 sexual activity you weaken the body. You change your exterior appearance to hide your passions within you. Filled with desires, you seek
excess; you practice counterfeits to make yourself famous. When rulers
are set up, tyranny arises; when officials are established, thieves are
210 born. You idly ordain rites and laws to bind the lowly common people.
You cheat the stupid and fool the unskilful, and hide your knowledge
to make yourselves appear to be like spirits. The strong look fierce and
215 are oppressive; the weak shiver with anguish and are servile. You pretend
to be honest to attain your avaricious ends; you harbor dangerous
thoughts within you but appear benevolent to the outside world. When
you commit some crime you do not repent of it, but when you
220 encounter some good fortune you take it as a matter for personal pride.
Because you pursue these things to the exclusion of all else [?], you
become stagnant and do not develop.

'Now, if there were no honors, those in low position would bear no
grudges; if there were no riches, the poor would not struggle [to obtain
225 them]. Each would be satisfied within himself and would have nothing

else to seek. If liberalities and favors did not bind one to [a sovereign],
there would be no reason [to expose oneself to] death and defeat
against [his] enemies. If rare music were not performed, the ear's hear-
230   ing would not be altered; if lascivious views were not shown, the eye's
sight would not be changed. If the ear and the eye were not altered and
changed, there would be no way to disrupt the spirit. This was the perfection arrived at in former times. But now you honor merit to make
235   one another exalted; you compete with your abilities to set one above
the other; you struggle for power to make one rule over another; and
you esteem honors so that you can offer them to one another. You
encourage the whole world to pursue these aims, and the result is that
240   the upper and lower classes harm one another. You exhaust all the
creatures of the universe to their very limits in order to purvey to the
endless desires of your senses. This is no way to nourish the common
people! And then you fear the people will understand what is going on,
245   so you add rewards to please them and strengthen punishments to keep
them in awe. But when there is no more wealth, rewards can no longer
be given; when there are no more punishments, sentences cannot be
carried out. Then begin the calamities of ruined states, assassinated
rulers and armies defeated and dispersed. Are these things not caused by
250   you gentlemen? Your rites and laws are indeed nothing more than the
methods of harmful robbers, of trouble-makers, of death and destruction. And you, you think they form an inalterable way of excellent conduct: how erroneous you are!
255   'Now I am going to soar about outside the universe, with the creation
as my friend. In the morning I will breakfast in T'ang Valley,[20] and in
the evening drink at the Western Sea. I will transform and change, and
260   begin anew again with the *tao*. How could this be other than beneficial
to the creatures of the world?[21] Those who do not understand spontaneity cannot talk of the *tao*; those who are blind to what is clear[22] can-
265   not be said to be perfectly intelligent. And these remarks refer to you,
[gentlemen]!'
      When the Master had answered, those in the world who took pleasure
in curiosities thought him exceptional; those who were of an impetuous,
270   liberal nature esteemed him. But they did not understand his essence,
nor see his true condition; they only guessed at his *tao*, falsely giving it
a vain name. No one recognized his real nature, nor understood his true
275   character. Though they thought him exceptional and esteemed him,
they, like those mentioned earlier who criticized or thought him
280   strange, were negligible. The Perfect Man is estimable when he is not
known and is spirit-like when he is not seen. When the spirit-like and
estimable *tao* is hidden within him, all creation will move about without
him. Thus his function will not be known, even until the ends of time.[23]
285   [The Master then] relaxed in Sung, in the wilds of Fu-yao.[24] There

was a hermit there who, when he saw the Master, was happy, thinking
they were of similar aspirations and conduct. He said: 'How good it is to
290 see you! When I look upon you I feel my pent-up indignation relieved!
The primeval and pure *tao* of remote antiquity has been rejected and
[only] its last branches and discarded flowers flourish now. [Men today
are like] panthers and tigers in their cruelty to the innocent creatures of
295 the world. "Harm" [to others] is mistaken for "profit" [to themselves]
and men's natures and bodies are both ruined and destroyed. I could
300 not bear to look upon this, so I left to dwell here. I refuse to have men
as my companions: I prefer the trees and rocks as neighbors. An-ch'i
fled to Mount P'eng;[25] Lu-li hid near Cinnabar River;[26] Pao Chiao[27]
305 took his stand and withered away; Lai Wei[28] left and died on the road.
All these men acted for reasons similar to mine. I will raise up my
ambitions to be brilliant and superior, and thus end my days here. I will
live like a bird, die like a beast, burying my body here, leaving behind
310 my bones. I shall never again return to my former life. Now, men of the
same ambitions seek one another out; men who like to be together
adjust their characters to one another. I would like to throw my lot in
with yours!'
Thereupon the Master unfurled a rainbow to protect himself from
315 the dust and tilted a parasol of snow to shade himself from the light. He
leaned on the jewelled luggage rack of his carriage and drove to and fro,
advancing slowly, taking all the reins into his hands. And then he turned
320 and said to the hermit: 'The True Man of the Great Beginning is the very
Root of Heaven![29] When he concentrates his breath and unifies his will,
the whole of creation takes its being from him. When he retires, you do
325 not see his back; when he advances, you do not observe his face. His
constructions [?] begin in the northwest, while his gate opens in the
southeast [i.e. he is omnipresent?]. For him the *tao* is subtle and, by its
virtue he can amuse himself for long [?]. He spans the universe and
330 dwells in the place of honor. It is thus that his [literally, 'my'] body is
achieved. He dwells without avoiding other beings and remains calm
wherever he gazes. Since he is not bound by other beings, he succeeds
wherever he goes. Simply wandering back and forth is enough to satisfy
his desires, and floating up and down is enough to suit his feelings. Thus
335 the Perfect Man has no home: he is a guest in the entire universe. The
Perfect Man has no Master: the universe is his territory. The Perfect Man
340 has no affairs: the universe is his concern. He knows no distinctions of
"true" and "false", no differences between "good" and "bad". Thus
the whole world receives his favors and all its creatures flourish because
345 of him. You, however, despise others and esteem yourself; you say you
are right and the others wrong. Your anger is aroused in your struggle to
obtain things; you esteem your ambitions and despise your body: you
350 "live like a bird and die like a beast". How can you still think you will

"be brilliant" and glorious? How sad to use your mind as you do! By despising that which will profit you and bring you peace, you neglect your vital energies; by making the pursuit of fame your principal concern, you ruin your body. As a matter of fact nothing really pits you against the others in the world; there is no reason for you to "wither

355 away and die on the road". It's hardly worth discussing your preferences: I am going to take leave of you!'

The [Great Man] raised his eyebrows, opened wide his eyes, shook

360 his sleeves and smoothed his robe. He loosened the reins and let go of his whip, rising with the wind and swooping in the clouds. The man [he had just left] looked up towards him and shed tears, feeling pained at

365 the [poverty] of his own ambitions. He clothed himself with bark and grasses, crouched down under a precipice, feared he would not live the whole night through, and died.

The Master passed over the spirits' palace and rested, rinsed his

370 mouth in the Spring of Wu[30] and went on, turning about on his way and gazing at the sights as he roamed. He saw a man picking up firewood on a hill and said, sighing, 'How could you end your days doing that?' To

375 which the woodgatherer replied: 'Whether I end my days doing this or not makes little difference: the saint takes nothing to heart; how could he ever be sad? Prosperity and decay, change and transformation: there

380 is no constancy here. I hide my talents within myself and keep low, awaiting the proper time. Sun [Pin] had his feet amputated by P'ang [Ch'üan] whom he later caught in battle;[31] [Fan] Chü's ribs were

385 broken, but later he prospered.[32] Pai-li [Hsi] was in dire straits and then became Prime Minister of Ch'in;[33] it was only after [Lü] Ya was aged that he aided Chou.[34] These men had been defeated before they rose again; clearly they reaped [their successes] only after having first suf-

390 fered poverty. The Ch'in destroyed the Six Kingdoms and united their territories. They exterminated the nobility, turned their faces to the south and [their duke] proclaimed himself emperor. They boasted of the beauties they had assembled in great numbers and accumulated

395 luxuries. They cut into the Southern Mountain and made it their gate tower, and made their entrance gate border the Eastern Sea.[35] There were unending series of chambers within their walls; their plan was to go on inexhaustibly, for ever and ever. They embellished the rooms of

400 their palaces and filled them with curtains and hangings, struck the gongs and drums to proclaim their splendor. They broadened the parks and deepened the ponds, and promoted the north of the Wei where they built Hsien-yang, [their capital]. But before the trees[36] [they

405 planted] had grown into forests, brambles had already grown thick in their A-p'ang Palace. The proper time comes only by alternation: those who find it first, lose it later. Bandits from the east of the mountains then arose and became the kings of the earth [founding the Han dyn-

410 asty]. When we look at these facts, how can we hope to know who will
fail and who will succeed? The saint, moreover, sets his mind only on
the *tao* and its virtue; he has no ambition for riches and honors. For

415 him, nothingness is useful: he does not concern himself with human
affairs. Esteem and eminence carry no weight for him; he does not think
more lightly of himself for being poor and lowly. If he loses, he does
not consider it a personal dishonor; and if he wins, he does not consider
it a personal glory. The roots of a tree may be straight and firm and the

420 branches may spread far; but when its leaves abound, its flowers will
fall. Unending death is no different from living one morning: it is useless

425 to try to prolong one's years.'[37]
    Thus [the woodgatherer] sighed and sang:
'The sun sets near Pu-chou;[38]
    The moon rises out of Tan-yüan.[39]
When the sun is hidden

430 It is the moon we see in all its splendor,
Splendor that lasts only an instant,
    For the sun will come to the east again in all its glory.
We melt away or coalesce like clouds or mist,
    Come and go like a whirling wind.

435 Riches and honors are a moment's matter:
    Why should poverty and low condition last forever?
The Lord of Liu began as a runaway outlaw,
    But his martial air [later] overawed the wild barbarians.[40]
Shao P'ing was enfeoffed as [Marquis of] Tung-ling,[41]

440 And then suddenly was reduced to a commoner's status.
    Branches and leaves depend upon the trunk and root;
    Life and death are the same as flourishing and decay.
When one achieves one's ambition, one rises with one's fate;
    When one loses power, one goes down with one's times.

445 Cold and heat move on, one after the other;
    The transformations of the world continue, one succeeding the
        other.
There is no constant rule governing good and bad fortune:
    Why grieve that one has nowhere to return?
Since this is the case . . . [one character is missing],

450   Why worry, either, that one must carry firewood on one's
        back?'
    When the Master heard this, he laughed and said: 'Even though you

455 have not attained greatness, you have more or less avoided mediocrity!'
And he sang:
'The heavens and earth become undone;
    The six directions spread apart;
The stars and their constellations drop;

The sun and the moon tumble down.
460 I will leap up into the heights:
       What would I take to heart?
     My robes are not lined, and yet I am splendidly garbed;
       My belt has no ornaments, and yet is gorgeous of itself.
     I will wander aimlessly up and down:
465   Who will know where I stay?
     Then I will leave and float far away,
       Setting up a cloud carriage under a parasol of vapor,
     Soaring about here and there,
       Beyond the limitless vast expanses.
470 I will raise up a comet as my flag,
       And strike the resounding thunder.
     I will set off from Pu-chou and leave my carriage,[42]
       Striding along the vast plains of the Nine Wilds.[43]
     I will sit in the Middle Province and look back once,
475   Gaze off towards the high mountains and turn about.
     I will set straight my insignia and let fly my standard,
       Releasing my thoughts at the ends of the world.
     I will liberate myself from those who preceded us and not follow
           their example,
       Running among the ignorant and travelling far.
480 I shall reject the multifarious activities of the world:
       How could such small things be worth my while?
     I shall empty my bodily form and rise up lightly;
       My essence will be marvellous and my spirit abundant.
     I will summon I-i[44] to make the sun go slowly,
485   And command Hsin-lai[45] to calm the wind.
     I will climb the high branches of the Fu-sang tree[46]
       And ascend the heights of Fu-yao,[47]
     Jump into the darkness of the hidden whirlwind
       And wash in shining light.
490 I will leave behind my clothing and not wear it
       And wear cloud vapors and go on in that way.
     In the morning I will take my carriage to T'ang Valley[48]
       And in the evening let my horses rest at the Long Springs.[49]
     Then on Yen-tzu[50] I will renew my breath
495   And make the Jo flowers[51] shine to brighten the darkness.
     I put Red Yang on my left to hold high my banner
       And, on the right, Dark Yin to raise my flag.[52]
     I change my appearance and correct my attitude,
       And then jump up furtively for a long trip.

500 The *yin* and the *yang* change and succeed one another in their
           march;

The four seasons go headlong in their race, one after the other.
I think of the suddenness of the immortals' transformations;[53]
    My heart is not happy with long lingerings.
A sudden wind springs up and I leave behind joy;
505   Although the clouds arise I forget my sadness.
Suddenly the lightning disappears and my spirit is at ease;
    I pass through boundless space and roam afar.
I wear the sun and the moon at my waist to spread their light;
    I mount playfully and float on high.
510 I will advance along that road [?],
    And walk on foot in the empty province.
I will sweep out the Purple Palace[54] and spread out the mats,
    Sit in the emperor's chamber and . . . [55] pledge him with wine.
An orchestra is assembled to perform music,
515   And a voice, startling and immense, reverberates in the distance.
The Five Emperors dance and then assemble together;
    The Six Spirits sing in alternating stanzas.[56]
The music is like the sound of cicadas or of the flapping of bird
      wings,
Going to the deepest parts of the heart and spirit.
520 It passes over far into the vast distance:
The heart goes out to it and forgets to return.
The thoughts expand and the ambitions swell with pride.

Then [I], the Great Man, become subtle and do not return;
    I raise cloud vapor and spread it above.
525 I summon the Jade Woman of Great Darkness[57]
    And meet the Beauty of the King Above.
Their bodies are as soft and pliant as cloud vapors,
    And their clothes, the chaste truth of the Great Purity.
We unite our happy passions and communicate subtly;
530   In an overflow of voluptuousness we become like spirits.
Their loveliness shines out
    And both sparkle in their bright beauty.
They incline their dark locks and let hang the hair on their temples;
    Their bright faces shine and they renew their [graces].
535 Then it becomes dark and they prepare to move on;
    The wind swirls about and shakes their clothing.
The cloud vapors divide and the fog leaves;
    The haze disperses and recedes.
My heart is troubled and my thoughts go far;
540   I turn my eyes far away, but see nothing.
I stir up a cool breeze and use it as my banner,
    Winging my way sinuously and with complete indifference,
        now here, now there.

I have Yen-yang[58] leap up beyond the boundaries;
Command Chu-jung[59] to go off on a mission.
545   I urge Hsüan-ming[60] to take my armour,
And have Ju-shou[61] bring forth my spear.
     Kou-mang[62] is my coachman
As we float in the morning mist.
     The vast spaces, townless, are wide without end;
550   Without a companion, I stand distant and alone.
     I lean on my carriage's jewelled luggage rack and look back,
Pained at the withering away I see in the land below.[63]
     There they divide things into "good" and "bad" and conduct
        themselves accordingly:
     But how could they serve as an example for me?
555   My rainbow flag swirls in the wind and my cloud banner trails
        behind:
     How happy to roam, to go beyond the outer rim of heaven!'
Master Great Man lets his hair fly loose on his shoulders and on his
temples. He wears Fang-li [?] clothing and girds a ceremonial [?] sash,
560 keeps rare mushrooms in his mouth, munches sweet flowers, sucks in
the floating mist and nibbles on the celestial vapors. He raises the morning cloud and makes the spring wind swirl. He burst into light east of the
565 Great Summit and roams west of K'un-lun. He lets go of the reins and
drops his whip, looking off towards the capitals of T'ang and Yü. As if
abstracted in his thoughts or lost in some painful melancholy, he says,
570 sighing impulsively: 'Ah! A season is not worth a year, a year not worth
575 heaven, heaven not worth the *tao*, and the *tao* not worth Spirit: Spirit
is the root of Spontaneity. Those twisted, narrow men think they are
580 honored in the world: how would they know the world is not worth
this? Thus they fight for honors with the world, but their honors are
not worth esteeming; they fight for riches with the world, but their
585 riches are not worth prizing. You must transcend the world and break
from the crowd, leave the vulgar and go off alone, climbing up beyond
the Great Beginning, gazing upon the commencement of Chaos,[64] your
thoughts flowing throughout "that which has nothing outside it", your
590 will immense and free, as you soar in the four seasons, flying and swooping in the eight cardinal points. The desires have full rein to roam at will,
throughout the vast expanses [of the universe] without hindrance. You
595 should not be blamed for [neglecting] the small rules of conduct, nor
praised for being a saint or a sage. Change with the transformations of
the world, supported by Spiritual Brightness.[65] Expand yourself broadly
into that which has nothing outside it and take that as your dwelling;
embrace the entire universe and take it as your humble cottage.
600 Strengthen the Eight Cords that support the world and live in peace;
rely on the Regulator of Things[66] and live forever. Then one may speak

of being rich and honored! Do not match your virtue with Yao's and
605   Shun's, nor pit your merit against T'ang's and Wu's. Wang [Ni] and Hsü
[Yu][67] are not worthy of being your peers, nor could [Li Po-]yang or
[K'ung] Ch'iu[68] keep in step with you! Heaven and earth will not live
longer than you will, nor would Kuang-ch'eng tzu[69] have been able to
610   compare [his longevity] with yours. Whip up the winds of the eight
directions to carry aloft your voice; follow the high traces of Great
Fortune [rather than those of the Ancients]. Wear the Nine Heavens on
your shoulders to open [your path?]; make cloud vapors your carriage
to drive the flying dragons. Unite that which is above [heaven] with
615   that which is below [earth] to rule them together; differ from both the
ancients and the moderns [in your acts]. How could worldly fame and
profit bind you to them? Lift up Ch'i and walk in Ch'u; take up Chao
620   and trample through Ch'in, and, before the morning is over there will be
no one left in the world: to the east, west, south or north, you will have
not a single neighbor. Alas, [woodgatherer,] what does all your culti-
625   vation of yourself amount to when you see it from my point of view?'
     The Master left him, and, tumultuously in the vast distances, his
tracks obscure, wildly and extravagantly, he scanned deep abysses,
630   striding across the blue sky. He turned and looked about him, for he
was to roam for endless years. From non-existence he suddenly coagu-
635   lates and then disperses and rises on high, abruptly splitting and leaving
[?]; limitless, he surges up like a whirlwind and floats on the clouds,
reaching the Pole Star. Then straightway he speeds to the midst of the
640   Great Beginning and relaxes in the Palace of Non-activity. What is the
Great Beginning like? It has neither 'after' nor 'before': no one can
645   plumb its farthest point. Who would know its origin? Distant and vast,
going on without end until it returns to the great *tao*: no one can
explain its limits.[70] Who could understand its origin? He opens the Nine
650   Spirit [Hall][71] and searches: how could this suffice to exalt himself?
[?] He mounts the ten thousand heavens and looks to infinity, bathing
in the pleasant wind of the Great Origin,[72] floating, roaming, going far,
655   following the endless great road. He leaves behind T'ai-i, the King of
Heaven,[73] and does not serve him; transcends heaven and earth and goes
straight on, leaping over primeval chaos and setting his traces far away.
On the left it is vast, endless, without a shore; on the right, dark and
660   distant, without direction. Above, he casts his hearing afar, but there is
no sound; below he looks into the distance, but there is no brightness.
He sets up nothingness and there lodges his spirit; preserving Great
Purity,[74] he lets himself go within it. In the towering precipices of high
665   mountains black clouds arise; the northern wind cuts crosswise bitterly,
and white snow swirls. Ice drifts high as hills and how the cold does
sting! The *yin* and the *yang* have gone awry; the sun and the moon have
fallen! The earth cracks open; rocks split; the trees of the forest break

asunder. Fire becomes cold; the *yang* freezes: how the cold stings the
670   breast! Spring-like *yang* becomes feeble and weak; flourishing *yin* is
exhausted. The ocean freezes over and no longer flows; cotton threads
break; one cannot breathe: how the cold stings and splits! The breaths
[of the *yin* and the *yang*] each come in turn, changing with spirit [-like
675   rapidity]; the cold begins; the heat follows: how they hurt and sting!
With the True Man I happily hold the Great Purity in my breast;
    My essence and spirit are concentrated on the One and thus
        my thoughts are calm.
There is no harm from heat or cold; I am calm, unruffled.
    Worry and harm have no hold on me: my pure breath is calm.
Floating on mist, leaping to heaven, letting myself to wherever I
    pass,
680   Back and forth in the Mystery, never upset on the way.
My tastes and pleasures are not of this world: what quarrel could
    I have with it?
When all others die, I alone will remain alive! [75]
The True Man is roaming, [76]
685   Driving eight dragons,
Shining in the sun and moon,
    Carrying a flag of cloud,
Going back and forth,
    Happy wherever he goes!
690   The True Man is roaming
    In the great staircase of heaven [...]. [77]
The flat plain unfolds;
    The Gate of Heaven opens;
The rain falls in a drizzle;
695   The wind begins to blow.
He climbs the Yellow Mountain
    And leaves his retreat.
The Yangtze and Yellow Rivers become clear,
    And the mud settles out of the Lo. [78]
700   The clouds disappear.
    The True Man is coming!
The True Man is coming!
    All is joy!
The seasons and generations change;
705   Goodness and joy decline.
The True Man is leaving,
    Returning with Heaven,
Going back to the Unending
    To prolong his years.
710   Alone, sublimely indifferent to the world,

He looks off towards me [and leaves]:
When will he come back?
He gallops off into the distance,
And the road gets longer and longer as the days go by.
715   Thereupon the Master went away and no one in the world knows
where he finally ended his days. I suppose he leapt up above heaven and
earth and floated along with them, brightly roaming without beginning
and without ending, the Absolute Reality of Spontaneity. The warbler
720   does not cross the Chi, nor does the badger traverse the Wen.[79] The
ordinary men of the world are very much like these animals: unable to
comprehend a small region of the earth's surface, how much less are
they able to reach beyond the Four seas or the very outer rim of the
universe! But for a man like the Master, the universe is no bigger than
725   an egg! How sad it is when some small creature, some minute person
tries to talk about the Great Man's strong and weak points or to criticize
730   what he does as 'right' or 'wrong'!

The 'Biography of Master Great Man' is one of Juan Chi's most famous and
important works, the work that is most often quoted to describe his 'philosophy'. How, then, are we to explain the contradictions between its untrammelled 'Taoism' and the anguished 'Confucianism' we have seen in so many
other works? Yoshikawa Kōjirō notes that Juan Chi's 'prose works', the
'biography' and the 'On understanding Chuang-tzu' in particular, present
coherent, relativistic Taoist philosophy, while the pentameter poetry is full of
contradictions. He explains this contrast as being the result of the differences
in the literary genres Juan Chi is using. He says (pp. 244–5 of vol. 7 of his
collected works) that prose and poetry demand different attitudes of their
authors: the former eschews ambiguity; the latter thrives upon it. This is unexceptionable, the statement of one of the essential differences between
poetry and other forms of expression: poetry (and art in general) attempts to
describe life *whole*, by an intuition of the truth with all the contradictions
and nuances 'truth' can have in real life; scientific or philosophical prose
attempts to analyze that 'truth' objectively and without contradictions. Stu-
dents of Milton's *Paradise lost* who despair at the internal contradictions in
the poem and at the clashes with Milton's prose works ought to meditate
upon this distinction. If Milton chose a poetic form to justify God's ways to
man, he did so surely because he knew that prose would be unable to do it,
that divine truth was not, ultimately, amenable to human logic. But, profound
and important as Yoshikawa's distinction is, I don't believe it explains away
the real contradictions in Juan Chi's work.

In the first place, the 'Biography of Master Great Man' and 'On understanding Chuang-tzu' are hardly 'philosophical prose'. They are artistic prose –

almost poetry in themselves. In the second place, and more importantly (the appreciation of what is 'artistic' and what is 'philosophical' prose being somewhat subjective), the contradiction between these two works and other 'prose' works ('Essay on music', 'On understanding the *I ching*') is equally great: it is not simply a question of consistency in the prose works and contradiction and ambiguity in the poetry. Juan Chi does seem to present two distinct and often contradictory attitudes in his works, and, to a lesser degree, in his life. In the 'Biography' and the 'Chuang-tzu', as in so many of his strange antics in society, he is expressing his 'Taoism', his yearning for absolute freedom, for spontaneity, for the kind of mystical flights so magnificently described in *Chuang-tzu*; in the 'Essay on music', 'On understanding the *I ching*', and in so much of his poetry that bemoans the passage of time, the fall of the dynasty, the inhumanity of man, as in his filial piety towards his mother, he is expressing his 'Confucianism', his yearning for purity, for his sovereign, for life in society helping his fellow man to live in peace and happiness. I believe there is no way to reconcile these two poles of his being, except perhaps to say that they are both very human, that they are found, in greater or lesser degree, in all of us, and that there was no recognized religious tradition in China at the time of Juan Chi might have helped him to bridge the gap between his religious and his worldly desires.

The theme of the Great Hero haunts much of the work we have already read, sometimes negatively in Juan Chi's pessimistic poems (the vast majority) in which he laments the lack of any lasting glory in this world, sometimes more positively in his mystical *fu* and his poems of immortality. In the poems we are about to read (close to a quarter of his pentameter poetry) he questions whether such a being could exist in a human world, extols the idea of a Great Man in heroic verse, and wonders whether he should follow him or stay in a humble rank among his peers. These poems are contradictory, often obscure and almost always difficult to interpret, but reading them grouped together helps to understand them better and to feel the anguish and pathos that underlie so many of them. I have been unable to give these poems anything but the semblance of an order, vaguely grouping together poems that seem to shed light upon one another. The first nine all contain, either as the main theme or a subordinate one, meditations on the contrast between the great and the small, the heroic and the mediocre.

In these first poems, the Great Man (or one of his symbols, the phoenix or immortal plants) is seen, unlike Master Great Man, in a political context: he is the constant hero, indifferent to worldly changes, and faithful to his allegiances.

26

In the morning I climb to the top of a great slope,

> And at dusk look off towards the Western Mountains.
> Brambles and thorns cover the plains
> Where the flights of birds flit lightly through the air.
> 5 But the phoenix is a bird who nests apart:
> There is something in its nature that makes it so.
> The Central Tree is unapproachable;
> The *yeh-kan* still graceful and lithe.
> But look at the creeping plants in the forests,
> 10 How they spread, linked together, one to another!

The 'Western Mountains' in line 2 is ambiguous: they are the paradise of the Immortals, as they are the mountain of retirement from politics. The brambles and thorns that cover the plains (line 3) suggest bad times, when peasants are unable to cultivate their fields. The phoenix, whose solitary life contrasts with the 'flights of birds' in line 4, are the *luan-i* 鸞 鷖 , a term coined by Chang Heng in his 'Ssu-hsüan fu' (*Wen hsüan* 15, p. 2a), the symbol of steadfast superior gentlemen, as Li Shan says in his commentary. The Central Tree of line 7 appears twice in the *Shan-hai ching*: first (chapter 10, p. 4a) on the banks of the Jo 弱 , and then (chapter 18, pp. 3b–4a) in some indeterminate place. T'ai-hao (Fu-hsi) passed by this tree and the Yellow Emperor took care of it. The *Lü-shih ch'un-ch'iu* 13, p. 126, says it was located at the center of heaven and earth and the Han commentator adds that the celestial emperors (*ti*) used the tree as a means of rising up to and descending from heaven. There are conflicting descriptions of the *yeh-kan* 射 干 of line 8. *Hsün-tzu* 1 says it is a tree four inches high (*sic*), unable to grow any taller because it is placed on the edge of a deep abyss. It is also given as the name of a plant and as the name of a *tall* tree in *Pen-ts'ao kang-mu* 17 B, p. 987b, which quotes Juan Chi's Poem 45 as the source for its definition. The 'creeping plants', *ko* 葛 , in line 9 are a kind of vine (*pueraria thunbergiana, Benth.*) used for food and weaving which is mentioned several times in the *Shih ching* (in the titles of Poems 2, 71, 107 and 124) where it is often symbolical of subjects clinging to their lord (e.g. in *Shih ching* 4). Here, too, they seem to represent the common run of man, gregariously growing together in the forest, very different from the phoenix in its splendid isolation.

The poem is thus made up of a series of contrasts: 'flights of birds' contrast with the 'phoenix', the 'Central Tree' with the *yeh-kan*, and these two with the 'creeping plants in the forests'; and the meaning of the poem is precisely in the contrast between the majestic, but fundamentally sad, solitude of the phoenix (for the Chinese, solitude *is* sadness) and the happy prosperity of the lowly creeping plants. Chu Chia-cheng sees the poem as referring to the 'small fry who achieve their power by collaborating, and to the Perfect Man who stands alone, without altering his standards'. The 'lady-like gracefulness', *shan-*

chüan 嬋娟, of the *yeh-kan* perhaps implies political toadying near the otherwise unapproachable Central Tree with its 'imperial' connotations. Ku Chih's comments go in this direction; Chiang Shih-yüeh seems to take the *yeh-kan* as an 'immortal', high mountain plant like the Central Tree. The poem thus describes the contrast between the superior man who, during the troubled times implied by line 3, lives as a hermit (like Po I and Shu Ch'i in the Western Mountains of line 2), while small men prosper and enjoy themselves together. The veiled satire adds to the pathetic effect, and the obscurity of the symbolism of the 'creeping plants' makes their spreading through the forest, linked together in a lowly, choking invasion, all the more ominous.

They appear again, together with the *yeh-kan*, in the following even more obscure poem.

45

    I cannot wear the hidden orchid at my waist;
        For whom would the scarlet plant break into flower?
    The tall bamboo hides in the shade of the mountains;
        The *yeh-kan* is near the Tiered Walls,
5   While creeping plants spread across the hidden valley
        And melons, one by another, on long stems grow.
    When joy is extreme it melts away the spirit;
        When sorrow is profound it wounds the affections.
    In the end we must realize anguish is of no avail;
10   How much better to give ourselves up to Great Purity!

The first line is taken almost word for word from the 'Li sao' (*Ch'u tz'u*, p. 31). In it Ch'ü Yüan laments that he is forbidden to wear the 'hidden orchid' at his waist by evil politicians in power at the court. The 'scarlet plant' in line 2 is an auspicious plant said to flower when the sovereign is virtuous. The *Wei lüeh* quoted in the *T'ai-p'ing yü-lan* 873, p. 7a, and the *Sung shu* 29, p. 37b, both mention scarlet plants growing next to the Wen-ch'ang Palace at the beginning of the reign of the Wei emperor Wen, Ts'ao P'i (*c.* A.D. 220). The 'Tiered Walls' in line 4 are generally identified as a place in the immortals' K'un-lun Mountains (*Ch'u tz'u*, 'T'ien wen', Hawkes translation, p. 49); it is also given as the name of a Han imperial palace. Line 5 echoes *Shih ching* 2 and 4, and line 6, *Shih ching* 237. These first six lines are surely satirical and might be paraphrased as follows. The court is in the hands of evil men; the sovereign is unworthy (lines 1 and 2). True gentlemen are in hiding; only small men, opportunists are near the imperial palace (lines 3 and 4). In their contexts in the *Shih ching* the next two lines seem to refer to the common people; with Ch'en Tso-ming and Tseng Kuo-fan, I believe they are here the image of the intriguing opportunists who swarm to the usurpers.

But how are we to understand the final quatrain? Juan Chi seems to stand back from the picture he has drawn of current political life and to ask himself what he can do about it, how he should feel about it. Should he rejoice with the small men so busily engaged in their profitable collaboration? Should he pine away with the true gentleman who retires rather than compromise himself? Either of these alternatives carried to an extreme would harm his psychosomatic equilibrium. The 'anguish', *yu* 憂 , of the following line 9 seems to be the result of all that precedes it: 'when "anguish is of no avail", that is true anguish brought to its highest pitch' (Ch'en Tso-ming). The poet reaches a state of complete despair whose only outlet is mystical escape. 'Great Purity', *t'ai-ch'ing* 太 清, is a term that appears in *Chuang-tzu* 14 (Legge translation, p. 349) and *Huai-nan-tzu* 2, p. 23, and 7, pp. 104, 107, as an epithet for the *tao* (Morohashi Tetsuji) or some mystical state of purgation. It also appears in Pan Ku's 'Tung-tu fu', *Wen hsüan* 1, p. 20a, where it may have a more moralistic overtone. In suggesting mystical escapism Juan Chi is not far from the philosophy of Master Great Man. But the latter arrives at his conclusion by a kind of aloof and superior indifference; Juan Chi's mysticism is born out of complete despair.

The difficulty of seeing the relation of the last four lines to the rest of the poem has prompted Huang Chieh and Huang K'an to different interpretations. The former suggests that the 'joy' and 'sorrow' refer only to the first two plants: the joy refers to their beauty, the sorrow to the fact that they cannot be seen or worn. The latter says this poem and the next (Poem 44) are illustrations of Chuang-tzu's relativity: since each plant has its own place in the scheme of things and cannot go against its destiny, it is better to forget all worries and return to the Great Purity. These conflicting theories serve to remind us that the poem is not crystal clear, and that the obscurity is functional: it helps give the poem a satirical cast and actually to heighten the pathos in the last quatrain.

Poem 44 is again concerned with the contrast between various plants, but it is only superficially related to Poem 45.

44

Species differ in their ends and their beginnings
    And live long, or short, each in its own way.
Pearly tree coral grows in the high mountains;
    Magic mushrooms shine in the scarlet hall.
5   The faintly glimmering blossoms of peach and plum
        Are close to death when a small path is beaten to them:
How could they dare to hope for a real road
    When they shine so feebly in spring?

Since they are not trees that can weather the wind
10   They wither: how could they last forever?

The first two lines are so concise as to be slightly obscure. 'Long' and 'short' in line 2 may refer not to longevity, but to the size of the 'different species'. 'Pearly tree coral', *lang-kan* 琅 玕, is spoken of in the *Shan-hai ching* now as a mineral (2, p. 16a), now as a tree (11, p. 5a) whose fruit the commentators say resembles pearls. The magic mushrooms, *chih* 芝 , in line 4 (as in Poem 24) are said to be an auspicious sign; there are five cases of their appearance recorded in *Sung shu* 29, p. 36b. These two 'immortal' plants contrast with the fragile blossoms of the peach and plum in lines 5–8. The allusion in these lines, as in Poem 3, is to the saying (*Han shu* 54, p. 2469): 'the peach and plum do not talk, yet a path forms under them', made by people coming to admire their flowers. The flowers' moment of glory is ephemeral, so they cannot hope for anything more than a small path, and not a 'real road' (accepting Huang Chieh's emendation of 千 into 阡 in line 7). And lines 9 and 10 present the final contrast, with another kind of 'immortal' tree, the pine, evergreen in spite of seasons.

These contrasts of 'differing species' of plants and trees are not simply botanical. Juan Chi is also contrasting hidden, steadfast beings with those who shine and attract attention to themselves, beings who can weather changes in seasons without losing their 'constancy' (*ch'ang* 常 , translated 'forever' in line 10), and others who are content to shine for a brief space of time and then wither away. Is Juan Chi depicting himself in the role of a 'tree that can weather the wind' as Tseng Kuo-fan says? Or is he saying, 'In a disordered world it is a blessing to be able to die', as Wang K'ai-yün would have it? Or is this an ostensibly dispassionate description of two careers open to an honest gentleman: short-lived brilliant service or longevity in solitary retirement? The lines 'Constancy is the great man's way./He does not fear ending his life in hardship . . . ' in Poem 16 are both echoed in the last line of this poem ('hardship' = 'they wither'; 'constancy' = 'forever'). The symbolism, as so often, remains 'distant and abstract', and if Juan Chi ultimately takes sides with the 'tree that can weather the wind', it is in sorrow, not in triumph.

Such is the attitude, too, in the very similar Poem 82.

82

What is it that glimmers faintly before the tombs?
        The hibiscus' bright scarlet blossoms.
But their glory hardly lasts the morning
        For gust after gust will make the flowers fall.
5   How could they compare with the plants of the Western Mountains,
        Pearly tree coral or Cinnabar Grain?

They cast shadows near the Tiered Walls
 As their overflowing brightness glows on the Nine Slopes.
Not even the young
10 Could help but sigh at the end of the day.

The hibiscus is the *hibiscus syriacus*, the Rose of Sharon or *althea*, whose flowers are indeed short lived. The Cinnabar Grain grows near the 'pearly tree coral' in the K'un-lun (*Shan-hai ching* 2, p. 16a). The Nine Slopes, Chiu-e 九 阿, are also in the Far West: they were visited by Emperor Mu in his famous westward voyage (*Mu t'ien-tzu chuan* 5, p. 5b). In the last two lines I have followed Huang Chieh's readings (微 = 無 ; 難 = 歎).

As in the previous poems, short-lived, faintly shining flowers – tomb flowers this time – are compared with brightly glowing 'immortal' blooms in the Western Mountains. Again Juan Chi does not take sides: he simply underlines the precariousness of our mortality by having a youth sigh at the end of the day. Both Tseng Kuo-fan and Huang Chieh point out the resemblance of this poem with Poems 44 and 71, but the former goes so far as to say that 'the reduplication of language and ideas in the poems and the lack of any real core of meaning make me wonder if Poem 82 has not been added by some later hand'.

In the following poem the contrast between ephemeral and long living plants again plays an important role.

18

The Hanging Chariot lies in the southwest,
 Hsi Ho about to drive it down to rest.
Light flows from it and shines upon the Four Seas,
 But suddenly dusk and darkness are upon us.
5 It brightened Hsien-ch'ih in the morning
 And [then] the banks of the Meng received its glow.
How can we know that a man who has his failures and successes
 Once dead is not reborn again?
Like the blossoms of the peach and plum
10 No one can remain sparkling and fresh for long.
Where can I find a good man?
 How I sigh never to have met him!
I lift up my eyes toward the pines of Mt Ching
 To bring comfort to my feelings.

The first six lines describe the setting of the sun in traditional language borrowed from the *Huai-nan-tzu* 3, p. 45 (and above, chapter 3 note 45), and the *Ch'u tz'u* (Hawkes translation, pp. 28, line 95, 47, line 15). Lines 5 and 6 describe the two poles of the sun's journey: Hsien-ch'ih in the morning, where

it takes its bath, and then the banks of the Meng, where it sets. They prepare
the lines to come: the daily 'birth and death' of the sun at once symbolize
and, since they are the ultimate cause of the passage of time and the seasons,
they are also the cause for human death and the death of the spring flowers.
Line 11 is difficult indeed to interpret without seeking some satirical explanation. What would a 'good man', a *chün-tzu* 君 子, a sage or a superior man,
teach the poet that he sighs because of his absence? The penultimate line hints
at the answer. He would teach him constancy, endurance, solidity in a world
of change, for the pine trees on Mt Ching are perfect symbols of these virtues.
In the first place they are traditional, and obvious, symbols of constancy,
being the only trees not to lose their greenery in the winter months; in the
second place, they have been on Mt Ching from time immemorial, since they
are mentioned in the Shang odes in the very last poem (no. 305) of the *Shih
ching*. Mt Ching is to the south of Yen-shih, some thirty kilometers to the
southeast of Lo-yang in the group of mountains belonging to the Sung-shan
chain. The 'good man' Juan Chi is seeking is thus a man of constant purpose,
a man whose aims do not change when he sees some opportunity for personal
profit.

The commentators, Chiang Shih-yüeh, Ch'en Tso-ming and Chu Chia-
ch'eng, are in general agreement. They see the setting of the sun described in
the first lines as a hidden allusion to the disappearance of the Wei dynasty. Ku
Chih, furthermore, would have the 'good man' be the Seven Sages of the
Bamboo Grove, perhaps because he has interpreted the characters I have translated as 'met' in line 12, *ho-ping* 合 幷, as 'assemble together'. But there is a
very good precedent to my translation in a famous poem by Wang Ts'an (*Wen
hsüan* 29, p. 13a) where the characters refer to meeting a longed-for ideal
figure, symbolized by a 'bird who nests apart'. The yearning, in lines 7 and 8,
for what amounts to resurrection of the dead, certainly seems to point towards
satire, to yearning for some martyr to the Wei cause, as Ch'en Tso-ming
suggests. But the suggestion is far from explicit and the poem remains slightly
obscure, a yearning for constancy in an inconstant world.

These poems contrasting various plants should be compared with a certain
number of poems contrasting two types of birds. We have already seen such a
contrast in Poem 8, between the Yellow Crane and the swallows and wrens;
the following poem is quite similar.

43

One after the other the Great Cranes go flying,
    Flying to the very ends of the world.
Their wings lift them high into the great wind,
    A myriad miles in an instant.

5   In the morning they breakfast on coral tree fruit
        And they pass the night on Mt Cinnabar's rim.
     They raise themselves up amidst the blue clouds:
        What net could catch *them*?
     How could they hobnob with country bumpkins,
10   Holding their hands, pledging their hearts?

There is perhaps an allusion in line 5 to a fragment from *Chuang-tzu* now found in the *I-wen lei-chü* 90, p. 3a, which speaks of a phoenix fed with the fruit of the 'tree coral'. 'Mt Cinnabar' in the following line we have already encountered in the *fu* 'Purifying the thoughts' (cf. chapter 7, note 25).

The 'Great Crane' is the first cousin to the 'Yellow Crane' of Poem 8 and a clearly recognizable figure in Chinese verse. He is a great, heroic figure capable of ruling the empire, whose ambitions are as great as his capabilities. He is very much a Great Man; he is, in fact, a 'crane' only by the necessity of attaching the name of some large bird to him, for the Chinese term is not to any specific genus of large birds. His mobility, his freedom, all point to his resemblance to Master Great Man, and the last two lines show we should not place too much importance on his wings and bird-like characteristics. The Chinese does not use any pronouns, of course, and my 'they' could be read 'you' or 'one' or 'we', drawing a human moral from the animal world, but the ambiguity seems more in keeping with the poem. The idea of an emperor who assembles men of great talent 'with a net' (line 8), is, for example, a commonplace in Chinese (as in Ts'ao Chih's 'Letter to Yang Hsiu', *Wen hsüan* 42, p. 12b).

The commentators all see the poem as a satire, either as the expression of Juan Chi's desire to flee the world (Chu Chia-ch'eng) or as a denunciation of the Ssu-ma and their clique of hangers-on (Ch'en Tso-ming and Wang K'ai-yün). This is all suggestive and has the merit of showing the relation of this poem to Poem 21, but it requires a great deal of imagination and (as we shall see in the next poem) juggling of symbols from one poem to the next. It seems better to me to take Juan Chi at his word and see this poem as the exaltation of a great heroic figure, not necessarily himself, not necessarily some frustrated loyalist revolutionary, and leave the hypothetical political allusions unexplained.

The following poem, very similar, and very contrasting, becomes easier to interpret and more meaningful in the context of Juan Chi's work if we take it, too, at its face value.

46

The little turtle doves fly as far as the mulberries and elms;
    The Sea Bird moves over the Great Ocean.

Of course they know how vast and wide the Ocean is,
> But their wings are not suited for it.
5 They cannot soar about in a vast roaming:
> It's best for them to perch on the branch of a tree,
So that, flying down, they can flock together among the weeds,
> Or, rising up, play in the garden hedges.
They find satisfaction enough in this alone,
10 As they go about, followed by their young.

The contrast between the great and small is the theme of this poem, as it is of Poem 49, but this time the point of view is that of the 'small'. The inspiration for the poem is *Chuang-tzu* 1, which begins with a description of a giant, sea-spanning phoenix, which Chuang-tzu calls a *p'eng*, but the philosophy it preaches is very different from Chuang-tzu's, much more like that of the commentary to Chuang-tzu by Kuo Hsiang (as Huang Chieh points out). Whereas Chuang-tzu is allegorically attempting to show that small intelligences find the great mystic's understanding of the *tao* incomprehensible, Kuo Hsiang twists the sense to mean that all understanding and all values are relative: the great bird's mystical flight wins no more 'happiness' for him than do the flittings about from tree to tree of small, domestic wrens and sparrows. Here Juan Chi seems to be indulging in the same sort of philosophy (especially in lines 3 and 4), a philosophy by no means incompatible with his Confucianist essays on music and on the *I ching*, but quite against the Taoist and mystical 'Biography of Master Great Man'.

The poem may, of course, be interpreted politically: Ch'en Tso-ming, Tseng Kuo-fan and Wang K'ai-yün all believe Juan Chi to be stating that he, like the small birds, has no great desires for high position and will live out his life in cautious retirement. Chiang Shih-yüeh and Huang Chieh compare this poem with no. 8 which shows a similar preference for small birds against the great 'heroic' Yellow Crane.

The last line, like so many last lines, is not clear. Huang Chieh's understanding of the first word, *yung* 用 , as an interrogative is arbitrary, as is his interpretation of the second word, *tzu* 子 (which can mean 'child' or 'you'), as referring to the Sea Bird: 'How could I seek out and follow you, [Sea Bird] ?' The meaning is not far from my own more straightforward translation, but the difficulty of the line again points up the difficulty of the interpretation of these poems, and the ambiguity of Juan Chi's own personality. Still, perhaps the most important thing to point out about these two poems is the contrast between them. In Poem 43 Juan Chi disdains the 'country bumpkins' and exalts the Great Cranes; in Poem 46 he sides with the small birds. There is no reason why he should not present these differing views in two different poems written, possibly, at different times in his life, but they show how very conscious he was of both philosophies of life, perhaps even how undecided he was as to which to choose.

There is even the temptation of interpreting Poem 46 ironically, to say Juan Chi is making fun of the small birds as he makes fun of his interlocutors in his 'Taoist' essays'. But the contrast between large and small birds also forms the subject of the following two obscure poems, and it is their *tone* that inclines me to believe that Juan Chi is not being ironical.

47

When was the hour of my birth?
    Sad and lonely, tears wet my lapels.
The High Bird soars over the mountain crests;
    The swallows and wrens nest in the forest below.
5   A blue cloud throws my garden into the shadow;
    The plain zither pains my heart.
There is a crane singing in the lofty mountain:
    How could I go looking for him?

The first line contains an echo of *Shih ching* 197: 'When heaven gave me life/What was the hour?' Juan Chi uses a more complicated term, *sheng-ming* 生命, for the word I have translated as 'birth'. It means, more precisely, 'the destiny of [my] birth', 'of my lifetime'. The rest of the poem is held together so tenuously that there certainly seems to be some hidden allusion. The contrast between great and small birds (lines 3 and 4) we have seen in the poems we have just read, and we have seen the impossibility of seeking after the former (lines 7 and 8) in Poem 8, but what are we to make of lines 5 and 6? Clouds passing before the sun may mean the eclipse of the emperor or of good government or some sort of backbiting; the 'plain zither' of line 6 may refer to the kind of zither used during the mourning period (*Li chi*, Couvreur, vol. 2, p. 702), but these possible allusions do not help us understand the poem much better. Perhaps we should not try to interpret too much and see this poem as a general lamentation for Juan Chi's 'mortality': by the destiny of his birth he is cut off from high flying beings (birds, immortals and officials high in government), and in this poem he expresses his sadness about it, a sadness that 'cannot be explained in ordinary words' (Huang K'an).

Huang Chieh and Ku Chih both attempt to explain the poem as a satire. The former says Juan Chi is thinking of his father, a virtuoso zither player who, in his poem 'Yung-shih shih', says that the sighs of the men who heard a famous would-be regicide, Chien-li 漸離, singing, formed 'blue clouds'. The 'singing crane' in the penultimate line would be an allusion to the *I ching*,

Hexagram 61: 'When the singing crane is in the shadow (= in hiding), its child answers it'. Ku Chih believes the poem is a hidden lament for Juan Chi's friend Hsi K'ang, executed in 262.

The next poem, in spite of its obscurity, seems to show that Juan Chi considered himself a complete 'outsider', neither the Great Crane of Poem 43 nor one of the small, happy birds of Poem 46.

48

The singing turtle dove plays in the garden trees;
   The *chiao-ming* roams in the floating clouds.
How could one see a bird flying alone,
   Flitting about without companion or flock?
5   Death after life is in the order of nature
   [And yet], how confusedly destruction seems to strike!

The *chiao-ming* 焦 明 is again an heroic bird which appears in Ssu-ma Hsiang-ju, 'Shang-lin fu' (Hervouet, p. 120) and the *Ch'u tz'u*, 'Chiu t'an' (Hawkes translation, p. 168). In this poem the *chiao-ming* and the small birds each lead a happy, normal life in their particular spheres. But there are other birds, not in their normal places, birds who have left their flocks and who are not able to soar in the floating clouds high above the world. They fly dangerously, unnaturally alone. There is every possibility that their life will not follow a natural order and that they will die before their term.

This poem is printed at the end of Poem 47 as part of that poem (the rhyme is the same) in the collection *Han Wei shih chi* 漢 魏 詩 集 according to Huang Chieh. Tseng Kuo-fan thinks this poem is a fabrication of later men, the first two lines presenting two incongruous groups of birds and the last four having nothing to do with the first two. Huang Chieh opposes this idea, correctly I believe, and he presents the hypothesis that the poem was written on the same occasion of the killing of Juan Chi's pet doves that inspired the 'Doves' *fu*. For him this poem contrasts the longevity of the *chiao-ming* phoenix with the early death of the singing doves. I prefer to see the solitary bird of lines 3 and 4 as a symbol of Juan Chi himself, or of some contemporary who has not taken sides.

The 'heroic bird' is again the subject of the next poem.

79

There is a rare bird in the forest
   Who calls himself a phoenix.
In the clear morning he drinks from a sweet spring
   And at the eve of day he nests on the mountain's crest.
5   When he sings his high song, his voice reaches to the ends of the empire;

And when he stretches his neck, he can look off to the ends of the
   earth.
But when he meets the autumn wind rising
   His very wings [seem to show] his inner sorrow.
Once he has gone off west of the K'un-lun,
10   When will he come soaring back again?
But alas! that he must stay where he does not belong!
   The utter sadness of it wrings my heart!

The 'phoenix', *feng-huang* 鳳 凰 , in China is known as a miraculous bird
who appears in the world of men as a sign that the government is saintly. In
lines 5 and 6 we can see that the phoenix is another name for Juan Chi's hero
whose world-spanning vision makes him a close relation to Master Great Man.
In this poem his flight from our world shows how inauspicious a place it really
is. The 'autumn wind' he meets in line 7 is the same the doves met in the *fu*
quoted earlier (p. 19), with the same possible satirical connotations of the
advent of a new dynasty. His going off to the 'west of the K'un-lun' is another
indication of the inauspiciousness of the world because there is no place
further to go. The strangeness of having the phoenix go off to the west of the
K'un-lun has probably made Shen Te-ch'ien suggest the penultimate line refers
to the fact that there is no place for him to roost *there*. As Huang Chieh
remarks, this penultimate line is ambiguous and either interpretation finds
support in other poems by Juan Chi. The ambiguity gives the poem an even
greater feeling of despair: there is no place for a hero in this world or out of it.
   Another bird-hero is the subject of the next poem.

21

I cherish this moment of time in my heart,
   Just as the sun is about to darken,
Shake my sleeve, fondle my long sword
   And gaze up where the floating clouds march past.
5 There is a Black Crane among the clouds
   Who, with all his might, gives forth a wail of woe.
In one flight he reaches the blue heavens
   And will never sing again until the end of time.
How could he play with the quail,
10   Flapping his wings with theirs as they sport in the courtyard together?

The emotions and motions described in the first four lines can easily be set
in the context of contemporary politics. The movement of thought towards
the floating clouds is at once towards high ambitions, and away from earthly
realities. 'Moment of time' in line 1 is, literally, 'an inch of shadow': 'The saint
does not value a foot of jade but considers an inch of shadow [on the sundial]

as important' (*Huai-nan-tzu* 1, p. 10). Line 7 is a near citation of *Shih chi* 126, p. 3, where a 'great bird' is used as a symbol of a hero in retirement (?) in an enigma told to arouse the King of Ch'u to action (cf. also *Shih chi* 40, p. 18). The bird that the poet sees in the sky (or that he imagines there) is of course his hero, and the sound of woe it makes is probably a cry of revolt against the corruption of the world. Chiang Shih-yüeh would like to see the poem as a satire, the description of Ch'en T'ai 陳泰 , a man who was to speak back courageously to Ssu-ma Chao after the assassination of Ts'ao Mao and then 'spit blood and die', but the image is surely used more abstractedly here. Hsi K'ang, for example, uses the same in his essay 'Pu i' 卜 疑 : 'Is it better to hide my scales and splendor like the dragon in an abyss, or to spread my wings and raise my voice like a great bird among the clouds?' (*Hsi K'ang chi chiao-chu* 3, p. 137).

In the context of the poem, 'just as the sun is about to darken', the great Black Crane's single cry and subsequent silence show it unable to cope: it can no longer live in a world of small men and opportunists. But the next three poems present a more positive view of the hero, a more traditional one, and, ultimately, probably an even more imaginary one.

39

How expansive are a hero's feelings:
    He sets his mind to over-awing all to the very ends of the earth!
He speeds in his carriage for a long tour of duty,
    Intent upon forgetting himself when he receives his orders.
5   He grasps 'Crow-caw', his trusty bow, under his arm,
    And his shining armor has a sparkling brightness.
Faced with danger, he cares not a whit for his life,
    The death of the body, the flight of the soul.
How could he try to keep himself intact?
10   He gives up his life on the field of battle!
His loyalty will be the glory of countless eras;
    His sense of duty make his honored name renowned.
His fame handed down to succeeding eras
    Will make his ardent constancy eternal!

Line 1 is reminiscent of the definition in the *Shuo-wen chieh-tzu* 10 B, p. 11b, of the term *k'ang-k'ai* 慷 慨 or 慷 忼 . Translated here as 'expansive . . . feelings', it is there glossed as 'a hero's not realizing the ambitions within his breast'. The term is also used by Juan Chi in Poems 71, 78 and 80, and the kind of 'boiling indignation' or energetic passion it describes is the ruling force behind much early Chinese poetry. Ts'ao Chih (whose 'Pai-ma p'ien' is perhaps the inspiration for this poem) speaks, in a poem sent to Hsü Kan, of 'a piece of literature writing itself' under the influence of this emotion. In line 5, 'Crow-caw', *wu-hao* 烏 號 , was a mythical bow, said to have belonged to the Yellow Emperor, about which there are a variety of fantastic etymologies; cf. *Shih chi* 28, p. 66, J.R. Hightower, *Han-shih wai-chuan* 8, pp. 281–2. The words *wu-hao* can also be translated 'cry of sorrow'.

Juan Chi owes much, in this poem, to his great predecessor Ts'ao Chih, but the accent is personal; the poem is a logical development of Juan Chi's yearning for heroic action, for absolute values, as it is of the traditionalistic side of his philosophy, his devotion to his sovereign and to Confucianistic virtues. And yet there is an obvious contradiction between the sentiments expressed in this poem and those in the very numerous poems (42, 35, 6, and so many others) that preach flight from commitment, retirement and retreat. We can probably only consider Poem 39, like the 'Biography of Master Great Man', to be a kind of wishful thinking, a literary sublimation of deep desires.

It is perhaps of the following very similar 'heroic' poem that the *Chin shu* (*chiao-chu* 49, p. 5b) is speaking when it says: '[Juan Chi] once ascended Kuang-wu and looked down upon the field where Ch'u and Han confronted one another in battle. He sighed and said: "There are no heroes in our times, so they make worthless idiots famous!" He ascended Mount Wu- [read Hu- 虎] lao, looked off towards the capital and sighed. That is when he recited (and composed) his poem "Great heroes".' Mt Kuang-wu 廣 武 was located near the Yellow River, to the east of the Fan-shui, and was the scene in 203 B.C. of a famous encounter between the two contenders for the throne, Hsiang Yü and Liu Pang, who spoke to one another across a ravine (*Shih chi* 7, p. 61; 8, p. 57). Juan Chi's sarcasm is perhaps based on the story of P'ang Ch'üan to which he alludes in the 'Biography of Master Great Man' (above, note 31). The Hu-lao 虎 牢 Pass, to the west of Kuang-wu, is about seventy kilometers to the northeast of Lo-yang.[80]

38

Flaming rays stretch on for a myriad miles
    And swollen rivers flood their rocky rapids.
I hang my bent bow on the Fu-sang tree
    And lean my long sword out beyond heaven.
5   Mount T'ai will be my whetstone,
    The Yellow River a sash for my robe.
Look at Master Chuang Chou
    [Who said] we cannot rely upon the blooming and withering [we
        call life].
He threw his body away, abandoned it in the wilds
10   Where crows and kites could do their harm.
How can he be compared to a glorious hero

The fame of whose deeds is heightened by this [kind of death in the field]!

The first two lines set the scene as one of natural grandeur such as described at the beginning of chapter 17 in *Chuang-tzu*, 'Autumn floods'. They tell us this is a poem of greatness, of heroism. The hero is described in quasi-cosmic terms in lines 3–6. Lines 5 and 6 are almost word for word from *Shih chi* 18, p. 2, where, however, they are used in an entirely different way as part of an oath of allegiance. Line 7 shows that the grandeur of the images in the first lines of the poem do indeed set the scene for Chuang-tzu himself. There is perhaps no writer who has influenced Juan Chi more than Chuang-tzu, no writer he quotes more often, and yet here (as in 'On understanding Chuang-tzu', above, pp. 102–9) he is clearly critical of him. And his criticism is of that aspect of Chuang-tzu's thought that brought the most opprobrium from critics throughout the Middle Ages: the medieval immortality seekers objected to Chuang-tzu's equation of life and death.[81] Chuang-tzu was interested in the objective existence of the truth, what he called the *tao*; Juan Chi and his contemporaries were no longer satisfied with what to them must have seemed 'cold' reasoning. They wanted subjectively to assimilate themselves to the *tao*, to become *tao*-like themselves. Juan Chi has wholeheartedly accepted Chuang-tzu's ontological view of the universe, but he cannot accept the logical results of that view to the extent of equating life and death. Chuang-tzu lived out his philosophy to the end and, when he was about to die, showed his indifference to all worldly things in the following scene found in chapter 32 of the work ascribed to him:

> When Chuang-tzu was about to die his disciples thought of giving him a splendid funeral, but Chuang-tzu said to them: 'Heaven and earth will be my coffins, the sun and the moon my jade tablet, the stars my pearls, and the whole of creation my mourners. Are not my funeral preparations complete?' His disciples replied: 'We are afraid the crows and kites will eat you.' To which Chuang-tzu replied: 'If I am above the earth I will be eaten by the crows and kites; if below, by the ants: you take from one to give to the other — why this prejudice?'

The last two lines of the poem ask how Chuang-tzu's death could be compared to the death of a hero who like him is left unburied in the open, but who, unlike him, receives a kind of immortality for his sacrifice. Juan Chi nowhere goes farther than in this poem to negate Taoist philosophy and to assert traditional Confucianism. Heroism, posthumous fame *are* immortality for orthodox Confucianists, and Juan Chi shows himself purely orthodox in this poem. But he also contradicts statements he has made elsewhere, statements denying any interest in fame or glory (Poem 41), the whole 'pacific-istic' Poem 61, and so many other Chuang-tzu-like declarations of indifference to worldly life and desire for obscurity and retreat. These two poems show how passionately, how contradictorily he desired to reach some kind of great-ness, absolute greatness. Even if they may be in part praise for contemporary loyalist revolutionaries like Kuan-ch'iu Chien 毌 丘 儉 (Ch'en Tso-ming, Tseng Kuo-fan), they cannot be written off as set pieces, however clearly they fit into a tradition of heroic verse extending from the 'Hymn to the fallen' of the 'Chiu ko' to the great T'ang 'frontier poems' (Fang Tung-shu): Juan Chi has again stamped them with his individuality and his passion.

The following poem carries the theme of the great hero even further into heroic fantasy.

58

My high-cocked hat splits the floating clouds
    And my long sword sticks out beyond heaven.
I worry not one whit over small affairs,
    For with one high step I straddle the whole world!
5   Fei-tzu is my driver
    As I playfully roam about the rim of the world.
Looking back as I take leave of Hsi-wang-mu,
    I will pass on further from here!
How could I stay with a man in a thatched hut,
10   Strumming a zither, pledging my heart to him?

Fei-tzu, in line 5, is a famous horse-raiser of antiquity, said to be the ances-tor of the house of Ch'in (*Shih chi* 5, pp. 8–9). Juan Chi has already made allusion to him, indirectly, in Poem 66, line 11. The first two lines of the poem allude, by their language, to the poem 'She Chiang' in the 'Chiu chang' of the *Ch'u tz'u* (Hawkes translation, pp. 63–5), a poem which describes a loyal, frustrated official leaving the court to retire in the distant wilderness. Juan Chi's poem is ostensibly a disparagement of simple retirement from pol-itical life (lines 9 and 10). His is to be a life of heroic, cosmic wandering, indifferent to space and time, even turning his back on the Queen of the immortals, Hsi-wang-mu, on the western rim of the world. He describes a life very much like that of the Great Cranes of Poem 43 (Ch'en Tso-ming) or of Master Great Man (Chiang Shih-yüeh), a life in the Absolute, infinitely higher than any partisan politics. So high, in fact, that it must make us wonder to what extent it is meant to be taken seriously, to what extent it is bluff or eye-wash meant to hide Juan Chi's more down-to-earth aspirations and defeats. Is this absolute abandon and freedom a tragi-comic attempt to express absolute despair at finding some sort of peace in this world (as Huang K'an says of Poem 38), or is it a serious, mystical attempt at some union with the universe? Or are the two questions two sides of the same coin?

There is one poem that does throw some light on this problem, and I think it shows us Juan Chi's attitude was ambiguous, mock-heroic and deadly serious at the same time.

54

Boastful talk relieves pent-up indignation;
    Negligent laziness irritates the heart.
In the northwest I climb Pu-chou;
    In the southeast I look towards Teng Forest.
5   Endless wilderness covers the Nine Provinces;
    Exalted mountains lift up their high crests.
A myriad generations? A short meal time for me.
    A thousand years? The time to bob up and down once as I float
        along!
Who says jade and stone are the same?
10   My tears fall and I cannot stop them!

'Boastful talk' is surely the kind of Chuang-tzu-like 'Great Man' exaggeration that characterizes the poems we have just been reading. Such boasting can, at least for a time, relieve one's feelings of frustration, or indignation by transporting one to an imaginary world and enabling one to see the causes of these frustrations and indignation *sub specie aeternitatis*, as the relative, temporal phenomena they ultimately are. The second line can be read simply as presenting an alternative to 'boastful talking' – doing nothing, being lazy, not climbing mythic mountains or striding across sidereal plains. But it can also be understood as complementary rather than contrasting: 'boastful talking' *is* a kind of laziness and will ultimately lead to irritation for not having accomplished anything with one's life. The second interpretation of the line is particularly suited to the variant reading of the first character, *ch'ing* 情 , 'feelings', for 'laziness', and is adopted by Huang K'an.

Lines 3 to 8 are an example of 'boastful talking' and show Juan Chi rising above all the apparent immensity of space (lines 3–6) and time (lines 7–8), as he has in his works most inspired by Chuang-tzu's dialectics, the 'On understanding Chuang-tzu' and the 'Biography of Master Great Man'. Pu-chou, the 'truncated mountain' (*Shan-hai ching* 16, p. 1a) and Teng Forest, metamorphosed from the staff of K'ua-fu, the 'Boaster' (above, pp. 162, 179), set the proper mythical background. But K'ua-fu's Teng Forest was said to have been north of the North Sea; Juan Chi, perhaps deliberately, has confused it with a southern forest bearing the same name mentioned in the *Shih chi* 23, p. 14, so that his view of the world can be all-encompassing, from the northwest corner of the world, where Mt Pu-chou is said to be, to the southeast.

The first two lines of this poem suggest that what follows is only 'boastful talking'; they throw a certain doubt on the reality of the description of the Great Man's cosmic navigation in the next lines. But the last two lines must be interpreted as throwing more than doubt on the reality of the Great Man's dream: they show that Juan Chi felt despair at the thought that 'jade and stone are the same', that is, in the context of the poem, that the Great Man he is masquerading as could be the same as ordinary humanity, that his Great Man boasting is, after all, idle posturing. He cries because, in the final analysis, he knows he is not made of the jade of 'greatness', but is of common human stone.

Juan Chi's weeping, like his drinking and his anti-ritualism, is one of his most famous attributes in history. He describes himself as actually crying or sobbing in six of his poems (11, 15?, 37, 49?, 54, 66). One of the stories told about him, one that has inspired a great number of poets throughout history, shows him in just such a posture: 'From time to time, as his fantasy led him, he would ride out alone, not following the by-paths. When the car tracks gave out he would cry passionately and without restraint and then return.'[82]

Like the Confucian gentleman he was, Juan Chi 'did not follow by-paths' (*Lun yü* 6, 12); he follows the Great Road, the *tao* of both Confucianists and Taoists. But what is the meaning of his strange behavior 'at the end of the road'? The great Chinese poets who have echoed this anecdote in their poetry — Li Po,[83] Tu Fu,[84] Su Shih,[85] to mention only three of the very greatest — all allude to the anecdote as if it meant he was bemoaning his failure to travel far on the road to political success, to fulfil his destiny and realize all his potentialities. This interpretation is unexceptionable as far as it goes, but I wonder if Juan Chi's action doesn't have even greater resonances. In the *Shih-shuo hsin-yü* commentary this anecdote is quoted just before the description of Juan Chi's visit to Sun Teng translated on pp. 150–51 above, placing it in a particularly 'philosophical' atmosphere. It seems to me that Juan Chi's tears are more than tears of sorrow over the appalling contemporary political conditions or for his own frustrated career, just as his poetry is more than pure political satire.[86] When he cries so disconsolately, he is crying because the great road he has travelled stops on the edge of human civilization, because he cannot ride out upon it into the wilderness inhabited by the immortals, and beyond into the cosmic spaces he travelled so freely in his imagination. There can be little doubt that the Ssu-ma's usurping and the mediocre band of opportunists that supported it made political action impossible for Juan Chi; but he remained a man attached to antique 'Confucian' values, down-to-earth social values, and was unable to make the great leap of the spirit that might have satisfied at least the part of his complicated mind that yearned for the freedom of the soul. Tears are the only release left to him to resolve the irresolvable contradictions that find such passionate expression in his poetry.

He expresses a feeling somewhat similar to this frustration, albeit without tears, in one of the most evocative of his poems.

5

Long ago, when I was young
    And frivolous and fond of music and song,
I roamed to the west, to Hsien-yang
    Where I hobnobbed with the Chaos and the Lis.
5   But before our games were ended
    The bright sun suddenly disappeared.
I urged on my horse to take me home again,
    Then turned around to look out at the Three Rivers.
I'd spent a fortune in gold:
10   There were always so many things to spend it for!
Towards the north I approached the T'ai-hang Road:
    I'd lost my way! And what shall I do now?

By placing the scene of his poem in Hsien-yang, Juan Chi seems to be suggesting some kind of historical or allegorical setting. Hsien-yang was, in fact, an important capital only half a millenium before Juan Chi's time, under the Ch'in dynasty in the third century B.C., and it was far to the west of the contemporary capital, Lo-yang. The two names dropped in line 4, too, suggest an historical setting, but opinion is sharply divided as to their reference. The problem is marginal, at most, because Juan Chi is obviously suggesting a stereo-type of rich, high-living personalities. The earliest and most generally accepted identification is that of Yen Yen-chih, in the *Wen hsüan*, who says they refer to two particularly famous Han imperial concubines, Chao Fei-yen 趙 飛 燕, empress of Ch'eng-ti (reigned 32–6 B.C.), and Madame Li 李 夫 人, favorite of Wu-ti (reigned 140–86 B.C.), both of whom were especially esteemed for their ability to sing and to dance. Ku Yen-wu 顧 炎 武 (A.D. 1613–1682), however, in his *Jih-chih lu* 日 知 錄 27, shows there is no need to commit the anachronism of yoking together two women who lived almost a century apart since the names 'Chao' and 'Li' are coupled at least twice in the *Han shu* (85, pp. 3460, 3465; 100, p. 4200), and refer to contemporaries, Ch'eng-ti's empress Chao Fei-yen and concubine Li P'ing 李 平, and their highly placed relatives. The references in the *Han shu*, moreover, are to their carousals and general unseemly behavior within the palace precincts, making them particu-larly apt for Juan Chi's poem.[87] I prefer Ku Yen-wu's suggestion because the idea of 'hobnobbing' with two anachronistic imperial concubines seems too farfetched to me; but the actual identity of the historical models for the stereotype is unimportant.[88]

Juan Chi also refers to the 'Three Rivers', as he does in line 8, in Poem 13; it is probable that he has the same locality in mind here, the heartland of ancient China which included his own native place of Ch'en-liu and the capital, Lo-yang. The surface meaning of the poem, up until the last two lines, thus seems fairly clear. The repentant playboy, having wasted his youth in frivolity in the west, realizes time is passing and decides to return home; he looks upon his homeland, and finds he is penniless. Although the last two lines contain an allusion, their surface meaning seems equally clear, and is basic to the understanding of the poem. The repentant playboy turns away from the Three Rivers, his homeland and the center of political life, towards the north and the road to the T'ai-hang Mountains, a chain rising just north of the Yellow River between Lo-yang and his native place. It was in these mountains that Sun Teng is supposed to have lived when Juan Chi visited him (above, pp. 149ff). The speaker of the poem thus turns his back on politics and society and looks towards the wilderness. But his renunciation is not one of an eager immortality seeker or of a man happy to flee society; it is of a bankrupt, disillusioned man who has lost his way.

The allusion in the penultimate line is to a story in the *Chan-kuo ts'e* (Crump translation, No. 372) which describes a man attempting to reach the southern state of Ch'u by travelling northward on the Great Highway, *ta hsing* 大 行, or on the road to the T'ai-hang 太 行 Mountains, depending upon how you want to interpret the characters. The allusion would thus add to the feeling of a man who is fleeing something, but who is obstinately going the wrong way. The whole effect of frustration and helplessness is greatly heightened by the allusion. The temporal progression in the poem is not explicit. The first line sets it resolutely in the past and the last line suggests the future. The rest is left vague.

By placing the beginning of the poem in Hsien-yang and alluding rather cryptically to the 'Chaos' and the 'Lis' and the 'Three Rivers', Juan Chi leaves open the door of political allusion and previous commentators have not hesitated to enter it. Most of them, like Liu Lü, think Juan Chi is lamenting his early, unthinking allegiance to the Ssu-ma clique, finding it impossible to extricate himself once the legitimate dynasty became only a figurehead and he discovered himself employed by usurpers. Ch'en Hang believes the first four lines refer not to Juan Chi himself, but to the Wei dynasty, personified as a feckless playboy until the death of Emperor Ming (line 6). The rest of the poem also allegorically uses the poet's (or his persona's) own biography as a hidden description of the fall of the Wei: the dangers of political life once the dynasty had lost power are presented as the dangers of the T'ai-hang Road.

Ku Chih suggests the poem is a satire of the playboy emperor Ts'ao Fang, Prince of Ch'i. To the extent that Juan Chi espoused the cause of the house of Wei, these speculations have a certain veracity. They remind us, in any case, of how intimately Juan Chi's thinking was bound up with current politics and attempt to carry through the hint of satire in the placing of the playboy's early excesses in Hsien-yang.

But, like all the other attempts at deciphering Juan Chi's satires, these fail. The poem is not a simple satire to be explained away once and for all by an identification; it is a complex statement that no amount of 'elucidation' can exhaust. It tells us, as nothing else today can, of Juan Chi's frustration and, in the wonderful last two lines, of his feeling of ever-increasing disorientation in a wasted life.

Poem 5 can be called symbolic of the failure of Juan Chi's entire life. Frustrated in politics by the presence of a corrupt, usurping government, incapable of finding any lasting joy in social life, ultimately sceptical of achieving immortality, and unsatisfied with a purely meditative, inactive life of mystical meditation, Juan Chi seems to have failed in all the aims he describes in his writings. And yet his life can hardly be said to have been a 'failure', for in the description of his anguish, his frustrations and his sorrows, he has left us a rare monument in the history of Chinese literature, his poetry.

11
POETRY

It is hard to know just how much of what Juan Chi wrote has been lost. The earliest bibliography that mentions him is in the *Sui shu* 35, p. 4b, where it is said that his collected works in the Sui library occupied ten *chüan*, and that, a century earlier, under the Liang, they occupied 13 *chüan* + one *chüan* of table of contents. The *Hsin T'ang shu* 60, p. 12b, lists only five *chüan*, but the *Sung shih* 208, p. 1b, and other Sung catalogues all describe his works as being in ten *chüan*. Ten *chüan* represent a fairly sizable oeuvre, quite a bit more than the twenty-odd prose works, *fu*, poetry and the fragments that remain today. And yet the only fragments or titles of any interest that are quoted in early books are the frustratingly short snippets from his works on Lao-tzu and Confucius (discussed above on pp. 112–13). Aside from a few lines of an *I-yang chi* 宜 陽 記 (presumably a geographical work describing the region near his native place) quoted in *T'ai-p'ing yü-lan* 42, p. 5a, all the other works quoted in early books still exist, and the texts seem almost identical. We may wonder, then, if anything of real interest has been lost. His pentameter poetry, in any case, seems to have survived intact. Two early historical works both speak of his having composed eighty-odd 'Poems which sing of my innermost thoughts'. The seventh-century *Chin shu* (*chiao-chu* 49, p. 6a) does not specify the meter, but an earlier work, another 'Chin shu', but by Tsang Jung-hsü (415– 488), quoted in the *Wen hsüan* 21, p. 16b, says they were pentameter poems. (I discussed the problem of the thirteen tetrameter poems, of which only three remain in current editions, above, in chapter 3, note 56.) He also adds an interesting remark on how Juan Chi wrote: 'with no painful premeditation, he finished his piece right off, with ease.' There are eighty-two pentameter poems in Juan Chi's works today and, although there may be some doubt about whether or not two of them (Poems 47 and 48) should be telescoped into one or others omitted altogether (Poems 64 and 82), I believe they have come down to us in fairly good condition.[1]

Until now we have been reading Juan Chi's poetry mainly for what it has to tell us about his ideas, and above all about his feelings. I have seldom felt it opportune to remark on characteristics of the verse as poetry, on its structure, its rhythm, its images or symbolism. I have refrained for two reasons. First, because his poetry, on the prosodic level, is relatively straightforward and uninventive: he left pentameter poetry formally as he received it from his predecessors. One might even say that, as a technician, he was inferior to at least one of them, Ts'ao Chih. In the second place I have felt that structural analysis in a foreign language is so difficult and so complicated that, if it doesn't actually defeat its own purpose, it would at least hold up progress in my explanation of the meaning of the poems. But, despite its formal traditionalism, Juan Chi's poetry is highly original, so original as to be, in the opinion of a large number of critics, epoch-making. A study of this originality will not only add to our understanding of the history of Chinese poetry; it will bring us closer to getting the feel of Juan Chi's verse, to appreciating it for what it is in itself, distinct from the forerunners that it superficially resembles so greatly.

As far as I have been able to see, it was Hu Shih 胡適 (1891–1962) who first pointed out where the greatest originality of Juan Chi's verse lay. His remarks are typical of the combination of inaccuracy and seminal intuition that characterizes so much of his work:

> Pentameter verse arose among the anonymous poets of the Han dynasty, and, after receiving the favor of the poets of the Chien-an period, was formally established only by Juan Chi. He is the first man to have written pentameter poems with the full concentration of his energies. Pentameter poetic style only became formally established with him, and the scope of the poetry only became all-embracing with him.[2]

Most of these remarks are inaccurate: the poets of the Chien-an period do not seem inferior to Juan Chi in the 'energy' used to write their poems, nor is their poetry formally immature. And yet Hu Shih's statements are highly suggestive. They show, albeit rather incoherently, that he has understood Juan Chi is an epoch-making figure in Chinese poetry, and he has hinted at where his importance really lies: in the fact that he has widened the scope of pentameter poetry, that he has made it 'all-embracing'. But even here we must be more explicit. Juan Chi has not 'widened the scope' of poetry thematically to its fullest range (there is a multitude of subjects that he has not touched on that will be developed later in Chinese poetry); he has widened it, or deepened it, philosophically; he has raised it to a new plane of universality. Poets before Juan Chi spoke almost exclusively of themselves, of their own lives. Their poetry was close to the story-telling verse of the folk poets who originated the pentameter form. When they wrote about women (the abandoned or lonely wife was a favorite theme), the woman usually symbolized their own separation from their sovereign or, if one refuses to accept this traditional interpretation, these women represented the poets themselves, or an actual abandoned woman, not 'solitude', not anything approaching a universal or abstract or philosophical point of view. When such points of view are found in the verse, they are usually tags on the shortness of life or the sadness of separation, nuggets of wisdom that are not really the subject of the poem, do not show the poet struggling with what is at once a personal and a universal problem.[3]

Perhaps the best way to show what I mean is to compare some of the poetry written before Juan Chi with his own, and perhaps the best examples to use are those belonging to a well defined theme, the theme of insomnia and what one might call 'midnight anguish', the theme of the first and most famous of Juan Chi's pentameter poems, a poem we have not yet read. The theme appears in many poems of the Chien-an period, perhaps inspired by the last of the Nineteen Old Poems (*Wen hsüan* 29, pp. 8ab).[4] In any case they all borrow very freely from one another, and all the elements in Juan Chi's poem, almost without exception, are borrowed from the other poems of the tradition, sometimes with only slight variations in the order of the words in the line. These poems present a traveller away from home who, unable to sleep, gets out of bed and paces back and forth disconsolately in the moonlight. There is never any doubt about what the poet is getting at: he is describing his solitude away from his home and friends. The poem may be complicated by political considerations, but it remains a personal outpouring of an individual's sadness because of some particular, easily definable reason.

Now let us see what Juan Chi has done to the theme.

1

It is the middle of the night and I cannot sleep;
　　I sit up to strum my singing zither.
My thin curtains reflect the shining moon;
　　A pure breeze blows against my breast.
5　In the distant moors a solitary wild goose cries,
　　As swooping birds sing in the northern wood.
Back and forth I pace: what more is there to see?
　　Sad thoughts wring my lonely heart.

Contemporary readers would have recognized this poem immediately as being in the 'insomniac' tradition I mentioned above. Are the first lines not almost word for word from Wang Ts'an's 'Alone at night I cannot sleep;/I gather up my robes and rise to strum my zither'? Or from Ts'ao Jui's 'In the tranquil night I cannot sleep/And listen to the birds at their song'? And the whole poem can be said to be inspired by the first four lines of the last of the 'Nineteen Old Poems':

How brilliant the shining moon
　As it beams upon my gauze bed curtains.
Sad and anguished, I cannot sleep;
　I gather my robes together and arise to pace back and forth.

Wang Ts'an's poem, too, mentions a 'flying bird swooping over its old forest'.
There can be no doubt that Juan Chi is writing in a close-knit tradition.

But he has breathed new life into the tradition, inspired every line with
resonances they never had previously, and most important, widened his viewpoint to make this poem, too, an illustration of his epoch-making originality.
Lines 3 and 4 are particularly interesting. Juan Chi has deliberately avoided
the parallelism of 'shining moon' and 'pure breeze', and at the same time,
shifted the interest to the 'thin curtains'.[5] These lines, which at first glance
seem banal and purely traditional, reveal themselves richer on closer scrutiny.
The word I have translated 'reflect', *chien* 鑑 , is translated 'see' by Yoshikawa
Kōjirō and glossed 'shine' by Li Shan. One could thus translate: 'I see the
bright moon in (or through) the thin curtains', or 'the thin curtains shine in
the bright moonlight'. The curtains are, as we saw in the quotation from the
'Nineteen Old Poems', bed curtains. Chinese beds were generally four-posters,
hung with curtains or actually closed in with ventilated walls (like some old
beds in Brittany). The curtains thus surround the poet entirely and seem
almost to be an extension of his own being. Their thinness and the fact that
they reflect, or let one see, or shine in, the bright moonlight make them symbolic of the poet's own attitude toward nature and the outside world. They
show his acute awareness of what is going on around him and his mirror-like
reaction to what he sees – his absolute vulnerability. And the following line
(line 4) emphasizes this openness, while insisting upon the 'purity' of his intentions. Here again he puts a modest barrier between himself and the outside
world, for the word I have translated as 'breast' is literally 'the lapels of my
robe'. A romantic poet would perhaps have said he 'bared his bosom to the
cold winds'. I have deliberately preserved the meaning 'pure' for *ch'ing* 清 in
spite of the fact that it often means 'cool' or 'fresh' when it modifies 'wind'.
Even if it does have that meaning here, it retains its basic meaning of purity,
as it does when Juan Chi uses the two words together again in the last line of
Poem 42.

Lines 5 and 6 tell us what he hears and sees and add a note of mystery. The
'solitary wild goose' and 'swooping' (variant: 'northern') 'birds' suggest
allusions. Birds, again, are part of the tradition Juan Chi is writing in, but in
his predecessors' poems they are birds flying to their 'old forest' (Wang Ts'an)
or 'a swallow who has lost its flock' (Ts'ao Jui), and the 'solitary wild goose,
swooping alone towards the south' (Ts'ao P'i), is symbolic of the poet's desire

to 'swoop' towards home himself. Here no such symbolism is possible. The
poet has not told us he is abroad and there is nothing in these lines to suggest
that the birds symbolize a yearning for home. What then do they suggest? The
'wild goose' is generally the symbol of some kind of great or outstanding man;
it is to be put into the same category as the Yellow Cranes and Sea Birds of
his other poems, and, like them, it is not really a generic name for any particular bird; the term used for it, *hung* 鴻 , can be translated 'swan' or, simply, as
an adjective, 'great'. The critics are divided as to how to interpret these birds,
or rather, they are divided as to whether or not they should be strictly interpreted as definite symbols at all. The earliest to see them as definite, contrasting symbols is Lü Hsiang, one of the Wu ch'en commentators:

> The 'solitary wild goose' is a metaphor for the good officials who, in
> their loneliness, expelled from the court, cry painfully. The 'swooping
> birds' are birds of prey who love to fly in circles: they symbolize the
> men in power, close to the throne, that is to say, Ssu-ma Chao.

The 'northern wood' does suggest the emperor, since he stayed to the north of
his subjects, facing them to the south, in a ritualistic, kingly position inherited
from the earliest period of Chinese civilization. There is, too, a children's song
referred to in the *Tso chuan*, Chao 25 (Legge translation, p. 709), in which a
sovereign is said to have been forced to live 'in the distant moors', *wai yeh*
外 野 , as here. Liu Lü follows this interpretation and even Yoshikawa Kōjirō,
who usually abstains entirely from any precise identification of political
allusion, says that the 'solitary wild goose' is a 'symbol of misfortune in the
world' and the 'swooping bird', 'a symbol of the evil in the world'. Ku Chih
refers us to *Shih ching* 26 as a distant ancestor of this 'insomniac' poetic tradition ('Wide awake, I cannot sleep/As if I had some hidden woe'), and insists
upon the fact that the traditional interpretation of the *Shih ching* poem is
that it represents the words of a good man bemoaning the fact that the sovereign has taken small men as his counsellors.

    All this is extremely suggestive and very much in keeping with what we
know of Juan Chi's works. But Ho Cho asks a very pertinent question: 'Juan
Chi's "sad thoughts" are those of a man whose life is too much with him: how
can the commentators know just what he means?' And indeed, if the 'solitary
wild goose' does seem to suggest some heroic figure rejected in the far distance,
it is less easy to know what the 'swooping birds' (or 'bird') represent. The fact
that Juan Chi uses the same word to describe their singing and that of his lute,
ming 鳴 , is striking in this short poem. Could not the swooping bird symbolize himself, close to the de facto ruler in the 'northern wood'? Must the
bird (or birds) be singing 'for joy' (Chiang Shih-yüeh)? I ask these questions
not because I think I have a new solution to this old riddle, but because I

think they show Juan Chi's allusions are ambiguous. It seems wrong to me to attempt to see these two lines as representing some kind of Manicheism between the 'good' and 'bad' forces at work. And yet Juan Chi is surely alluding to present political conditions; if it is wrong to attempt to define them too precisely in the imagery of this poem, it seems even worse to me to ignore the political background altogether.[6] The poem is a suggestive one, delicate and tense, and in its haunting ambiguity, a truly fitting introduction to the entire series – in spite of Wu Ju-lun's warning that the eighty-two poems that make it up are the fruit of Juan Chi's entire lifetime and cannot be read as if they were written in any particular order.

But, even if we accept the narrower of the political interpretations of this poem, it is still very different from the other poems in the tradition it superficially belongs to, and different, too, from the tradition of Ch'ü Yüan and his epigones who describe the corruption in court and their personal inability to reach their sovereign. However you interpret it, Juan Chi's poem remains abstract; his point of view, general and philosophical. If the birds he hears symbolize those who are in and out of the graces of the court, the last two lines remain obstinately abstract: his melancholy may be inspired by current political conditions, or simply by the avian night noises that accompany his insomnia, but it remains an abstract *Weltschmerz*, not the limited, distinctly personal and contingent homesickness or disappointment that inspired his predecessors.

And this is equally true for his other poems. No. 2 in the series bemoans the lack of lasting friendship or of true constancy in human relations; no. 3, the danger of life in the world of politics; and so on throughout the series. Nos. 38 and 39 exalt heroism very much as Ts'ao Chih does in his 'Pai-ma p'ien',[7] but while the latter tells the story of brave northern horsemen ready to risk their lives for their sovereign and their country, Juan Chi raises his poems to a veritable metaphysical level, turning Ts'ao Chih's brave horsemen into cosmic heroes whose sacrifice (in Poem 38) gives the lie to Chuang-tzu's theories of relativity. But these comparisons with earlier poets do not mean that Juan Chi's poetry is 'better' than theirs because it is more 'advanced' or more 'sophisticated'. The new qualities I ascribe to Juan Chi's poetry have enriched it, made it more complicated and intellectually mature, but they have robbed it, at the same time, of some of the freshness and directness that make the poetry of the Chien-an period so appealing. A broad philosophical viewpoint is surely not a necessary adjunct of poetry, and it is not because Juan Chi introduced this element into Chinese poetry that he is a great poet, but the way he used it in his verse.

Few critics have remarked on Juan Chi's technique as such. Perhaps the earliest to touch on the subject[8] was Chung Jung 鍾 嶸 (469–518) in the

first chapter of his *Shih p'in* 詩 品 , the chapter in which he describes the
poetry of the poets of the first rank. I will translate the passage in full since it
is probably the most frequently quoted appreciation of Juan Chi we have. At
the beginning of all his critical judgements Chung Jung attempts to place the
poet in question into a poetic tradition stemming from the *Shih ching*, from
some early poet, or from folk verse.

> The origins of Juan Chi's verse are to be sought in the 'Minor Odes' of
> the *Shih ching*. His poetry is not ornate and yet his 'Songs of my inner-
> most feelings' are capable of liberating the spiritual energies and dissi-
> pating our deepest broodings. His words stay within the sphere of what
> we can see and hear, but his feelings soar out beyond the fringes of the
> universe! So magnificent is his verse that it can be compared with the
> 'Airs of the kingdoms' or the 'Odes' of the *Shih ching*! It makes us
> forget our petty narrowness and lets us reach out to what is distant and
> great. It is full of lines choked with despair. His ideas are so deep and
> untrammelled that it is difficult to know what he is getting at. Yen Yen-
> chih wrote a commentary to the verse saying Juan Chi was afraid to tell
> his aspirations outright.[9]

Chung Jung has probably chosen the 'Minor Odes' as Juan Chi's distant
model because it is in that part of the *Shih ching* (Poems 161 to 234) that
satires abound, according to traditional interpretation. By naming the 'Minor
Odes' at the beginning of his paragraph, Chung Jung immediately alerts his
reader to the type of poet he is dealing with: a satirist, a poet whose theme is
politics. And if he singles out the fact that Juan Chi's style 'is not ornate', he
is not tacitly comparing him with the highly sophisticated poets of his own
day who would make any third-century poet seem sober. As can be seen from
the fact that he calls Ts'ao Chih's style 'highly colored and ornate', he is
singling out Juan Chi's style as being particularly bare, even in his own
period.[10] In spite of the spareness of his style, Juan Chi is still said, in two
magnificent lines, to transport our thoughts to the very confines of the universe. Chung Jung is praising Juan Chi in the highest terms when he compares
his work with the 'Airs of the kingdoms' and the 'Odes' of the *Shih ching*; he
is perhaps echoing Ssu-ma Ch'ien's praise for the 'Li sao' in *Shih chi* 84, p. 4,
where the latter says Ch'ü Yüan has combined the 'sensuality without
licentiousness' of the 'Airs of the kingdoms' and the 'bitter censoriousness
without subversion' of the 'Minor Odes'. But Chung Jung's allusive style has
endless reverberations.

As 'unornate' as it is, Juan Chi's poetry is still far from being 'simple' or
'prosaic'. He has not enriched poetic technique very much, but he does have a
very personal way of leaping from one thought to another, of dividing his
poems into apparent stanzas that are not really stanzas by the movement of

his closely linked thought.[11] Some critics have even seen his verse as antici-
pating tonal parallelism in poetry. Weng Fang-kang 翁 方 綱 (1733–1818),
a well known epigraphist and poetical theorist, in his 'Wu-yen shih p'ing-tse
chü-yü' 五 言 詩 平 仄 舉 隅 (preface dated 1792, printed in 1793),
singles out seven of Juan Chi's poems (1, 5, 6, 8, 9, 11 and 16) to begin his
essay on the 'prehistory' of regulated verse.[12] His remarks are limited to pointing out the contrasts in tones of words in key positions in various lines. This is
also the aim of Huang Chieh, who declares that the two couplets in lines 3–6
of Poem 1 are at the beginning of the poetic evolution which would eventually
lead to regulated verse.[13] But the analysis of these tonal contrasts is extremely
subtle, so subtle in fact that Weng Fang-kang and Huang Chieh do not single
out the same characters as showing contrasting tones! In any case they are
subtle enough to make me admit to being insensitive to their discoveries.
These critics do not claim to make Juan Chi an 'ornate' poet, however, or a
technical innovator aside from his anticipation of tonal contrast. They, and
most other critics, would probably subscribe to the remark made by Yen Yü
嚴 羽 (fl. 1200) in his *Ts'ang-lang shih-hua* 滄 浪 詩 話 : 'After the Huang-
ch'u era (220–226) only Juan Chi's work, the "Songs of my innermost
thoughts", attains to the limits of that which is "lofty" and "antique" in art;
it retains, in its feeling and in its structure, something of the Chien-an era
(196–219).'[14] Besides flattering Juan Chi by saying he has retained the qualities of his predecessors, Yen Yü is also suggesting that he is to be considered
with them as an inheritor rather than as an innovator or as a precursor. Only
Hu Ying-lin (1551–1602), in his *Shih sou* 2, p. 28, chides Juan Chi for being
over-ornate, too heavy on style, too narrow in meaning, closer to his Chin
successors in language and form than to his Wei predecessors, and all the
worse for it.[15]

Other examples of Juan Chi's lack of inventiveness in poetic technique are
his attitude towards nature in his poetry and his handling of symbolism. If we
can believe the *Chin shu*: ' . . . he would climb upon the heights to look down
upon the mountains and rivers for days on end, forgetting to return home.'[16]
This passage has been interpreted as showing that Juan Chi was the originator
of the fad of scenery viewing, the fad that was to begin to play such an
important role in Chinese intellectual life in the fourteenth century.[17] It is all
the more surprising, then, when we turn to his actual treatment of nature in
his verse, to see that he has again followed his predecessors and treated nature
merely as a reflection of his own feelings, as a kind of 'pathetic fallacy'.[18]
Autumn, evoked so often, is not really described for itself, but as a symbol of
the passage of time: the coming of winter and the death of nature (and/or the
Wei dynasty). In Poem 1, which we have just read, all seems symbolical: the
birds, the breeze, the moonlight; nothing seems to be evoked for itself, for its

intrinsic beauty or interest. In Poem 17 he sees an *empty* landscape, a *lonely* bird, an animal *separated* from its flock, all external manifestations of his own solitude. Even when, in Poem 7, his description of nature is one of summer calm, it is again to underline the season's fragility, to lament that it will soon pass away with the inexorable evolution of the seasons. I would like to quote two lines from the poetry of T'ao Yüan-ming to show the tremendous gulf between the two poets in their appreciation of nature. At the end of the first stanza of a tetrameter poem on a subject dear to the heart of Juan Chi, 'The revolution of the seasons', 'Shih yün', T'ao Yüan-ming writes:

> There comes a wind from the south
> That touches the young sprouts with its wings.

There is a delight in nature for itself in these wonderful lines that is different from anything in Juan Chi's verse.

In his symbolism, too, Juan Chi is hardly original. His phoenixes and pine trees are both symbols of moral superiority and steadfastness that appear as early as the *Lun yü* (9, 8; 9, 27), and his other 'symbols', if they deserve that name, can really be understood only within the context of each poem, varying with their mood, never explicit, always delicate to interpret. His birds, for example, appear, according to one (unverified) account, fifty-six times in his poetry,[19] but they are hardly 'symbols of freedom and longed-for escape'.[20] Poem 1 would suffice to show how arbitrary his bird symbolism is: neither the lonely wild goose nor the swooping bird could be said to symbolize freedom or longed-for escape, and, although there are many examples of such bird symbolism in his verse (Poems 24, 46, 49, etc.), there are as many that show birds as symbols of fragility, animals, like his own tame doves, easily destroyed in our dangerous world (Poems 11 and 48) or as subject to its disappointments as humans are (Poems 65 and 79).

Just as the birds defy a definite categorization, so do the immortals, their feathered companions of the air. As we have seen in the last chapter, it is not by any means easy to assign them once and for all the role of allegorical figures, of simple symbols of escape from a dangerous political world. Juan Chi often really seems to have us take them for what they are: men so purified of worldly desires as to be superhuman, ego-less, united with the cosmos.

The most pervasive of all symbols, however, are those that describe the passage of time: the moving sun, autumn, the short lived hibiscus flowers and the peach and plum blossoms, the frost, the quickly dried dew, the graveyard, the rosy cheeks of youth. All these symbols, like the birds, are used naturally, almost naïvely, their symbolic meaning springing out of their reality and their context in the poem. Juan Chi is no symbolist, even if his intensive introspection, his constant concern with his own anguish, his twisting of nature to reflect his own soul's dark moods, sometimes make his poetry resemble that of the symbolists.

Juan Chi's position in the history of Chinese poetry was truly crucial, and one of the proofs of this is the fact that his influence has been so pervasive and so long-lasting. One finds traces of his works in countless medieval poets[21] and they are often quoted in prose works and in the *Wen hsüan*.[22] But perhaps the most striking examples of Juan Chi's influence are the large number of poets who have deliberately imitated his verse, or attempted to describe him in verse resembling his own. The earliest poet to have described Juan Chi in his verse was Yen Yen-chih (384–456), who was also the first of his commentators. In 426 Yen Yen-chih was called back from exile in the far south where he had been sent four years earlier, the victim of a *coup d'état* against his friends in court. He found life difficult after his return and, gifted with a wicked tongue, he struck out against the men in power who kept him from rising in the official hierarchy. The reaction came rapidly and Yen Yen-chih was again sent away from the capital (Nanking) and named governor of Yung-chia (the present Wen-chou, in Chekiang). To express his scorn of his oppressors he wrote a series of poems called 'Songs of the Five Princely Men', 'Wu-chün yung' 五 君 詠, describing five of the Seven Sages of the Bamboo Grove — Wang Jung and Shan T'ao, the only two of the seven to have risen in rank in the official hierarchy, are deliberately ignored, and thus snubbed as being somewhat less than princely.[23] The Princely Five are all praised for having remained aloof from the vulgar crowd. The first poem is in honor of Juan Chi:

'Infantry' Juan

Although Lord Juan kept his actions hidden from men's eyes,
    He was not only wise in the ways of the world, but clear-sighted as
        well.
His deep drunkenness was a way of hiding his intelligence;
    His allusive literature, an attempt at satire.
5   He whistled long, as if he were yearning for a friend,
    Transgressed the rites and of course shocked the common run of men.
Since he could not discuss the why and wherefore of things,
    How could he keep from sobbing at the end of the road?[24]

The 'why and wherefore of things' literally translates *wu-ku* 物 故 ; the traditional meanings of the term are 'death' and 'an accident', 'a happening', 'an affair'. Yen Yen-chih is describing Juan Chi's frustration at being unable to participate openly in the affairs of state. The ambiguity of the term is surely deliberate: the pall of 'death' hung over the 'affairs' and 'happenings' of the end of the Wei! Every line of this poem would require an extended commentary to someone unfamiliar with Juan Chi's life and work, which shows how intimately the men of Yen Yen-chih's time knew both.

Twenty years younger than Yen Yen-chih, Pao Chao 鮑 照 (405–466) is the first poet to have imitated one of Juan Chi's poems. His 'Imitation of Lord Juan's "It is the middle of the night and I cannot sleep" ' follows Juan Chi's Poem 1 step by step. The words are all different, as is the style (much more sophisticated), but the meaning of each couplet is so close to Juan Chi's that his readers, who most probably knew the original by heart, received a delicious *frisson* as they compared the original in their memories with Pao Chao's new version of it. Here is a fairly literal translation:

> The waterclock marks midnight and I cannot lie down;
> > I pour out some wine to scatter my all too plentiful woes.
> The soft wind, carried by the night, becomes cool,
> > As the moonlight flows through the chinks in the wall.
> 5   I hear the singing crane only once now:
> > Within a thousand miles he has not a single companion.
> Long I stand here, waiting for whom?
> > In my solitude I vainly taste my self-imposed sadness.

A near contemporary of Pao Chao, Wang Su 王 素 (418–471) of Lang-yeh, also wrote a poem 'in the style of Juan Chi'. Little is known of Wang Su, except that he was a hermit much admired for his purity and disinterestedness (his biography is in *Sung shu* 93, pp. 19b–20a, and *Nan shih* 24, pp. 18ab). His poem (found in *Ch'üan Sung shih* 5, p. 721) is full of echoes of Juan Chi's whole cycle, and preaches a message of purity. A phoenix and an immortal woman (the daughter of Duke Mu of Ch'in; cf. *Lieh-hsien chuan*, Kaltenmark translation, pp. 125–7) singing in the clouds send a message to a man of high principles warning him of the inconstancies of public life and darkly hinting, in the final couplet, that one must choose between purity and compromise – 'as it is said in the decade of songs called "East wind" ' in the *Shih ching* (the Minor odes).

In the generation immediately following Wang Su, a poet famous for his imitations devoted no less than sixteen poems to imitations of Juan Chi. That poet was Chiang Yen 江 淹 (444–505) and he is said to have 'loved Juan Chi above all the others'.[25] His 'Fifteen pieces written in imitation of Lord Juan's poems'[26] are quite different from the imitations by his predecessors. They are much freer, less dependent upon the sophisticated, just off center echoes of Juan Chi's lines that seem to be the principal motive his predecessors had for writing their imitations. There are parallels, but they are fewer and more spontaneous. Chiang Yen seems to be more interested in achieving something close to the total effect of Juan Chi's poetry than simply to provide

little electric *frissons* for those who recognize his learned allusion. His most
famous imitation of Juan Chi is not one of the fifteen, but one of a series
called 'Thirty pieces of poetry in the "miscellaneous style" ', 'Tsa-t'i shih san-
shih shou'雜 體 詩 三 十 首, contained in *Wen hsüan* 31, pp. 8a—30b;
the poem in imitation of Juan Chi is on p. 13b. Although it perhaps imitates
Juan Chi's verse a bit more closely than the group of fifteen, it is interesting
in itself, and also for the light it throws on Juan Chi's thought.

> **Infantry [Colonel] Juan, 'A song of my innermost thoughts'**
> The Blue Bird roams over the sea,
>> While the little doves fly in the weeds.
> What suits the one doesn't suit the other;
>> Each has wings in accord with its species.
> 5　[The doves] live out their lives flitting here and there;
>> And [the Blue Bird], from his vast heights, is also at ease, indifferent
>> to the values set by the world.
> Thanks to her [endless] transformations, Chao-yün
> Shone forth with a beauty the world has rarely seen.
> The Ching-wei bird holds wood and stones in its beak:
> 10　Who can fathom the hidden subtleties [of these phenomena]?

The first four lines of this poem are an obvious allusion to Juan Chi's Poem
46, with the Sea Bird of Juan Chi's poem transformed into the mythological
Blue Bird who appears at the end of Poem 22. The substitution is meaningful,
as we shall see. In the following lines there are also allusions or echoes: line 5,
to Poem 36; line 7, to Poem 11; line 9, to the *fu* 'Purifying the thoughts',
lines 11—14. But perhaps the most extraordinary allusion to Juan Chi's poetry
is the obscurity of the poem, the seeming lack of continuity between the first
six lines and the last four. The first six are straightforward enough: they
preach the philosophy of Chuang-tzu as modified by Kuo Hsiang that we also
saw in Juan Chi's Poem 46 (alluded to here in the first four lines). According
to this philosophy, Chuang-tzu's relativism is pushed to absurdity: even the
mystical roaming of the great Sea Bird is equated with the grasshopping of the
little doves; each contents itself with its allotted share of 'happiness'. Line 6 is
slightly ambiguous, very much as some of Juan Chi's are (e.g. Poem 23, line
11; 46, line 5); it can be taken as an affirmative declaration: 'From such vast
heights one is at peace equally with all the world's contradictions'; or as a
rhetorical question implying a negative answer: 'How could one take sides
with any mundane faction from such vast heights?' The overall meaning is the
same.

　　But what do the last four lines have to do with what precedes? And what
exactly do they mean? Chao-yün is the nymph in the 'Kao-t'ang fu' whose

name has become synonymous with amorous dalliance. As she herself explains in the *fu*: 'At dawn I am the morning Cloud [= Chao-yün], and at eve I fall as rain', and the poet describes her as the mist on the mountain constantly changing its form, 'limitless transformations in an instant' (*Wen hsüan* 19, p. 2a, and above, chapter 7, note 32). Ching-wei 精 衛 is a bird, the mythological princess Nü-wa metamorphosed after she had drowned in the Eastern Sea (above, chapter 7, note 14). She spends her days filling up the sea with sticks and stones that she carries in her beak. These three lines, then, are the 'hidden subtleties' referred to in the last line, the strange occurrences we read of in the *Shan-hai ching* and the other old books of mythology. And they give the meaning to the poem: the comfortable philosophy described in the first six lines is not all; the equation of the gigantic Sea Bird with tiny sparrows is not the end of the matter. There are things on earth undreamed of by Kuo Hsiang and his group of philosophers: miracles, spiritual wonders — jade is *not* simple stone, as Juan Chi exclaims in Poem 54. In Poem 22 Juan Chi asks the Blue Bird to show these wonders to him. Perhaps it is not a coincidence that Chiang Yen has substituted this mythological messenger of Hsi-wang-mu for the Sea Bird in his imitation. He has alerted us in the very first words that his subject is not quite what it seems to be at first glance, that it is something uncanny, not of the relativistic world described by the rest of the opening lines.

This is the most obvious reading of the poem, and a reading that is very much in keeping with the other of Chiang Yen's imitations of Juan Chi found in his collected works, and in particular with no. 5 which begins:

> We cannot know [all the movements] of the *yin* and the *yang*:
> Ghosts and spirits remain dark and obscure . . .

There is nothing quite like this in Juan Chi's works. Chiang Yen is obviously extrapolating from his own intellectual climate, so much more permeated with religion and delight in the supernatural than was Juan Chi's. But I think he has seen an aspect of Juan Chi's works that the other commentators (aside from Huang K'an) adamantly refuse to acknowledge: a real interest in religion, in the world of the spirit, and of the spirits.[27]

Chiang Yen's admiration for Juan Chi is not an isolated case. The greatest poet of the age succeeding his, the last great poet of the pre-T'ang era, Yü Hsin 庚 信 (513–581), wrote a series of twenty-seven poems under the title of Juan Chi's 'Songs of my innermost thoughts' and began the first poem of the series with an allusion to the 'Infantry [Colonel, Juan Chi]'.[28] Chang Cheng-chien 張 正 見 (died between 569 and 582) wrote a poem inspired by line 3 of Poem 1 ('The thin curtain reflects the bright moon') and Chiang Tsung 江 總 (519–594) four lines inspired by line 2 of the same poem. And their admiration for Juan Chi shows how tenacious his influence was, for at the end of the Six Dynasties period, when they lived, interest in the kind of poetry he wrote, still close to the vigorous, but, for their taste, uncouth origins of the pentameter line, had waned considerably, to be awakened only a century later with the early T'ang masters. Ch'en Tzu-ang 陳子昂 (661–701), in particular, is known as the first champion of a revival of the older verse, and he is also known as a poet profoundly influenced by Juan Chi,[29] whom he himself mentions in a letter as a kind of unattainable model for the 'singing of his innermost thoughts'.[30] Ch'en Tzu-ang's masterpiece, the series of thirty-eight poems called 'Kan yü' 感遇 , 'Frustrations', is clearly influenced by Juan Chi in the themes of many of the poems, as in the satirical atmosphere that reigns throughout them, but they are formally of a truly new era.

Ch'en Tzu-ang's championing of Juan Chi and of early pentameter poetry is the prelude to the glorious period of T'ang poetry where we again find Juan Chi cropping up constantly in the greatest of the great poets of the era: Tu Fu quotes him by name at least ten times and alludes to him much more often; Li Po is often spoken of as writing in the tradition of Juan Chi's verse, as are Chang Chiu-ling and Wei Ying-wu.[31] In fact, so pervasive is his influence that it is useless to continue citing his admirers. I would like to quote only one more poem, written by Jao Tsung-i 饒宗頤 in 1960, to show how Juan Chi's 'aura of purity has shone down countless generations' (Poem 42) to our own times.[32] This poem is neither an imitation of Juan Chi's poetry nor a description of his character, but a poem written upon the rhymes of Poem 1, what the Chinese call *ho*[4]-*yün* 和韻, 'echoing the rhymes' of another's poem. The practice began in mid-T'ang times and there are three ways of carrying it out. The poet wishing to 'echo' the rhymes of another either writes a poem using the same rhyme category and the same number of lines, or, and this is infinitely more difficult, he will use the actual rhyme words in his new poem, either in the original order or in a new order. Professor Jao has chosen the most difficult of these methods, respecting all of Juan Chi's rhyme words in their original order in the eighty-two poems, an amazing virtuoso performance. He himself describes the background in two short prefaces to the 'Ch'ang-chou chi' 長洲集, his collection of poems echoing Juan Chi's rhymes:

> ... Among the poets of the Wei and Chin periods, only Juan Chi was able to plumb the depths of his passion and T'ao Yüan-ming to plumb the depths of his entire human nature. When Su Tung-p'o was exiled to the south he wrote 'echoes' of all of T'ao Yüan-ming's works. I am particularly fond of Juan Chi's poetry and wanted to express what I had stored up in my heart by following his rhymes. Perhaps, by unstinting effort, I have been able to attain to an infinitesimal amount of the

passion he expressed. On New Year's Eve (according to the solar calendar) I had taken temporary lodging in Ch'ang-chou, [an island near Hongkong], and I took my zither to dwell in [the house of a friend called] Twin Jade Hall. My room was surrounded by the sound of the rolling waves: they were like the wild goose singing in the outer moors and made me melancholic. There was a copy of the 'Poems which sing of my innermost thoughts' on the table and I echoed their rhymes in the same order, finishing the work in five days . . .

My poems do not imitate Juan Chi's style: they only follow his rhymes and describe my own thoughts and pains, to fix them thus [in words] for a short while . . .

Here is the first of Professor Jao's poems. The words at the end of the couplets are those common to both Juan Chi's and this poem. I felt I should use the same words as in my translation of Juan Chi's poem (virtuosity *oblige*); they are in fact all translations of the original Chinese rhyme words (zither, breast, wood, heart).

> Now that the cold waves have purified my ears
>> I can stop the strings of my singing zither.
> I hear the sound of a wind come from afar
>> To cleanse, for a while, my troubled breast.
> 5   The banana trees show forth their new-grown greenery;
>> There are only two or three, not enough to form a wood.
> Just by looking at one another we seem to have become friends;
>> I would like to bind us together into a brotherhood of true hearts.

The poem is redolent with allusions, but is, if anything, less allusive than most of Professor Jao's sensitively erudite verse. The allusion of greatest importance for understanding the poem is in line 1. 'Purified [literally, 'washed out] my ears' refers to the story alluded to by Juan Chi in Poem 74 in which the hermit Hsü-yu 'washes out his ears', *hsi-erh* 洗 耳, after Yao has soiled them by offering the empire to him. The banana trees in line 5 are a common Buddhist symbol of the essential unsubstantiality of the soul; just as the banana plant stem is made up of successive layers with no real core, so is man an assemblage of 'aggregates' with no real, lasting soul. The sage realizes this and looks upon the banana plant as the symbol of the ideal human condition, of essential purity and disinterestedness. The poem is thus, from the first line to the last, a hymn to purity, to purity in a troubled world, a world that has soiled the poet's ears and that only the sound of cold waves or the breath of a breeze 'come from afar' can cleanse. Formally, superficially, the poem, in spite of the 'echoed rhymes', is very different from Juan Chi's. It is set at a much lower pitch, and the dénouement, while far from being optimistic or joyful, is the kind of graceful conceit that Juan Chi ignores. And yet underneath it all there is a basic communion between the two poets, between two men of different ages and (in all probability) of quite different temperaments. There is an interiority in both poems, and a moral sensitivity bruised by a hostile world that draw the two men together across so many generations into their essential common humanity.

CONCLUSION

There can be no doubt that the usurpation of the Wei throne by the Ssu-ma family was the single most important event in Juan Chi's life, however unlikely that may seem to a modern Westerner. The divinity of kingship, so obvious in the most ancient Near Eastern societies, maintained its central importance for the Chinese long after it had become secondary (if hardly forgotten) in the Mediterranean world. Juan Chi, by his father's post and friendship with the imperial family, was morally attached to the Wei dynasty. The Ssu-ma usurpation, moreover, was a sordid affair, full of cheating and hypocrisy, bloodshed and violence, nothing like the gentlemanly accession of the Wei to the throne of the dying Han in 220. The Ssu-ma acted so skilfully that Juan Chi was a member of their party in all probability before he knew of their aims, and, once enrolled in their headquarters, his possibilities of action were severely restricted. He had only three alternatives open to him: collaboration with the usurpers, resistance (and retirement from politics could be considered resistance), and a kind of passive resistance in which he could 'serve without serving'. Collaboration meant moral resignation; outright resistance or 'retirement' meant certain death for himself and his entire family. Juan Chi chose the last alternative and played his difficult role with great ability. He was a constant guest at the usurpers' table, and yet took no part in political life. Very few historians have criticized him for his action.[1]

The hypocrisy of the political world rubbed off on to contemporary society. The Ssu-ma called themselves staunch Confucianists, saviors of the state against the libertine views of Ts'ao Ts'ao and his descendants, and their partisans seem to have indulged in ostentatious ritualism and demonstrations of filial piety. But the decay of morality was not due entirely to political instability; both were manifestations of the tremendous changes taking place in Chinese society, transforming it into the family-centered quasi-feudal system characteristic of the Chinese 'Middle Ages'. Again Juan Chi had a number of different alternatives open to him: give in to the reigning hypocrisy, oppose it outright, or play the clown. That he chose the last shows that he was not fundamentally anti-social, that he was truly attached to human society. To have given in to hypocrisy would mean that he was at bottom indifferent to society, and to oppose it outright would again have brought exile or even death to him and to his entire family. By playing the clown he could attempt to show up his contemporaries' excesses and to force them towards more reasonable, more natural moral reactions.

Juan Chi's clowning was in the Taoist tradition and most of the authors who have studied his period place him in the camp of the 'Taoists',[2] almost always coupling his name with that of his friend, the philosopher Hsi K'ang, or within the group of the Seven Sages of the Bamboo Grove, as partisans of 'spontaneity', *tzu-jan*, or 'freedom', *k'uang-ta* 曠 達.[3] And yet the two thinkers are in fact very dissimilar, as is to be expected of two such original and creative geniuses. Hsi K'ang was, I believe, as close to being a true 'Taoist' as any Chinese thinker in the period. But the case of Juan Chi is very different, and more typical. He was not a great philosopher, although he has been highly praised for his philosophical essays,[4] and his philosophical position was much closer to traditional Confucianism than to 'Taoism'. One of his most astute commentators, in fact, speaks of him as a 'pure Confucianist' and I wonder if he was not right.[5] Like Hsi K'ang he was a partisan of 'spontaneity' against the rigid formalism of contemporary Confucianism, but Hsi K'ang seems to have been heart and soul an admirer of the ancient Taoists and their philosophy in almost all his works, whereas Juan Chi's 'Taoist' works are limited to 'On understanding Chuang-tzu' and the 'Biography of Master Great Man'. Juan Chi was too attached to society, and to the antique social virtues, to be able to give himself over entirely to the kind of primitive anarchism preached by the ancient Taoists.

Neither can Juan Chi's interest in the search for immortality be considered as a sure indication of 'Taoist' proclivities. Whether it grew up independently of Taoism or not, the search for immortality certainly became imbued with Taoist thought and terminology in the Han dynasty, but immortality became an exceedingly common goal among medieval Chinese, a goal that in itself did not preclude other orientations in other fields; many of the most ardent searchers after immortality were strong opponents of Chuang-tzu's philosophy and staunch Confucianists in their official life. Juan Chi was indeed a 'pure Confucianist', but one who yearned to supplement Confucianism with something new, one who had what we would call 'religious aspirations', and it was only in Taoism and the search for immortality that he could find elements that seemed to satisfy them. He yearned for an impossible synthesis of antique ethics and medieval religion, a synthesis he was perhaps born too early to achieve.

The Chinese commentators have been most struck by the fact that so much of Juan Chi's verse is 'political', that it is concerned with the change in dynasty that took place under his eyes. Shen Te-ch'ien perhaps put it most forcibly: 'It was inevitable that, living at the time he did, Master Juan should have written the poems he wrote.'[6] If this is more than a truism (any poet is part of the period in which he lives), it should probably be interpreted as meaning that the strong satirical element in Juan Chi's verse was inevitable to any 'right-minded' poet, one who would oppose the unworthy usurpation of the Ssu-ma; it was natural that there should be poetry full of obscure satire against the evil-doers when it was impossible to speak out clearly. But the commentators have attempted to cope with this satire in two ways. They have either considered the satire so veiled as to be impossible to understand in any but the most general way (Yen Yen-chih, Shen Te-ch'ien himself) or they have attempted to identify the butts of even the most obscure allusions (Ch'en Hang, Ku Chih).[7] It is natural to attempt to come as close as we can to what Juan Chi really meant, and so, it seems to me, it is natural to attempt to identify the men to whom he is alluding. But it is absurd to believe that we today can find the key to puzzles that were meant to baffle his own contemporaries. His poetry must be read as poetry first, with the search to identify allusions strictly subservient to the cause of understanding the true pulse of the verse. The more extended attempts to identify satirical allusions by Ku Chih and some of the blunter equations of Ch'en Hang are absurd, risible, and give the Western student of Chinese poetry a pitiful opinion of Chinese criticism – until he stops to think of the similar absurdities still practiced in the lower reaches of Elizabethan studies (and elsewhere) in the West! But with Chinese commentators the question is further complicated by their unwillingness to believe that a poet (or anyone else) can be interested in anything but politics. Ch'en Hang says Juan Chi's verse is 'the expression of the indignation of a man of goodness and of ideals', and he adds: 'How could it be nothing more than complaints about the sadness of life?'[8] His judgement is typical of the majority of Chinese commentators who cannot imagine that Juan Chi's sadness could ever spring from anything other than the fall of the Wei dynasty.

And yet Juan Chi's sadness was more complex. He attempted to reach out perhaps not 'beyond' politics, but to something that would contain politics and yet penetrate into another sphere. He was rather incoherently groping towards some kind of religion, something that would lead him out beyond 'the end of the road', and this search to attain to some new level of meaning in life is, I believe, what led to his broadening and deepening the pentameter form, raising it to the place of pre-eminence that it has occupied in the history of Chinese poetry. He is no longer content to see himself as a wanderer far from home, or as a disappointed official rejected by his sovereign; he is also a man alone in the universe: his home-sickness is truly metaphysical. Other poets had versified philosophy before him (usually in *fu* rather than in regular verse), but for him it was no longer a question of simple, objective philosophy. He has put all his passion into his verse, all his passion into his desire to know who he is, where he is going. Other poets had wandered to Heaven and supped with its King, dallied with the immortal maidens in the Pure Capital and tasted the delights of the rapture of the soul, but Juan Chi wants to know if all these mystical voyages are really possible for him, if they will lead him to an eternal life, and not simply vanish when he awakes.

This broadened interest is not really philosophical; it is more deeply human and passionate. When Liu Hsieh 劉 勰 (born in 464?) says: 'Juan Chi wrote his poetry with his vital breath (*ch'i*)' (*Wen-hsin tiao-lung* 47), he is probably saying something similar. Juan Chi writes with his soul. He 'plumbs the depths of his passion', as Jao Tsung-i has said, and his poetry is truly intimate and passionate, the 'tensest' in Chinese verse according to Yoshikawa Kōjirō.[9] Only his mystical exaltation and his 'immortal' yearnings provide temporary solace, ultimately unsatisfactory. Hsi K'ang, thirteen years his junior, was a 'firm believer' in immortality seeking (*Hsi K'ang chi chiao-chu* 2, p. 123), a truly religious personality. Perhaps Juan Chi lived too early, was too strongly attached to traditional values to be able to shake himself free of them. Whatever the reason, his ambiguous, tortured verse seems torn between the two worlds: full of the righteous indignation of the antique patrician civil servant, it is also incoherently groping towards some kind of metaphysical salvation that would take him forever out of time and corruption and the relativity of the world here below.

NOTES

Introduction

1   *Chu-lin ch'i-hsien lun*, quoted in *Shih-shuo hsin-yü* C (Section 23), p. 38a. The reader will find bibliographical descriptions of the *Chu-lin ch'i-hsien lun* and similar fragmentary works in the list of *Fragmentary sources quoted*.

2   The members of the Juan family are said to be descended from the Shang 'Lords of Juan' mentioned in *Shih ching* 241 whose fief was located in southeastern Kansu. This genealogy is given in the tomb inscription for Juan Chi (of doubtful authenticity) by Chi Shu-liang 稽 叔 良 (probably Hsi 嵇 Shu-liang). According to Yen K'o-chün (*Ch'üan San-kuo wen* 53, pp. 3b–4b), the inscription is found only in the Ming anthology *Kuang wen-hsüan* where it is anachronistically ascribed to Chi Shu-yeh, i.e. Hsi K'ang (cf. *Ssu-k'u ch'üan-shu tsung-mu t'i-yao* 192, pp. 5–6 of the Wan-yu wen-k'u edition). This genealogy is also mentioned in the *Yüan-ho hsing-tsuan* 6, p. 35b (1880 edition) and *T'ung chih* 26, p. 453c (Commercial Press edition). Fictitious genealogies of this kind were extremely common during the Middle Ages when one's official career depended entirely upon the antiquity and rank of one's family.

3   Cf. *Yüan-ho hsing-tsuan, loc. cit.* Two other members of the Juan family of Juan Tun's generation, Juan Ch'en 阮 諶 and Juan Lüeh 阮 略 , are listed in the 'Shih-shuo hsin-yü jen-ming p'u' (photographic reproduction of the Sung edition, Peking, 1962, p. 67b) by Wang Tsao 王 藻 (1079–1154). Juan Ch'en is listed as Minister, *nei-shih* 內 史 , of the principality of Ch'i. (A variant says he was Prefect, *t'ai-shou* 太 守 , of the commandery of Ch'i, but Ch'i was a principality under the Latter Han until 206; cf. *Hou Han-shu chi-chieh, chih*, 22, p. 3944 of the Kuo-hsüeh chi-pen ts'ung-shu edition.) According to a history of the Juan family, the *Juan-shih p'u* (quoted in *San-kuo chih chi-chieh* 16, p. 27b), Juan Ch'en never accepted the official posts that were offered to him and was the author of a work on ritual called the *San-li t'u* 三 禮 圖 . But the *Sui shu* 32, p. 19a, lists this work (in 9 *chüan*) as being by Cheng Hsüan, the 'Hou Han *shih-chung* 侍 中 Juan Ch'en and others'. The title given to him here implies that Juan Ch'en did serve in an official post and that he was also given the honorific title of *shih-chung*, 'Gentleman-in-Waiting at the Court'. (On the *San-li t'u* and Juan Ch'en's role in its composition, see *Sung shih* 431, pp. 3ab, and P. Demiéville, *BEFEO* 25 (1925) p. 216, reproduced in *Choix d'études sinologiques* (Leiden, 1973), p. 578.)

4   *San-kuo chih chi-chieh* 1, p. 17b. The *Yüan-ho hsing-tsuan* and the *T'ung chih* say that Juan Tun was magistrate at Pa-wu 巴 吾, obviously a mistake for Chi-wu 己 吾 ; cf. Ts'en Chung-mien, *Yüan-ho hsing-tsuan ssu chiao-chi* (Kuo-li chung-yang yen-chiu yüan li-shih yü-yen yen-chiu so chuan-k'an 29, Shanghai, 1948), p. 643.

5   The two most complete accounts of Juan Yü's life are by Yoshikawa Kōjirō,
     Yoshikawa Kōjirō zenshū 7 (Tokyo, 1968) pp. 112–17, and Nakagawa Kaoru,
     'Kenan bunjin den (2) : Gen U den', *Tottori daigaku gakugei gakubu kenkyū
     hōkoku : Jimbun shakai kenkyū* (Tottori) 14 (1963) pp. 1–20. The most recent
     study of Juan Yü, and the most thorough treatment of his poetry, is Shimosada
     Masahiro, 'Gen U no gogonshi ni tsuite', *Chūgoku bungaku hō* (Kyoto) 24 (1974)
     pp. 24–47.

6   His letter to Sun Ch'üan is contained in *Wen hsüan* 42 and has been translated by
     E. von Zach, *Die chinesische Anthologie* (Harvard-Yenching Institute Series XVIII,
     1958) 2, pp. 773–8. There is an imaginary answer written to this letter by Su
     Shih (1037–1101) in *Ching-chin Tung-p'o wen-chi shih-lüeh* 58 (Peking, 1957)
     pp. 961–6.

7   *San-kuo chih chi-chieh* 21, p. 10a.

8   *Wen hsüan* 42, p. 9b; 52, p. 7a.

9   *Tien lüeh*, quoted in *San-kuo chih chi-chieh* 21, p. 10a. The letter in question may
     be the letter Ts'ao Ts'ao sent to the warlord Han Sui in the autumn of 211 as a
     ruse, trying to separate him from his allies before the battle of the Wei; cf. *San-
     kuo chih chi-chieh* 1, p. 85a.

10   *San-kuo chih chi-chieh* 21, p. 9a. These posts were respectively of the fifth and
     seventh grades; cf. Hung I-sun, *San-kuo chih-kuan piao*, p. 13a and c (Erh-shih-wu
     shih pu-pien edition, p. 2743a and c). In the *San-kuo chih* 21, the first of these
     posts is called *chün-mou* 謀 *chi-chiu*, perhaps to avoid the taboo of the name of
     Ssu-ma Shih, but this taboo is not avoided in *San-kuo chih chi-chieh* 1, p. 39b,
     where it is stated that the post was created by Ts'ao Ts'ao in 198.

11   *San-kuo chih chi-chieh* 21, p. 10a. There were *ts'ang-ts'ao* in various of the central
     government bureaus (*t'ai-wei, ssu-k'ung*) as well as in the provincial administrations.
     Hung I-sun, *op. cit.*, p. 13c, says (rightly I believe) that Juan Yü was in the *ssu-
     k'ung*'s (i.e. Ts'ao Ts'ao's) bureau. It was a seventh rank post.

12   *San-kuo chih chi-chieh* 14, p. 23b, and *passim*.

13   Juan Yü's early death would account for the low grade posts he occupied, if indeed
     he did die young, as this text and the early age of his son at his death seem to
     show. Nakagawa, in the article quoted above, on the strength of a poem of Juan
     Yü's describing an aging, white-haired man, insists at great length that he could
     not have died before middle age, but his arguments are not entirely convincing.

14   *Wen hsüan* 16, p. 19b, and, for the second sentence, *I-wen lei-chü* 34, p. 7b
     (photographic reproduction of a Sung edition, Peking, 1959).

15   *Wen-shih chuan* quoted in *San-kuo chih chi-chieh* 21, p. 9b.

16   *Hou Han-shu chi-chieh* (*chih*) 29, pp. 4249–50.

17   See P'ei Sung-chih's discussion, *San kuo chih chi-chieh* 21, p. 9b.

18   *San-kuo chih chi-chieh* 1, p. 95b.

19   The story of men being burned out of mountains (and usually burned to death) is
     known in Chinese antiquity; see, for example, *Hsin hsü* 7, pp. 13ab (Ssu-pu
     ts'ung-k'an edition), for one version of the story of Chieh-tzu T'ui, and the dis-
     cussion in *Jih-chih lu* 25, pp. 81–4 (Wan-yu wen-k'u edition).

20   There is an entire chapter devoted to these hermits in *Hou Han-shu* 113 (*Hou
     Han-shu chi-chieh* 83, pp. 3035–63).

21   *Shih-shuo hsin-yü* C (Section 33), p. 93a.

Chapter 1

1   Lu K'an-ju and Feng Yüan-chün, *Chung-kuo shih shih* (Peking, 1957), pp. 334–5.

2   *Wen hsüan* 23, pp. 2a and b. In the Wu-ch'en edition of the *Wen hsüan* the second
     of these comments is attributed to Li Shan (died 689). This is probably an error
     of the Wu-ch'en editors. Li Shan's edition states at the outset that the commen-

tary to Juan Chi's poems is by 'Yen Yen-nien, Shen Yüeh, *et al.*', although he sometimes adds the words 'Shen Yüeh says' or 'Yen Yen-nien says', he sometimes prefaces the comments with no attribution at all. Are these remarks his own, as the Wu-ch'en editors believe, or are they 'Yen Yen-nien's *et al.*', as I suggest here? Various later commentators have chosen one or the other of these two alternatives. I base my conclusion that the comments are not by Li Shan on two facts: (1) Li Shan himself, in his own edition, introduces his comments with the words 'Shan says' (as in *chüan* 23, pp. 4a, 4b, 5b, etc.); (2) as Professor Jao Tsung-i has pointed out to me in private conversation, the comments are very unlike Li Shan's which are usually simple references to parallel texts. Interesting material on Li Shan's commentary is given in Obi Kōichi, 'Monzen Ri Zen chū insho kōshō kō', *Hiroshima daigaku bungakubu kiyō* 26, 1 (1966) pp. 101–5.

3 According to Wan Ssu-t'ung, *Wei fang-chen nien-piao* (Erh-shih-wu shih pu-pien edition), pp. 2618 and 2619, Wang Ch'ang was governor of Yen-chou from 226 to 241. Juan Chi could have been to see him at any time during this period, but the scene depicted in the anecdote makes one feel that it was as a very young man that he accompanied his uncle to Tung-chün. Liu Ju-lin, *Han Chin hsüeh-shu piennien* 6 (Shanghai, 1935), p. 111, places the anecdote in 225.

4 Ssu-ma I recommended him to the emperor in 236; cf. *San-kuo chih chi-chieh* 27, p. 14a.

5 The westernmost part of central Shantung. The capital of Yen-chou was Yen 鄄 , some twenty kilometers southeast of the present P'u-hsien, Shantung.

6 *Wei-shih ch'un-ch'iu* quoted in *Shih-shuo hsin-yü* A (Section 1), p. 5b. The first line is taken from the *Chin shu* (cf. *Chin-shu chiao-chu* 49, p. 1b). Another version of this interview, slightly abridged, is to be found in the *Chin shu* by Tsang Junghsü quoted in the *T'ai-p'ing yü-lan* 512, p. 5b (p. 2332a of the re-edition made in Peking, 1960).

7 Cf. D. Holzman, 'Les débuts du système médiéval de choix et de classement des fonctionnaires', in *Mélanges publiés par l'Institut des Hautes Etudes Chinoises* (Paris, 1957), pp. 401–3.

8 Strictly speaking, Wei should be referred to as a kingdom, one of the Three Kingdoms, but each of the Three Kingdoms pretended it was the legitimate inheritor of the Han empire and set up an imperial system in imitation of the Han.

9 The *Wei-shih ch'un-ch'iu* says he may have been a grandson of Ts'ao Chang (*San-kuo chih chi-chieh* 4, p. 1a), but see the discussion by Lu Pi, *ibid.* 3, p. 36a, who insists that the child was really of unknown origin.

10 Cf. H. Maspero, *La Chine antique* (Paris, 1955), p. 326.

11 The popularity of these lines in the Middle Ages can be seen from the fact that they are quoted (ironically) by the rebel Huan Hsüan 桓 玄 as he prepared to enter Chien-k'ang (Nanking) in 402 to take the Chin throne (*Shih-shuo hsin-yü* B (Section 13), p. 104a) and by Li Tao-yüan in the *Shui-ching chu*, 22, p. 42.

12 The most famous of the towers, the T'ung-ch'üeh t'ai, was celebrated in a *fu* by Ts'ao Ts'ao's eighteen-year old son, Ts'ao Chih. The *fu* is contained in the *Ts'ao-chi ch'üan-p'ing* 2, p. 20 (Peking, 1957 edition). The building of the three towers is discussed in *San-kuo chih chi-chieh* 1, pp. 78a and 100b. The T'ung-ch'üeh t'ai was in Ts'ao Ts'ao's mind shortly before he died; his tomb, the Hsi-ling, could be seen from it. Cf. Wang Chung-lao, *Ts'ao Ts'ao* (Shanghai, 1956), p. 119.

13 The character 妖 is actually substituted for 魅 (as in Juan Chi's text if my emmendation is correct) in Li Hsien's commentary to the 'Ying chien' 應 閒 (*Hou Han-shu chi-chieh* 59, p. 2064), the work by Chang Heng referred to.

14 The various myths concerning these figures are discussed in some detail in M. Granet, *Danses et légendes de la Chine ancienne* (Paris, 1959), pp. 352–60.

15 They seem to be quoting from the Ssu-k'u ch'üan-shu version of this work, the

only version that bears the exact title of *Shih-hua pu-i*; the more current editions of Yang Shen's literary criticism, the *Sheng-an shih-hua* and its *pu-i*, do not contain an entry dealing with this poem by Juan Chi.

16 The only exception to this statement known to me is the eulogy of Ho Yen's administration by Fu Hsien 傅 咸 (239–294) found in the *Chin shu* (*Chin-shu chiao-chu* 47, p. 15a). Recent Chinese historians of the period, always on the watch for reformist movements, tend to see the Ts'ao Shuang clique in a highly favorable light; see Hsü Te-lin, *San-kuo shih chiang-hua* (Shanghai, 1955), pp. 106–7.

17 *San-kuo chih chi-chieh* 4, p. 9a. The *t'ai-wei* occupied the third highest post in the empire at this time, after the *t'ai-fu* Ssu-ma I and the *ta chiang-chün* Ts'ao Shuang.

18 Tsang Jung-hsü, *Chin shu*, quoted in *Wen hsüan* 40, p. 30a. The term translated 'municipal offices' is *tu-t'ing* 都 亭 , and it is somewhat obscure. It would seem to have been some kind of administrative center which included an official hostelry, jail, post office and barracks. Was it for the postal service that Juan Chi visited it in this quotation? The term has been studied by a large number of scholars, and a bibliography has been established by Y. Hervouet, *Un poète de cour sous les Han: Sseu-ma Siang-jou* (Paris, 1964), pp. 37–8, to which should be added the works quoted by Moriya Mitsuo, 'Sō Gi shakusei ni kansuru ni san no kōsatsu', *Tōyōshi kenkyū* 20 (1962), p. 393.

19 When he retired after the death of Confucius, Tzu-hsia, one of Confucius's disciples, became the teacher of Wen, the Marquis of Wei. The Hsi was an old name for the portion of the Yellow River that runs along the western Shansi border. Cf. *Shih chi* 67, pp. 29–30.

20 Tsou-tzu (or Tsou Yen) was a philosopher of the Warring States period whose most famous exploit was the changing of the climate of a cold northern valley which made it possible to grow millet there. He was for a time the teacher of Chao, Prince of Yen (311–279 B.C.). Cf. *Shih chi* 74, p. 8; trans. D. Bodde, in Fung Yu-lan, *The history of Chinese philosophy*, vol. 1, p. 161.

21 Officials wore silk clothing and ornate belts of untanned leather.

22 If he had accepted an official post Juan Chi would have been exempt from taxes.

23 *Wen hsüan* 40, p. 30b–31a. There is a translation of this text by E. von Zach, *Die chinesische Anthologie* 2, pp. 767–8

24 Tsang Jung-hsü, *Chin shu*, quoted in *Wen hsüan* 40, pp. 30ab.

25 Wang Jung (234–305) was fourteen years old when he first met Juan Chi, who was then a Secretary of the Minister of State Affairs, *shang-shu lang*; cf. *Chu-lin ch'i-hsien lun*, quoted in *Shih-shuo hsin-yü* C (Section 24), p. 49a.

26 *Chin-shu chiao-chu* 49, p. 2b.

27 *Ts'an-chün* was a low (seventh grade) post of relative importance, since its duties were to advise the *ta chiang-chün* on military affairs. The *Shui-ching chu* 16, p. 80, says that Juan Chi's 'old home' (not his ancestral home) was at a bend ('Juan's Bend') of the Ku River (the present Chien River), not far to the southeast of Lo-yang.

28 *Chin-shu chiao-chu* 49, p. 2b; cf. *Wei-shih ch'un-ch'iu*, quoted in the *San-kuo chih chi-chieh* 21, p. 20b.

29 *Chin-shu chiao-chu* 1, p. 36a.

30 Hsi Ts'o-ch'ih, *Han Chin ch'un-ch'iu*, quoted in *San-kuo chih chi-chieh* 28, p. 3b.

31 Cf. Ho Ch'ang-ch'ün, *Wei Chin ch'ing-t'an ssu-hsiang ch'u-lun* (Shanghai, 1947), p. 45 and note 10, p. 53.

32 Cf., for example, T'ang Yung-t'ung and Jen Chi-yü, *Wei Chin hsüan-hsüeh chung ti she-hui cheng-chih ssu-hsiang lüeh-lun* (Shanghai, 1956), pp. 5–6.

33 Cf. Wang Chung-lao, *Wei Chin nan-pei ch'ao Sui ch'u-T'ang shih* 1 (Shanghai, 1961) p. 61, who also insists upon the 'nobility' of the wives of the Ssu-ma. His

demonstration of this latter point, however, is directly contradicted in the case of Ssu-ma I's mother-in-law (who was of the Shan 山 family) by the *Chin shu* of Yü Yü quoted in the *Shih-shuo hsin-yü*, A (Section 3), p. 51b, according to which Ssu-ma I himself made fun of Shan T'ao, a member of the same Shan family, saying he came from a 'small clan'. The problem is a complex one and I doubt that we have enough historical materials to draw definitive conclusions.

34 Chang Chih-yüeh, 'Lüeh-lun Juan Chi chi ch'i "Yung-huai shih" ', *Wen-hsüeh i-ch'an tseng-k'an* 11 (Peking, 1962) pp. 76—8.

35 Cf. Ho Tzu-ch'üan, *Wei Chin nan-pei ch'ao shih-lüeh* (Shanghai, 1958), pp. 28—9.

36 Chang Chih-yüeh, p. 74, suggests that the low grade of his father's position in Ts'ao Ts'ao's 'Military Government' and the fact that he died before the accession of the new (Ts'ao-Wei) dynasty weakened Juan Chi's ties with that dynasty, to the extent at least that the Ssu-ma could consider him as a possible ally, as they could not consider Hsi K'ang who was related to the Ts'ao family by marriage. The Juan, however, as we have seen (above, p. 3), were intimates of the Ts'ao, and it seems doubtful to me that his father's hierarchical grade or early death could have influenced Juan Chi's own loyalty to their dynasty.

37 There is one character too many in the second line, showing probable textual corruption.

38 To make them even more inaccessible to hunters; cf. *Hsün-tzu* 30, p. 351.

39 This is an allusion to a story found in the *K'ung-tzu chia-yü* 18 (trans. R. Wilhelm, *Kungfutse : Schulgespräche*, Jena, 1961, p. 96) describing the sadness of a mother bird as she takes leave of her four fledglings when they fly away from the maternal nest on Mt Huan to the four corners of the world.

40 Cf. Wang Yün-hsi, *Yüeh-fu shih lun-ts'ung* (Shanghai, 1958), pp. 58—9, and *Sung shu*, pp. 24a—26a (T'ung-wen shu-chü edition). The symbolism of white doves is applied to the Chin (Ssu-ma) dynasty by Tso Chiu-p'in 左 九 嬪 (i.e. the poetess Tso Fen 左 芬) in a *fu* dated 272 whose preface can be found in *T'ai-p'ing yü-lan* 921, pp. 7ab. But even more significant is the fact that Ts'ao Chih lists doves as signs of 'Wei's virtue' in the set of tetrameter verses appended to his essay 'Wei te lun': *Ts'ao-chi ch'üan-p'ing* 9, p. 165.

41 Cf. D. Holzman, 'Les premier vers pentasyllabiques datés dans la poésie chinoise', in *Mélanges de sinologie offerts à Monsieur Paul Demiéville* (Paris, 1974), vol. 2, pp. 96—7.

42 Cf. *San-kuo chih chi-chieh* 3, p. 42a.

43 Cf. *Ch'un-ch'iu fan-lu* 59; Fung Yu-lan, *The history of Chinese philosophy* (Princeton, 1953), vol. 2, p. 22.

44 The texts of Juan Chi's *fu* are translated from his works in the Han Wei liu-ch'ao pai san ming-chia collection (Sao-yeh shan-fang edition, Shanghai, 1925, as the basic edition). Nakajima Chiaki, 'Gen Seki no "ron" to "fu" to ni tsuite', *Nihon Chūgoku gakkai hō* (Tokyo) 9 (1957) pp. 37—48, interprets 'The doves' as a satire against Ssu-ma Shih, Ssu-ma I's son and successor (p. 48).

45 A sixth-grade advisory post; the *Chin-shu chiao-chu* 49, p. 2b, says Ssu-ma Shih took him into his bureau as *ta ssu-ma ts'ung-shih chung-lang* which is probably an error, since Ssu-ma Shih was *ta chiang-chün* ('generalissimo') and never *ta ssu-ma*.

46 *San-kuo chih chi-chieh* 9, pp. 55b—56a. The conflicting versions of this event are all translated in A. Fang, *The Chronicles of the Three Kingdoms*, vol. 2, pp. 161—3, 169—7.

47 *San-kuo chih chi-chieh* 4, p. 33b.

48 *Shih chi* 61, pp. 9—10.

49 *Lun yü* 5, 22; 7, 14; 16, 12; etc.

50 Bronzes from Shang or Western Chou times have been found in these hills, but their celebrity as a burial place seems to date from the Latter Han times; cf.

Morohashi Tetsuji, *Dai Kan Wa jiten* 2, p. 455b. According to the *Yüeh-fu shih-chi* 94, p. 7a, ballads bearing the name 'Pei-mang hsing' (Mt Shou-yang is a peak in the Pei-mang range) were funeral hymns, but it only quotes two examples, both dating from the T'ang dynasty.

51 Strictly speaking, the first year of the Cheng-yüan era had no autumn; it began in the tenth lunar month, the first month of winter. Was Juan Chi attempting, by this anachronism, to place the scene of his poem as close as possible to the events of the deposition?

52 Juan Chi was *ts'ung-shih chung-lang* from 251 to 254 or 255.

53 I.e. Ssu-ma Shih's headquarters. Ssu-ma Chao's headquarters (perhaps the same one that was used later by his brother Ssu-ma Shih) still existed centuries later during the Northern Wei dynasty when it was used as an armaments depot; cf. *Lo-yang ch'ieh-lan ahi chiao-chi* (Peking, 1958), p. 39.

54 There have been at least five mountains called Shou-yang (which means 'first light', the first to catch the light of the sun in the morning) in China. Po I and Shu Ch'i's is undetermined, but Juan Chi's still bears the same name and is about seven kilometers northwest of Yen-shih hsien, Honan, about ten kilometers northeast of the old town of Lo-yang. According to the *Shui-ching chu* 1, p. 77, there was a temple in honor of Po I and Shu Ch'i on the mountain erected during the Latter Han dynasty.

55 Echoes Chang Heng, 'Ssu-hsüan fu', *Wen hsüan* 15, p. 2b; trans. von Zach, p. 218.

56 These two lines echo the 'Yüan ssu' in the 'Ch'i chien' attributed to Tung-fang Shuo; *Ch'u tz'u*, p. 128.

57 The phrase 'the two old men' in Han and pre-Han texts usually refers to Po I and T'ai-kung Wang (Lü Shang): cf. *Meng-tzu* 4A, 13; *Han shu* 87B, p. 3568. In later texts, as here, it often refers to Po I and Shu Ch'i.

58 *Ch'üan San-kuo wen* 44, pp. 8b–9a, adds eleven characters at the end of this *fu* that obviously belong to some old commentary.

59 Cf. P. Demiéville, 'La montagne dans l'art littéraire chinois', *France-Asie/Asia* 183 (1965) pp. 13–18; below, pp. 234–51.

60 Cf. *Hou Han-shu chi-chieh* 60B, p. 2140.

61 *I-wen lei-chü* 37, p. 5b.

62 *Chuang-tzu* 8, pp. 273–5. In *Chuang-tzu* 28, pp. 163–5, Po I and Shu Ch'i are praised very highly.

63 *Han shu* 65, p. 2874 (Pan Ku's appreciation of Tung-fang Shuo's character); elsewhere, *Han shu* 65, p. 2870, and the 'Ch'i chien' in the *Ch'u tz'u*, p. 124 (of very doubtful authenticity), Tung-fang Shuo's attitude is less critical or frankly eulogistic.

64 The *Yüeh-fu shih-chi* 37, pp. 3ab, contains an 'old' (= anonymous) ballad called 'Pu-ch'u Hsia-men hsing' and ballads using the same title by Ts'ao Ts'ao and Ts'ao Jui (the latter actually begins with an excursion to Mt Shou-yang). The thirteenth of the 'Nineteen old poems' begins with a similar line: 'I speed my carriage out the Upper Eastern Gate', and many, many other ballads use similar opening lines. There is an interesting parallel to this use of a popular ballad line by a man of letters in W.H. Auden's first poem in 'Songs and other musical pieces' in *The collected poetry of W.H. Auden* (New York, 1945), pp. 197–9, which begins with the line 'As I walked out one evening', imitating a line from the popular ballad 'The sailor's return' included in W.H. Auden, ed., *The Oxford book of light verse*. The ballad begins: 'As I walked out one night'.

65 Cf. the preface, p. 2, of the *Lo-yang ch'ieh-lan chi* which quotes this poem by Juan Chi; the poem is also quoted in *Shui-ching chu* 16, p. 72.

66 Cf. Fung Yu-lan, *The history of Chinese philosophy*, vol. 2, pp. 13–16; M. Granet, *La pensée chinoise* (Paris, 1934), pp. 213 ff. Juan Chi's contemporaries believed

that the rise of the 'breath' at the middle of the month reached a point at which it caused ashes stuffed into pitch pipes specially buried in the earth to fly out into the air. Cf. D. Bodde, 'The Chinese cosmic magic called watching the ethers', *Studia Serica Bernhard Karlgren dedicata* (Copenhagen, 1959), pp. 14–35. I have adopted Shen Yüeh's interpretation of 汸汸 as 由 in line 11.

67 A.H. Smith, *Chinese characteristics* (New York, 1894), p. 240.

68 The medieval practice of equating autumn with sadness is discussed at length by Obi Kōichi in an article included in his *Chūgoku bungaku ni arawareta shizen to shizen kan* (Tokyo, 1962), pp. 52–109 (this poem by Juan Chi is quoted as an example on pp. 82–3).

69 *Tso chuan*, Legge translation, p. 146.

70 The second character of the term, as it stands in all the texts of Juan Chi's poem known to me, has the radical of the 'woman' at the left. The *Ch'u tz'u*, 'Ai shih-ming' (Hawkes translation, p. 140), uses a two-character term quite similar to Juan Chi's except that the second character has the 'heart' radical. The term in this case is taken to mean 'anguish' (Hawkes translation: 'ill at ease'). I would much prefer to read the term thus, and translate line 9: 'The man filled with anguish at the side of the road'. Such a translation makes the identification with Juan Chi himself much easier and actually makes the poem read better, but the text as it stands is intelligible and the two-character term translated as 'graceful beauty' is a very common one so that I hesitate to make the change.

71 *San-kuo chih chi-chieh* 4, pp. 26ab; cf. Fang, *The Chronicles of the Three Kingdoms*, vol. 2, p. 165.

Chapter 2

1 The most recent study of these knighthoods is by Moriya Mitsuo, 'Sō Gi shakusei ni kansuru ni san no kōsatsu', *Tōyōshi kenkyū* 20, 4 (1962) pp. 383–412. To the references he gives can be added Yü Cheng-hsieh, *Kuei-ssu lei-kao* 11 (Shanghai, 1957), pp. 403–8. E. Balazs, *Traité économique du Souei chou* (Leiden, 1953), p. 191, says the knighthood was given for military action. This may have been true during Ts'ao Ts'ao's times, but was not true later in the dynasty. Balazs also errs in stating that the title was originated by Ts'ao Ts'ao (cf. *San-kuo chih chi-chieh* 1, p. 120a); it was an old title going back to Ch'in times.

2 These posts are mentioned in the *Chin shu* 49 (*Chin-shu chiao-chu* 49, p. 2b). It is the *Chu-lin ch'i-hsien chuan*, quoted in *I-wen lei-chü* 48, p. 16b, and in *Pei-t'ang shu-ch'ao* 58, p. 9b, which says he did not like the post of *san-ch'i ch'ang-shih*.

3 Ho Ch'i-min, *Chu-lin ch'i-hsien yen-chiu* (Taipei, 1966), pp. 154–5, 230, suggests Juan Chi received his title as payment for the role he played in the deposition of Ts'ao Fang and in the accession of Ts'ao Mao. He quotes a text dated 16 November 254 (*San-kuo chih chi-chieh* 4, p. 35a) which states that an official was ordered to establish a 'merit list' for knighthoods and advancement in rank based upon the role played during these events. This is at best circumstantial evidence, but there may be some truth in it. Or was Juan Chi rewarded for his passivity, simply for keeping aloof from these events?

4 Cf. Hsi K'ang, 'Yü Shan Chü-yüan chüeh-chiao shu', *Wen hsüan* 43, p. 4a.

5 *Wen-shih chuan* quoted in *Shih-chuo hsin-yü* C (Section 23), p. 37a. Parallel texts or fragments can be found in *Chin-shu chiao-chu* 49, p. 3a; *T'ai-p'ing yü-lan* 498, p. 3b; 901, pp. 1b–2a.

6 Yen K'o-chün, *Ch'üan San-kuo wen* 53, p. 3b. The *Shih-shuo hsin-yü* text, which reads *t'ai-shou* 太守 for 'governor' here is erroneous; Tung-p'ing was a principality (*kuo*) at this time and the 'governor' of a principality was known as a *hsiang* 相 . Cf. Yen Keng-wang, *Chung-kuo ti-fang hsing-cheng chih-tu shih*, shang pien 3 (Taipei, 1963), pp. 225ff.

7 Given in Yen K'o-chün, *Ch'üan San-kuo wen* 44, p. 12.
8 This is quite consistent with traditional Chinese beliefs; cf., for example, *Kuan-tzu* 14 (Section 39), p. 2b (1875 ed.; translation D. Bodde, in Fung Yu-lan, *The history of Chinese philosophy*, vol. 1, p. 167), where the quality of a region's water is said to dictate the character of the people.
9 Chü-yeh swamp is a well known area that was located to the northeast of Chi-ning. It has long been identified with the area called Ta-yeh 大 野 in the 'Yü kung' chapter of the *Shu ching* (Legge translation, 3, pp. 105–6). The Chi River became the lower reaches of the Yellow River in the middle of the nineteenth century.
10 Chin-hsiang 金鄉 was (and is) some forty kilometers to the southeast of Chi-ning. Kao-p'ing 高平, under the Latter Han, was a marquisate located to the southwest of the present Tsou-hsien 鄒縣, some forty kilometers due west of Chi-ning.
11 I have not been able to identify Ming-chiu 鳴鳩. Ch'ü-ch'eng 曲城 is in all probability not the Han marquisate of Ch'ü-ch'eng 曲成 (present I-hsien), far to the east, but Ch'ü-fu 曲阜, some forty kilometers to the northeast.
12 These are two fiefs whose lords were famous figures at the end of the Chou dynasty; the former received a large fief to the north of the Huai and the latter inherited his father's fief at Hsüeh 薛, some twenty kilometers to the southeast of the present T'eng-hsien 滕縣, which would have made it some thirty kilometers southeast of K'ang-fu.
13 These are respectively to the southeast and northwest of Chi-ning (K'ang-fu). The city on the Hsüeh probably refers to Meng Ch'ang's fief mentioned above; Shan-yang was a commandery located some twenty kilometers to the northwest of Chin-hsiang or some sixty kilometers to the northwest of K'ang-fu.
14 This is the traditional interpretation of these two words as they appear in the *Tso chuan*, Hsüan 15: 'Cheng is enlightened and Sung is benighted (literally: deaf)'.
15 Cf. H. Wilhelm, 'The scholar's frustration: Notes on a type of fu', in Fairbank (ed.), *Chinese thought and institutions* (Chicago, 1957), p. 317. Nakajima Chiaki, 'Gen Seki no "ron" to "fu" to ni tsuite', *Nihon Chūgoku gakkai hō* 9 (1957) pp. 37–48, upon which some of the following material is based, does not mention this possible source of Juan Chi's *fu*.
16 Cf. in particular the *Ch'en-liu feng-su chuan* 陳留風俗傳 by Chüan Ch'eng 圈稱 listed in *Sui shu* 33, p. 22b. Chüan Ch'eng lived at the end of the Latter Han; cf. *San-kuo chih chi-chieh* 22, p. 24b.
17 *Sui shu* 30, p. 10b (cf. E. Balazs, *Traité économique du 'Souei chou'*, p. 314).
18 This is the opinion of Nakajima Chiaki, *op. cit.*, p. 46.
19 We should perhaps compare the evil state of K'ang-fu society with the ideal society described in Juan Chi's 'Essay on music' studied below, pp. 88–93.
20 The Nine Provinces and Nine Wildernesses can refer either to the entire universe or to China's nine ancient provinces (*Shih chi* 74, p. 7). The *Lü-shih ch'un-ch'iu* 13, p. 1, uses these two terms to refer to the Nine Provinces of the earth and the Nine Fields of the heavens that correspond to them.
21 The suggestion that 'rare and bizarre sights' in a landscape 'cannot be shown on a map' proves that the impetus for landscape painting was already in existence at least a century earlier than the earliest examples of landscape art noted in M. Sullivan, *The birth of landscape painting in China* (Berkeley and Los Angeles, 1962), pp. 79–80.
22 Ling-lun is a mythical figure who is said to have fixed the musical scale by blowing into bamboo pipes and listening to the song of the phoenix; cf. *Lü-shih ch'un-ch'iu* 5 (Section 5), pp. 51–2.
23 Tsou Yen 鄒 (or 騶) 衍 was a late fourth/early third century B.C. proto-scientist (cf. Fung Yu-lan, *The history of Chinese philosophy*, vol. 1, pp. 160–62) who has

many legends attached to his name. The one referred to here, that of his blowing a flute in the musical mode that provoked warm weather, is also mentioned by Juan Chi in his letter to Chiang Chi, above, chapter 1, note 20.

24   All I know of Po-kao is that he was a friend of the legendary Yellow Emperor; cf. *Lieh-tzu* 2 (Graham translation, p. 35; *Kuan-tzu chi-chiao* 77, p. 1145). I do not know where the heights of Shang-chi were.

25   Hsien-men is a famous immortal thought to have lived in the Three Isles of the Blessed off Shantung; cf. *Shih chi* 28, pp. 21, 23.

26   'Mysterious garden', in the K'un-lun; *Ch'u tz'u*, 'Chiu huai', Hawkes translation, p. 143.

27   A miraculous forest; cf. *Shan-hai ching* 8, p. 2b, and below, pp. 161–2.

28   On this term, *heng-shu* 橫 術 , see below, p. 115.

29   A-chen 阿 甄 is most probably Chen-ch'eng 鄄 城 which was located some ten kilometers to the east of the present P'u-hsien, ninety kilometers to the west of Tung-p'ing on the Hopeh border. Ch'i-p'u is probably the ancient Ch'i 戚 which was located north of the present P'u-yang 濮 陽 , Hopeh, twenty kilometers to the west of P'u-hsien.

30   A reference to *Li chi*, 'Yüeh chi', Couvreur vol. 2, p. 49. The phrase is a common-place meaning 'dissolute music' which would lead a country to ruin. Some authorities take the words 'among the mulberries' as a place name, 'Sang-chien', located some twenty kilometers to the west of the general area described here.

31   Three of the vassals of ancient Chin revolted and dismembered the state, setting themselves up as the Han, Wei and Chao states. Part of their territory was in this region; cf. *Meng-tzu* 1A, p. 11b, commentary of Chao Chi (1815 edition). Parts of the earlier states of Cheng and Wei, proverbial centers of dissoluteness, were also located in this region.

32   This line is defective. I read 土 for the 士 of all the texts, but without great conviction.

33   Liu Pang, founder of the Han dynasty, was from P'ei in northern Kiangsu, some one hundred and fifty kilometers to the south of Tung-p'ing.

34   There were several Lu families of this name. I do not know to which Juan Chi is referring here, or to what event.

35   Hsiang Yü divided Ch'i into three states; cf. *Shih chi* 7, pp. 46–7. Ch'i was to the east of Tung-p'ing, but Tsou and Lu were not to the west of it.

36   There is perhaps some allusion to historical figures here that I have not understood. The words 'small towns' imply towns that were not administrative centers and that were, presumably, very backward and rustic.

37   Both the Yellow River and the Chi were, at this time, to the north of Tung-p'ing, the Chi running south and parallel to the Yellow River.

38   The Wen divided into several streams before entering into at least two different lakes, Chü-yeh tse 鉅 野 澤 and Mao-tu ting 茂 都 淀 . Today it flows into the Shu-shan hu 蜀 山 湖 to the south of Tung-p'ing.

39   Another name for T'ai-shan, less than a hundred kilometers to the northeast of Tung-p'ing.

40   This is an allusion to *Chuang-tzu* 25 (Legge translation, 2, p. 126): just as old folk sayings or adages contain the wisdom of many men, so does the great man amalgamate in himself the variety of the wide world; he encompasses all differences in his deep understanding of the basic relativity of all things.

41   The cinnabar tree grows in the Western Mountains, on the top of Mt Mi 崃 (*Shan-hai ching* 2, pp. 13b–14a; cf. also p. 29a); but I do not understand these two lines. Is there perhaps an allusion to 'Yüan yu' and to the cassia tree (not cinnabar tree) that blooms in winter (*Ch'u tz'u* p. 84, line 44)?

42   Allusions to *Shih ching* 40 and *Shih ching* 197. These two poems are by virtuous

officers who have been misunderstood by their sovereigns. They introduce a long series of analogies showing the uselessness of virtue in certain situations.

43   *Lieh-tzu* 2 (Graham translation, p. 45). A sea gull played on the sea shore with an innocent young child because he knew he was naturally good and would do him no harm, but when the child's father asked to see him, he flew away.

44   The Ch'in-p'i (for 玊 read 鵁) is a mythological animal mentioned in the *Shan-hai ching* 2, p. 15a. It is probably the same as the K'an-p'i 堪 ·坯 who, in *Chuang-tzu* 6 (Legge translation, 1, p. 244), is said to be lord of the K'un-lun.

45   *Chuang-tzu* 17 (Legge translation, 2, p. 381) makes a similar comparison: excellent coursers 'could in one day gallop one thousand *li*, but for catching rats they were not equal to a wild dog or a weasel . . . '

46   Cf. *Chuang-tzu* 1 (Legge translation, 1, p. 172).

47   An immortal; cf. M. Kaltenmark, *Le Lie-sien tchouan* (Peking, 1953), pp. 190–94.

48   These lines are reminiscent of *Lao-tzu* 13: 'The reason I am in great distress is because I have a personality. Once I have no personality, how could I be distressed?' 'Emptying the heart' (or the 'mind') and 'losing the personality' should both be understood mystically as losing the 'self'.

49   The characters translated 'And I say again [in my Envoi]', 重 日 , also appear in *Ch'u tz'u*, 'Yüan yu', where Hawkes (Textual notes, p. 196) says they are meaningless. Either he is wrong or Juan Chi has servilely imitated the accepted text of the 'Yüan yu', not realizing he was repeating a textual corruption. Wang I's interpretation of the words in the 'Yüan yu' is that they show the poet 'stating again the indignation he had not completely expressed'. Perhaps this is Juan Chi's meaning. It is fairly clear that he has this section of the 'Yüan yu' in mind here: the evocation of Wang-tzu Ch'iao is similar, as is the basic idea of leaving a corrupt place for a mystical roaming. I feel, however, that, unlike the 'Yüan yu', where the words 重 日 appear too early in the poem, here the words mean something like 'Envoi'; they introduce the final section of the poem.

50   'Heaven's dividing lines', *chien-wei* 間 維 , are glossed by Yen K'o-chün (*Ch'üan San-kuo wen* 44, p. 7b) as being similar to *k'un-wei* 坤 維 , that is the great ropes that support the earth. But the term *chien-wei* itself appears in the 'Yüan yu' (Hawkes, p. 86, line 84) where it is explained in a sub-commentary as the six lines that separate the seven heavenly mansions. 'Great Wind' is a character from *Chuang-tzu* 11 (Legge translation, 1, pp. 322–4) who himself asks questions of a great Taoist spirit.

51   The *fu-yao* is a divine tree that grows in the Eastern Sea (*Chuang-tzu* 11, Legge translation, 1, p. 300) and the Ho-hsü Mountains, according to the *Shan-hai ching* 14, p. 3a, 'are at the place where the sun and the moon rise', that is, they are both located in the east.

52   Lake Hsien-ch'ih is where the sun takes his evening bath and Tseng-ch'eng is in the K'un-lun. Both are thus in the west. Juan Chi spans the universe in these two lines.

53   *Chuang-tzu* 32 (Legge translation, 2, p. 204) describes the ideal man as one who 'drifts like a vessel 舟 loosed from its moorings that emptily (= aimlessly) 虚 wanders about', and later texts speak of 'an empty vessel' as meaning a person without worldly attachments of any kind.

54   These strange sentences seem to mean that the Perfect Man in question was at the same time 'metaphysical', in that he could touch the supernatural K'ung-sang Mountains (*Shan-hai ching* 3, p. 19a, but there are a number of other possible places going under the same name), while maintaining a 'physical' identity in the midst of the cultivated fields of the everyday world.

55   I don't know why. In Poem 19 (below, p. 144) he speaks of an immortal beauty who wears a pair of jade half-discs in her belt. Perhaps they were common parts of the immortals' costume.

56 Chuan-hsü 顓 項 was the grandson of the Yellow Emperor. His tomb was on Mt Fu-yü according to the *Shan-hai ching* 13, p. 3b (in other passages in the *Shan-hai ching* different forms of the characters for the name of this mountain are given). The exact location of the mountain is doubtful, but Ho I-hsing, in his sub-commentary to the *Shan-hai ching*, thinks it is P'u-yang, about a hundred kilo-meters to the west of Tung-p'ing.

57 *Chuang-tzu* 24 (Legge translation, 2, pp. 96—7) tells the story of a divine child who, having fatigued his eyes with cosmic voyaging, was advised by an elder to relax by 'riding in the chariot of the sun and roaming in the wilds of Hsiang-ch'eng'.

58 The 'Tung-p'ing fu' is reproduced in the *Tung-p'ing hsien-chih* 17, pp. 45a—47a (first edition 1936, reproduced in Taipei, 1968). The text given is quite corrupt. It is followed (pp. 47a—49a) by a continuation of the 'Tung-p'ing fu' by Shen Wei-chi 沈 維 基, governor of Tung-p'ing chou at the end of the eighteenth cen-tury, meant to 'correct' some of Juan Chi's 'errors', fill in his omissions and bring the history of the region up to date. He begins his 'Continuation of the Tung-p'ing fu' with some biting sarcasms against Juan Chi who, according to him, could hardly hope to see the details of Tung-p'ing from the dizzy metaphysical heights he was wont to inhabit. According to the *Chung-kuo hsin-wen* (London) 678 (1 February 1972) pp. 11—12, a newsletter in Chinese published by the consulate of the People's Republic in England, before 1949 Tung-p'ing and the region around it were plagued by catastrophic floods during the rainy season, to the extent that the population had, for the most part, fled. Today, according to the report, in autumn the region is like a sea — of golden grain!

59 Liu Ju-lin (vol. 4, ch. 7, pp. 19—21) says that Juan Chi was given this post in 256, but Hung I-sun, *chung*, p. 48a, lists the dates as 'during the Chia-p'ing era (249—253)'. It is more probable, as Liu says, that Juan Chi was given his last post after having been governor in Tung-p'ing in 255.

60 *Wei-shih ch'un-ch'iu* quoted in *San-kuo chih chi-chieh* 21, p. 20b. Another anec-dote from *Shih-shuo hsin-yü* C (Section 24), pp. 48b—49a, showing Juan Chi imbibing is translated in D. Holzman, 'Les Sept Sages de la Forêt des Bambous et la société de leur temps', *T'oung Pao* (Leiden) 44 (1956) pp. 342—3.

61 Ch'ü-ch'eng 曲 成 (or 城) was a Han marquisate in Shan-tung (present I-hsien). There seems to be some doubt as to the actual identity of the master swordsman of this name. Waley (*Chinese Poems*, p. 202) says it was a man who lived in 112 B.C. (presumably Liu Wan-sui 劉 萬 歲, *Shih chi* 21, p. 43, Marquis of Ch'ü-ch'eng). Liu P'an-sui in a note to *Lun heng* 13 (Section 38), p. 275 of his edition, says the swordsman Wang Ch'ung is referring to is the first Marquis of Ch'ü-ch'eng, Ch'ung Ta 蟲 達, ennobled by Kao-tsu (*Shih chi* 18, pp. 44—5), but his reasons are not convincing. I believe both Wang Ch'ung and Juan Chi refer to a man men-tioned in *Shih chi* 127, p. 13, as Chang Chung 張 仲 of Ch'i, Marquis of Ch'ü-ch'eng. This man, otherwise unknown, is said to have attained world-wide fame because of his swordsmanship. No one with this name held the marquisate of Ch'ü-ch'eng in Han times, however, so that he must have lived earlier.

62 Cf. Lao Kan, '*Shih chi* Hsiang Yü pen-chi chung "hsüeh-shu" ho "hsüeh-chien" ti chieh-shih', CYYY 30 (1959) pp. 499—510.

63 Cf. *Chün cheng* 軍 政 quoted in *Sun-tzu* B, pp. 36b—37a (Sung edition, repro-duced in Peking, 1961).

Chapter 3

1 *San-kuo chih chi-chieh* 4, p. 78a.

2 He helped Ssu-ma I against Ts'ao Shuang in 249 and was enfeoffed by Ssu-ma Shih for his help in quelling the revolt of Kuan-ch'iu Chien in 255.

3 *Chin-shu chiao-chu* 39, p. 1b. Perhaps one should say, more exactly, a preliminary

draft of such a history, some kind of *shih-lu*, since the dynasty was still in existence during his lifetime.

4   *Shih t'ung* 8 (Section 29), pp. 7ab.

5   *Shih t'ung* 12 (Section 2), p. 8a.

6   Juan Chi died in the winter of the fourth year of Ching-yüan (18 November 263 – 15 February 264). The letter was written in November–December 263 (cf. *Chin-shu chiao-chu* 2, p. 28a, pp. 31b–32a). It is thus quite possible that Juan Chi died in early 264 and not in 263 as is generally stated.

7   On the Nine Distinctions, *chiu hsi* 九 錫 , cf. C.S. Goodrich, 'Bow-and-arrow gifts in the *Tso Chuan*', JAOS 78 (1958) p. 45, n. 22; W. Eberhard, 'The political function of astronomy and astronomers in Han China' in J.K. Fairbank (ed.), *Chinese thought and institutions* (Chicago, 1958) p. 348, n. 42; and, especially, Miyakawa Hisayuki, *Rikuchō shi kenkyū* (Tokyo, 1956), pp. 73–172.

8   This is an anachronism. Cheng Ch'ung, according to *San-kuo chih chi-chieh* 4, p. 46b, became *ssu-t'u* at a date corresponding to November–December 256. He had been *ssu-k'ung* from December–January 252–252 (*ibid*. p. 19a), until that time, and became *t'ai-pao* at the beginning of 264. He should therefore be called *ssu-t'u* here.

9   Yüan Chun 袁 準 was a scholar who, like Juan Chi, never assumed high office under the Wei. He came from a famous family and left an appreciable amount of writing, most of which has perished; cf. *San-kuo chih chi-chieh* 11, pp. 5ab.

10 *Shih-shuo hsin-yü* A (Section 4), pp. 78ab; cf. R.B. Mather, 'Chinese letters and scholarship in the third and fourth centuries: 'The "Wen-hsüeh p'ien" of the *Shih-shuo hsin-yü*', JAOS 84 (1964) pp. 374–5.

11 The *Chin shu* version of this story (*Chin-shu chiao-chu* 49, pp. 3b–4a) suggests that Juan Chi had been asked to write the text earlier and was so drunk that he simply 'forgot' to do it.

12 *Wen hsüan* 40, pp. 21b–24a; translation by E. von Zach in *Die chinesische Anthologie*, vol. 2, pp. 760–62.

13 *Chin-shu chiao-chu* 2, pp. 31b–32b.

'14 Shu actually fell only a very short time after this letter was written, at the end of December, 263.

15 Chih-po refers to Tzu-chou Chih-po 子 州 支 伯 who refused to accept the throne when Shun offered it to him; see *Chuang-tzu* 28 (Legge translation, 2, p. 149). The 'azure beach' seems to be Juan Chi's invention (much imitated later as the name of a place where hermits live); the 'azure' refers to the color of the water, not of the sand.

16 Yao attempted to resign his throne to Hsü-yu who promptly refused and went off to the foot of Chi Mountain to hide away; cf. *Lü-shih ch'un-ch'iu* 22, p. 293.

17 A near quotation from *Chuang-tzu* 20 (Legge translation, 2, p. 30). The Marquis of Lu, receiving instruction from a Taoist sage, is told to retire to a distant region. The marquis is worried that he will have no neighbors, but this of course is the whole idea: he should have none so that he can be free in the heart of nature. Von Zach follows the *Wen hsüan* commentator Lü Hsiang and translates my 'neighbor' as 'equal': 'Who could equal him?', which can perhaps be defended, but in the next line he translates the word 'petty' as if it referred to the honors offered to Ssu-ma Chao. This makes the sentence much more polite, but the words 'petty refusals', *hsiao jang* 小 讓 , have their canonical authority (*Li chi*, 'Ju hsing', Couvreur, vol. 2, p. 602), and in this context (as in *Shih chi* 7, p. 33) they are pejorative.

18 Liu Ch'en-weng 劉 辰 翁 (1232–1297) quoted in the commentary of the *Shih-shuo hsin-yü pu* 5, p. 2b (Japanese edition whose preface is dated 1779). Ho P'an-fei, in his 'Juan Chi yen-chiu', *Wen-hsüeh nien-pao* 3 (1937) pp. 177–200, quotes

traditional scholars who have attacked and defended Juan Chi for having written this letter. Chang Chih-yüeh, 'Lüeh lun Juan Chi chi ch'i "Yung-huai shih" ', *Wen-hsüeh i-ch'an* 11 (1962) p. 75, goes so far as to suggest that Juan Chi's death was caused, directly or indirectly, by the writing of this letter: it was only in death that he could find a solution to the contradiction between his actions in serving the Ssu-ma and his loyalistic feelings.

19   This last is the theory of Jen Pan-t'ang, in *T'ang hsi-nung* (Peking, 1958), pp. 393–412. This very long, two-volume work is polemical in nature, attempting to establish the fact that true theater really existed during the T'ang dynasty (cf. P. Demiéville, in *Revue bibliographique de sinologie* 4, No. 660). The author is at great pains to show that 'monkey theater' was in fact true theater, with monkeys trained to *act*, and that it was an important missing link in the pre-T'ang history of the theater. His arguments are far from convincing, but the large number of sources quoted make it clear that monkeys, as pets or as some sort of 'proto-comedians' (whatever that may mean) were very popular in China at the time of Juan Chi. Jen Pan-t'ang quotes Juan Chi's 'The monkey' on pp. 399–400. Chang Heng, in his 'Hsi-ching' *fu*, describes men disguised as apes used in entertainments (see the translation by E. von Zach, *Die chinesische Anthologie*, vol. 1, pp. 14–16).

20   Cf. *Shu ching* 5 (Legge translation, p. 77).

21   Cf. *Tso chuan*, Hsüan 3 (Legge translation, pp. 292–3).

22   Cf. *Chuang-tzu* 20 (Legge translation, 2, p. 29).

23   *Shan-hai ching* 12, p. 3a, describes a fabulous, precious, multi-colored beast, whose tail is longer than its body, and calls it a *tsou-wu* 騶吾 . The commentary identifies the beast with the *tsou-yü*. The animal is the subject of *Shih ching* 25 (in the traditional interpretation).

24   One of the several meanings of this word is 'the name of an animal'; cf. *Lü-shih ch'un-ch'iu* 22, p. 292.

25   The present text reads *tu-lu* 獨鹿, 'lone deer'. I follow Nakajima Chiaki, 'Gen Seki no "Bikō no fu" ni tsuite', *Chūgoku chūsei bungaku kenkyū* 5 (1966) p. 18, who suggests that the original may have been inspired by the *lu-shu* 鹿蜀, a fabulous animal mentioned in *Shan-hai ching* 1, p. 1b. Nakajima's article contains a useful translation of this *fu* into Japanese.

26   These fabulous beasts are described in *Shan-hai ching* 14 and 15, pp. 3a and 3b.

27   Nakajima (1966), says this passage refers to *Chuang-tzu* 24 (Legge translation, 2, pp. 102–3). He changes the 狙 into 狙 and 功 into 巧 and reads: 'Should the bear or monkey roam near the river and show their cleverness they will put their lives into danger.' The line is very possibly corrupt and needs some correction of this sort.

28   The *k'uei* was a one-legged beast whose movements into and out of the water pro-voked the wind and the rain. The Yellow Emperor made a drum of his skin; cf. *Shan-hai ching* 14, p. 3b.

29   Cf. *Chuang-tzu* 7 (Legge translation, 1, p. 260).

30   This is an allusion to events recorded at least twice in the *Ch'un-ch'iu*: sacrificial animals were ruined when their horns were gnawed upon by mice; cf. *Tso chuan*, Ch'eng 7 (Legge translation, pp. 361–2) and Ting 15 (Legge, pp. 789–90).

31   Han Fei-tzu was imprisoned and forced to commit suicide in Ch'in in 233 B.C.; cf. *Shih chi* 63, p. 28.

32   These two lines are extremely difficult to understand. Nakajima (1966), p. 20, says there is an allusion to a story in *Han Fei-tzu* 7 (Section 22, Liao translation, p. 241). A man has realized that his neighbor has 'dynastic ambitions' and he also knows that his neighbor's view is impeded by his forest. Should he cut down the trees of the forest, he would please his neighbor, but would also show him he feared him and understood his hidden designs. Better to leave the trees and keep

his knowledge to himself. The relation of this story to the plight of Han Fei-tzu imprisoned in Ch'in can be understood: Han Fei-tzu was forced to commit suicide to keep him from disclosing Ch'in's projects to annex his home state of Han. His going to Ch'in to offer his services showed he realized what Ch'in was up to — he had 'cut down the trees'. But the meaning of line 38 escapes me. Perhaps it means simply that he had been safe ('surrounded by a hedge') when he was in his native forest (in his native Han, for Han Fei-tzu), but by showing off (cf. *Chuang-tzu* 24, Legge translation, 2, pp. 102—3), he 'cut down his trees'.

33 Hsiang Chi (Hsiang Yü) once said, nostalgically, 'To be rich and honored and not return home [to be admired by one's friends and loved ones[is like wearing embroidered robes and going abroad at night: [in either case] who is there to admire you?' (*Shih chi* 7, p. 36). The passage continues: 'A critic said "There is a saying that men from Ch'u are nothing more than monkeys with bonnets on." This is, after all, true [as we can see from the example of Hsiang Yü, who was from Ch'u].'

34 Ch'ang-ch'ing is the *tzu* of the famous poet Ssu-ma Hsiang-ju who was renowned for his beauty.

35 Cf. *Lun yü* 6, 14: Confucius said that 'without the speech of the litanist T'o or the beauty of Sung Chao, it is difficult to get by in the present world.'

36 The Teng Forest is an immortal forest often invoked by Juan Chi; see below, p. 162.

37 Fragments can be found in *I-wen lei-chü* 95, *Ch'u-hsüeh chi* 29, and *T'ai-p'ing yü-lan* 910, and there is a translation by A. Waley, *Chinese poems* (London, 1948), pp. 72—4.

38 Aside from Jen Pan-t'ang, p. 400, who suggests that these comparisons with famous courtiers, 'although they do not actually show that these personages were acted on the stage, *are extremely suggestive hints!* The indistinct outlines of true monkey theater can definitely be seen in them' (Jen Pan-t'ang's italics).

39 Nakajima Chiaki (1966), pp. 21, 26—7.

40 *Shih-shuo hsin-yü* A (Section 1), p. 5b. The bracketed words are from the commentary.

41 'Letter to Shan Chü-yüan', *Hsi K'ang chi chiao-chu* 2, p. 118. The following words in the letter (also describing Juan Chi) are translated below, p. 82. The term trans- lated 'extremely broad-minded', *chih-hsing* 至 性 , is a difficult one. It also means 'extremely filial'; we shall see in the next chapter that Juan Chi was also renowned for his filial piety, but in this context I prefer the reading given. It is also followed by the Wu-ch'en commentary in *Wen hsüan* 43, pp. 4b—5a.

42 *Chin-shu chiao-chu* 49, p. 3a.

43 Cf. *Wen hsüan* 20, p. 10b. The letter, full of 'abstract and distant' praise for Lu Po, is contained in Juan Chi's works. Another case of recommendation, in *Yü lin*, is quoted in the *Shui-ching chu* 16, p. 68: 'Ch'en Hsieh 陳 協 had presented the Infantry Colonel Juan with wine on several occasions. When Ssu-ma Chao wanted to repair the Nine Dragon barrage, Juan Chi recommended him and he was used for the job.' The barrage seems to have been to the west of Lo-yang, on the Ku River.

44 *Chin-shu chiao-chu* 36, p. 29b. At the time Chang Hua, who was undoubtedly one of the most brilliant men of the early Chin period, was unknown. The text in the *I-wen lei-chü* 56, quoting the *Chin shu* by Wang Yin, says Juan Chi based his appreciation solely upon Chang Hua's *fu* called 'Chiao-liao', 'The small bird': an interesting illustration of the importance of literature in politics at this very early date. However, Hayashida Shinnosuke, 'Gi Shin Nanchō bungaku ni shimeru Chō Ka no zahyō', *Nihon Chūgoku gakkai hō* 17 (1965) p. 70, doubts that the *Chin shu* version of this anecdote is correct. It seems 'too appropriate' for him that

Juan Chi should discover the man who was to become the most eminent statesman of his generation when he was totally unknown. He feels that the remarks in the Tsang Jung-hsü *Chin shu* quoted in *Wen hsüan* 13, p. 23b, which would date the 'Chiao-liao fu' from after 264, and thus after the death of Juan Chi, may be closer to the truth. And yet in his note 3, p. 90, Hayashida shows that Chang Hua's future father-in-law knew Juan Chi's father well, and that thus there were ties uniting the two men. According to Hayashida, if the *Chin shu* version is correct, Juan Chi's appreciation must be dated 254 (when Chang Hua was twenty-two years old).

45 *Shan-hai ching* 9, pp. 3ab. Originally, to 'hang up one's chariot', *hsüan ch'e* 懸車, meant 'to retire'; thus 'the hanging chariot' is an epithet usually applied to the sun when it is about to set in the west, as in Poem 18, below, pp. 211–12. Presumably Juan Chi has 'perched' it in the Fu-sang tree while it is waiting to take the sun on its westward journey.

46 Cf. Chang Heng, 'Ssu-hsüan fu', *Wen hsüan* 15, p. 2a.

47 This term, *yüan-tu* 怨毒, comes from *Shih chi* 66, p. 23, and is used again in Poem 69, p. 114 below, where it is translated as 'bitter grudges'.

48 *Shih chi* 87, p. 43.

49 According to Shen Yüeh, *san ho* 三河, the Three Rivers, is cognate with *san ch'uan* 三川, the name of a Ch'in commandery comprising the region to the north, south and east of the great bend in the Yellow River. In *Chan-kuo ts'e* (Crump translation, no. 66), *san ch'uan* refers to the region of the capital (Lo-yang). But the term *san ho* itself is used to refer to the 'home provinces', the relatively small area in which the earliest dynasties founded their capitals; cf. *Shih chi* 129, p. 19.

50 *Wei-shih ch'un-ch'iu* quoted in *San-kuo chih chi-chieh* 21, p. 20b.

51 *Chin shu*, quoted in *Wen hsüan* 40, p. 30b.

52 *Han Wu-ti ku-shih*, quoted in the *Shui-ching chu* 19, p. 116. The text of the *Shui-ching chu* quotes Juan Chi's poem.

53 Suzuki Shūji, 'Kei Kō, Gen Seki kara Tō Emmei e', *Chūgoku bungaku hō* 18 (1963) p. 33.

54 Cf. Huang-fu Mi, *Kao-shih chuan*, quoted in Chang Shou-chieh's commentary of the *Shih chi* 61, p. 6. These two figures perhaps really represent the faint echo of prehistoric tribal life when it was indeed difficult to find a man willing to accept the dangers and duties of the chieftain's rank; cf. C. Lévi-Strauss, *Tristes tropiques* (Paris, 1955), p. 330. Some editions read 揚 for 楊 in line 6 and take the line to refer not to Yang Chu, but to Ning-tzu, reading: 'But who would be willing to sacrifice himself with the song he sang?' As Tseng Kuo-fan (who follows this interpretation) says: 'Juan Chi is showing himself contemptuous of Ning Ch'i . . . '

55 Including *Tso chuan*, Wen 18 (Legge translation, p. 282); *Shih ching* 235, 266, 299 (same quotation); and *Shang shu*, 'I chi' (Legge translation, p. 90).

56 There appear to be thirteen tetrameter poems by Juan Chi, but none of the current editions print more than three. According to Hsiao Ti-fei, *Tu-shih san cha-chi* (Peking, 1957), p. 20, Huang Chieh made a commentary to these thirteen poems as they appear in an edition by P'an Ts'ung 潘璁 which he had in his possession. Hsiao Ti-fei quotes snatches of these poems in his essay, and Huang Chieh himself quotes an entire poem in his commentary to Poem 64. The existence of these thirteen poems is mentioned by Ch'en Chen-sun (first half of the thirteenth century) in his *Chih-chai shu-lu chieh-t'i* 19, p. 525 (Ts'ung-shu chi-ch'eng edition), and by Miao Ch'üan-sun, *Yün tzu-tsai k'an sui-pi* (Peking, 1958), p. 163. Try as I may, I have been unable to procure an edition of these thirteen poems. Yoshikawa Kōjirō, *Yoshikawa Kōjirō zenshū* 7, p. 192, gives additional bibliographical information on these tetrameter poems, but says that he, too, has failed in his attempts

to get to see them. Aside from the poem quoted by Huang Chieh in his commentary to Poem 64 and some more or less isolated lines quoted by Hsiao Ti-fei (pp. 14, 16, 20, 21), four lines of a fragmentary tetrameter poem are quoted in *T'ai-p'ing yü-lan* 1, p. 6a.

Chapter 4

1   *Shih-shuo hsin-yü* C (Section 23), p. 37b. Juan Hsien was Juan Chi's nephew, the son of his elder brother Hsi 熙 . Ho Ch'ang-ch'ün quotes this passage to show that the social importance of belonging to a 'first-class noble family' did not depend upon being rich; both branches, rich and poor, of the family were in the front rank of Lo-yang society. Cf. his *Han T'ang chien-feng chien t'u-ti so-yu-chih hsing-shih yen-chiu* (Shanghai, 1964), p. 187.

2   Cf. H. Franke, 'Some remarks on the interpretation of the Chinese dynastic histories', *Oriens* (Leiden) 3 (1950) pp. 120–21.

3   From the *Chu-lin ch'i-hsien lun* by Tai K'uei, quoted in the *Shih-shuo hsin-yü, loc. cit.*, and in several encyclopedias (cf. *Ch'üan Chin wen* 137, p. 11a). The citation is from *Lun yü* 13, 8. The *Chu-lin ch'i-hsien lun* quotation in the *Shih-shuo hsin-yü* continues: 'Only Juan Hsien's family honored Taoism and rejected the world's affairs, were fond of wine and poor.' But in the version given in *T'ai-p'ing yü-lan* 31, p. 9b, the words for 'Juan Hsien's family' 咸 一 家 are given as 'Juan Chi's lane' 籍 一 巷 .

4   *T'ung chih* 26, p. 453 (Shanghai, 1935 edition).

5   Thus Juan Chi and Hsi K'ang, who both died before the advent of the new dynasty, are often referred to as 'men of Chin', perhaps because they both have biographies in the *Chin shu*.

6   Wang Su-ts'un, *Hsing lu* (Taipei, 1960), p. 218.

7   Cf. Yü Ying-shih, 'Han Chin chih chi shih chih hsin tzu-chüeh yü hsin ssu-ch'ao', *Hsin Ya hsüeh-pao* (Hongkong) 4, 1 (1959) pp. 25–144, and the numerous articles in Chinese and Japanese he refers to.

8   The medieval dynastic histories, beginning with the *Hou Han-shu* 69 and with the exception of the *San-kuo chih* and the *Pei Ch'i shu*, all contain chapters devoted to filial sons, and there have been innumerable popular stories describing filial actions written throughout the centuries, one of the most famous being the (at least) early T'ang work *Hsiao-tzu chuan* 孝 子 傳 . A sampling of the stories can be found in E. Chavannes, 'Confucius', *Revue de Paris* (1903) pp. 136–42. The subject of the rise of filial piety and its perversion is treated in Okazaki Fumio, *Gi Shin Nambokuchō tsūshi* (Tokyo, 1954), pp. 423 ff, 436; and Hsiao Kung-ch'üan, *Chung-kuo cheng-chih ssu-hsiang shih*, vol. 3, p. 376 and notes 66, 68.

9   The *locus classicus* for this ritualistic law is *Li chi* 1, Couvreur, vol. 1, p. 29.

10 *Shih-shuo hsin-yü* C (Section 23), p. 37b.

11 *Shih-shuo hsin-yü* C (Section 23), p. 37b.

12 Wang Yin, *Chin shu*, quoted in *Shih-shuo hsin-yü* C (Section 23), p. 37b. According to Liu Chih-chi, *Shih t'ung* 12, p. 9b, Wang Yin presented his *Chin shu* to the throne in 340.

13 *Chin-shu chiao-chu* 49, p. 3b.

14 *Chuang-tzu* 29, Legge translation, 2, p. 171; cf. also J.J.L. Duyvendak, *The Book of Lord Shang* (London, 1928), p. 225.

15 *Li chi*, 'Wen sang', Couvreur, vol. 2, p. 552.

16 *Ibid.*, 'San-nien wen', Couvreur, vol. 2, p. 581; cf. also 'Sang ta-chi', Couvreur, vol. 2, pp. 222–3.

17 *Li chi*, "T'an kung", Couvreur 1, p. 246.

18 Cf. M. Granet, *La civilisation chinoise*, pp. 390 ff.

19   Date determined by Liu Ju-lin, *Han Chin hsüeh-shu pien-nien* 7, pp. 19–21; also
      see below, notes 25, 29.

20   *Shih-shuo hsin-yü* C (Section 23), p. 37b.

21   Teng Ts'an, *Chin chi*, quoted in *Shih-shuo hsin-yü*, *loc. cit.*; cf. Yoshikawa Kōjirō,
      'Gen Seki den', *Yoshikawa Kōjirō zenshū* 7, p. 183.

22   Teng Ts'an, whose biography is found in *Chin-shu chiao-chu* 82, pp. 22b–23a,
      flourished around 380. His *Chin chi*, from which this anecdote is quoted, is
      praised by Liu Hsieh in *Wen-hsin tiao-lung* 4 (Section 16), p. 286 (of the *Wen-hsin
      tiao-lung chu* edition, Hongkong, 1960; translation of V. Shih, p. 90), for having
      renewed the annalistic style by modelling himself on the ancients. But he also says
      Teng Ts'an's work served as a model to Sun Sheng 孫 盛 who seems clearly to
      have lived a generation earlier, so that his judgement need not be taken too
      seriously. Liu Chih-chi, *Shih t'ung* 4 (Section 10), p. 4b, on the contrary, con-
      demns him for being 'prolix and lacking in concision'. P'ei Sung-chih has not used
      any of his works in his commentary to the *San-kuo chih*.

23   Yang Lien-sheng, *Studies in Chinese institutional history* (Harvard-Yenching
      Institute Series XX), pp. 119–20. The anecdote is included in the present *Chin-
      shu chiao-chu* 49, pp. 4ab.

24   *Shih t'ung* 20 (Section 12), pp. 8a–9a. Liu Chih-chi quotes the anecdote from the
      '*Hsin*' *Chin-shu*, as our present *Chin Shu* was called when it first appeared. His
      argument that Juan Chi could hardly 'waste away' eating meat and drinking wine
      is hardly convincing as a proof that the anecdote is not historical.

25   This permits us to date these anecdotes approximately. P'ei K'ai died in 291 or
      292 at the age of 54 (*Chin-shu chiao-chu* 35, pp. 22a–23a). He was thus nineteen
      (*jo-kuan*) in 256 or 257. The *Shih-shuo hsin-yü* version of this anecdote anachron-
      istically calls him by the title he received in the last year of his life, *chung-shu ling*
      中 書 令 , Head of the State Secretarist.

26   Either the hut in which filial sons lived after the death of a parent or one of the
      ritualistic positions a mourner was supposed to occupy when he received callers
      and accompanied them to the main hall; cf. *T'ung tien* 83, pp. 449–50, where the
      ritual for condolence calls for this epoch is quoted from Wei, Chin and Liu-Sung
      sources. The newly orphaned son is supposed to cry ritually at certain moments of
      the visit.

27   *P'ei K'ai pieh-chuan* quoted in *T'ai-p'ing yü-lan* 561, p. 7b.

28   *Shih-shuo hsin-yü* C (Section 23), p. 38a. For the beginning of this anecdote I
      have preferred the *P'ei K'ai pieh-chuan* version because of the date it alludes to
      and also because it seems less purely 'anecdotal'; the *Shih-shuo hsin-yü* version
      shows 'Juan Chi drunk, his hair down and sitting unceremoniously on his bed
      with his legs stretched out in front of him'.

29   Ho Tseng occupied this post 'for several years' (*Chin-shu chiao-chu* 33, p. 14a)
      beginning either 'during the Chia-p'ing period' (*ibid.*, p. 13a), i.e. from 249 to
      254, or 'during the Cheng-yüan period' (Kan Pao, *Chin chi*, quoted in *San-kuo
      chih chi-chieh* 12, p. 24a), i.e. from 254 to July 256. He vacated the post some-
      time before July 256 (*Chin-shu chiao-chu* 33, p. 14a), so that the anecdote, and
      Juan Chi's mourning, should probably be dated in the first half of the year, or per-
      haps late in 255.

30   Quotation from *Li chi*, 'Sang ta-chi', Couvreur, vol. 2, p. 226.

31   *Shih-shuo hsin-yü* C (Section 23), p. 36a; cf. also *Chin-shu chiao-chu* 33, p. 13b;
      Wen hsüan 43, p. 4a.

32   *Chin pai-kuan ming*, quoted in *Shih-shuo hsin-yü* C (Section 24), p. 49b; also in
      Chin-shu chiao-chu 49, p. 5a.

33   Cf. D. Holzman, *La vie et la pensée de Hi K'ang* (Leiden, 1957), pp. 32–4; Fukui

Fumimasa, 'Chikurin shichiken ni tsuite no ichi shiron', *Philosophia* (Tokyo) 37 (1959) pp. 75–102.

34 Hou Wai-lu *et al.*, *Chung-kuo ssu-hsiang t'ung-shih* 3 (Peking, 1957), p. 156.

35 Ho Ch'i-min, *Chu-lin ch'i-hsin yen-chiu*, pp. 152–7, sees Hsi K'ang as 'pro-Wei and anti-Chin'; Juan Chi as actually 'anti-Wei, feigning to be pro-Chin as if he could not do otherwise'; Shan T'ao as 'anti-Wei and pro-Chin'; and the others as servants of the Chin by opportunism, or because they were born too late to have any choice. He is right to point out the Seven Sages' variety of political opinion, but surely wrong to attempt to analyse the nuances of their innermost feelings with such precision.

36 The discovery was first described in *Wen-wu* 1960, 8/9, pp. 37–42, and discussed by A.C. Soper in *Artibus Asiae* 24 (1961) pp. 79–86.

37 'Yü Shan Chü-yüan chüeh-chiao shu' in *Wen hsüan* 43 and *Hsi K'ang chiao-chu* 2, p. 118. There are translations by von Zach, *Die chinesische Anthologie*, vol. 2, p. 785, and J.R. Hightower, in C. Birch (ed.), *Anthology of Chinese literature* (New York, 1965), pp. 162–6.

38 Pp. 1a–3b. Yen K'o-chün says it appears in the *Juan Ssu-tsung chi*, but I have never seen it in any edition of Juan Chi's works I am familiar with. Nakajima Chiaki, 'Chō Ka no "Shōryō no fu" ni tsuite', *Shinagaku kenkyū* (Hiroshima) 32 (1966) pp. 29–32, contains extracts of this letter, and of Juan Chi's reply to it, in résumé and in Japanese translation.

39 This description of a magical beast who surpasses human understanding is reminiscent of the pseudo-Confucius's description of Lao-tzu in *Chuang-tzu* 14, Legge translation, 1, p. 358, and in the *Shih chi* 63, p. 5. Perhaps all the description beginning at the colon refers only to the dragon and alludes to these descriptions of Lao-tzu.

40 The text has 'dove and phoenix *yüan*' 鶠 , a heroic bird mentioned in *Chuang-tzu* 17, Legge translation, 1, p. 391. This would indeed be a strange combination, but Morohashi has included it in his *Dai Kan Wa jiten*. I prefer reading 鶉 , 'quail', for 鶠 , and believe the parallelism of the text requires some such emendation. The quail is often used as a symbol of small, unimportant entities (e.g. *Chuang-tzu* 1).

41 Unknown elsewhere; this probably means the shores of the seas that enclose the world.

42 Many different enumerations of the 'six breaths' are given. According to the *Tso chuan*, Chao 1 (Legge translation, p. 581), they are *yin*, *yang*, wind, rain, cloudy and clear weather; according to other texts they refer to the air at different hours of the day, etc.

43 The Somber Net is not attested elsewhere; but cf. *Lao-tzu* 73, 'Heaven's Net is wide; though its meshes are loose, nothing escapes it'; and *Chuang-tzu* 14 (Legge translation, 1, p. 345).

44 *Shih-shuo hsin-yü* A (Section 1), p. 5b. (Also quoted above, p. 58).

Chapter 5

1 Yü Ying-shih, article quoted in chapter 4, note 7, p. 98 and his note 140. Mr Yü's argument is that a few phrases attributed to Juan Chi's 'Yüeh lun' that do not appear in the work as we have it are quoted in the *Wen hsüan* 18, p. 20a, and 26, p. 30a. He very prudently suggests that the 'Yüeh lun' must therefore be fragmentary and that we should not use it to define Juan Chi's philosophical position. But the phrases quoted in the *Wen hsüan* are not from Juan Chi at all; they are from Hsi K'ang's essay' 'Sheng wu ai-le lun', a slip of Li Shan, showing, incidentally, that he probably quoted from memory. There is a reconstruction of Juan Chi's 'Yüeh lun' pieced together with fragments quoted in early encyclopedias and

the like (including one passage from Li Shan's commentary to the *Wen hsüan*) in *Han Wei i-shu* 10, pp. 1a–3b, by Wang Mo.

2   Aoki Masaru, *Shina bungaku shisō shi* (Tokyo, 1948), p. 339; cf. also Chou Shaohsien, *Wei Chin ch'ing-t'an shu-lun* (Taipei, 1966), pp. 79–81.

3   There is a useful annotated version of the essay with a translation into the vernacular (not devoid of errors) by Chi Lien-k'ang in an appendix to his *Hsi K'ang: Sheng wu ai-le lun* (Peking, 1964), pp. 72–92, and an unpublished thesis containing a French translation by Mlle Martine Blum, presented to the University of Paris VII in 1970.

4   *Li chi*, 'Ching chieh', Couvreur, vol. 2, p. 358; *Hsiao ching* 12.

5   The 'eight instruments' (mouth organ, flute, battery, strings, etc.) are put into general relation with the 'eight winds' (of the different seasons and half-seasons of the year) in *Tso chuan*, Yin 5, Legge translation p. 19, and there are one-to-one relations established in later texts such as the commentary by Kao Yu 高 誘 (end of second century) to *Huai-nan-tzu* 3, p. 38: the wind which blows forty-five days after the winter solstice corresponds to the mouth organ, etc.

6   The lowest tube in the scale, and the one that set the pitch for the other notes of the scale.

7   The sacrifices to heaven were made on a round altar, those to earth on a square; cf. *Chou li*, 'Ch'un kuan', 'Ta-ssu yüeh', Biot translation, vol. 2, pp. 34–5.

8   *I ching*, 'Hsi tz'u' A, Legge translation, p. 349.

9   This term, *p'ing-tan* 平 淡 , seems to be original with Juan Chi; it has a vaguely Taoist tinge and can be compared with *Lao-tzu* 35.

10   A common play on words: *yüeh* (*ngâk*) means 'music'; the same character, 樂 , pronounced *le* (*lak*), means 'joy'.

11   *Lü-shih ch'un-ch'iu* 5 and 22; *Han shu* 21 A, pp. 1 ff; etc.

12   Literally, 'the degree *kung* (= prime) of the first tube of the scale, *huang-chung*'. The *Lü-shih ch'un-ch'iu* 5 ('Ku-yüeh'), p. 52, says that this is 'the basis of the musical tubes', and the term plays a central role in the equivalences made between music and natural phenomena (cf. M. Courant, 'Essai historique sur la musique classique des Chinois', in *Encyclopédie de la musique* [Paris, 1912], p. 93).

13   'Shun tien', Legge translation 1, pp. 47–9, and 'I chi', pp. 81, 87–9. The passages have had signal importance in the history of Chinese literary criticism and are discussed in detail in a large number of works; for a bibliography and further discussion, see Chow Tse-tsung, 'The early history of the Chinese word *shih* (poetry)', in Chow Tse-tsung (ed.), *Wen-lin* (Madison, Wis., 1968), pp. 152–5.

14   Chapter 18 of *Chuang-tzu* is entitled 'Supreme joy', using the same characters as 'Supreme music' here. There is perhaps a subtle allusion.

15   Cf. Jao Tsung-i, 'Lu Chi Wen-fu li-lun yü yin-yüeh chih kuan-hsi', *Chūgoku bungaku hō* (Kyoto) 14 (1961) pp. 27–30. Juan Chi's opposition to this attitude is discussed on p. 30.

16   Two examples are taken from Han history: emperors Huan (147–167) and Shun (126–144) mistook the sad sounds they heard for 'music-joy'. The implication is that by giving their imperial guarantee to this heretical form of music they were hastening the fall of their dynasty. The sentences from Juan Chi's essay referring to emperor Huan have been accurately quoted by Liu Chao 劉 昭 (*c.* 510) in his commentary to the treatises of the *Hou Han-shu* (*Hou Han-shu chi-chieh* (*chih*) 18, p. 3787).

17   Cf. *Li chi*, 'Yüeh chi', Couvreur, vol. 2, p. 65.

18   Hsia-hou Hsüan, 'Pien-yüeh lun' 辨樂論 , quoted in *T'ai-p'ing yü-lan* 16, pp. 7ab. I follow the text of the Sung edition of the *TPYL* (Peking, 1960) for the last word, rather than the *Ch'üan San-kuo wen* 21, pp. 7ab.

19   Cf. Holzman, *La vie et la pensée de Hi K'ang*, pp. 68–72. Aoki Masaru, *Shina*

bungaku shisō shi, p. 379, suggests that Hsi K'ang wrote his essay to oppose Juan Chi's; his aim was to attack Confucianist theories of music as Juan Chi attacks ritualism in other essays.

20 Honda Wataru, *Ekigaku: Seiritsu to tenkai* (Kyoto, 1960), p. 138: 'The core of the essay on the *I ching* by Juan Chi is an amplification of the "Hsü kua".'

21 'The reasoning in the entire essay ['On understanding the *I ching*'] is clear and solid; in every respect it represents the speech of a Confucianist': Chou Shao-hsien, *Wei Chin ch'ing-t'an shu-lun*, p. 76.

22 The *Chin shu* says merely that Juan Chi 'wrote the "Ta Chuang lun" to describe the value of non-activity (*wu-wei*)'; *Chin-shu chiao-chu* 49, p. 6a. Nakajima Chiaki (1957), pp. 37–8, barely touches on the essay; Fukunaga Mitsuji (1958), pp. 167 ff, emphasizes its religious Taoist aspects; and Mou Tsung-san, *Ts'ai-hsing yü hsüan-li* (Kowloon, 1963), pp. 297–302, reproduces it with short interlinear comments.

23 The *Chin shu* authors already believed the text of the 'Ta Chuang lun' to be incomplete; cf. *Chin-shu chiao-chu* 49, p. 6a.

24 Nakajima Chiaki thoroughly describes the various works that may have influenced Juan Chi in this essay and in the 'Ta-jen hsien-sheng chuan' in his 1957 article, pp. 37–41.

25 Kuo Hsiang says that (during his youth, at the time of Juan Chi?) before he had read Chuang-tzu he took him to be a sophist, because of what he had heard said of him during *ch'ing-t'an* discussions; cf. Liu Wen-tien, *Chuang-tzu pu-cheng* (Shanghai, 1947), 10B, p. 24a. (This note was kindly communicated to me by M. P. Demiéville.)

26 Fukunaga Mutsuji (1958), p. 168, equates *tzu-jan* with *tao* in this context — rather too hastily to my mind.

27 Fukunaga (1958), p. 169, invokes *Lao-tzu* 42 as an explanation. The phrase is, perhaps, an echo of the last of Hui-shih's paradoxes in *Chuang-tzu* 33.

28 Cf. P. Demiéville, 'Langue et littérature chinoise', *Annuaire du Collège de France* 48, pp. 158–60, for a discussion of this term.

29 But cf. Ho Ch'i-min, *Chu-lin ch'i-hsien yen-chiu*, p. 159, who believes Juan Chi is clearly berating Confucianism in favor of Chuang-tzu's philosophy in precisely this passage.

30 Fukunaga (1958) also emphasizes the resemblance between these two essays (p. 172), but he reads them both as being much more 'Taoist' than I do.

31 This interest in Taoist 'religion' is even more evident in the 'Ta-jen hsien-sheng chuan', below, pp. 187ff.

32 These are two adjoining mansions that Jupiter goes through in its twelve-year journey around the heavens. Juan Chi has used archaic, 'fancy' names for these mansions, and seems to want to suggest the Master's indifference to time: he wanders about quite indifferent to what the year or (in the next lines) season may be.

33 This and the other place names mentioned are imaginary immortal haunts, mainly found in the K'un-lun Mountains. I will identify them only by mentioning earlier texts that also name them. The Red River is named in *Chuang-tzu* 12, Legge translation, 1, p. 311, and in the 'Li sao', *Ch'u tz'u*, p. 33.

34 *Chuang-tzu* 22, Legge translation, 2, p. 57.

35 *Chuang-tzu* 4, Legge translation, 1, p. 217.

36 Cf. *Lun yü* 10, 3: '[Confucius] hastened forward [with his arms spread out] like the wings of a bird.'

37 That is, the mythical emperors of the Golden Age, Yao and Shun.

38 The great founders of the Chou dynasty who lived over a thousand years after the legendary emperors.

39   Successors of the previous who reigned, according to traditional chronology, from 1115 to 1053 B.C.
40   The actual date is left vague.
41   As insignia of rank?
42   Cf. *Chuang-tzu* 2, Legge translation, 1, p. 183: 'Heaven and earth are a single finger; the ten thousand creatures a single horse.'
43   A mountain in the immortals' K'un-lun range; cf. 'Li sao', *Ch'u tz'u*, p. 29.
44   This seems to be an echo of *Chuang-tzu* 1, Legge translation, 1, p. 172, concerning the 'man from Sung who did trade in ceremonial caps and went with them to Yüeh . . . where they had no use for them'.
45   Cf. *Chuang-tzu* 17, Legge translation, 1, p. 381: 'The horses Ch'i-chi and Hua-liu could run a thousand *li* in a day but were not as good as a wild dog or a weasel for catching rats.'
46   Mythical localities in the K'un-lun mentioned in *Shui-ching chu* 1, p. 1.
47   The dragon of Chung Mountain whose eyes shone so brightly they made it seem light as day, and dark as night when they were closed; cf. *Shan-hai ching* 8, p. 1a; 17, pp. 7ab.
48   I do not understand this line. Chung Mountain is another name for the K'un-lun and is where the Torch Dragon lives, but nowhere does it say he 'speaks'. Is it a volcano?
49   *Wu-wai* 無 外 , 'limitless', a term borrowed from Hui Shih; cf. *Chuang-tzu* 33, Legge translation, 2, p. 229.
50   Perhaps we are to understand this passage as the kind of cosmogony found in *Lao-tzu* 42. It is, in any case, not clear. If we understand 'heaven and earth' as the 'universe' or 'cosmos', 'all that is', a kind of hypostasis of spontaneity, but one which is differentiable, it perhaps becomes clearer; both being 'absolutes', they can be considered to be ultimately 'without differences'. But what follows shows that Juan Chi wants us to understand the 'unity' (or lack of 'differences') on another plane.
51   In Five Element theories the earth is considered *yin* and damp, heaven, *yang* and dry: hence the translation. This and the succeeding paragraph seem strongly influenced by Han scholasticism (cf. Tung Chung-shu, *Ch'un-ch'iu fan-lu* 58, Fung, *The history of Chinese philosophy*, vol. 2, pp. 21–22). The world is described as a constantly evolving series of contrasting or harmonizing elements, based upon a common substratum, 'breath', *ch'i* 氣 .
52   Based upon the description in the 'Hsi tz'u' of the *I ching*, Legge translation, p. 353.
53   Another echo of the 'Hsi tz'u', Legge translation, p. 348.
54   The 'Essay on music' contradicts this; cf. above, p. 88.
55   Perhaps, with lines 125–6, an echo of Hui Shih's paradox: 'Mountains are on the same level as marshes'; *Chuang-tzu* 33, Legge translation, 2, p. 229.
56   Cf. *Chuang-tzu* 5, Legge translation, 1, p. 224, with the difference noted above, p. 101.
57   The relation between man's nature, his emotions, organs etc, and the Five Elements is described in detail in *Po-hu t'ung* B, ch. 'Ch'ing-hsing' 情 性 .
58   In *Chuang-tzu* 11, Legge translation, 1, pp. 294–5 (for example), it is the 'heart' or 'mind', *hsin* 心 , that is described as riding through the universe, not the 'spirit', *shen* 神 ; cf. also *I ching*, Legge translation, p. 354.
59   Close imitation of *Chuang-tzu* 2, Legge translation, 1, p. 188.
60   The *I ching, Shu ching, Shih ching, Ch'un ch'iu, Li ching* and *Yüeh ching*.
61   Shang Yang (Duyvendak, p. 14) divided the population into mutually responsible groups of five and ten families.
62   During the Ch'in dynasty, the residents of the small wards of Chinese towns were

divided, for conscription purposes, into two groups depending upon whether they lived to the right or to the left of the central lane of the ward; cf. *Shih chi* 48, p. 3.

63   *Chuang-tzu* 11, Legge translation, 1, pp. 297–300, describes a sage who achieves a kind of bodily immortality through ataraxia and who is visited by Huang-ti.

64   *Chuang-tzu* 12, Legge translation, 1, p. 311. Hsüan-yüan is an appellation of Huang-ti. 'Root', *ken* 根 , rhymes with 'gate', *men* 門 ; it is difficult to see for what other reason it is used here.

65   The spirit of the Yellow River; cf. *Chuang-tzu* 6, Legge translation, 1, p. 244.

66   *Chuang-tzu* 17, Legge translation, 1, pp. 374–5 ff. (Legge's translation here is very faulty.)

67   *Chuang-tzu* 11, Legge translation, 1, pp. 300–3. Hung-meng shows Yün-chiang how to live as a Taoist; the latter can perhaps be said to have 'lost the argument'.

68   These seemingly un-Taoistic lines (the Taoist exalts *wu* 無 , 'what they do not have') probably are supposed to elucidate the lines that precede: one should base one's actions on one's actual potentialities, on one's pettiness in the cosmos, not on the ideas one might have of one's own importance.

69   The sun is bathed in Hsien Lake before it undertakes its daily journey across the sky; cf. above, p. 60, note 45.

70   These paradoxes are inspired by Juan Chi's interest in the *I ching* and are not typical of Chuang-tzu's philosophy.

71   Cf. *I ching*, Hexagram 11, Legge translation, p. 281.

72   Allusion to *Chuang-tzu* 29, Legge translation, 2, p. 174. Wei-sheng died under a bridge, drowned by the incoming tide because he refused to leave the place. He was supposed to meet a girl who had given him a rendez-vous there. Chuang-tzu castigates him as being vainglorious.

73   Reference to the eldest son of the duke of Chin (reigned 676–651); forced to strangle himself by his step-mother, his ghost threatens Chin with ruin; cf. *Ch'u tz'u*, 'Tien wen', Hawkes translation, p. 56.

74   The terms usually refer to immortals ('Yüan yu', *Ch'u tz'u* p. 83).

75   Ch'ü Yüan refused to 'expose his purity to the dust and mud of the world'; *Ch'u tz'u*, 'Yü fu', Hawkes translation, p. 91.

76   This sentence is from *Tso chuan*, Chao 31, Legge translation, 2, p. 738.

77   According to *Shih chi* 3, p. 33, 'When Chou's armies were defeated, he . . . clothed himself in his jewel bedecked garments and walked into fire and died.' Other traditions (*Shih chi* 2, p. 49) say he drowned in a lake.

78   For Po I, see above, p. 21; for Yen Yüan, see *Lun yü* 6, 9.

79   Cf. *Chuang-tzu* 11, Legge translation, 1, p. 296.

80   These two famous culture heroes of the Golden Age of both Taoisn and Confucianism are spoken of as living in a period of primitive simplicity in *Chuang-tzu* 10, Legge translation, 1, pp. 287–8.

81   Juan Chi seems to insist upon the necessity of following these primitive cultural leaders more than the Taoists do. The latter actually decry their 'inventions' that tend to destroy primitive simplicity.

82   *Chuang-tzu* 24, Legge translation, 2, p. 112.

83   The Sophists are here called the 'hard and the white', one of the most famous theses of Kung-sun Lung.

84   The great schools of thought of ancient China were traditionally divided into two opposing camps: the eastern, Confucianist schools of Ch'i and Lu, and the more disparate group of Confucianists, Sophists and Legalists of central China, the ancient state of Chin.

85   The text seems corrupt here and throughout the following eleven lines where the subject changes abruptly to the theme of the 'usefulness of the useless', with echoes of *Chuang-tzu* 1, 2 and 20.

86 Cf. *Chuang-tzu* 11, Legge translation, p. 296.

87 The *Lü-shih ch'un-ch'iu* was posted on the gate of Hsien-yang with one thousand pieces of copper hanging over it to be given to anyone capable of adding or subtracting a single character; cf. *Shih chi* 85, p. 10.

88 King Hsüan of Ch'i gathered scholars here in an academy late in the fourth century B.C.; cf. *Shih chi* 46, p. 31.

89 Chapter 48 of the *Mo-tzu* is devoted to Kung-meng. The third conversation (Mei translation, pp. 231–3) concerns ritual robes and whether the gentleman should wear them before or after he acts. Mo-tzu takes the position that it is a matter of indifference when he puts them on.

90 *Huai-nan-tzu* 12, p. 195. Rather than repress Kung-tzu Mou's un-Taoist desire to serve in government, Chan Ho tolerated it so the damage to his psyche would be simple rather than double: better to let oneself go than repress one's desires.

91 This seems to be a reference to later 'religious' Taoist works which began to flourish only centuries after the time of Chuang-tzu.

Chapter 6

1 Cf. Fung Yu-lan, *The history of Chinese philosophy*, vol. 2, pp. 169 ff.

2 Cf. *Tao-te chen-ching chuan*, Preface, p. 2b, in the Chih hai (1839–46) edition reproduced in Taiwan as part of the Wu-ch'iu-pei chai Lao-tzu chi-ch'eng, and Wang Chung-min *Lao-tzu k'ao* 1 (Peking, 1927?), pp. 170–71. The work also appears in the Tao tsang, vol. 93 (Wieger No. 679). This reference was kindly given to me by Mme Robinet of Paris.

3 Yü Kuan-ying, *Han Wei Liu-ch'ao shih lun-ts'ung* (Shanghai, 1953), pp. 45–6, quotes Juan Chi's usage of this binomial expression in Poem 80 (below, p. 177) as an example of such an expression composed of words with contrasting meanings of which only one is used.

4 This is not the only time Juan Chi has been charged with homosexuality; Gulik, *Sexual life in ancient China*, p. 93, makes a similar accusation with, if anything, even less evidence.

5 This interpretation agrees with the old *Wen hsüan* 23, p. 4a, commentary. In the Li Shan edition of the *Wen hsüan* the commentary is not identified, probably meaning that Li Shan ascribes it to 'Yen Yen-nien, Shen Yüeh and others', since the entire *Wen hsüan* 'Yung huai shih' commentary is ascribed to them. At the end of the (old) commentary to this poem, Li Shan adds a note of his own, prefaced by the usual words 'Shan yüeh'. In the *Wu-ch'en chu wen-hsüan* 23, pp. 3b–4a, the entire note is preceded by the words 'Shan yüeh'. This is further proof that the Wu ch'en are careless in their ascriptions of the commentary (cf. above, p. 7). Von Zach (p. 354) believes the general meaning of the poem is 'the perishableness of all beauty', a meaning which becomes clear, according to him, in the following poem in the *Wen hsüan*, No. 4 in the traditional order. If the two poems were a 'pair', meant to be read together, this interpretation *might* be defended, but as far as we know they are not and each poem must be interpreted independently.

6 Most versions of the story name Ch'eng Chi, the younger brother, the assassin; only the *Wei-shih ch'un-ch'iu* and *Wei-mo chuan* accuse the two brothers of the actual crime (cf. *San-kuo chih chi-chieh* 4, pp. 57b–58a).

7 Juan Chan was the son of Juan Chi's nephew, Juan Hsien. He lived *c.* 280–*c.* 310. His biography, like Juan Chi's, Hsieh K'un's and Hu-wu Fu-chih's, is in *Chin shu* 49. Wang Ch'eng was Wang Jung's nephew.

8 Wang Yin, *Chin shu*, quoted in *Shih-shuo hsin-yü* A (Section 1), p. 7b. The terms 'Universal', *t'ung* 通, and 'Enlightened', *ta* 達, are probably from *Chuang-tzu* 2 (Legge translation, p. 184); cf. Ho Ch'ang-ch'ün, *Wei Chin ch'ing-t'an ssu-hsiang ch'u-lun* (Shanghai, 1947), p. 49, n. 2, and p. 53.

9   He was from Wu; cf. *Chin-shu chiao-chu* 92, pp. 19b–21a.

10   *Shih-shuo hsin-yü* C (Section 23), p. 40a.

11   Kan Pao 干 寶 (fl. 320), '*Chin-chi* tsung-lun', *Wen hsüan* 49, p. 16a. The poet Liu K'un 劉 琨 (270–317) in a letter to Lu Ch'en 盧 諶 (*Wen hsüan* 25, pp. 6b–7a) says that it was during the wars at the end of the Western Chin that he realized that the philosophies of Juan Chi, Lao-tzu and Chuang-tzu were false.

12   Ku Yen-wu, *Jih-chih lu* 13, p. 41 (Wan-yu wen-k'u edition).

13   Ch'ien Ta-hsin, 'Ho yen lun', *Ch'ien-yen t'ang chi* 2, p. 13b (Ssu-pu ts'ung-k'an edition).

14   *Shih-shuo hsin-yü* C (Section 23), p. 38b.

15   Ho Ch'i-min, *Chu-lin ch'i-hsien yen-chiu*, pp. 158–9, basing himself on this poem (which I discuss on pp. 163–5 below), says that there is an evolution in Juan Chi's thought from his early 'Confucian' years, still inspired by his family education (his father was a student of the great Confucian scholar Ts'ai Yung), and the essay on the *I ching*, still purely Confucian, through the syncretism of the 'T'ung Lao lun', to the pro-Taoist, anti-Confucian [*sic*] position of the essay on Chuang-tzu. This is all very pat and convenient, but it is far from incontrovertible. I much prefer the position of T'ang Chang-ju, *Wei Chin Nan-pei ch'ao shih lun-ts'ung* (Peking, 1957), pp. 327–8, who strongly underlines the Confucian bias of the essays on the *I ching* and on music, and then contrasts them with the essay on Chuang-tzu and (especially) with 'The biography of Master Great Man', suggesting that there may be a chronological sequence, the latter two works being a product of his maturity and his disillusionment with Confucianism. T'ang Chang-ju then adds, however, the following sentence with which I concur wholeheartedly: 'But it is extremely difficult to say whether or not Juan Chi, at the bottom of his heart, really agreed with [the strong anti-Confucianism of 'The Biography of Master Great Man']; it is better to say that in these works he is stigmatizing the kind of false gentleman represented by men like Ho Tseng.'

Chapter 7

1   Juan Wu 阮 武, the son of Juan Ch'en 阮 諶, was actually Juan Chi's uncle. In the *Ch'en-liu chih* (quoted in *Shih-shuo hsin-yü* B (Section 8), p. 47b) he is said to have admired Juan Chi when the latter was quite young and as yet unknown.

2   *Chin-shu chiao-chu* 49, p. 1b.

3   Cf. R.H. van Gulik, *The lore of the Chinese lute* (Tokyo, 1940), pp. 88 ff and *passim*; M. Freeman, 'Yen Hsi-chai, a seventeenth century philosopher', *Journal of the North China Branch of the Royal Asiatic Society* 57 (1926) p. 79.

4   The term for 'stupidity' used in the *Chin shu, ch'ih* 癡, was also applied to the great painter and eccentric Ku K'ai-chih (341?–401?) in the *Chung-hsing shu* (quoted in *Shih-shuo hsin-yü* A (Section 4), pp. 86ab). Ling Shao-k'uei, 'T'an Ku K'ai-chih ti ch'ih', in *Ta-lu tsa-chih* (Taipei) 6, 8 (1953) pp. 17, 32, believes it refers to an assumed stupidity, useful, like Juan Chi's drunkenness, for keeping away from political entanglement.

5   The attribution is doubtful; cf. Y. Hervouet, *Sseu-ma Siang-jou* (Paris, 1964), p. 142.

6   Cf. K.P.K. Whitaker, 'Tsaur Jyr's Loushern Fuh', *Asia Major* N.S. 4 (1954) pp. 36–56.

7   This sub-tradition is very well studied by J.R. Hightower, 'The *fu* of T'ao Ch'ien', *Harvard Journal of Asiatic Studies* 17 (1954) pp. 169–230. He dissociates the two traditions with more rigor than I think necessary (p. 192); there can be no question of the fact that in the case of Juan Chi (mentioned by Hightower on pp. 180–81), at least, the two traditions are intermingled.

8   Which has earned him (unjustifiably, I believe) very bad marks from A. Waley (*The temple*, London, 1925, p. 55) and Hightower, *loc. cit.*

9   This mystical view resembles the view stated earlier (pp. 91–2) that music should be appreciated for its 'structure' rather than for its actual sound. It suggests that true beauty is something that surpasses sensual apperception. The examples that follow attempt to 'prove' this theory by showing that the most marvellous music and the greatest beauties of the past were only dimly perceived by the eye and ear.

10   Cf. *Shih chi* 28, p. 66.

11   One character is missing here. In the anecdote in *Chuang-tzu* 14 (Legge translation, 1, pp. 348–51) in which the Yellow Emperor 'describes' his mystical, *tao*-like music, it is said he performed it in the open country near Lake Tung-t'ing.

12   Shun's music-master; cf. *Shu ching*, 'Shun tien', Legge translation, p. 47.

13   A famous ancient virtuoso zither player, mentioned for the first time in *Hsün-tzu* 1, p. 6.

14   Cf. *Shan-hai ching* 3, p. 16b. Nü-wa was Yen-ti's youngest daughter who drowned in the Eastern Sea, was metamorphosed into a bird called the Ching-wei, and then carried wood and stones from the Western Mountains to fill up the sea: *Lieh-hsien chuan* (Kaltenmark translation, pp. 39–40). It seems to me that Juan Chi is definitely referring to this story here, but his text (especially the next two lines) is obscure and probably corrupt. What is 'hung-hsi'? West of the Hung, river or mountain? The variant 'Hsi shan', 'Western Mountains', found in Li Shan's commentary to *Wen hsüan* 31, p. 13b, is probably a preferable reading.

15   'Jewelled terrace' has many meanings, but here probably signifies a tower inhabited by immortals.

16   Reading 李 for 季.

17   Allusion to the séances held by a magician from Ch'i to summon up the image of Mme Li who had been an imperial concubine and favorite of Emperor Wu (and who was given posthumous rank as an empress). The séance was held at night and the spirit of Mme Li (or a 'pretty girl who looked like her', as Pan Ku sceptically puts it) was seen only distantly and through veils. Cf. *Han shu* 97A, p. 3952.

18   Perhaps a reference to Li Yen-nien, Mme Li's elder brother, who was instrumental in drawing the emperor's attention to her. In all these examples, Juan Chi aims at showing the beauty of the invisible and the inaudible: Mme Li was close to invisible; perhaps her brother's singing was close to inaudible?

19   These four lines are unintelligible to me as they stand. The first of them seems to refer to Tsou Yen's ability to make the air warm in Cold Valley (cf. chapter 1, note 20 above). A character is missing in the second line which seems totally unintelligible. The four lines, in this context, *seem* to refer to the extraordinary power of the emotions when they are aroused.

20   Cf. *Lao-tzu* 32 and 44.

21   I.e. the passage of time will not upset you; cf. the poem of Chiang Yen in imitation of Kuo P'u in *Wen hsüan* 31, p. 19b.

22   It is so quiet that even the clams' respiration is audible and sounds like singing.

23   The identity of the star (or planet) called T'ai-yin is debatable. The most complete account of the debate can be found in Kao Pu-ying, *Wen hsüan Li-chu i-shu* 7, pp. 6b–7a (Taipei, 1966), commentary to Yang Hsiung, 'Kan-ch'üan fu'. The term is alternately interpreted as Jupiter or its 'consort' star.

24   It was at the famous Yün-meng Swamp that Sung Yü described the meetings of the nymph Chao-yün in the 'Kao-t'ang fu' and the 'Shen-nü fu' (*Wen hsüan* 19). These *fu* describe the meetings in the form of mildly erotic dreams. Juan Chi here expressly links his poem with the Sung Yü tradition.

25   An immortal abode (as in Poem 43, below). There are a number of 'Cinnabar

Mountains' in Chinese tradition. The one referred to here is probably the 'Cinna-bar Cave Mountain' of *Shan-hai ching* 1, p. 9a.

26 K'ua-fu died while attempting to race with the sun; he died of thirst before he was able to reach the Great Swamp after having drunk the Wei River dry. His staff was metamorphosed into the Teng-lin (Teng Forest); cf. *Shan-hai ching* 8, p. 2b. Ch'in-p'i (reading 鴆 for 邳), together with the supernatural child of Mt Chung, killed Pao (or Tsu) Chiang on the sunny side of the K'un-lun. The Heavenly Emperor (*ti*) then slaughtered them on the east of Mt Chung at a place called Mountainous 嶓 Cliff 崖 or (as here) Jewelled 瑤 Bank 岸 . He was metamor-phosed into a Great Osprey; cf. *Shan-hai ching* 2, pp. 15ab. The evocation of these two unhappy mythological figures suggests that Juan Chi's appreciation of the music is passionate, sad, and somehow unsatisfied.

27 The Heavenly Emperor's garden on Huai-chiang Mountain; cf. *Shan-hai ching* 2, pp. 16ab. It is elsewhere called the Somber 玄 or Hanging 縣 Garden. There were extensive views in the four directions (on the K'un-lun, Great Swamp, etc.), according to the *Shan-hai ching*.

28 Cf. *Shan-hai ching* 3, p. 10a; identified with the Yü-yen shui 於 (or 于) 延 水 in the *Shui-ching chu* 13, p. 18. This latter is identified with the Tung-yang ho or Ch'ao-ho ho, north of T'ien-chen hsien, beyond the Great Wall in Chahar Province (cf. *Han-shu pu-chu* 28B, p. 22a). But it should be remembered that for Juan Chi these place names refer to some fairy-like never-never land.

29 The old Wei river is identical with the upper course of the present river of the same name rising in the foothills of Mt Sung in Honan. A widening and deepening of the river just southwest of the old town of Hsin-cheng (southwest of the present town) was called the Wei Deeps, Wei-yüan, which is referred to here; cf. *Shui-ching chu* 5 (22), p. 35.

30 Morohashi Tetsuji, *Dai Kan Wa jiten*, under 'chiu-ying' 九 英 , quotes this passage and suggests the 'Nine splendors', by analogy with the Nine stars, means the stars of the Little Dipper. The following line supports this interpretation.

31 Polaris, the seventh star in the Little Dipper (Ursa Minor).

32 Morning Cloud, Chao-yün 朝 雲 , is the nymph who united with the King of Ch'u at Kao-t'ang in the *fu* of that name attributed to Sung Yü. During the day she took the form of mist (or cloud) on the mountain and in the evening fell as rain upon it. These two lines suggest the immortal in Juan Chi's *fu* was transcendently beautiful, combining all aspects of the world's beauty in her complex, variegated form.

33 In *Shan-hai ching* 15, pp. 5ab and 16, p. 5a, Ch'ang-i 常 儀 or Ch'ang-hsi 常 羲 is said to have been the mother of the moons; she is here put in the role of the go-between, an essential element in any Chinese marriage.

34 Probably equivalent to the 'Jewelled Bank' discussed in note 26, above.

35 Ling-yang was an immortal (*Lieh-hsien chuan*, Kaltenmark translation, pp. 183–7) who gave his name to a piece of music; cf. Hsi K'ang, 'Ch'in fu', translated in van Gulik, *Hsi K'ang and his essay on the lute* (Tokyo, 1941), p. 65.

36 There is perhaps a suggestion in these two lines of the exchange of vital powers during the sexual act as it was described in old Taoist handbooks; cf. H. Maspero, 'Les procédés de "nourrir le principe vital" dans la religion taoïste ancienne', in *Le taoïsme et les religions chinoises* (Paris, 1971), pp. 553 ff; R.H. van Gulik, *Sexual life in ancient China* (Leiden, 1961), chapter 4, *passim*.

37 Perhaps because, as in the 'Lo-shen fu', the two lovers are not both mortals. The theme of the danger of union with spirits (fox fairies and the like) is very common in later literature.

38 Cf. *Shan-hai ching* 7, p. 1a.

39 Like the Hsia emperor's in the preceding note.

40 There is a 'thing' named 'the corpse of the Yellow Chü 姐 ' (variant, 'Yellow Dame') in *Shan-hai ching* 16, p. 5b. Perhaps she (or 'it'?) is Juan Chi's 'Yellow Creature'.
41 The Thunder Master appears in 'Li sao', *Ch'u tz'u*, p. 28, and 'Yüan yu', *Ch'u tz'u*, p. 85. The falling rain is reminiscent of the nymph of the 'Kao-t'ang fu', Chao-yün, who was a cloud in the morning and fell as rain at night.
42 Li-lun 離侖 is a spirit, the demon of the sophora tree, 槐鬼 , who lives on Mt Chu-pi. The characters here are not exactly the same: Juan Chi writes 倫 . Cf. *Shan-hai ching* 2, p. 16b.
43 Unknown. These two names could be read as allegorical figures (as often in *Chuang-tzu*): 'Li-lun' is 'Leaving social relations' and 'Ying-ku', 'Cleaving to commerce'.
44 Lu K'an-ju and Feng Yüan-chün, *Chung-kuo shih-shih* (Peking, 1957), pp. 322–3.
45 Li Chou-han 李周翰 , in his commentary to the 'Kao-t'ang fu' (*Liu-ch'en chu Wen-hsüan* 19, p. 7b) interprets *mi-chieh* 弭節 as 'in a short time', a meaning that would fit well here; but his reading is based upon a variant Li Shan (who reads 何節) did not know, and seems suspect, textually, to me.

Chapter 8

1 Kung is now Hui-hsien 輝縣 , N. Honan. Chi commandery had its seat in Chi-hsien 汲縣 during the T'ang when the *Chin shu* was written. Other sources state that his place of origin was unknown.
2 R.H. van Gulik, *The lore of the Chinese lute* (Tokyo, 1940), writes of Sung Teng's zithers on pp. 174–5 and reproduces what he seems to believe are two of their backboards in illustrations I and II (facing p. 196). These do not seem to be one-stringed instruments; cf. also the same author's *Hsi K'ang and his poetical essay on the lute* (Tokyo, 1941), p. 34.
3 The *T'ai-p'ing kuang-chi* 9, p. 63 (Peking, 1961 edition), is even more explicit: 'No one ever saw him eat.'
4 To the west of the present I-yang 宜陽 , southwest of Lo-yang.
5 *Chin-shu chiao-chu* 94, pp. 1b–2a.
6 Cf. D. Holzman, *La vie et la pensée de Hi K'ang* (Leiden, 1957), pp. 42–3.
7 But the *Wei-shih ch'un-ch'iu* quoted in *T'ai-p'ing yü-lan* 392, p. 3a, says the encounter took place during Juan Chi's 'youth'. The *Shih-shuo hsin-yü* C (Section 18), p. 14a, quoting this same passage from the *Wei-shih ch'un-ch'iu*, has 'once' 嘗 for 'youth' 少時 .
8 Quoting Tsang Jung-hsü, *Chin shu*; cf. *Shui-ching chu* 15, pp. 48–9.
9 *Shih-shuo hsin-yü* C (Section 18), p. 13b; Sun Ch'o, *Hsü kao-shih chuan* (quoted in *Shui-ching chu, loc. cit.*); *Chu-lin ch'i-hsien lun*, quoted in *T'ai-p'ing yü-lan* 392, p. 4b.
10 It is possible, of course, that both are correct and that Juan Chi met with several 'immortals' in the mountains near Lo-yang.
11 Other, only slightly differing versions are: *Wei-shih ch'un-ch'iu*, quoted in *Shih-shuo hsin-yü, loc. cit.*; Ts'ang Jung-hsü, *Chin shu*, quoted in *Shui-ching chu, loc. cit.*; *Sun Teng pieh-chuan*, quoted in *T'ai-p'ing yü-lan* 392, pp. 4ab; *Wei-shih ch'un-ch'iu* (another version), quoted in *T'ai-p'ing yü-lan, loc. cit.* It should be noted that in neither the *Shih-shuo hsin-yü* nor the *Wei-shih ch'un-ch'iu* versions is the immortal named.
12 See the discussion below, pp. 151–2.
13 Cf. the beginning of *Chuang-tzu* 6. 'True Man' in this context is another name for a Taoist immortal: he is a man true to his own essence, to his integrity, the totality of his natural self, untainted by desires or attachment to the outside world.
14 Northwest of Hui-hsien, Honan, where Sun Teng is said to have lived.

15   Very unceremonious behavior; cf. *Li chi* 1, Couvreur, vol. 1, p. 27. The term *chi-chü* 其踞 , which I have translated 'with legs spread out fan-wise', is sometimes taken to mean 'with legs crossed, tailor fashion', since both of these positions can conceivably be construed as resembling a *chi*, a 'winnowing basket', triangular in shape.

16   Legendary emperors.

17   The Hsia, Shang and Chou.

18   Variant: 教 for 外 . 'He described the doctrine of activity', i.e. Confucianism.

19   Taoist psychosomatic regimens.

20   The character for 'flowing', 嚼 , I have been unable to find in any dictionary. It is probably an onomatopoeic expression.

21   *Shih-shuo hsin-yü* C (Section 18), p. 13b.

22   *Feng-shih wen-chien chi chiao-chu* 5, pp. 44–5 (Peking, 1958).

23   E.D. Edwards, *Chinese prose literature of the T'ang dynasty* 1 (London, 1937), pp. 178–80. A colophon dated 1520, by Tu Mu 杜牧 , is quoted as saying the latter, having read in the 'Hsiao chih' of Sun Teng and Juan Chi, two famous singers of ancient times, paid a visit to Su-men Hill near Lo-yang and there attempted to find traces of them, but without success.

24   Cheng Hsüan, commentary to *Shih ching* 22; Ch'eng-kung Sui, 'Hsiao fu', *Wen hsüan* 18, pp. 26a–30b.

25   The oldest meaning of the word *hsiao* (*Shih ching* 22, 229 and 69) seems clearly to have been 'to wail' (cf. B. Karlgren, *Bulletin of the Museum of Far Eastern Antiquities* 16 (1944) pp. 104–5). By the time of Cheng Hsüan, Juan Chi and Ch'eng-kung Sui, it seems to have broadened its meaning to include 'whistling'. The Japanese translators of the *Shih-shuo hsin-yü* translate *hsiao* as *usobuku*, 'to roar, to wail', and add in the notes that it is a 'form of whistling', *kuchibue; Chūgoku ko shosetsu shū* (Sekai bungaku taikei 71), Tokyo, 1964, p. 174. The problem has been studied by Aoki Masaru, ' "Shō" no rekishi to jigi no hensen', *Ritsumeikan bungaku* (Kyoto) 150–1 (1957) pp. 179–87. Cf. also Funazu Tomihiko, 'Gi Shin bungaku ni okeru shōgo ni tsuite', *Tōyō bungaku kenkyū* (Tokyo) 11 (1963) pp. 34–50, who shows that, in binomial expressions at least, *hsiao* still maintains its early meaning of 'wail, roar'. M. Kaltenmark, *Le Lie-sien tchouan*, pp. 74–6 (on the immortal 'Hsiao-fu' 嘯父), does not choose between the two meanings of the word. Encyclopedia articles concerning *hsiao* (beginning with the *I-wen lei-chü*) can be found in *Chung-kuo ku-tai yin-yüeh shih-liao chi-yao* 1 (Peking, 1962), pp. 48, 106, 345–6, 359, 1048.

26   Yü Ying-shih, 'Life and immortality in the mind of Han China', *Harvard Journal of Asiatic Studies* 25 (1964–1965) pp. 80–122, especially pp. 89 ff, is an important article full of interesting facts about early immortality seeking. It also contains insights into the attitude of modern Chinese toward immortality and religion in general, as on pp. 106–7 where the author says: 'While there is no reason to doubt the sincerity of people like Han Wu-ti and Liu An in seeking immortality, it is certainly beyond anyone's comprehension why they should be interested in becoming traditional *hsien* (= immortals) at the cost of all their earthly pleasures.'

27   Cf. David Hawkes, 'The supernatural in Chinese poetry', *University of Toronto Quarterly* 30, 3 (1961) pp. 311–24; there is a good translation of Juan Chi's Poem 35 on p. 322. The immortals are said to play a role in Chinese poetry somewhat similar to that played by antique gods and goddesses in Western poetry. Funazu Tomihiko, 'Sō Shi no Yūsenshi ron', *Tōyō bungaku kenkyū* (Tokyo) 13 (1965), pp. 49–65, describes and attempts to date Ts'ao Chih's ballads that take immortality as their theme. He quotes the texts relevant to Ts'ao Chih's scepticism of the existence of immortality.

28   Ts'ao Chih, for example, in his ballads that sing of immortality, never puts their

existence into doubt; it is in his prose and in other poems that he expresses his scepticism.

29 Cf. *Huai-nan-tzu* quoted in *Ch'u-hsüeh chi* 1, p. 5. This usage of the words is a commonplace in poetry, but the editors of the useful handbook, *Wei Chin Nan-pei ch'ao wen-hsüeh shih tzu-liao* (Peking, 1962), p. 77, understand the words 'mulberry and elm' as the names of two stars (?) and their error has been repeated by many Western translators.

30 For 'Leaving my banners', *li hui* 離麾 , Huang Chieh suggests that *hui*, 'banner', is a mistake for *mi* 靡 , a very similar character, especially in the form it is given in the *Shuo-wen chieh-tzu*. *Li-mi* is an onomatopoeic doublet that has, as far as I can see, two meanings: 'excessively beautiful', and 'spreading about all over without interruption' (like undergrowth). The line might then read: 'Ranging without end below Jade Mountain'. Ku Chih suggests another substitution, but his reasoning is wildly unscientific.

31 Some authors (including Arthur Waley) believe that Emperor Wu of the Han dynasty was willing to wage costly wars to be able to import these horses because he believed they were actually 'heavenly' and could help him reach the paradise of Taoist immortals; cf. the references given in the article by Yü Ying-shih in *HJAS* 25, pp. 97, n. 72, and 98, n. 75.

32 Cf. P. Demiéville, 'Préface' to Chow Yih-ching, *La philosophie morale dans le néo-confucianisme* (Paris, 1954), pp. xi–cii, on the evolution of the term 'great summit', *t'ai-chi*. There is a good translation of Poem 35 by Hawkes in his article mentioned in note 27, above.

Chapter 9

1 If Juan Chi has actually borrowed this imaginary toponymic from *Lieh-tzu*, this would be an argument in favor of that book's authenticity, but of course there may very well be a common source. Chang Ping-lin states that Juan Chi (with the rest of his contemporaries) never quotes *Lieh-tzu* (quoted by A.C. Graham, 'The date and composition of Liehtzyy', *Asia major* N.S. 8 (1961) p. 145).

Chapter 10

1 On the theme of the indifference of the Great Man, cf. P. Demiéville, 'L'esprit de bienfaisance impartiale dans les civilisations de l'Extrême-Orient', *Revue inter-nationale de la Croix-Rouge* (Geneva) 404 (1952) pp. 670–78, reprinted in *Choix d'études sinologiques* (Leiden, 1973), pp. 113–20. Fukunaga Mitsuji, 'Daijin fu no shisōteki keifu : Jifu no bungaku to Rō Sō no tetsugaku', *Tōhō gakuhō* (Kyoto) 41 (1970) pp. 97–126, discusses the philosophical background of the 'Biography of Master Great Man'; Nakajima Chiaki, 'Gen Seki no "ron" to "fu" ni tsuite', *Nihon Chūgoku gakkai hō* (Tokyo) 9 (1957) pp. 41–4, describes the other influences apparent in the work, the hagiographies (such as the *Lieh-hsien chuan* and Hsi K'ang's *Kao-shih chuan*) and the series of 'questions and answers' by such authors as Tung-fang Shuo, Yang Hsiung and Pan Ku who, by answering questions asked by imaginary figures, actually give an apology of their own way of life, for their refusal or inability to engage in an official career. Cf. also Nakajima Chiaki (1966), pp. 33–4. As early as the fourth century Juan Chi was being compared to Ssu-ma Hsiang-ju 司馬相如, presumably because of the resemblance of Juan Chi's 'Biography of Master Great Man' with Ssu-ma Hsiang-ju's *fu* 'The Great Man' ('Ta-jen fu'). Wang Kung 王恭 (d. 398) asked Wang Ch'en 王忱 to compare Juan Chi to Ssu-ma Hsiang-ju, which he did in the following wise: 'Juan Chi bears sorrows [literally, 'clods' or 'lumps'] within his breast that he must moisten with wine.' (*Shih-shuo hsin-yü* C (Section 23), p. 48a).

2 Cf. above, pp. 149–52. The *Chin-shu chiao-chu* 49, p. 6b, and the *Chu-lin ch'i-*

hsien lun quoted in *Shih-shuo hsin-yü* C (Section 18), p. 14a, both state that Juan Chi's encounter with Sun Teng (or the 'Master of Su-men Mountain') was the inspiration for his 'Biography of Master Great Man'.

3 This is the theory of Yoshioka Yoshitoyo, *Dōkyō to bukkyō* (Tokyo, 1959), pp. 50–51; cf. A.K. Seidel, *La divinisation de Lao tseu* . . . (Paris, 1969), pp. 88–9.

4 Fukunaga Mitsuji, 'Chūgoku ni okeru tenchi hōkai no shisō: Gen Seki no "Daijin sensei ka" to To Ho no "Tō Jionji tō shi" ni yosete', in *Yoshikawa hakase taikyū kinen Chūgoku bungaku ronshū* (Kyoto, 1968), pp. 171–3, shows that the idea of the end of the world was present in ancient Taoism, but only as an illustration of the fragility of all that was not the *tao*. He later (p. 183) very sensitively stresses the 'religious' quality of Juan Chi's 'Biography' and remarks on the surprising resemblances of parts of it with the *Book of Revelations*. His opinion is very gratifying, for I had come to the same conclusion independently. The Buddhist idea of the end of the world at the end of a *kalpa* was adapted by the Taoists at least as early as the *Wei shu* 114, p. 25b (T'ung-wen edition), i.e. the second half of the sixth century.

5 Cf. Jung Chao-tsu, *Wei Chin ti tzu-jan chu-i* (Shanghai, 1935), pp. 42–3; Lin Mousheng, *Men and ideas* (New York, 1942), pp. 151–2; Hsiao Kung-ch'üan, *Chung-kuo cheng-chih ssu-hsiang shih* vol. 3 (Taipei, 1954), pp. 370–72. T'ang Yung-t'ung and Jen Chi-yü, *Wei Chin hsüan-hsüeh chung ti she-hui cheng-chih ssu-hsiang lüeh-lun* (Shanghai, 1962), pp. 26–35, discuss Hsi K'ang and Juan Chi as representative thinkers in the quarrel between the 'Doctrine of Names' and 'Spontaneity'. They make the error of treating Hsi K'ang's and Juan Chi's philosophies as being close to identical. When they say (p. 30): 'Superficially their [i.e. Juan Chi's and Hsi K'ang's] political thinking looks like a reappearance of Lao-tzu's and Chuang-tzu', but in reality it is, on the contrary, a mutation of Confucian thought', I believe they are right as far as Juan Chi is concerned. But their attempt to prove (p. 33) that the 'Biography of Master Great Man' is Confucian, and its anarchism is illusory, by quoting sentences out of context and confirming them with references to the essays 'On understanding the *I ching*' and 'On understanding Chuang-tzu' (both rightly treated as 'Confucian'), is unacceptable, and is very aptly criticized by Hsiao Hsüeh-p'eng, 'Juan Chi shih-lun', which first appeared in *Chung-shan ta-hsüeh hsüeh-pao* (*she*) (Canton) 4, 1956, and is reprinted in *Wei Chin Liu-ch'ao shih yen-chiu lun-wen chi* (Hongkong, 1969), pp. 49–58 (the discussion of the 'Biography' is on pp. 53–4).

6 It should not be forgotten that the concept of 'spirit', *shen*, plays an important role in later ancient Confucian philosophy, in the 'Hsi tz'u' chapter of the *I ching*, for example: 'We shall call "spirit" that which we cannot fathom in the [interaction] of the *yin* and the *yang*' (Legge translation, p. 357). It becomes so important, in fact, that Ch'ien Mu, 'Chung-kuo ssu-hsiang shih chung chih kuei-shen kuan', *Hsin Ya hsüeh-pao* (Hongkong) 1, 1 (1955) pp. 19–21, suggests that it becomes characteristic of later Confucian philosophy, as distinguished from later Taoist philosophy: the Confucianists at the end of the Chou dynasty and thereafter posit an undefinable moral power, *shen*, in the world, while the Taoists (Beginning with the *Lao-tzu*) insist that the world is ruled by *wu* 無 , a basic 'nondifferentiation'. Juan Chi's cryptic use of the concept of *shen* coupled with his avowed interest in the *I ching*, thus again point to his Confucianist tendencies, even in such a purely 'Taoist' work as the 'Biography of Master Great Man'. Ch'ien Mu's discussion of Kuo Hsiang's philosophy (*Chung-kuo ssu-hsiang shih*, Taipei, 1952, pp. 94–105) strikes me as being very much to the point.

7 The *T'ai-p'ing ching* 56–64 presents the following hierarchy: *shen-jen* 神人 , *chen-jen* 真人 , *hsien-jen* 仙人 , *sheng-jen* 聖人 , *hsien-jen* 賢人 , *min-jen* 民人 , *nu-pi* 奴婢 (cf. Wang Ming (ed.), *T'ai-p'ing ching ho-chiao*, Peking,

1960, p. 221). The fact that the 'Spirit Man' and the 'True Man' head the list is another indication that Juan Chi has been influenced by religious Taoism.

8   This is the gist of the opinion given on Juan Chi's whole life and works by a funerary inscription written for him by a certain Chi Shu-liang 嵇叔良 who is otherwise almost unknown. (Yang Shen, *Tan-ch'ien tsung-lu*, quoted in *Ch'üan San-kuo wen*, says he was prefect of the province of Tung-p'ing.) The inscription, 'Wei San-ch'i ch'ang-shih Pu-ping hsiao-wei Tung-p'ing hsiang Juan Ssu-tsung pei' 魏散騎常侍步兵校尉東平相阮嗣宗碑, is found no earlier than the Ming *Kuang wen-hsüan* and is reproduced in *Ch'üan San-kuo wen* 53, pp. 3b–4b.

9   The *Chin shu* and the *Shih-shuo hsin-yü*, as quoted in note 2 above, both insist upon the fact that the Great Man represents Juan Chi's own views.

10   The text followed is that of the Sao-yeh shan-fang (Shanghai, 1925) edition of the Han Wei Liu-ch'ao pai-san ming-chia chi, with the following variants (mainly from the *Ch'üan San-kuo wen* 46, pp. 5a–11a, version): line 261, for 之 read 通 ; line 285 宗 read 宋 ; line 321 大 read 天 ; line 332 道 read 迺 ; line 361 今 read 令 ; line 662 水 read 氷 ; line 673 correcting 莫 as 寞 ; line 706 add 去 after 我 . (Only these last two corrections are my own suggestions, not based on variants in the *Ch'üan San-kuo wen*.) Juan Chi often breaks out into short sections of irregular rhymed verse that I have not always translated as such.

11   Li Mu 李牧 was a famous general in Chao during the Warring States period. In spite of his brilliant service against the Hsiung-nu and the Ch'in, he was executed by the sovereign of Chao who believed a calumny against him; cf. *Shih chi* 81, p. 24.

12   Po Tsung 伯宗 was an outspoken courtier of the state of Chin during the Ch'un-ch'iu period who was killed, with his family, because his frankness irritated less scrupulous courtiers than himself; cf. *Tso chuan*, Ch'eng 15, Legge translation, p. 389.

13   The analogy of lice in a pair of drawers, the most famous part of the 'Biography', was probably inspired by a passage in *Chuang-tzu* 24 (Legge translation, 2, p. 109) in which a class of men are compared to lice living on a pig; the 'great fire' is probably also inspired by that passage, and should be read with the fall of dynasties in lines 154 ff in mind. I cannot accept the explanation of the *Wei Chin Nan-pei ch'ao wen-hsüeh ts'an-k'ao tzu-liao* editors (p. 200) who interpret 'hills of flame' as 'the southern regions'.

14   Literally '*yang* crow'. This seems to be the earliest usage of this term as an heroic bird (like the phoenix or roc), a usage found often in later poetry. The comparison between heroic and small birds is based on the first chapter of *Chuang-tzu*. Like so many of the creatures referred to by Juan Chi, the Sun Crow was probably a well known mythological animal, perhaps the black crow often shown against the sun in early (Former Han) paintings; cf., for example, the illustrations of the silk painting found in Ma-wang tui, Changsha, reproduced in *K'ao-ku* 1973, 1, p. 44 and Plate 7, and a Latter Han version on p. 50. Archeological discoveries of this type continue to show us that so many of the strange birds and beasts Juan Chi delights in mentioning were an important, perhaps even a commonplace part of contemporary daily life.

15   Traditionally in 1766 B.C.

16   The Chou were actually defeated by the Ch'in in 255 B.C. and the latter by the Han in 206 B.C., but Master Great Man can hardly be expected to take a mere half century into account!

17   Said to be the capital of the Shang king Tsu-i 祖乙 (reigned 1525–1505 B.C.); cf. *Shih chi* 3, p. 18, commentary of Ssu-ma Chen.

18   Po 薄 is in all probability Po 亳 , the three capitals of the founder of the Shang dynasty, T'ang, variously located near Lo-yang; the two characters are commonly confused in old texts (*Hsün-tzu, Li chi*, etc.).

19 The capital of the early kings of the Chou dynasty, in the northwest of Ch'ang-an; cf. *Shih chi* 4, pp. 15, 96.

20 Where the sun rises; cf. *Shan-hai ching* 9, p. 3a.

21 By participating in the natural course of the universe the Great Man actually helps it evolve as it should rather than going against it and setting it awry as do the ritualists. He resembles the 'spirit-like men' in *Chuang-tzu* 1, Legge translation, 1, pp. 170–71, who were able, by 'freezing their spirit, to protect the world from disease and bring a yearly harvest'.

22 *Chuang-tzu* 22, Legge translation, 2, p. 63: 'What is clear was produced from what is obscure; what has order from that which has no form.'

23 Like the *tao* itself, the Perfect Man is indescribable, unanalyzable; he can carry out his function as a kind of demiurge only if he remains, like the *tao*, an Absolute, undiminished by well- or evil-meaning critics attempting to define (and thus reduce) him.

24 This sentence, and thus this whole section, begins very abruptly. There is perhaps a hiatus in the text. Fu-yao 扶搖 is said to have two meanings in *Chuang-tzu*: a rising wind (*Chuang-tzu* 1, Legge translation, 1, p. 165), and a sacred tree that grows in the Eastern Sea (*Chuang-tzu* 11, Legge translation, 1, p. 300). It is difficult to know what it means here. Sung is not on the Eastern Sea, nor does grammar permit the translation: 'in wilds swept by a rising wind'. The word is probably used to suggest some distant fairy land.

25 An immortal said to have lived on Mount P'eng-lai, in the Eastern Sea; cf. *Shih chi* 28, p. 48.

26 Lu-li 角 or 甪 里 was one of the Four White Heads who retired when the Ch'in came to power and who spent the remainder of their lives in the mountains; cf. *Han shu* 72, p. 3056. The Cinnabar River is an immortal haunt often referred to by Juan Chi, but it does not seem to have been associated with Lu-li or the Four White Heads elsewhere.

27 Pao Chiao 鮑焦 is said to have lived at the time of Confucius and to have allowed himself to starve to death rather than serve a corrupt sovereign. He first appears in *Chuang-tzu* 29 (Legge translation, 2, p. 173) where he is said to have 'died with his arms around a tree'. A more extended version is in *Han-shih wai-chuan* 1 (Hightower translation, pp. 35–6) and in the commentary to *Shih chi* 83, p. 5.

28 Lai Wei 萊維, as far as I know, appears in no other text. He may be Lao-lai-tzu 老萊子, a famous recluse and filial son who, assisted by his equally famous wife, fled political commitment and lived out his life as a poor farmer; cf. *Shih chi* 63, p. 7, with the commentary.

29 This sentence and the next few lines are difficult to understand and probably contain corruptions. I have marked the completely incomprehensible passages with question marks between square brackets. The general meaning of the passage is, however, clear: the Perfect Man, or True Man, is above any partisan action and makes no personal choice. The 'Great Beginning', *t'ai-ch'u* 泰初, appears in *Chuang-tzu* 12, Legge translation, 1, p. 315.

30 Unknown elsewhere.

31 Sun Pin 孫臏 and P'ang Ch'üan 龐涓 studied military arts together, but the latter, knowing the former was more proficient at them than himself, had Sun Pin's feet amputated. Sun Pin made his way to a neighboring kingdom and defeated P'ang Ch'üan, forcing him to commit suicide, his last words being: 'And this is how I make that worthless idiot famous!' Cf. *Shih chi* 65, pp. 5–11.

32 Fan Chü 范雎 (sometimes called Fan Sui 睢), suspected of treason, is flogged until his ribs are broken and his teeth are pulled out. He manages to escape and

later becomes a high dignitary in Ch'in; cf. *Shih chi* 79, pp. 2 ff. H. Maspero (*La Chine antique*, 1955, p. 335, n. 2) suspects he is a fictional figure.

33 Pai-li Hsi 百里傒 when he was seventy years of age, was ransomed from the prison in Ch'u where he was being held and employed in the service of the Ch'in (clan name Ying 嬴, as in Juan Chi's text) whom he raised to the position of leader after seven years of service; cf. *Shih chi* 5, pp. 23 ff.

34 Lü Ya 呂牙 was the *tzu* of Lü Shang 呂尚, better known as T'ai-kung Wang. Different versions of his life are given, almost any of which would explain the present allusion: either he was raised from poverty late in life by King Wen of the Chou dynasty, or he switched to Chou late in life after having unsuccessfully tried to serve the last Shang ruler. Cf. *Shih chi* 32, pp. 2—5, with the commentaries.

35 A near citation of *Tso chuan*, Hsiang 29, Legge translation, p. 550, but the word *piao* 表 is used in a different meaning. The meaning Juan Chi gives to the words is also found in the pseudo-*Tzu-hua-tzu* 子華子 6, p. 1b (Pai-tzu ch'üan-shu, Sao-yeh shan-fang, 1931, edition): 'The state of Ch'i borders the sea . . .'.

36 The character 麗, modifying the word for 'tree', is not attested elsewhere, making it impossible to translate it here.

37 These last sentences underline the relativistic, cyclical philosophy of the wood-gatherer: flourishing leads only to decay, birth to death. Lines 427—36 are quoted in *Wei-shih ch'un-ch'iu*; cf. *Shih-shuo hsin-yü* C (Section 18), p. 14a.

38 Pu-chou 不周 is a mythical mountain in the northwestern K'un-lun range; cf. *Shan-hai ching* 16, p. 1a.

39 Tan-yüan 丹淵, the Cinnabar Depths, is mentioned in Poem 23, above, p. 174, and in *Han shu* 21B, p. 1013, as a fief given by Yao when he abdicated in favor of Shun.

40 One of the most famous lieutenants of the founder of the Han dynasty, Chang Liang 張良, Marquis of Liu 留, at the beginning of his career had to change his name and hide because of an attempt at the life of the First Emperor of the Ch'in. His later success is probably characterized here as extending his charisma to the very frontiers of the empire; cf. *Shih chi* 55.

41 Cf. above, Poem 6, pp. 116ff.

42 See above, note 38, for Pu-chou. 'Leave my carriage' translates *ch'u-ch'e* 出車 which is actually the title of Poem 168 in the *Shih ching* where, however, it means 'take my carriage out'.

43 The uncultivated wilderness of the Nine Provinces that make up the civilized world.

44 I 羿, the archer, is especially famous for having shot down nine of the ten suns that appeared during Yao's reign. He is called I-i 夷羿, as here, in *Tso-chuan*, Hsiang 4, Legge translation, p. 424, and in the 'T'ien wen' of the *Ch'u tz'u* (Hawkes translation, p. 50). For a general discussion, cf. M. Granet, *Danses et légendes de la Chine ancienne* (Paris, 1959), pp. 376—81.

45 I have been unable to identify this name which means, literally, 'Come joyously'.

46 The mythical tree of the east where the suns perched before setting off on their diurnal voyage; cf. above, p. 60, chapter 3 note 45.

47 Cf. above, note 24.

48 Cf. above, note 20.

49 One would expect the 'Long Springs' to be located in the far west, on the opposite side of the world from T'ang Valley, where the sun rises, but the term does not seem to have any special significance as a proper noun. It is used by Yüan Hung 袁宏 in his 'Tung-cheng fu' (*Ch'üan Chin-wen* 57, p. 1a) as a place name near the Yangtze around Lake Tung-t'ing and by Ku K'ai-chih in his 'Ping fu' (*Ch'üan Chin-wen* 135, p. 3a), but not as a proper noun. Perhaps Juan Chi is referring to

the springs of the great Chinese rivers that are indeed located in the K'un-lun in Chinghai?

50 Yen-tzu 崦 嵫 is, in fact, according to the *Shan-hai ching* 2, p. 29a, the western-most of the Western Mountains.

51 The flowers of the Jo 若 tree, a glowing tree in the Kun-lun mountains, are said to illuminate the underworld; cf. *Ch'u tz'u*, 'T'ien wen' (Hawkes translation, p. 49).

52 The 'Red *yang*' and 'Dark *yin*' represent the two aspects of the universe whose respective waxings and wanings produce the changes in the seasons. They are here shown as subordinate to the Great Man.

53 Fukunaga Mitsuji, in his 1958 article, pp. 164−5, insists upon the importance of this line for the understanding of Juan Chi's attitude towards the immortals and the mystical experience: the split-second ecstatic experience is what interests him, not the prospect of immortality itself. But can the word 'transformation', *hua* 化 , mean 'ecstasy'?

54 The Purple Palace is the name of a star, of the emperor's dwelling place, and of the palace of the immortals; all three meanings are more or less appropriate here.

55 The character *hu* 忽 seems to be superfluous here.

56 The *wu ti* 五 帝 and *liu shen* 六 神 are glossed in the *Ch'u tz'u*, 'Chiu chang', 'Hsi sung' (Hawkes translation, p. 60), as the gods of the five directions (north, east, south, west and center) and the spirits of the seasons, the sun, the moon, etc. I read 代 for 伐 in the second line (with the *Ch'üan San-kuo wen*), but am still not sure of the meaning of *tai chou* 代 周 .

57 The country of the Great Darkness is said, in *Shan-hai ching* 18, p. 8b, to be located in the North Sea. The Jade Woman, is mentioned in Yang Hsiung, 'Kan-ch'üan fu', *Wen hsüan* 7, p. 8b. The 'Beauty of the King Above', mentioned in the next line, is unattested.

58 *Yen-yang* 炎 陽 literally means 'flaming *yang*' and usually refers to the heat in midsummer; it should probably be read as Yen shen 炎 神 or Yen ti 炎 帝 , the spirit of the South who, like the divinities mentioned in the following lines, appears in *Ch'u tz'u*, 'Yüan yu' (Hawkes translation, p. 85, 1. 73).

59 Attendant of the preceding; spirit of the south, of fire and summer; cf. *ibid.*, p. 86.

60 Attendant of the spirit of the north; cf. *ibid.*, p. 86.

61 Spirit of the west; cf. *ibid.*, p. 85.

62 Spirit of the east; *ibid.*, p. 84. These spirits are also mentioned in the 'Yüeh ling' chapter of the *Li chi* with approximately the same functions as in the 'Yüan yu'. There is a discussion of them in some detail in Granet, *Danses et légendes*, pp. 255−8 and *passim* (see index).

63 This looking down and being pained at the suffering on earth below is typical of the ecstatic voyage and can be seen in 'Li sao' (*Ch'u tz'u*, p. 34), 'Yüan yu' (*Ch'u tz'u*, p. 85). But here it leads to the purely philosophical comment in the follow-ing line.

64 The term *hu mo* 沕 漠 also appears in the 'Tung-p'ing fu' where it is translated as 'the endless desert'; cf. above, p. 40.

65 'Spiritual brightness', *shen-ming* 神 明 , is a term sometimes used in the *Chuang-tzu* to mean 'an intuition of the *tao*'; cf. *Chuang-tzu* 33, Legge translation, 2, p. 225.

66 I do not know what the 'Regulator of things', *chih-wu* 制 物 is, but the 'Eight Cords', *pa wei* 八 維 , are referred to in the *Ch'u tz'u*, Ch'i chien', 'tzu pei' (Hawkes translation, p. 130), as cosmic cords supporting the earth in each of the eight directions.

67 Wang Ni 王 倪 is the Taoist master of Nieh Ch'üeh 齧 缺 who, in turn, was the master of Hsü Yu 許 由 , who, finally, was the master of Yao; cf. *Chuang-tzu* 12, Legge translation, 1, p. 312.

68   Li Po-yang 李伯陽 is Lao-tzu; K'ung Ch'iu 孔丘, Confucius.

69   Kuang-ch'eng-tzu 廣成子 was a great sage consulted by Huang-ti; cf. *Chuang-tzu* 11, Legge translation, 1, pp. 297–300.

70   There are echoes of *Lao-tzu* 6 in this passage. The Great Beginning seems to be a hypostasis of the *tao* through which the Great Man passes to reach his union with the Absolute.

71   In later religious Taoism the 'Chiu-ling chih kuan' 九靈之館, 'Hall of the Nine Spirits', was under the jurisdiction of Hsi-wang-mu; cf. *Yün-chi ch'i ch'ien*, quoted By Morohashi Tetsuji, vol. 1, p. 386a.

72   The Great Origin, *t'ai shih* 太始, mentioned here after the Great Beginning, *t'ai ch'u* 太初, makes one think of the cosmogonies current at the end of the Han dynasty. The Great Beginning describes the 'beginning of breath', *ch'i* 氣; the Great Origin, the beginning of forms, *hsing* 形. Cf. Yasui Kōzan and Nakamura Shōhachi, *Isho shūsei* (Tokyo, 1960) vol. 1, p. 40. The passage also appears in *Lieh-tzu* 1.

73   An important divinity in Han official religion: the spirit of the Pole star, King of Heaven, etc. (*Han shu* 25A, pp. 1218–20), who later came to play a central role in Taoist religion; cf. H. Maspero, *Le taoïsme et les religions chinoises* (Paris, 1971), pp. 389, 398–9.

74   The term 'Great Purity', *t'ai-ch'ing* 太清, has different meanings; here it seems to be another epithet for the *tao*, as it is in *Chuang-tzu* 14, Legge translation, 1, p. 349. Juan Chi uses it again in line 522, above, and in line 671, below, and in Poem 45, below, p. 208.

75   There is perhaps an echo here of *Chuang-tzu* 11, Legge translation, p. 300: 'Men will all die and I alone will remain.'

76   The prosody and even some of the vocabulary of these three syllable verses (lines 678–709) are reminiscent of the fourteenth of the eighteen 'Han nao-ko'; cf. Wang Hsien-ch'ien, *Han nao-ko shih-wen chien-cheng* (1872), pp. 62a–64a.

77   A character is missing here, or perhaps in the next line.

78   A traditional way of saying 'until the ends of time' is 'when the Yellow River becomes clear'; cf. *Tso chuan*, Hsiang 8, Legge translation, p. 435.

79   According to the *Chou li* 39, 'K'ao-kung chi', p. 2a: 'When the mandarin orange is [transplanted] north of the Huai it becomes a trifoliate orange. The warbler does not cross the Chi; when the leopard crosses the Wen it dies.'

80   It is also possible to interpret Juan Chi's words in the past tense: 'There were no heroes in their times, so they made worthless idiots famous!' According to this interpretation he is making fun (in Master Great Man fashion) of two of China's greatest heroes, Liu Pang and Hsiang Yü, and not of his contemporaries. Li Po, in a poem entitled 'thoughts about antiquity after having ascended to the old battle-field at Kuang-wu', prefers this latter interpretation of Juan Chi's words and severely rebukes him for his lèse-majesté against Liu Pang. Su Shih, in turn, re-bukes Li Po for not having understood Juan Chi's words correctly. Hung Mai 洪邁 (1123–1202) and Hsiao Shih-yün 蕭士贇 (fl. 1250) follow Su Shih's interpretation, but the latter says Li Po's poem must be a forgery. Cf. *Li T'ai-po ch'üan-chi* 21, pp. 17b–20b (Peking, 1957 edition).

81   The most famous example is Ko Hung who severely took Chuang-tzu to task for 'equating life and death . . . considering existence as a corvée and death as a rest'; *Pao-p'u-tzu*, Nei-p'ien 8, p. 34. Cf. also H.G. Creel, *Journal of the American Oriental Society* 76 (1956), pp. 151–2.

82   The same text is ascribed to the *Wei-shih ch'un-ch'iu* in both the *Shih-shu hsin-yü* C (Section 18), p. 14a, and *San-kuo chih chi-chieh* 21, p. 21a.

83   In 'Ku feng' 古風, No. 54; cf. Takebe Toshio, *Ri Haku* 2 (Chūgoku shijin senshū, Tokyo, 1958), pp. 180–81.

84 Cf. Ogawa Tamaki, 'Wo tao ch'ang yu-yu: To Ho no jikkau', *Chūgoku bungaku hō* (Kyoto) 17 (1962) p. 5.

85 In the poem 'Huang-chou han-shih' 黃州寒食 . Cf. D. Holzman, *Etudes song in memoriam Etienne Balazs*, Série II, 2 (Paris, 1976).

86 Cf. Huang K'an, quoted by his disciple Shen Tsu-fen in Ch'eng Ch'ien-fan and Shen Tsu-fen, *Ku-tien shih-ko lun-ts'ung* (Shanghai, 1954), pp. 119–20.

87 And for Wang Wei's 'Lo-yang nü-erh hsing' 洛陽女兒行 which echoes it; cf. *Wang Yu-ch'eng chi chien-chu* 6 (Peking, 1961), pp. 99–100.

88 Other theories can be found in Yang Shen 楊慎 , *Tan-ch'ien yü-lu* 丹鉛餘錄, quoted in the Han Wei Liu-ch'ao pai san ming-chia chi edition of Juan Chi's works, pp. 20b–21a; Ku Ch'i-yüan 顧起元 (1565–1628), quoted by Huang Chieh; and Liang Chang-chü, *Wen-hsüan p'ang-cheng* 21, pp. 14ab.

Chapter 11

1 I say this in spite of the remark made by the Ming anthologist Feng Wei-ne in his *Shih chi*: 'The Ts'ao family of the Capital possesses a copy of the *Juan Pu-ping shih* 阮步兵詩 in one *chüan*. It is in T'ang handwriting and differs widely from the editions now current.' (Quoted by Yao Chen-tsung and Lu Pi in the works mentioned below.) I have not been able to use Feng Wei-ne's work, but the variants reproduced in the editions of Juan Chi's poetry available to me (Huang Chieh's in particular), whose editors used Feng Wei-ne's anthology, seem to be relatively unimportant; that is, with only a few exceptions noted in my commentary, they do not greatly change the meaning of Juan Chi's poems. If Feng Wei-ne did not use the variants from the Ts'ao family's T'ang MS in his *Shih chi*, it is of course possible that it represented an entirely different textual tradition that is now lost. There are no notes on the textual history of Juan Chi writings in the standard bibliography of Chinese works, the *Ssu-k'u ch'üan-shu tsung-mu t'i-yao*, perhaps simply because no edition worthy of inclusion in the Ssu-k'u ch'üan-shu collection was submitted to the Ch'ien-lung emperor when he called up the works that were to form the basis of his gigantic bibliographical project. The most complete account is in *Sui-shu Ching-chi chih k'ao-cheng* 30 by Yao Chen-tsung (1842–1906), Erh-shih-wu shih pu-pien 4, pp. 5718–19 (Peking, 1956). Cf. also Lu Pi, *San-kuo chih chi-chieh* 21, p. 22a. The earliest complete editions of Juan Chi's works I have seen are both of Ming date: the *Juan Ssu-tsung chi* 阮嗣宗集 in two *chüan* in the Han Wei Liu-ch'ao wen collection by Wang Shih-hsien 汪士賢 (preface dated 1543; according to Yokota Terutoshi, 'Bai Teiso no sōshū hensan', *Shinagaku kenkyū* 30 (1965), p. 25, the *Juan Ssu-tsung chi* in this collection was edited by Ch'eng Jung 程榮), and the *Juan Pu-ping chi* in one *chüan* in Chang P'u's Han Wei Liu-ch'ao pai-san ming-chia chi. The earliest commented edition of the poetry is by Chiang Shih-yüeh (1799), a copy of which was kindly lent to me for photo-copying by Professor Yoshikawa Kōjirō. Descriptions of the other commentaries and editions used will be found in the Bibliography and in the Finding list.

2 *Pai-hua wen-hsüeh shih* (preface dated 1928), p. 51.

3 Cf. Yoshikawa Kōjirō, 'Gen Seki no Eikaishi ni tsuite', *Yoshikawa Kōjirō zenshū* 7, pp. 193–6.

4 The following poems, in their entirety or in part, are members of this tradition: Ts'ao P'i, 'Tsa shih', 'Man-man ch'iu-yeh ch'ang' (*Weh hsüan* 29, pp. 13b–14a); Wang Ts'an, 'Ch'i ai', 'Ching-man fei wo hsiang' (*Wen hsüan* 23, p. 16a); Ts'ao Jui, 'Ch'ang-ko hsing' (Huang Chieh, *Wei Wu-ti, Wei Wen-ti shih chu*, Peking, 1958, pp. 63–4). Another poem in this tradition is called an anonymous *yüeh-fu* entitled 'Shu-ko hsing' in *Wen hsüan* 27, p. 16b, and is also sometimes ascribed to Ts'ao Jui (Huang Chieh, pp. 71–2).

5   Cf. the discussion of these lines by Huang Chieh in the notes assembled by his student, Hsiao Ti-fei, *Tu-shih san cha-chi* (Peking, 1957), p. 17. Huang Chieh also suggests that Juan Chi has avoided placing the words 遵 and 我 in the same position in the lines (penultimate) for tonal reasons (they are both inflected tones). Chang Cheng-chien 張 正 見 (d. c. 575) has used this line as the title of a short poem of his own (*Ch'üan ch'en-shih* 2, p. 1402).

6   As do Yü Kuan-ying, *Han Wei Liu-ch'ao shih hsüan* (Peking, 1958), p. 146, and H. Frankel, review of J.J.Y. Liu, *The art of Chinese poetry*, in *Harvard Journal of Asiatic Studies* 24 (1962–1963) pp. 267–8. For the former the words 'pace back and forth' refer not only to the poet but to the wild goose and the swooping birds as well; it is this moonlit insomniac movement that calls forth the sadness in the poet. Professor Frankel gives an accurate and sensitive reading of the poem but is hindered by the fact that he has confined himself to the rhymed, and very free translation in J.J.Y. Liu's book (*The art of Chinese poetry*, Chicago, 1962, p. 113).

7   Or in no. 5 of his Miscellaneous poems ('Tsa shih') as Li Chih-fang, *Han Wei Liu-ch'ao shih lun-kao* (Hongkong, 1967), p. 78, points out. Li Chih-fang makes similar comparisons between Juan Chi's poems and those of his predecessors on pp. 76–80 of his book, but not always with as much felicity.

8   I have quoted the remarks of Yen Yen-chih, Juan Chi's first commentator, above, on p. 7. He says nothing about Juan Chi's technique as such.

9   Cf. Takamatsu Kōmei, *Shihin shōkai* (Horisaki, 1959), pp. 30–31.

10   Ch'en Tso-ming makes a similar statement in his *Ts'ai-shu t'ang ku-shih hsüan* 8 (quoted in *Wei Chin Nan-pei ch'ao wen-hsüeh shih ts'an-k'ao tzu-liao*, p. 206).

11   Hsiao Ti-fei (quoting Huang Chieh), pp. 18–19.

12   In *Hsiao-shih-fan t'ing chu-lu* 3, reprinted in Ting Fu-pao, Ch'ing shih-hua 1.

13   Hsiao Ti-fei, p. 17.

14   Kuo Shao-yü, *Ts'ang-lang shih-hua chiao-shih* (Peking, 1965), p. 142. 'Lofty' and 'antique' 高 古 and 'feeling and structure' 風 骨 are technical terms. For the former, see G. Debon, *Ts'ang-lang's Gespräche über die Dichtung* (Weisbaden, 1962), p. 60 and note 50; for the latter, Kōzen Hiroshi, *Bunshin chōryū* (Sekai koten bungaku zenshū 25, Tokyo, 1970), p. 357, note 1. In the next line Yen Yü couples Juan Chi with T'ao Yüan-ming as being the greatest poets of the 'Chin' dynasty. In his note 448, Debon acutely refers to the article of Yoshikawa Kōjirō mentioned in note 3 above to suggest that Yen Yü's view is contradicted by Yoshikawa's on the broadened scope of Juan Chi's verse. Yen Yü's terminology is so vague, however, that I believe his 'feeling and structure' can be interpreted as referring primarily to the technical aspects of Juan Chi's verse.

15   Hayashida Shinnosuke, 'Gen Seki Eikaishi kō', *Kyūshū Chūgoku gakkai hō* (Fukuoka) 6 (1960) p. 68, who ignores the pejorative part of this citation, takes it to signify that Hu Ying-lin has recognized Juan Chi's originality, the fact that he has 'transcended the Chien-an poets, the direct inheritors of the plain, unvarnished *yüeh-fu* ballads', to transform pentameter verse into a truly 'literary' medium. Juan Chi is a crucial figure in the history of pentameter verse, but Hu Ying-lin is wrong, it seems to me, to describe his originality as being in language and form rather than in scope and content.

16   *Chin-shu chiao-chu* 49, p. 1b. There is a variant from the *Ch'i-hsien chuan* in *T'ai-p'ing yü-lan* 611, p. 7a, which reads ' . . . he would roam about the hills and forests for days on end and not go back.'

17   Obi Kōichi, *Chūgoku bungaku ni arawareta shizen to shizen kan* (Tokyo, 1962), pp. 134–5.

18   *Ibid.*, and Tsuru Haruo, 'Tō Emmei no egaku shizen ni tsuite', in *Yoshikawa hakase taikyū kinen Chūgoku bungaku ronshū* (Tokyo, 1968), pp. 215–19.

19   B. Watson, *Chinese lyricism* (New York and London, 1971), p. 70.

20   *Ibid*. This error is not typical of the interesting short remarks that accompany B. Watson's excellent translations of the poems by Juan Chi included in his book.

21   Li Chih-fang, *op. cit.*, pp. 85–99, discusses his influence, but often in a very formal way, accounting any poem which uses Juan Chi's general title, 'Poems which sing of my innermost thoughts', as being influenced by him.

22   Twice in the *Shih-shuo hsin-yü*; six times in the *Shui-ching chu*; and over thirty times in the *Wen hsüan*.

23   *Sung shu* 73, pp. 2b–3a; cf. Takahashi Kazumi, 'Gan Enshi no bungaku', *Ritsumeikan bungaku* (Kyoto) 1960, pp. 474–95, and the good abstract by P. Demiéville, *Revue bibliographique de sinologie* 6 (Paris and The Hague, 1967), No. 454.

24   *Wen hsüan* 21, pp. 16ab; von Zach translation, p. 323; commentary by Yü Kuan-ying, *Han Wei Liu-ch'ao shih hsüan* (Peking, 1958), pp. 229–30.

25   Ch'en Tso-ming, *Ts'ai-shu t'ang ku-shih hsüan* 24, quoted in *Wei Chin Nan-pei ch'ao wen-hsüeh shih ts'an-k'ao tzu-liao*, p. 642.

26   *Chiang Li-ling chi* 江醴陵集 2, pp. 11a–12a (of the Sao-yeh shan-fang edition of the Han Wei Liu-ch'ao pai-san ming-chia chi).

27   E. von Zach, *Die chin. Anthologie* 1, p. 588, translates the poem as a political satire: Juan Chi hates the Ssu-ma as the Ching-wei hates the Eastern Sea. This is without support from the *Wen hsüan* commentators whom von Zach usually follows.

28   These poems should not be taken as 'imitations' of Juan Chi's as they are sometimes titled; cf. Feng Shu, *Shih-chi k'uang-miu*, p. 23 (Ts'ung-shu chi-ch'eng edition).

29   Cf. Chiao-jan 皎然 (late eighth century), *Shih shih* 3, p. 1b (Shih wan chüan lou ts'ung-shu, Third Series, edition); and Hu Ying-lin, *Shih sou* ('Nei pien' 2), p. 35.

30   *Ch'en Tzu-ang chi* 10, p. 231 (Peking, 1960); cf. the essay by Wang Yün-hsi, p. 291 of this edition.

31   Cf. Li Chih-fang, *op. cit.*, pp. 93–4.

32   In his 1966 Preface to the *Ch'ang-chou chi* 長洲集 in which this poem is contained, Professor Jao lists seven poets who have imitated Juan Chi's works, four who lived during the Ming dynasty and three later poets, including the philosopher Wang Fu-chih 王夫之 (1619–92) who wrote no less than eighty-two imitations; cf. *Wang Ch'üan-shan shih-wen chi* (Peking, 1962), pp. 196–9, 373–80.

Conclusion

1   For the names of some who have, see above, chapter 3, note 18; chapter 6, notes 13–14. The list could be extended. Yeh Meng-te 葉夢得 (1077–1148), for example, called Juan Chi a traitor to the Wei dynasty in his *Shih-lin shih-hua* C, pp. 8b–9a (in the Li-tai shih-hua of Ho Wen-huan, Taipei, 1971). The mid-eighteenth-century Manchu writer Ch'ang-an 常安 , probably referring to this passage, asks a very pertinent question: 'Evil-doers must profit from their actions if they are to do them. Since Juan Chi took no part in court affairs, where was the profit he received from engaging in evil-doing?' Cf. *Pa-ch'i wen ching* 19, pp. 9b–10a (a postface to the poems of Juan Chi).

2   Beginning with Ch'en Shou in the *San-kuo chih* (chi-chieh 21, p. 20a): 'Juan Chi took Chuang Chou as his model . . . '

3   Fung Yu-lan, *A short history of Chinese philosophy* (New York, 1948), chapter 20; T'ang Yung-t'ung, *Wei Chin hsüan-hsüeh lun-kao* (Peking, 1957), p. 127; Jung Chao-tsu, *Wei Chin ti tzu-jan chu-i* (Shanghai, 1935), chapter 2 (all the quotations illustrating Juan Chi's philosophy are taken from 'On understanding Chuang-tzu' and the 'Biography of Master Great Man'); Fan Shou-k'ang, *Wei Chin chih ch'ing-t'an* (Shanghai, 1936), chapter 4; T'ang I-chieh, 'Hsi K'ang ho Juan Chi ti che-

hsüeh ssu-hsiang', *Hsin chien-she* 9 (1962) pp. 25–30. This last is a very interesting essay, one of the very few to study Juan Chi's thought *per se*, but its usefulness is almost completely negated because of two grave errors. First, the author assimilates Juan Chi and Hsi K'ang too easily. (The fact that he recognizes the danger of such an assimilation in the footnote on the very title of the essay has not helped him avoid the danger inherent in it.) Second, he seems mainly interested in proving the two thinkers 'materialists joining forces against Wang Pi's and Ho Yen's subjective idealism'. These concepts simply have no meaning in third-century Chinese thought.

4   His contemporary Chung Hui 鍾 會 attempted to plagiarize his essays, according to Chiang Yen in his Preface to his 'Thirty pieces in miscellaneous style' found in his works, ch. 2, p. 6a, and in the Wu-ch'en edition of *Wen hsüan* 31, pp. 10b–11a (without a single word of commentary). Chang P'u 張 溥 (1602–1641), in his preface to Juan Chi's works in his Han Wei Liu-ch'ao pai-san ming-chia chi, puts his 'Essay on music' higher than Ssu-ma Ch'ien's (which actually is not by Ssu-ma ch'ien!) and his essays on understanding the *I ching* and Chuang-tzu in the same category as Wang Pi's and Kuo Hsiang's commentaries on those two works (cf. the Peking, 1960 commented edition of his prefaces by Yin Meng-lun, p. 189).

5   Huang Chieh, quoted by Hsiao Ti-fei, *Tu-shih san cha-chi*, p. 15.

6   Shen Te-ch'ien 沈 德 潛 , *Shuo-shih tsui-yü* 説 詩 晬 語 , quoted by Li Chih-fang, p. 89.

7   Cf. Ch'en Yen-chieh, *Shih-p'in chu* (Hongkong, 1959), p. 16.

8   *Shih pi-hsing chien* 2, p. 1a (edition whose postface is dated 1883).

9   *Yoshikawa Kōjirō zenshū* 7, p. 191.

BIBLIOGRAPHY

Editions of complete works consulted

Basic text: *Juan Pu-ping chi* 阮步兵集 in Chang P'u 張溥 (1602–1641), editor, Han Wei Liu-ch'ao pai san ming-chia chi 漢魏六朝百三名家集 in the Sao-yeh shan-fang (Shanghai, 1925) edition. This collection was copied into the Ssu-k'u ch'üan-shu and re-edited a number of times at the end of the nineteenth century. The title varies slightly according to the edition.

Juan Ssu-tsung chi 阮嗣宗集 in Wang Shih-hsien 汪士賢, editor, Han Wei chu ming-chia chi 漢魏諸名家集. Ming edition, preface dated 1543. See above, chapter 11, note 1. The title of this collection varies slightly, too.

List of Chinese commentators quoted

This list contains only those commentators who have actually been quoted by name in the body of the book. Other commentators will be found in the bibliography of Primary sources and traditional sinology listed under the titles of their works. The asterisks indicate works I have never seen and quote only from secondary sources (mainly Huang Chieh's commentary).

Ch'en Hang 陳沆 (1785–1826), *Shih pi-hsing chien* 詩比興箋 2, pp. 1a–13a (post-face dated 1883); reprint, Shanghai, 1959, pp. 40–51.

*Ch'en Tso-ming 陳祚明 (*fl.* 1655–1673), *Ts'ai-shu t'ang ku-shih hsüan* 采菽堂古詩選.

Chiang Shih-yüeh 蔣師爚 (*chin-shih* in 1780), *Juan Ssu-tsung Yung-huai shih chu* 阮嗣宗詠懷詩註 (1799).

Ch'iu Kuang-t'ing 丘光庭 (T'ang?), *Chien-ming shu* 兼明書. Remarks on Poem 6 in *chüan* 4, pp. 37–8 of the Ts'ung-shu chi-ch'eng edition.

*Chu Chia-cheng 朱嘉徵 (1602–1684), quoted by Huang Chieh.

*Fang Tung-shu 方東樹 (1722–1851), *Chao-mei chan-yen* 昭昧詹言 (1891).

Ho Cho 何焯 (1661–1722), *I-men tu-shu chi* 義門讀書記 (preface dated 1769), *Wen hsüan* 文選 2, pp. 3a–14a.

Hsiao Ti-fei 蕭滌非, *Tu-shih san cha-chi* 讀詩三札記. Originally published in *Hsüeh heng* 學衡 (Shanghai) 70 (1929); reprinted Peking, 1957. Pp. 10–21.

Huang Chieh 黃節 (1874–1935), *Juan Pu-ping Yung-huai shih chu* 阮步兵詠懷詩註 (preface dated 4 March 1926). Reprinted, with textual corrections by Hua Ch'en-chih 華忱之, Peking, 1957, and Hongkong, 1961.

Huang K'an 黃侃 (1886–1936), 'Yung-huai shih pu-chu' 詠懷詩補註, in *Chih-yen* 制言 (Soochow) 45 (1938) pp. 1–22. Originally written in 1916; posthumously published by his son, Huang Nien-t'ien 黃念田.

Ku Chih 古直, *Juan Ssu-tsung Yung-huai shih chien ting pen* 阮嗣宗詠懷詩箋定本, in Ts'eng-ping t'ang wu-chung 層冰堂五種, Peking, 1935; reprinted Taipei, 1966.

Li Shan 李善 (d. 689), commentary to *Wen hsüan* 23, pp. 2a–9b (see Finding list and bibliography of Primary sources under *Wen hsüan*).

*Liu Lü 劉履 (1317–1379), *Feng-ya i* 風雅翼, containing *Hsüan-shih pu chu* 選 詩補註, copied into the Ssu-k'u ch'üan-shu.

Lü Hsiang 呂向 (fl. 720), sub-commentary to *Liu-ch'en chu Wen-hsüan* 六臣註文 選 23, pp. 1a–11b (See Finding list and bibliography of Primary sources under *Liu-ch'en chu Wen-hsüan*).

Lü Yen-chi 呂延濟 (early eighth century), *ibid.*

Peking University, members of the Department of the History of Chinese Literature, *Wei Chin Nan-pei ch'ao wen-hsüeh shih ts'an-k'ao tzu-liao* 魏晉南北朝文學史參 考資料 1, Peking, 1962, pp. 175–91. Contains fourteen poems in the following order: 1–3, 5–6, 11, 16–17, 19, 31, 33, 39, 61, 67.

Shen Te-ch'ien 沈德潛 (1673–1769), *Ku-shih yüan* 古詩源 (1725), reprinted Peking, 1957. Contains twenty poems in the following order: 1–3, 5–6, 8–9, 11, 14–19, 21, 31–2, 60, 79–80.

Shen Yüeh 沈約 (441–513), quoted by Li Shan.

Tseng Kuo-fan 曾國藩 (1811–1872), *Shih-pa chia shih ch'ao* 十八家詩鈔 (1874), reprinted Taipei, 1966.

*Wang K'ai-yün 王闓運 (1833–1916). Quoted by Huang Chieh from manuscript marginal notes in the possession of Chou Ta-lieh 周大烈; cf. Huang's edition, p. 95 (note to Poem 78).

Wu-ch'en 五臣, the 'Five Officials', commentators, with Li Shan, in the *Liu-ch'en chu Wen hsüan*.

*Wu Ch'i 吳淇 (1615–1675), *Hsüan-shih ting-lun* 選詩定論

*Wu Ju-lun 吳汝綸 (1840–1903), quoted by Huang Chieh.

Yen Yen-chih 顏延之 (384–456), quoted by Li Shan.

Fragmentary sources quoted

The following is a descriptive bibliography of the fragmentary sources mentioned in the body of the book and in the notes. References to Yao Chen-tsung, followed by chapter and page numbers, refer to his *Sui-shu Ching-chi chih k'ao-cheng* in the Erh-shih-Wu shih pu-pien 4, pp. 5039–5904. References to a work with exactly the same title by Chang Tsung-yüan (Erh-shih-wu shih pu-pien 4, pp. 4943–5037) are made in the same way. Reconstructions have been made of most of the fragmentary Wei and Chin histories; I have mentioned only those published separately. A list of those published in *ts'ung-shu* can be found in *Chung-kuo ts'ung-shu tsung-lu* 2 (Shanghai, 1961), pp. 279, 297. See also R. de Crespigny, *The records of the Three Kingdoms* (Canberra, 1970).

Ch'en-liu chih 陳留志. A work in 15 *chüan* by Chiang Ch'ang 江敞 (also called Chiang Wei 微 and Chiang Cheng 徵) of the Eastern Chin. It is also called *Ch'en-liu jen-wu chih* 陳留人物志 and contained information on the geography and on eminent persons from Ch'en-liu, Juan Chi's home commandery. Members of the Juan clan are frequently named in the fragments that remain. Cf. Yao Chen-tsung 20, p. 5344bc.

Ch'i-hsien chuan 七賢傳. A work presumably devoted to stories about or biographies of the Seven Sages of the Bamboo Grove in five or seven *chüan* by Meng Chung-hui 孟仲暉 who lived in the middle of the sixth century in Northern Wei; a Buddhist layman, he is mentioned at the end of *Lo-yang ch'ieh-lan chi* 4. The work is also called *Chu-lin ch'i-hsien chuan* 竹林七賢傳. Cf. Yao Chen-tsung 20, p. 5354b.

Chin pai-kuan ming 晉百官名. *Pai-kuan ming* or *Pai-kuan chih* 志 and similar titles seem to have been generic names for compilations of thumb-nail descriptions of officials used by the Impartial and Just when he classified men according to the system of Nine Categories. Numerous compilations of this type for different periods are known; cf. Chang Tsung-yüan 10, pp. 5012a–5013b. They are all anonymous except for one that described the officials of the first part of the reign of Emperor Hui (290–307) attributed to Lu Chi 陸機 (261–303). The *Chin pai-kuan ming* is listed in the Sui and T'ang official bibliographies as having 30, 40 or 14 (an error for 40?) *chüan*. It is probably a compendium of a number of shorter collections for separate reign periods or eras. Cf. Yao Chen-tsung 20, pp. 5316c–5317b.

Chin chi 晉紀 . An annalistic history of the fifty-three years of the Western Chin in 22 or 23 *chüan* by Kao Pao 干寶 written soon after the exodus to the south and highly praised by contemporaries and by Liu Chih-chi. For Kan Pao's strong criticism of Juan Chi's anti-ritualism see p. 135 and note 11. Cf. Yao Chen-tsung 20, p. 5260bc.

Chin chi 晉紀 . An annalistic history of the Chin until 325 or a little later in 11 *chüan* by Teng Ts'an 鄧粲 (fl. 380). Cf. above, chapter 4, note 22, and Yao Chen-tsung 20, p. 5261c.

Chin shu 晉書 . A history of the entire Chin dynasty in 110 *chüan* by Tsang Jung-hsü 臧榮緒 (415–488) which was the main source used by the T'ang editors of the present *Chin shu*. Cf. Yao Chen-tsung 20, p. 5248bc.

Chin shu 晉書 . A history of the (Western?) Chin in 93 *chüan* begun around 318 on imperial command by Wang Yin 王隱 and Kuo P'u 郭璞 and submitted to the throne in 340 by Wang Yin alone. Wang Yin used, in part, material assembled by his father which became, in fact, the best part of his history according to the authors of the present *Chin shu* (*chiao-chu* 82, p. 11a). They say his own writing was pedestrian and incoherent. According to Liu Chih-chi, he was only interested in collecting local gossip. Cf. above, chapter 4, note 12, and Yao Chen-tsung 20, pp. 5246c–5247a.

Chin shu 晉書 . A history of the Chin until 326 in 44 *chüan* by Yü Yü 虞預 (fl. 325) who is said to have plagiarized Wang Yin and to have taken advantage of his aristocratic relations to have lowly born Wang Yin calumniated and removed from office. He hated metaphysical speculation and, like Ku Yen-wu and Ch'ien Ta-hsin (above, chapter 6 notes 12–13), he held Juan Chi (and in particular his nudity, above, p. 135) responsible for the invasion of China by the barbarians (*Chin-shu chiao-chu* 82, p. 15a). Cf. Lu Pi, *San-kuo chih chi-chieh* 21, pp. 23b–24a.

Chu-lin ch'i-hsien lun 竹林七賢論 . In two *chüan* by Tai K'uei 戴逵 (c. 335–395), an essay on the Seven Sages of the Bamboo Grove. Yen K'o-chün, *Ch'üan Chin-wen* 137, pp. 8a–11a, has assembled the remaining fragments. Tai K'uei was an artistically gifted Confucian scholar who refused, up until the end of his life, to enter into a career in the government; cf. above, p. 135.

Chung-hsing shu 中興書 , usually called *Chin* 晉 *chung-hsing shu*. A history of the Eastern Chin in 78 *chüan* usually attributed to Ho Fa-sheng 何法盛 (fl. 460), although an anecdote in *Wei shih* 33, p. 15a, says the work was originally written Hsi Shao 郗紹 and stolen by the former. Cf. Yao Chen-tsung 11, pp. 5247b–5248c.

Han Chin ch'un-ch'iu 漢晉春秋 (also called *Han Chin yang-* 陽 *ch'iu* to avoid a taboo). An annalistic (presumably) history of the period from the beginning of the Latter Han to the end of the Western Chin in 54 *chüan* by Hsi Tso-ch'ih 習鑿齒 (d. 384). The history is written with a distinct prejudice against the Wei dynasty, and attempts to show the Ts'ao were usurpers against the Han. Cf. above, pp. 16–17, and R.B. Mather in *Journal of the American Oriental Society* 84, 4 (1964) pp. 380–81.

Han Wu-ti ku-shih 漢武帝故事 (also called *Han Wu ku-shih*). A collection of anecdotes in 2 *chüan* about the famous Han emperor of unknown author and date. There may very well have been a work of this name circulating in Han times. Almost none of the quotations of the work in Six Dynasties texts appear in the work presently going under this title (translated in *Lectures chinoises* (Peiping) 1 (1945) pp. 28–91). This work is a later forgery often attributed (since the Sung dynasty) to Pan Ku. Cf. K.M. Schipper, *L'empereur Wou des Han dans la légende taoïste* (Paris, 1965), pp. 1, 8–9.

Hsü kao-shih chuan 敍高士傳 (more often called *Chih-jen kao-shih chuan tsan*

至 人 高 士 傳 讚). A short work in 2 *chüan* by Sun Ch'o 孫 綽 (*c.* 310–*c.* 397) which seems to have described (partly in tetrameter verses) 'Perfect Men and Eminent Gentlemen'. No fragments of a work by either of these titles remain, but Yen K'o-chün, *Ch'üan Chin-wen* 61, p. 7b, believes some verses by Sun Ch'o quoted in *Ch'u-hsüeh chi* 17, p. 12, to be from it and Chang Tsung-yüan 13, p. 5026b, adds a quotation in prose from the 'Hsi Chung-san chuan' found in the commentary of the *Wen hsüan* 21, p. 17a. On Sun Ch'o, see R.B. Mather, in *Monumenta serica* 20 (1961) pp. 226–45.

Juan-shih p'u 阮 氏 譜 . An anonymous history of the Juan family; cf. Chang Tsung-yüan 7, p. 5000b.

P'ei K'ai pieh-chuan 裴 楷 別 傳 .

Sun Teng pieh-chuan 孫 登 別 傳 . These two works belong to a large category of biographies by (usually) anonymous writers; cf. Yao Chen-tsung 20, p. 5857b. A biography of Sun Teng is said to have been written by Sun Ch'o in *Shui-ching chu* 15, p. 48.

Tien lüeh 典 略 . A history of China in 89 *chüan* by Yü Huan 魚 豢 about whom very little is known except that he lived during the Wei dynasty. *Tien lüeh* would seem to be the title he gave to his universal history of which the last 38 *chüan* were devoted to the Wei dynasty and are often called the *Wei lüeh*. The work was an important source for Ch'en Shou's *San-kuo chih* and is constantly quoted in P'ei Sung-chih's commentary. There is a reconstruction of the *Wei lüeh* by Chang P'eng-i 張 鵬, *Wei lüeh chi-pen* 魏 略 輯 本 in 25 *chüan* (1924). Cf. Lu Pi, *San-kuo chih chi-chieh* 1, pp. 86ab, 108ab; Edouard Chavannes, 'Les pays d'Occident d'après le Wei lio', *T'oung Pao* N.S. 6 (1905) pp. 519–20, corrected by Paul Pelliot, in *Bulletin de l'Ecole Française d'Extrême-Orient* 6 (1906) pp. 361–4.

Wei-mo chuan 魏 末 傳 . A history of the end of the Wei in 2 *chüan* by an unknown author. P'ei Sung-chih criticizes the work as being mendacious and vulgar. Cf. Yao Chen-tsung 13, p. 5279a.

Wei-shih ch'un-ch'iu 魏 氏 春 秋 (also erroneously called *Wei wu* 武 *ch'un-ch'iu*). A history of the Wei dynasty in 20 *chüan* by Sun Sheng 孫 盛 (307?–378?), who was an indefatigable soldier, statesman and scholar; P'ei Sung-chih deplores his lack of accuracy and desire to embellish. Cf. Lu Pi, *San-kuo chih chi-chieh* 1, pp. 45b and 10b.

Wen-shih chuan 文 士 傳 . A collection of biographies of famous men of letters in 50 *chüan* by an unknown author called Chang Yin 張 隱 or Chang Chih 騭 , the latter form being the most commonly encountered and being corroborated by Chung Jung in his *Shih p'in*. It is possible that the collection was added to after the date of the principal author, but the primitive work would seem to date no later than from the early fourth century since it is quoted by P'ei Sung-chih (372–451). The latter proves (*San-kuo chih chi-chieh* 21, pp. 3b–4a) that the anecdotes related are very often of no historical value. Cf. also *ibid.* 9, p. 23a. Some authorities believe the author of the *Wen-shih chuan* to have been Chang Yin 張 隱 , the son of the prefect of Lu-chiang, Chang K'uei 張 夔 , mentioned in *Chin shu* (*chiao-chu* 66, p. 21b) (cf. Ting Kuo-chün 丁 國 鈞 , *Pu Chin-shu i-wen chih* 補 晉 書 藝 文 志 2, p. 3669c). Chang Yin lived early in the fourth century, but there is no other reason to think he is the author of the book.

Yü lin 語 林 . A collection of anecdotes in 10 *chüan* assembled by P'ei Ch'i 裴 啓 (also called P'ei Jung 榮) in 362. This work seems to have provided the authors of the *Shih-shuo hsin-yü* with much of their material and was very popular until its veracity was contested by the great hero and *arbiter elegantiae* Hsieh An 謝 安 (320–385), when it immediately lost favor. Cf. *Shih-shuo hsin-yü* A (Section 4), p. 84a, and the commentary at C (Section 26), pp. 74ab; R.B. Mather, in *Journal of the American Oriental Society* 84, 4 (1964) pp. 383–4. There is a reconstruction of the work by Lu-hsün in his *Ku hsiao-shuo kou-ch'en* 古 小 說 鉤 沈 (Peking, 1954), pp. 5–36.

Primary sources and traditional sinology

This list and the following contain, with few exceptions, only works that have actually been quoted in the body of the book or in the notes. The lists are thus not meant to be exhaustive or to introduce the reader to the general literature on the Three Kingdoms period. They are meant to make it easy to determine the exact description of works quoted (sometimes by abbreviation) in the foregoing pages, and to include all works directly related to Juan Chi, excluding references to him in general histories of Chinese literature, works that I have found of no interest, and, of course, works I have inadvertently missed. The list of Primary sources and traditional sinology is arranged according to the title of the work in question; the Secondary sources, according to the author's name. The reference to a particular translation of a primary source does not necessarily mean that I have used that translation in the book; it is usually given to help determine the exact location of a quotation in an easily accessible Western publication. J. Legge's translation of *Chuang-tzu*, for example, is referred to only because I believe it is still more accessible than B. Watson's more recent and much better translation (New York and London, 1968). Mention is made of Chinese editions of primary sources only when references are made directly to them and not to translations in the text and notes. These editions, too, have for the most part been chosen for their accessibility. The lists do not contain references to the Chinese commentators quoted; these can be found in the special list devoted to them above.

Chan-kuo ts'e 戰國策 . J.I. Crump, Jr, trans., *Chan-kuo ts'e*, Oxford, 1970.

Ch'en Tzu-ang chi 陳子昂集 . Hsü P'eng 徐鵬 , ed., Peking, 1960. Contains an essay by Wang Yün-hsi 王運熙 on pp. 265–308.

Chiang Li-ling chi 江醴陵集 . The collected works of Chiang Yen 江淹 (444–505). Han Wei Liu-ch'ao pai-san ming-chia chi edition.

Ch'ien-yen t'ang chi 潛研堂集 , by Ch'ien Ta-hsin 錢大昕 (1728–1804). Ssu-pu ts'ung-k'an edition.

Chih-chai shu-lu chieh-t'i 直齋書錄解題 , by Ch'en Chen-sun 陳振孫 (*fl.* first half of the thirteenth century). Ts'ung-shu chi-ch'eng edition.

Chin shu 晉書 , by Fang Hsüan-ling 房玄齡 (578–648) and others. Quotations made from *Chin-shu chiao-chu* edition.

Chin-shu chiao-chu 晉書斠注 . Wu Shih-chien 吳士鑑 and Liu Ch'eng-kan 劉承幹 , eds., Peking, 1927; reproduced Taipei, n.d.

Ching-chin Tung-p'o wen-chi shih-lüeh 敬進東坡文集事略 by Su Shih 蘇軾 (1037–1011). Compiled by Lang Yeh 郎瞱 (Sung dynasty) and collated by P'ang Shih-chou 麗石帚 , Peking, 1957.

Ch'ing shih-hua 清詩話 . Compiled by Ting Fu-pao 丁福保 (1874–1952), Shanghai, 1916; reproduced Taipei, n.d.

Chou-i lüeh-li 周易略例 , by Wang Pi 王弼 (226–249). Han Wei ts'ung-shu edition.

Chou li 周禮 . Edouard Biot, trans., *Le Tcheou-li*, 2 vols. + index, Paris, 1851; reproduced Taipei, n.d.

Ch'u-hsüeh chi 初學記 . Compiled by Hsü Chien 徐監 (659?–729) and others, Peking, 1962.

Ch'u tz'u 楚辭 . David Hawkes, trans., *Ch'u Tz'u; The Songs of the South*, Oxford, 1959.

Chu-tzu chi-ch'eng 諸子集成 . 8 vols., Peking, 1954.

Chuang-tzu 莊子 . James Legge, trans., *The texts of Taoism* (Sacred books of the East, vols. XXXIX and XL), London, 1891; second impression, 1927.

Ch'un-ch'iu fan-lu 春秋繁露 , by Tung Chung-shu 董仲舒 (176?–104? B.C.). Han Wei ts'ung-shu edition.

Ch'üan Ch'en-shih 全陳詩 . See *Ch'üan Han Wei San-kuo Chin Nan-pei ch'ao shih*.

Ch'üan Chin-wen 全晉文. See *Ch'üan shang-ku san-tai Ch'in . . . wen.*

Ch'üan Han San-kuo Chin Nan-pei ch'ao shih 全漢三國晉南北朝詩. Compiled by Ting Fu-pao 丁福保 (1874–1952), Shanghai, 1916; reprinted in 2 vols., Peking, 1959.

Ch'üan Hou Han-wen 全後漢文. See *Ch'üan shang-ku san-tai Ch'in . . . wen.*

Ch'üan San-kuo wen 全三國文. See *Ch'üan shang-ku san-tai Ch'in . . . wen.*

Ch'üan shang-ku san-tai Ch'in Han San-kuo Liu-ch'ao wen 全上古三代秦漢三國六朝文. Compiled by Yen K'o-chün 嚴可均 (1762–1843), original edition of 1893 reproduced in 4 vols. with some corrections in the margins, Peking, 1958. (References are made to the various sections of the work: *Ch'üan Hou Han-wen, Ch'üan San-kuo wen, Ch'üan Chin-wen.*)

Ch'üan Sung-shih 全宋詩 . See *Ch'üan Han San-kuo Chin Nan-pei ch'ao shih.*

Ch'üan T'ang-shih 全唐詩. Compiled by P'eng Ting-ch'iu 彭定求 (1645–1719) and others, imperial preface dated 1707; reprinted in 12 vols., Peking, 1960.

Erh-shih-wu shih pu-pien 二十五史補編. 6 vols., Peking, 1956.

Feng-shih wen-chien chi 封氏聞見記, by Feng Yen 封演 (second half of eighth century). Chao Chen-hsin 趙貞信, ed., *Feng-shih wen-chien chi chiao-chu* 封氏聞見記校注 , Peking, 1958.

Han Ch'ang-li chi 韓昌黎集. The collected works of Han Yü 韓愈 (768–824). Kuo-hsüeh chi-pen ts'ung-shu edition; reproduced Hongkong, 1964.

Han Fei-tzu 韓非子. W.K. Liao, trans., *The complete works of Han Fei Tzu*, 2 vols., London, 1959.

Han nao-ko shih-wen chien-cheng 漢鐃歌釋文箋正. Wang Hsien-ch'ien 王先謙 (1842–1918), ed., 1872; reproduced Taipei, n.d.

Han-shih wai-chuan 韓氏外傳. James Robert Hightower, trans., *Han shih wai chuan: Han Ying's illustrations of the didactic application of the Classic of Songs* (Harvard–Yenching Institute Monograph Series, Volume XI), Cambridge, Mass., 1952.

Han shu 漢書, by Pan Ku 班固 (32–92), Peking, 1962.

Han-shu pu-chu 漢書補注. Wang Hsien-ch'ien 王先謙 (1842–1918), ed., Chang-sha, 1900.

Han Wei i-shu 漢魏遺書. Compiled by Wang Mo 王謨. Prefaces dated 1798 and 1800.

Han Wei Liu-ch'ao pai san ming-chia chi 漢魏六朝百三名家集. A collection of the complete works of authors who lived during the first five hundred years of the Christian era by Chang P'u 張溥 (1602–1641). Shanghai, 1925.

Han Wei Liu-ch'ao pai san chia chi t'i-tz'u chu 漢魏六朝百三家集題辭注. A commented edition of the prefaces to the individual works contained in Chang P'u's collection by Yin Meng-lun 殷孟倫. Peking, 1960.

Han Wei ts'ung-shu 漢魏叢書. Compiled by Ho Yün-chung 何允中, preface dated 1593; reproduced Shanghai, 1925.

Hou Han-shu chi-chieh 後漢書集解. The *Hou Han-shu* 後漢書 by Fan Yeh 范曄 (398–445) with commentary by Wang Hsien-ch'ien 王先謙 (1892–1918). Kuo-hsüeh chi-pen ts'ung-shu edition, Shanghai, 1940; reproduced Peking, 1959.

Hsi K'ang chi chiao-chu 嵇康集校注. The works of Hsi (or Chi) K'ang, edited and with a commentary by Tai Ming-yang 戴明揚, Peking, 1962.

Hsiao ching 孝經. The canonical book of filial piety contained in *Shih-san ching chu-shu* 十三經注疏. Lithographic reproduction of a Sung edition, 1887.

Hsiao shih-fan t'ing chu-lu 小石帆亭著錄, by Weng Fang-kang 翁方綱 (1733–1818). Originally printed 1793; extracts reprinted in Ch'ing shih-hua.

Hsin hsü 新序, by Liu Hsiang 劉向 (77?–6? B.C.). Ssu-pu ts'ung-k'an edition.

Hsin T'ang-shu 新唐書, by Ou-yang Hsiu 歐陽修 (1007–1072) and Sung Ch'i 宋祁 (998–1061). T'ung-wen shu-chü edition.

Hsün-tzu 荀子 . Chu-tzu chi-ch'eng edition.

Huai-nan-tzu 淮南子 , by Liu An 劉安 (d. 122 B.C.) and his courtiers. Chu-tzu chi-ch'eng edition.

I ching 易經 . James Legge, trans., *The Sacred Books of China, the texts of Confucianism, Part II: The Yï King* (The Sacred Books of the East, Vol. XVI), Oxford, 1899.

I Chou-shu 逸周書 . Han Wei ts'ung-shu edition.

I-wen lei-chü 藝文類聚 . Compiled by Ou-yang Hsün 歐陽詢 (557–641) and others. Reproduction of a Sung edition, Peking, 1959.

Jih-chih lu 日知錄 , by Ku Yen-wu 顧炎武 (1613–1682). Wan-yu wen-k'u edition.

Ku-shih lu 古詩錄 (full name *Wan-lin shu-wu* 宛鄰書屋 *ku-shih lu*). Compiled by Chang Ch'i 張琦 (1765–1833), preface dated 1815; Shanghai, 1926. *Chüan* 4 contains fifty-three poems by Juan Chi, the three tetrameter poems and the following in pentameter: 1–18, 20–24, 31–2, 35, 39, 41, 43, 45–7, 55, 58, 65, 71, 79–80, 26–8, 42, 60, 66, 19, 25, 54, 61, 73, 82.

Ku-shih shang-hsi 古詩賞析 . Compiled by Chang Yü-ku 張玉穀 (late eighteenth century), preface dated 1772; Kambun taikei edition, Tokyo, 1924. *Chüan* 10 contains the following poems: 1–3, 5, 8, 11, 15, 17, 21, 31, 79.

Kuan-tzu 管子 . Edition dated 1875.

Kuan-tzu chi-chiao 管子集校 . Kuo Mo-jo 郭沫若 , Wen I-to 聞一多 and Hsü Wei-yü 許維遹 , eds., Peking, 1956.

*Kuang wen-hsüan 廣文選 . Compiled by Liu Chieh 劉節 (late fifteenth century).

Kuei-ssu lei-kao 癸巳類稿 , by Yü Cheng-hsieh 俞正燮 (1775–1840), Shanghai, 1957.

K'ung-tzu chia-yü 孔子家語 . Richard Wilhelm, trans., *Kungfutse: Schulgespräche*, Jena, 1961.

Lao-tzu 老子 . J.J.L. Duyvendak, trans., *Tao Te Ching: The Book of the Way and its Virtue*, London, 1954.

Li chi 禮記 . S. Couvreur, *Li ki ou Mémoires sur les bienséances et les cérémonies*, 2 vols., Ho Kien Fou, 1913; reproduced in 4 vols., Paris, 1951.

Li T'ai-po ch'üan-chi 李太白全集 . The collected works of Li Po 李白 (699?–762?), Wang Ch'i 王琦 , ed., preface dated 1758; reproduced in 4 vols. from the Ssu-pu pei-yao edition, Peking, 1957.

Li-tai shih-hua 歷代詩話 . Compiled by Ho Wen-huan 何文煥 , preface dated 1770; reproduced Taipei, 1971.

Li-tai shih-hua hsü-pien 歷代詩話續編 . Compiled by Ting Fu-pao 丁福保 (1874–1952), Shanghai, 1915; reproduced under the title Hsü li-tai shih-hua 續歷代詩話 , Taipei, n.d.

Lieh-hsien chuan 列仙傳 . Max Kaltenmark, trans., *Le Lie-sien tchouan*, Peking, 1953.

Lieh-tzu 列子 . A.C. Graham, trans., *The Book of Lieh-tzu*, London, 1960.

Lieh-tzu chi-shih 列子集釋 . Yang Po-chün 楊伯峻 , ed., Shanghai, 1958; reproduced Hongkong, 1965.

Liu-ch'en chu Wen hsüan 六臣註文選 . The *Wen hsüan* (q.v.) with commentary by Li Shan and five others (the 'Wu ch'en'). Ssu-pu ts'ung-k'an edition, reproduced Taipei, 1964.

Lo-yang ch'ieh-lan chi 洛陽伽藍記 , by Yang Hsüan-chih 楊衒之 (*fl.* 530). References are made to Fan Hsiang-yung 范祥雍 , ed., *Lo-yang ch'ieh-lan chi chiao-chu* 洛陽伽藍記校注 , Peking, 1958.

Lun heng 論衡 , by Wang Ch'ung 王充 (A.D. 27–91). References are made to Liu P'an-sui 劉盼遂 , *Lun-heng chi-chieh* 論衡集解 , Peking, 1959.

Lun yü 論語 . Arthur Waley, trans., *The Analects of Confucius*, London, 1949.

Lü-shih ch'un-ch'iu 呂氏春秋 . Chu-tzu chi-ch'eng edition.

Meng-tzu 孟子. James Legge, trans., *The works of Mencius* (The Chinese Classics, Vol. II), Oxford, 1895.

Mo-tzu 墨子. Mei Yi-pao, trans., *The ethical and political works of Motse*, London, 1929.

Mu t'ien-tzu chuan 穆天子傳. Han Wei ts'ung-shu edition.

Nan Ch'i shu 南齊書, by Hsiao Tzu-hsien 蕭子顯 (489–537). T'ung-wen shu-chü edition.

Nan shih 南史. Edited by Li Yen-shou 李延壽 (c. 629). T'ung-wen shu-chü edition.

Pa-ch'i wen-ching 八旗文經. Edited by Sheng-yü 盛昱 (1850–1900). Printed in 1902.

Pao-p'u-tzu 抱朴子, by Ko Hung 葛洪 (284–363). Chu-tzu chi-ch'eng edition.

Pei-t'ang shu-ch'ao 北堂書鈔, by Yü Shih-nan 虞世南 (558–638). 1888 edition, reproduced Taipei, 1962.

Pen-ts'ao kang-mu 本草綱目, by Li Shih-chen 李時珍 (1518–1593). Edition dated 1885; reproduced Peking, 1957.

San-kuo chih 三國志, by Ch'en Shou 陳壽 (233–297). Quotations are made from *San-kuo chih chi-chieh*.

San-kuo chih chi-chieh 三國志集解. The *San-kuo chih* with a commentary by Lu Pi 盧弼, Peking, 1957.

San-kuo chih-kuan piao 三國職官表, by Hung I-sun 洪飴孫 (1773–1816). Erh-shih-wu shih pu-pien edition.

Shan-hai ching 山海經 Hao I-hsing 郝懿行 (1757–1825), ed., *Shan-hai ching chien-shu* 山海經箋疏. Ssu-pu pei-yao edition.

Sheng-an shih-hua 升菴詩話, by Yang Shen 楊慎 (1488–1559). In Li-tai shih-hua hsü-pien.

Shih chi 史記. Takigawa Kametarō 瀧川龜太郎, ed., *Shiki kaichū kōshō* 史記會注考證, 10 vols., Tokyo, 1932–1934; reproduced Peking, 1957.

Shih chi 詩紀 (also called *Ku-shih chi* 古詩紀). compiled by Feng Wei-ne 馮惟訥 (d. 1572).

Shih-chi k'uang-miu 詩紀匡謬, by Feng Shu 馮舒 (born 1593). Ts'ung-shu chi-ch'eng edition.

Shih ching 詩經. Bernhard Karlgren, trans., *The Book of Odes*, Stockholm, 1950.

Shih-hua pu-i 詩話補遺 by Yang Shen 楊慎 (1488–1559). Ssu-k'u ch'üan-shu version.

Shih-lin shih-hua 石林詩話, by Yeh Meng-te 葉夢得 (1077–1148). In Ho Wen-huan, Li-tai shih-hua.

Shih p'in 詩品, by Chung Jung 鍾嶸 (469–518). Ch'en Yen-chieh 陳延傑, ed., *Shih-p'in chu* 詩品注, Shanghai, 1927; Peking, 1958; Hongkong, 1959.

Shih shih 詩式, by Chiao-jan 皎然 (late eighth century). Shih wan chüan lou ts'ung-shu 十萬卷樓叢書 edition, containing the version in 5 *chüan*.

Shih-shuo hsin-yü 世說新語. Compiled by Liu I-ch'ing 劉義慶 (403–444); commentary by Liu Chün 劉峻 (462–521). Sung edition (1138) reproduced Peking, 1962, in 5 vols.

Shih-shuo hsin-yü pu 世說新語補. Japanese edition, preface dated 1779.

'Shih-shuo hsin-yü jen-ming p'u' 世說新語人名譜, part of the *Shih-shuo hsü-lu* 世說敘錄, by Wang Tsao 王藻 (1079–1154). Printed in vols. 4 and 5 of the *Shih-shuo hsin-yü*, Peking, 1962.

Shih sou 詩藪, by Hu Ying-lin 胡應麟 (1551–1602). Re-edition based on a Japanese edition dated 1686, Peking, 1958.

Shih t'ung 史通, by Liu Chih-chi 劉知幾 (661–721). Reproduction of an edition printed in 1577, Peking, 1961.

Shu ching 書經. James Legge, trans., *The Shoo-king* (The Chinese Classics, Vol. III, Parts 1 and 2), London, n.d.

Shui-ching chu 水經注 , by Li Tao-yüan 酈道元 (died 527). Kuo-hsüeh chi-pen ts'ung-shu edition in 2 vols.

Shuo-wen chieh-tzu 說文解字 , by Hsü Shen 許慎 (A.D. 30–124). Reproduction of 1873 edition, Peking, 1963.

Shuo yüan 說苑 , by Liu Hsiang 劉向 (77?–6? B.C.). Han Wei ts'ung-shu edition.

Ssu-k'u ch'üan-shu tsung-mu t'i-yao 四庫全書總目提要 by Chi Yün 紀昀 (1724–1805) and others. Wan-yu wen-k'u edition.

Sui shu 隋書 , by Wei Cheng 魏徵 (580–643) and others. T'ung wen shu-chü edition.

Sui-shu Ching-chi chih k'ao-cheng 隋書經籍志考證 , by Chang Tsung-yüan 章宗源 (1752?–1800). Erh-shih-wu shih pu-pien edition.

Sui-shu Ching-chi chih k'ao-cheng 隋書經籍志考證 , by Yao Chen-tsung 姚振宗 (1842–1906). Erh-shih-wu shih pu-pien edition.

Sun-tzu 孫子 . Early thirteenth-century edition, reproduced in 4 fasc., Peking, 1961.

Sung shih 宋史 , by T'o-t'o 托托 (1313–1355) and Ou-yang Hsüan 歐陽玄 (1274/5–1358). T'ung-wen shu chü edition.

Sung shu 宋書 , by Shen Yüeh 沈約 (441–513). T'ung-wen shu-chü edition.

Ta Tai li-chi 大戴禮記 . Han Wei ts'ung-shu edition.

T'ai-p'ing ching 太平經 . Wang Ming 王明 , ed., *T'ai-p'ing ching ho-chiao* 太平經合校 , Peking, 1960.

T'ai-p'ing kuang-chi 太平廣記 . Compiled by Li Fang 李昉 (925–996) and others, 10 vols., Peking, 1961.

T'ai-p'ing yü-lan 太平御覽 . Compiled by Li Fang 李昉 (925–996) and others, Shanghai, 1935 reproduction of a Sung edition, reproduced Peking, 1960.

Tao-te chen-ching chuan 道德真經傳 , by Lu Hsi-sheng 陸希聲 (T'ang dynasty?). Reproduced from the Chih hai 指海 (1839–1846) edition as part of the Wu-ch'iu pei chai Lao-tzu chi-ch'eng 無求備齋老子集成 collection, Taipei, n.d.

Ts'ao-chi ch'üan-p'ing 曹集銓評 . The works of Ts'ao Chih 曹植 (192–232) edited by Ting Yen 丁晏 (1794–1875), preface dated 1865; reprinted Peking, 1957.

Tso chuan 左傳 . James Legge, trans., *The Ch'un Ts'eu, with the Tso Chuen* (The Chinese Classics, Vol. V in 2 Parts), London, n.d.

T'ung chih 通志 , by Cheng Ch'iao 鄭樵 (1102?–1160?). Shanghai, 1935; reproduced Taipei, 1965.

Tung-p'ing hsien-chih 東平縣志 . 1936; reproduced Taipei, 1968.

T'ung tien 通典 , by Tu Yu 杜佑 (735–812). Shanghai, 1935; reproduced Taipei, 1966.

Tzu-chih t'ung-chien 資治通鑑 , by Ssu-ma Kuang 司馬光 (1019–1086). Achilles Fang, trans. (of chapters 69–78), *The Chronicles of the Three Kingdoms* (Harvard–Yenching Institute Studies VI), 2 vols., Cambridge, Mass., 1952, 1965.

Wang Ch'üan-shan shih-wen chi 王船山詩文集 , by Wang Fu-chih 王夫之 (1619–1692). 2 vols., Peking, 1962.

Wei fang-chen nien-piao 魏方鎮年表 , by Wan Ssu-t'ung 萬斯同 (1638–1702). Erh-shih-wu shih pu-pien edition.

Wei shu 魏書 , by Wei Shou 魏收 (506–572). T'ung-wen shu-chü edition.

Wen-hsin tiao-lung 文心彫龍 , by Liu Hsieh 劉勰 (b. 465?). (Fan Wen-lan 范文瀾), ed., *Wen-hsin tiao-lung chu* 文心彫龍注 , 2 vols., Shanghai, 1936; Peking, 1958; reproduced, without the editor's name, Hongkong, 1960. Vincent Yu-chung Shih, trans., *The Literary Mind and the Carving of Dragons*, New York, 1959.

Wen hsüan 文選 . Compiled by Hsiao T'ung 蕭統 (501–531), with commentary by Li Shan 李善 (died 689). Hu K'o-chia 胡克家 (1757–1816) reproduction in 1809 of an edition dated 1181; reproduced Taipei, 1967.

Wen-hsüan Li-chu i-shu 文選李注義疏 , by Kao Pu-ying 高步瀛 , preface dated 1929. Original edition reproduced in 8 vols. in Hsüan-hsüeh ts'ung-shu, Taipei, 1966.

Wen-hsüan p'ang-cheng 文選旁證 , by Liang Chang-chü 梁章鉅 (1775–1849).

First published 1838; reprinted 1882; reproduced from the second edition in the Hsüan-hsüeh ts'ung-shu, Taipei, 1966.

Wang Yu-ch'eng chi chien-chu 王右丞集箋注. The works of Wang Wei 王維 (701–761), edited by Chao Tien-ch'eng 趙殿成 (1683–1756), preface dated 1736; reprinted in 2 vols., Peking, 1961.

Yen-tzu ch'un-ch'iu chiao-chu 晏子春秋校注. Edited by Chang Ch'un-i 張純一, preface dated 1935; reprinted in the Chu-tzu chi-ch'eng.

Yü-t'ai hsin-yung 玉臺新詠. Compiled by Hsü Ling 徐陵 (507–583). See Secondary sources under Suzuki Torao. Chapter 2 contains two poems by Juan Chi, nos. 2 and 12.

Yüan-ho hsing-tsuan 元和姓纂, by Lin Pao 林寶. Preface dated 812; edition of 1880.

Yüeh-fu shih-chi 樂府詩集. Compiled by Kuo Mao-ch'ien 郭茂倩 (twelfth century). Reproduced in 4 vols. from Sung and Yüan editions, Peking, 1955.

Secondary sources

Aoki Masaru 月木正兒, *Shina bungaku shisō shi* 支那文學思想史, Tokyo, 1948.

—, ' "Shō" no rekishi to jigi no hensen' 嘯の歷史と字義の變遷, *Ritsumeikan bungaku* 立命館文學 (Kyoto) 150–151 (1957) pp. 179–87.

Balazs, Etienne, 'Entre révolte nihiliste et évasion mystique: Les courants intellectuels en Chine au IIIe siècle de notre ère', *Etudes Asiatiques* (Bern) 2 (1948) pp. 27–55. Translated by H.M. Wright, in *Chinese civilization and bureaucracy*, New Haven and London, 1964, pp. 226–54.

—, *Traité économique du 'Souei-chou'* (Etudes sur la société et l'économie de la China médiévale I), Leiden, 1953.

Birch, Cyril, Ed., *Anthology of Chinese literature*, New York, 1965.

Blum, Martine, 'Vertus et méfaits de la musique', unpublished Third Cycle doctorate thesis, University of Paris-VII, 1970. Contains a translation of Juan Chi's 'Essay on music'.

Bodde, Derk, 'The Chinese cosmic magic called watching the ethers', *Studia serica Bernhard Karlgren dedicata*, Copenhagen, 1959, pp. 14–35.

Chang Chih-yüeh 眾志岳, 'Lüeh-lun Juan Chi chi ch'i "Yung-huai shih" ' 略論阮籍及其詠懷詩, *Wen-hsüeh i-ch'an tseng-k'an* 文學遺產增刊 (Peking) 11 (1962) pp. 73–93.

Chavannes, Edouard, 'Confucius', *Revue de Paris* (1903) pp. 136–42.

—, 'Les pays d'Occident d'après le Wei lio', *T'oung Pao* N.S. 6 (1905) pp. 519–56.

Ch'en, Jerome and Michael Bullock, trans., *Poems of solitude*, London, New York and Toronto, 1960. Fifteen poems by Juan Chi are freely translated: 1, 5, 8, 10, 14, 17, 21, 33, 34, 38, 47, 50, 76, 62, 77.

Chi Lien-k'ang 吉聯抗, *Hsi K'ang: Sheng wu ai-le lun* 嵇康 (聲無哀樂論), Peking, 1964. Contains a translation into modern Chinese of Juan Chi's 'Essay on music' on pp. 79–92.

Ch'ien Mu 錢穆, *Chung-kuo ssu-hsiang shih* 中國思想史, Taipei, 1952.

—, 'Chung-kuo ssu-hsiang shih chung chih kuei-shen kuan' 中國思想史中之鬼觀, *Hsin Ya hsüeh-pao* 新亞學報 (Hongkong) 1, 1 (1955) pp. 1–43.

Chou Shao-hsien 周紹賢, *Wei Chin ch'ing-t'an shu-lun* 魏晉清談述論, Taipei, 1966.

Chow Tse-tsung, 'The early history of the Chinese word *shih* (poetry)' in Chow Tse-tsung, ed., *Wei-lin: Studies in the Chinese humanities*, Madison, Wis., 1968, pp. 151–209.

Chung-kuo hsin-wen 中國新聞, London, 1972.

Chung-kuo ku-tai yin-yüeh shih-liao chi-yao 中國古代音樂史料輯要 1, Peking, 1962.

Chung-kuo ts'ung-shu tsung-lu 中國叢書綜錄 , 3 vols., Shanghai, 1959–1962.

Chüan, T.K., 'Yüan Chi and his circle', *T'ien Hsia Monthly* (Shanghai) 9 (1939) pp. 469–83.

Courant, Maurice, 'Essai historique sur la musique classique des Chinois', in *Encyclopédie de la musique*, Paris, 1912, pp. 77–241.

Couvreur, S., see Primary sources, under *Li chi*.

Creel, H.G., 'What is Taoism?', *Journal of the American Oriental Society* (New Haven, Ct.) 76, 3 (1956) pp. 139–52.

de Crespigny, Rafe, *The records of the Three Kingdoms* (Occasional Paper No. 9), Canberra, 1970.

Crump, J.I., Jr, see Primary sources, under *Chan-kuo ts'e*.

Debon, Günther, *Ts'ang-lang's Gespräche über die Dichtung: Ein Beitrag zur chinesischen Poetik*, Wiesbaden, 1962.

Demiéville, Paul, *Choix d'études sinologiques (1921–1970)*, Leiden, 1973.

—, 'L'esprit de bienfaisance impartiale dans les civilisations de l'Extrême-Orient', *Revue internationale de la Croix-Rouge* (Geneva) 404 (1952) pp. 670–78; reproduced in *Choix d'études sinologiques*, pp. 113–20.

—, 'Langue et littérature chinoise', *Annuaire du Collège de France* (Paris) 48e Année (1948) pp. 158–62; reproduced in *Choix d'études sinologiques*, pp. 89–93.

—, 'La montagne dans l'art littéraire chinois', *France-Asie/Asia* (Tokyo-Paris) 183 (1965) pp. 7–32; reproduced in *Choix d'études sinologiques*, pp. 364–89.

—, Preface to Chow Yih-ching, *La philosophie morale dans le néo-confucianisme (Tcheou Touen-yi)*, Paris, 1954, pp. ix–xv.

—, résumés No. 660 in *Revue bibliographique de sinologie* (Paris and The Hague) 4 (1964); No. 454 in *ibid.* 6 (1967).

Diény, Jean-Pierre, *Les Dix-neuf Poèmes Anciens* (Bulletin de la Maison Franco-Japanaise, N.S., Tome VII, No. 4), Paris, 1963.

Duyvendak, J.J.L., *The Book of Lord Shang*, London, 1928.

—, see also Primary sources, under *Lao-tzu*.

Eberhard, Wolfram, 'The political function of astronomy and astronomers in Han China', in John K. Fairbank, ed., *Chinese thought and institutions*, Chicago, 1958, pp. 33–70.

Edwards, E.D., *Chinese prose literature of the T'ang dynasty* 1, London, 1937.

Fan Shou-k'ang 范壽康 , *Wei Chin chih ch'ing-t'an* 魏晉之清談 , Shanghai, 1936.

Fang, Achilles, see Primary sources, under *Tzu-chih t'ung-chien*.

Franke, Herbert, 'Some remarks on the interpretation of the Chinese dynastic histories', *Oriens* (Leiden) 3 (1950) pp. 113–22.

Frankel, Hans. H., review of J.J.Y. Liu, *The art of Chinese poetry*, in *Harvard Journal of Asiatic Studies* 24 (1962–1963) pp. 267–8.

Freeman, Mansfield, 'Yen Hsi-chai, a seventeenth century philosopher', *Journal of the North China Branch of the Royal Asiatic Society* 57 (1926) pp. 70–91.

Frodsham, J.D., 'The poet Juan Chi', *Majallah panti, Journal of the Chinese Language Society* (University of Malaya) 2 (1964/5) pp. 26–42. Contains translations of the following poems by Juan Chi: 15, 4, 5, 10, 1, 9, 3, 8, 21, 17, 60, 16, 11, 6, 59, 33.

—, and Ch'eng Hsi, *An anthology of Chinese verse: Han Wei Chin and the Northern and Southern Dynasties*, Oxford, 1967. Contains translations of the following poems by Juan Chi: 1–6, 8–10, 15–17, 21, 31–3, 38, 59–61, 71.

Fukui Fumimasa 福井文雅 , 'Chikurin shichiken ni tsuite no ichi shiron' 竹林七賢についての一試論, *Philosophia* (Tokyo) 37 (1959) pp. 75–102.

Fukunaga Mitsuji 福永光司 , Chūgoku ni okeru tenchi hōkai no shisō: Gen Seki no 'Daijin sensei ka' to To Ho no 'Tō Jionji tō shi' ni yosete" 中國に於ける天地崩壞の思想(阮籍の大人先生歌と杜甫の登慈恩寺塔詩によせて) in *Yoshikawa hakase taikyū kinen Chūgoku bungaku ronshū* 吉川博士退休紀念中國文學論文集, Kyoto, 1968, pp. 169–88.

—, 'Daijin fu no shisōteki keifu: Jifu no bungaku to Rō Sō no tetsugaku' 大人賦の思想的系譜 (辭賦の文學と老莊の哲學), *Tōhō gakuhō* (Kyoto) 41 (1970) pp. 97–126.

—, 'Gen Seki ni okeru osore to nagusame: Gen Seki no seikatsu to shisō' 阮籍における懼れと慰め (阮籍の生活と思想), *Tōhō gakuhō* 東方學報 (Kyoto) 28 (1958) pp. 139–74.

Funazu Tomihiko 船津富彦 , 'Gi Shin bungaku ni okeru shōgō ni tsuite' 魏晉文學における嘲傲について, *Tōyō bungaku kenkyū* 東洋文學研究 (Tokyo) 11 (1963) pp. 34–50.

—, 'Sō Shi no Yūsenshi ron: Toku ni setsuwa no tenkai o chūshin ni shuite' 曹植の遊仙詩論 (特に説話の展開を中心にして), *Tōyō bungaku kenkyū* 東洋文學研究 (Tokyo) 13 (1963) pp. 49–65.

Fung Yu-lan (D. Bodde, trans.), *The history of Chinese philosophy*, 2 vols., second edition, Princeton, N.J., 1952.

—, *A short history of Chinese philosophy*, New York, 1948.

Goodrich, Chauncey S., 'A note on the textual criticism of the formula for the bow-and-arrow gifts in the *Tso chuan*', *Journal of the American Oriental Society* (New Haven, Ct.) 78 (1958) pp. 41–9.

Graham, A.C., 'The date and composition of Liehtzyy', *Asia Major* N.S. 8 (1961) pp. 139–98.

—, see also Primary sources, under *Lieh-tzu*.

Granet, Marcel, *La civilisation chinoise* (L'Evolution de l'Humanité XXV), Paris, 1929; reprinted 1948.

—, *Danses et légendes de la Chine ancienne* (Annales du Musée Guimet, Bibliothèque d'Etudes, Tome LXIVe), Paris, 1926; reprinted 1959.

—, *La pensée chinoise* (L'Evolution de l'Humanité XXV bis), Paris, 1934.

van Gulik, R.H., *Hsi K'ang and his poetical essay on the lute*, Tokyo, 1941.

—, *The lore of the Chinese lute: An essay in ch'in ideology*, Tokyo, 1940.

—, *Sexual life in ancient China: A preliminary survey of Chinese sex and society from ca. 1500 B.C. till 1644 A.D.*, Leiden, 1961.

Hawkes, David, 'The supernatural in Chinese poetry', *University of Toronto Quarterly* 30, 3 (1961) pp. 311–24.

—, see also Primary sources, under *Ch'u tz'u*.

Hayashida Shinnosuke 林田慎之助 , 'Gen Seki Eikaishi kō: Sono kozetsu no ishiki ni tsuite' 阮籍詠懷詩考 (その孤絶の意識について), *Kyūshū Chūgoku gakkai hō* 九州中國學會報 (Fukuoka) 6 (1960) pp. 53–68.

—, 'Gi Shin Nanchō bungaku ni shimeru Chō Ka no zahyō' 魏晉南朝文學に占める張華の座標 *Nihon Chūgoku gakkai hō* 日本中國學會報 (Tokyo) 17 (1965) pp. 69–91.

Hervouet, Yves, *Un poète de cour sous les Han: Sseu-ma Siang-jou* (Bibliothèque de l'Institut des Hautes Etudes Chinoises, Vol. XIX), Paris, 1964.

Hightower, James Robert. 'The *fu* of T'ao Ch'ien', *Harvard Journal of Asiatic Studies* 17 (1954) pp. 169–230; reproduced in John L. Bishop, ed., *Studies in Chinese literature* (Harvard–Yenching Institute Studies XXI), Cambridge, Mass., 1965, pp. 45–106.

—, see also Primary sources, under *Han-shih wai-chuan*, and above (p. 295) under Birch, Cyril.

Ho Ch'ang-ch'ün 賀昌羣 , *Han T'ang chien feng-chien t'u-ti so-yu chih hsing-shih yen-chiu* 漢唐間封建土地所有制之形式研究 , Shanghai, 1964.

—, *Wei Chin ch'ing-t'an ssu-hsiang ch'u-lun* 魏晉清談思想初論, Shanghai, 1947.

Ho Ch'i-min 何啓民 , *Chu-lin ch'i-hsien yen-chiu* 竹林七賢研究 (Chung-kuo hsüeh-shu chu-tso chiang-chu wei-yüan-hui ts'ung-shu 中國學術著作獎助委員會叢書 24), Taipei, 1966.

—, *Wei Chin ssu-hsiang yü t'an-feng* 魏晉思想與談風 (Chung-kuo hsüeh-shu chu-tso chiang-chu wei-yüan-hui ts'ung shu 中國學術著作獎助委員叢書 32), Taipei, 1967.

Ho P'an-fei 何蟠飛 , 'Juan Chi yen-chiu' 阮籍研究 , *Wen-hsüeh nien-pao* 文學年報 (Peiping) 3 (1937) pp. 177–200.

Ho Tzu-ch'üan 何茲全 , *Wei Chin Nan-pei ch'ao shih-lüeh* 魏晉南北朝史略 , Shanghai, 1958.

Holzman, Donald, 'Les débuts du système médiéval de choix et de classement des fonctionnaires: Les Neuf Catégories et l'Impartial et Juste', in *Mélanges publiés par l'Institut des Hautes Etudes Chinoises* (Bibliothèque de l'Institut des Hautes Etudes Chinoises, Tome XI) 1, Paris, 1957, pp. 387–414.

—, 'Une fête à Houang-tcheou chez Sou Che', in *Etudes Song in memoriam Etienne Balazs*, Série II, 2, Paris, 1976.

—, 'Les premiers vers pentasyllabiques datés dans la poésie chinoise', in *Mélanges de sinologie offerts à Monsieur Paul Demiéville* (Bibliothèque de l'Institut des Hautes Etudes Chinoises, Volume XX) II, Paris, 1974, pp. 77–105.

—, 'Les Sept Sages de la Forêt des Bambous et la société de leur temps', *T'oung Pao* (Leiden) 44 (1956) pp. 317–46.

—, *La vie et la pensée de Hi K'ang (223–262 ap. J.-C.)*, Leiden, 1957.

Honda Wataru 本田濟 , *Ekigaku: Seiritsu to tenkai* 易學（成立と展開）(Sāla sōsho サーラ叢書 13), Kyoto, 1960.

Hou Wai-lu 侯外廬 and others, *Chung-kuo ssu-hsiang t'ung-shih* 中國思想通史 3, Peking, 1957.

Hsiao Hsüeh-p'eng 蕭學鵬 , 'Juan Chi shih-lun' 阮籍試論 , *Chung-shan ta-hsüeh hsüeh-pao (she)* 中山大學學報（社）(Canton) 4, 1956; reproduced in *Wei Chin Liu-ch'ao shih yen-chiu lun-wen chi* 魏晉六朝詩研究論文集, Hong-kong, 1969, pp. 49–58.

Hsiao Kung-ch'üan 蕭公權 , *Chung-kuo cheng-chih ssu-hsiang shih* 中國政治思想史 , 6 vols., Taipei, 1954.

Hsiao Ti-fei 蕭滌非 , see List of Chinese commentators quoted.

Hsü Te-lin 徐德嶙 , *San-kuo shih chiang-hua* 三國史講話 , Shanghai, 1955.

Hu Shih 胡適 , *Pai-hua wen-hsüeh shih* 白話文學史 , 1928; reproduced Taipei, n.d.

Huang Chieh 黃節 , ed., *Wei Wu-ti Wei Wen-ti shih chu* 魏武帝魏文帝詩注 , Peking, 1958.

—, see also List of Chinese commentators quoted.

Huang K'an 黃侃 , see List of Chinese commentators quoted.

*Imamura Yoshio 今村與志雄 , 'Chikurin no shichiken oboegaki: Gen Seki no shin' 竹林の七賢覺書（阮籍の慎）, *Bungaku* 文學 (Tokyo) 33, 5 (1965) pp. 65–73.

Jao Tsung-i 饒宗頤 , *Ch'ang-chou chi* 長洲集 , preface dated Paris, 1966; Singapore?, n.d.

—, 'Lu Chi Wen-fu li-lun yü yin-yüeh chih kuan-hsi' 陸機文賦理論與音樂之關係 , *Chūgoku bungaku hō* 中國文學報 (Kyoto) 14 (1961) pp. 22–37.

Jen Pan-t'ang 任半塘 , *T'ang hsi-nung* 唐戲弄 , 2 vols., Peking, 1958.

Jung Chao-tsu 容肇祖 , *Wei Chin ti tzu-jan chu-i* 魏晉的自然主義 , Shanghai, 1935.

*Kao Hai-fu 高海夫 , 'Lüeh-t'an Juan Chi chi ch'i Yung-huai shih' 略談阮籍及其詠懷詩 , *Jen-wen tsa-chih* 人文雜誌 (Sian) 2 (1959) pp. 55–9, 43.

Kaltenmark, Max, see Primary sources, under *Lieh-hsien chuan*.

K'ao-ku 考古 . Quarterly periodical published in Peking.

Karlgren, Bernhard, 'Glosses on the Siao ya odes', *Bulletin of the Museum of Far Eastern Antiquities* (Stockholm) 16 (1944) pp. 25–169; reproduced in *Glosses on the Book of Odes*, Stockholm, 1964.

—, see also Primary sources, under *Shih ching*.

Kawakatsu Yoshio 川 勝 義 雄 and others, trans., *Sesetsu shingo* 世 說 新 語 , in *Chūgoku ko shōsetsu shū* 中 國 古 小 說 集 (Sekai bungaku taikei 世 界 文 學 大 系 71), Tokyo, 1964.

Kōzen Hiroshi 興 膳 宏 , trans., *Bunshin chōryū* 文 心 雕 龍 (Sekai koten bungaku zenshū 世 界 古 典 文 學 全 集 25), Tokyo, 1968; second printing, 1970.

Kuo Shao-yü 郭 紹 虞 , trans., *Ts'ang-lang shih-hua chiao-shih* 滄 浪 詩 話 校 釋 , Peking, 1965.

Lao Kan 勞 幹 , 'Shih chi Hsiang Yü pen-chi chung "hsüeh-shu" ho "hsüeh-chien" ti chieh-shih' 史 記 項 羽 本 記 中 學 書 和 學 劍 的 解 釋 , *Chung-yang yen-chiu yüan li-shih yü-yen yen-chiu-so chi-k'an* 中 央 研 究 院 歷 史 語 言 研 究 所 集 刊 (Taipei) 30 (1959) pp. 499–510.

Legge, James, see Primary sources, under *Chuang-tzu, I ching, Meng-tzu, Shu ching, Tso chuan.*

Lévi-Strauss, Claude, *Tristes tropiques*, Paris, 1955.

Li Chi, 'The changing concept of the recluse in Chinese literature', *Harvard Journal of Asiatic Studies* 24 (1963) pp. 234–47.

Li Chih-fang 李 直 方 , *Han Wei Liu-ch'ao shih lun-kao* 漢 魏 六 朝 詩 論 稿 , Hong-kong, 1967.

Liao, W.K., see Primary sources, under *Han Fei-tzu.*

Lin Mou-sheng, *Men and ideas*, New York, 1942.

Ling Shao-k'uei 凌 紹 藥 , 'T'an Ku K'ai-chih ti ch'ih' 談 顧 愷 之 的 癡 , *Ta-lu tsa-chih* 大 陸 雜 誌 (Taipei) 6, 8 (1953) pp. 17, 32.

Liu Ju-lin 劉 汝 霖 , *Han Chin hsüeh-shu pien-nien* 漢 晉 學 術 編 年 , 4 vols., Shanghai, 1935.

Liu Wen-tien 劉 文 典 , *Chuang-tzu pu-cheng* 莊 子 補 正 , Shanghai, 1947.

Lu K'an-ju 陸 侃 如 and Feng Yüan-chün 馮 沅 君 , *Chung-kuo shih shih* 中 國 詩 史 , 3 vols., 1931–1935; new edition, Peking, 1956; second printing, 1957.

Lu-hsün 魯 迅 (Chou Shu-jen 周 樹 人), ed., *Ku hsiao-shuo kou-ch'en* 古 小 說 鉤 沈 , Shanghai, 1939; reprinted Peking, 1954.

Maspero, Henri, *La Chine antique*, first published Paris, 1927 (as Tome IV of Histoire du Monde); new edition Paris, 1955.

—, 'Légendes et mythes dans le *Chou king*', *Journal asiatique* 204 (1924) pp. 1–100.

—, 'Les procédés de "nourrir le principe vital" dans la religion taoïste ancienne', *Journal asiatique* 229 (1937) pp. 177–252, 353–430; reprinted in *Le taoïsme et les religions chinoises*, Paris, 1971, pp. 479–589.

Mather, Richard B., 'Chinese letters and scholarship in the third and fourth centuries: The "Wen-hsüeh p'ien" of the *Shih-shuo hsin-yü*', *Journal of the American Oriental Society* (New Haven, Ct.) 84, 4 (1964), pp. 348–91.

—, 'The mystical ascent of the T'ien-t'ai Mountains: Sun Ch'o's "Yu T'ien-t'ai shan fu" ', *Monumenta serica* (Tokyo) 20 (1961) pp. 226–45.

Mei Yi-pao, see Primary sources, under *Mo-tzu.*

Miao Ch'üan-sun 繆 荃 孫 (1844–1919), *Yün tzu-tsai k'an sui-pi* 雲 自 在 龕 隨 筆 , Peking, 1958.

Miyakawa Hisayuki 宮 川 尚 志 , *Rikuchō shi kenkyū* 六 朝 史 研 究 , Tokyo, 1956.

Morohashi Tetsuji 諸 橋 轍 次 , *Dai Kan Wa jiten* 大 漢 和 辭 典 , 13 vols., Tokyo, 1956–1959.

Moriya Mitsuo 守 屋 美 都 雄 , 'Sō Gi shakusei ni kansuru ni san no kōsatsu' 曹 魏 爵 制 に 関 す る 二 三 の 考 察 , *Tōyōshi kenkyū* 東 洋 史 研 究 (Kyoto) 20, 4 (1962) pp. 383–412.

Mou Tsung-san 牟 宗 三 , *Ts'ai-hsing yü hsüan-li* 才 性 與 玄 理 , Kowloon, 1963.

Nakagawa Kaoru 中 川 薰 , 'Kenan bunjin den (2) : Gen U den' 建 安 文 人 傳 (阮 瑀 傳), *Tottori daigaku gakugei gakubu kenkyū hōkoku: Jimbun shakai kenkyū* 取鳥大學學藝學部研究報告人文社會研究 (Tottori) 14 (1963) pp. 1–20.

Nakajima Chiaki 中島千秋, 'Gen Seki no "Bikō no fu" ni tsuite' 阮籍の獮猴の賦について, *Chūgoku chūsei bungaku kenkyū* 中國中世文學研究 (Hiroshima) 5 (1966) pp. 17–27. 中國世界文學研究

—, 'Gen Seki no "ron" to "fu" to ni tsuite' 阮籍の論と賦とについて, *Nihon Chūgoku gakkai hō* 日本中國學會報 (Tokyo) 9 (1957) pp. 37–48.

—, 'Chō Ka no "Shōryō no fu" ni tsuite' 張華の鷦鷯の賦について, *Shina-gaku kenkyū* 支那學研究 (Hiroshima) 32 (1966) pp. 28–41.

Numaguchi Masaru 沼口勝, 'Gen Seki no Eikaishi ni okeru shigo ni tsuite no ichi kōsatsu' 阮籍の詠懷詩における詩語についての一考察, *Jimbun ronkyū* 人文論究 (Hakodate) 29 (1969) pp. 15–27.

Obi Kōichi 小尾郊一, *Chūgoku bungaku ni arawareta shizen to shizen kan: Chūsei bungaku o chūshin to shite* 中國文學に現われた自然觀 (中世文學を中心として), Tokyo, 1962.

—, 'Monzen Ri Zen chū insho kōshō kō' 文選李善注引書攷證稿, *Hiroshima daigaku bungakubu kiyō* 廣島大學文學部紀要, 26, 1 (1966) pp. 101–35.

Ogawa Tamaki 小川環樹, 'Wo tao ch'ang yu-yu: To Ho no jikaku' 我道長悠悠 (杜甫の自覺), *Chūgoku bungaku hō* 中國文學報 (Kyoto) 17 (1962) pp. 1–8.

Okazaki Fumio 岡崎文夫, *Gi Shin Nambokuchō tsūshi* 魏晋南北朝通史, Tokyo, 1932; reprinted, 1954.

Pelliot, Paul, review of E. Chavannes, 'Les pays d'Occident d'après le Wei lio', in *Bulletin de l'Ecole Française d'Extrême-Orient* 6 (1906) pp. 361–400.

des Rotours, Robert, trans., *Courtisanes chinoises à la fin des T'ang, entre circa 789 et le 8 janvier 881: Pei-li tche (Anecdotes du quartier du Nord) par Souen K'i* (Bibliothèque de l'Institut des Hautes Etudes Chinoises, Volume XXII), Paris, 1968.

Schipper, Kirstofer Marinus, *L'Empereur Wou des Han dans la légende taoïste: Han Wou-ti nei-tchouan* (Publications de l'Ecole Française d'Extrême-Orient, Volume LVIII), Paris, 1965.

Seidel, Anna K., *La divinisation de Lao-tseu dans le taoïsme des Han* (Publications de l'Ecole Française d'Extrême-Orient, Volume LXXI), Paris, 1969.

Shen Tsu-fen 沈祖棻, 'Juan Ssu-tsung Yung-huai shih ch'u-lun' 阮嗣宗詠懷詩初論, in Ch'eng Ch'ien-fan 程千帆 and Shen Tsu-fen, *Ku-tien shih-ko lun-ts'ung* 古典詩歌論叢, Shanghai, 1954, pp. 91–120.

Shih, Vincent Yu-chung, see Primary sources, under *Wen-hsin tiao-lung*.

Shimosada Masahiro 下定雅弘, 'Gen U no gogonshi ni tsuite' 阮瑀の五言詩について, *Chūgoku bungaku hō* 中國文學報 (Kyoto) 24 (1974) pp. 22–47.

Smith, A.H., *Chinese characteristics*, New York, 1894.

Soper, Alexander Coburn, 'A new Chinese discovery: The earliest representations of a famous literary theme', *Artibus Asiae* (Ascona) 24 (1961) pp. 79–86.

Sullivan, Michael, *The birth of landscape painting in China*, Berkeley and Los Angeles, 1962.

Suzuki Shūji 鈴木修次, 'Kei Kō, Gen Seki kara Tō Emmei e: Mujun kanjō no bungakuteki shori ni okeru mittsu no kata 嵇康阮籍から陶淵明へ 矛盾感情の文學的處理における三つの型), *Chūgoku bungaku hō* 中國文學報 (Kyoto) 18 (1963) pp. 25–50. Translates the following poems by Juan Chi: 41, 37, 63, 70, 80.

Suzuki Torao 鈴木虎雄, trans., *Gyokutai shinei shū* 玉臺新詠集 (Iwanami bunko 岩波文庫 4975–4978), 3 vols., Tokyo, 1955–1956. Translates Poems 2 and 12 by Juan Chi.

*Syrokomla-Stefanowska, A.D., 'The third-century writer Juan Chi', *Journal of the Oriental Society of Australia* (Sydney) 2, 2 (1964?) pp. 20–28.

Takahashi Kazumi 高橋和已 , 'Gan Enshi no bungaku' 顏延之の文學 , *Ritsu-meikan bungaku* 立命館文學 (Kyoto) 1960 pp. 474–95.

Takamatsu Kōmei 高松亭明 , *Shihin shōkai* 詩品詳解 , Aomori, 1959.

Takebe Toshio 武部利男 , *Ri Haku* 李白 2 (Chūgoku shijin senshū 中國詩人選集), Tokyo, 1958.

T'ang Chang-ju 唐長孺 , *Wei Chin Nan-pei ch'ao shih lun-ts'ung* 魏晉南北朝史論叢 , Peking, 1955; second printing, 1957.

T'ang I-chieh 湯一介 , 'Hsi K'ang ho Juan Chi ti che-hsüeh ssu-hsiang' 嵇康和阮籍的哲學思想 , *Hsin chien-she* 新建社 (Peking) 9 (1962) pp. 25–30.

T'ang Yung-t'ung 湯用彤 , *Wei Chin hsüan-hsüeh lun-kao* 魏晉玄學論稿 , Peking, 1957.

—, and Juan Chi-yü 任繼愈 , *Wei Chin hsüan-hsüeh chung ti she-hui cheng-chih ssu-hsiang lüeh-lun* 魏晉玄學中的社會政治思想略論 , Shanghai, 1956.

Ts'en Chung-mien 岑仲勉 , *Yüan-ho hsing-tsan ssu chiao-chi* 元和姓纂四校記 (Kuo-li chung-yang yen-chiu yüan li-shih yü-yen yen-chiu-so chuan-k'an 國立中央研究院歷史語言研究所專刊 29), Shanghai, 1948.

Tsuru Haruo 都留春雄 , 'Tō Emmei no egaku shizen ni tsuite' 陶淵明の描く自然について , in *Yoshikawa hakase taikyū kinen Chūgoku bungaku ronshū* 吉川博士退休記念中國文學論集 , Tokyo, 1968, pp. 209–27.

*Tung, Constantine, 'Juan Chi, an escapist, and his inescapable world', *Journal of the Blaisdell Institute* 5, 2 (June 1970) pp. 9–22.

Waley, Arthur, *Chinese poems*, London, 1948. Translates Juan Chi's Poem No. 61.

—, *The temple*, London, 1925.

—, see also Primary sources, under *Lun yü*.

Wang Chung-lao 王仲犖 , *Ts'ao Ts'ao* 曹操 , Shanghai, 1956.

—, *Wei Chin Nan-pei ch'ao Sui ch'u-T'ang shih* 魏晉南北朝隋初唐史 , Shanghai, 1961.

Wang Chung-min 王重民 , *Lao-tzu k'ao* 老子考 , 2 vols., Peking, 1927?.

Wang Su-ts'un 王素存 , *Hsing lu* 姓錄 , Taipei, 1960.

Wang Yün-hsi 王運熙 , *Yüeh-fu shih lun-ts'ung* 樂府詩論叢 , Shanghai, 1958.

—, see also Primary sources, under *Ch'en Tzu-ang chi*.

Watson, Burton, *Chinese lyricism*, New York and London, 1971. Translates the following poems by Juan Chi: 3, 5, 6, 15, 7, 10; numbered according to the *Wen hsüan* order: 3, 8, 9, 11, 13, 16.

Wen-wu 文物 . Monthly periodical, published in Peking.

Wei Chin Nan-pei ch'ao wen-hsüeh shih ts'an-k'ao tzu-liao, see List of Chinese commentators quoted, under Peking University.

Whitaker, K.P.K., 'Tsaur Jyr's Loushern Fuh', *Asia Major* N.S. 4 (1954) pp. 36–56.

*Whitman, Chris, 'Constraint and escape in Juan Chi', *Dodder* (Ann Arbor, Mich.) 3 (1970) pp. 16–21.

Wilhelm, Hellmut, 'The scholar's frustration: Notes on a type of fu', in John K. Fairbank, ed., *Chinese thought and institutions*, Chicago, 1957, pp. 310–19.

Wilhelm, Richard, see Primary sources, under *K'ung-tzu chia-yü*.

Yang Lien-sheng, 'Notes on the economic history of the Chin dynasty', *Harvard Journal of Asiatic Studies* 9 (1945–1947) pp. 107–85; reproduced in Yang Lien-sheng, *Studies in Chinese institutional history* (Harvard–Yenching Institute Series XX), Cambridge, Mass., 1961.

Yasui Kōzan 安居香山 and Nakamura Shōhachi 中村章八 , *Isho shūsei* 緯書集成 , 8 vols., Tokyo, 1960.

Yen Keng-wang 嚴耕望 , *Chung-kuo ti-fang hsing-cheng chih-tu shih* 中國地方行政制度史 (Chung-yang yen-chiu yüan li-shih yü-yen yen-chiu so chuan-k'an 中央研究院歷史語言研究所專刊 45), 4 vols., Taipei, 1963.

Yin Meng lun, see Primary sources, under Han Wei Liu-ch'ao pai san ming-chia chi.

Yokota Terutoshi 横田輝俊 . 'Bai Teiso no sōshū hensan: Bunki o chūshin to shite' 梅鼎祚の總集編纂 (文紀を中心として), *Shinagaku kenkyū* 支那學 研究 (Hiroshima) 30 (1965) pp. 25–34.

Yoshikawa Kōjirō 吉川幸次郎 , 'Gen Seki den' 阮籍傳 (1950); reprinted in *Yoshikawa Kōjirō zenshū* 吉川幸次郎全集 7, Tokyo, 1968, pp. 180–91.

—, 'Gen Seki no Eikaishi ni tsuite' 阮籍の詠懷詩について (1956–1957); reprinted in *Yoshikawa Kōjirō zenshū* 7, pp. 192–247. The location of the poems translated can be found in the Finding list.

—, 'Sangoku shi jitsuroku' 三國志實錄 (1958); reprinted in *Yoshikawa Kōjirō zenshū* 7, pp. 3–132.

Yoshioka Yoshitoyo 吉岡義豐 , *Dōkyō to bukkyō* 道教と佛教 , Tokyo, 1959.

Yü Chia-hsi 余嘉錫 , *Yü Chia-hsi lun-hsüeh tsa-chu* 余嘉錫論學雜著 , 2 vols., Peking, 1963, pp. 660–61.

Yü Kuan-ying 余冠英 , *Han Wei Liu-ch'ao shih hsüan* 漢魏六朝詩選 , Peking, 1958. Commentaries on the following poems by Juan Chi: 1, 3, 5, 6, 8, 11, 15, 17, 31–2, 38, 58, 67.

—, *Han Wei Liu-ch'ao shih lun-ts'ung* 漢魏六朝詩論叢 , Shanghai, 1952; second printing, 1953.

Yü Ying-shih 余英時 , 'Han Chin chih chi shih chih hsin tzu-chüeh yü hsin ssu-ch'ao' 漢晉之際士之新自覺與新思潮 *Hsin Ya hsüeh-pao* 新亞學報 (Hong-kong) 4, 1 (1959) pp. 25–144.

—, 'Life and immortality in the mind of Han China', *Harvard Journal of Asiatic Studies* 25 (1964–1965) pp. 80–122.

von Zach, Erwin, *Die chinesische Anthologie: Übersetzungen aus dem Wen hsüan* (Harvard–Yenching Studies XVIII), 2 vols., Cambridge, Mass., 1958. Translations of the seventeen poems from the *Wen hsüan*, in the *Wen hsüan* order.

FINDING LIST

A list of the eighty-two poems in the traditional order followed by (1) the page number in this book of my translation; (2) page references to Chiang Shih-yüeh's edition; (3) the number of the poem in Wang Shih-hsien's edition; (4) page references (in the 1959 edition) to Ch'en Hang's thirty-eight poems; (5) the page in the *Yoshikawa Kōjirō zenshū* on which whole poems or long fragments are translated; (6) the order of the first seventeen poems as they are reproduced in the *Wen hsüan*.

Poem	My page	Chiang	Wang	Ch'en	Yoshikawa	*Wen hsüan*
1	229	1.1b	1		193	1
2	120	1.3a	4	45	215	2
3	155	1.5b	5	43	{ 205 240	3
4	158	1.13b	6	40	202	5
5	224	2.4b	7	41		8
6	116	2.6b	8	47	227	9
7	132	2.18a	9	43	210	13
8	117	2.19a	10	47		14
9	25	2.8a	11	48	240	10
10	161	2.1a	12	46	223	16
11	32	1.18a	13	41	222	17
12	123	1.7b	16	45	216	4
13	62	1.15a	17	46	214	6
14	133	1.16b	18	48	211	7
15	163	1.31a	19	50	243	11
16	28	2.3a	20	42	226	12
17	134	2.25a	45	44	196	15
18	211	1.10b	14	45		
19	144	1.11a	15		234	
20	122	1.12b	23	45		
21	217	2.12b	24			
22	178	1.19b	25			

Poem	My page	Chiang	Wang	Ch'en	Yoshikawa
23	174	1.20a	32		230
24	153	1.21b	34		
25	59	1.23a	37		218
26	206	1.24b	40		
27	146	1.25b	42		206
28	183	1.26b	55	50	
29	11	1.28a	57	44	
30	128	2.14a	58	48	
31	9	2.16b	59	41	208
32	159	2.17a	61	50	
33	131	2.21a	62	51	213
34	131	2.21b	63		
35	160	2.22b	71	48	212
36	129	2.23b	2		
37	130	2.24a	3		
38	219	3.1a	47	48	
39	218	3.1b	52		233
40	165	3.3a	68	49	203
41	180	3.4b	69		241
42	67	3.6b	70		
43	212	3.7b	80		
44	209	3.8b	21		235
45	208	3.9a	82		
46	213	3.10a	26		
47	215	3.11a	⎰ 27	49	
48	216	3.11b	⎱ 27		
49	61	3.12a	28	49	
50	157	3.13a	29		
51	126	3.14b	30	46	217
52	146	3.15b	31	44	
53	148	3.16b	33		
54	222	3.17b	35		246
55	53	2.10a	36	42	
56	125	2.11a	38		
57	156	3.19a	39		
58	221	3.19b	41		
59	115	2.13b	43		
60	111	4.1a	44	51	232
61	49	4.1b	46	49	
62	60	4.3a	48		218
63	65	4.3b	49		
64	27	4.4b	50		

Poem	My page	Chiang	Wang	Ch'en	Yoshikawa
65	51	3.5b	51	42	
66	64	4.5a	53	47	
67	110	4.6a	54	46	224
68	172	4.7b	56		
69	113	4.9a	60		
70	168	4.9b	64		
71	148	4.10b	65		207
72	119	4.11a	66		221
73	185	4.11b	67		
74	66	4.12a	72		231
75	30	4.13b	73		
76	167	4.14b	74		228
77	170	4.16a	75		
78	176	4.17a	76	51	239
79	216	4.17b	77		
80	177	4.18b	78		243
81	181	4.19b	79		
82	210	4.20a	81		

N.B. Wang Shih-hsien considers Poems 47 and 48 (in the traditional order) as one poem (No. 27 in his order). He makes up for the loss of one poem by printing the imitation of Juan Chi by Chiang Yen (above, p. 238) as what he calls Poem 22, as if it were actually a poem by Juan Chi.

The editions by Huang Chieh, Ku Chih (who does not include Poems 35 and 36), Huang K'an and Tseng Kuo-fan are not included here because they give the poems in the traditional order and are thus easy to refer to. The Peking University group's fourteen poems are given in a new order, but the traditional number of each poem is clearly indicated. References are not made to Western translations mentioned in the text because they are relatively easy to find: von Zach and Watson use the order of the *Wen hsüan*, Frodsham and Ch'eng, the traditional order. Complete bibliographical references to their translations and to other translations not mentioned in the text will be found in the Bibliography of Secondary sources, under the name of the translator, together with a list of the poems they have translated.

INDEX

The **bold face** numerals refer to the page on which the Chinese character for the word indexed can be found, or to the page on which the romanization or the translation of the word appears with reference to a note containing the character. The characters for book titles can be found in the bibliography. Italic is used in this index for cross-references and for titles of books and other publications.

27676543R00195

Printed in Great Britain
by Amazon